BRIDGE ACCOUNTING
Procedures, Systems, and Controls

J. EDWARD KETZ
Penn State University

JOHN WILEY & SONS, INC.
New York / Chichester / Weinheim / Brisbane / Singapore / Toronto

Acquisitions Editor   *Mark Bonadeo*
Marketing Manager   *Clancy Marshall*
Senior Production Editor   *Petrina Kulek*
Associate Editor   *Julie Kerr*
Senior Designer   *Madelyn Lesure*
Cover Photograph   *David Schultz/Stone*
Illustration Coordinator   *Sandra Rigby*
Photo Editor   *Sara Wight*

This book was set in 10/12 Times Roman by Matrix Publishing Services and printed and bound by Hamilton Printing Company. The cover was printed by Lehigh Press.

This book is printed on acid free paper. ∞

ISBN: 0-471-24228-4

Printed in the United States of America

10 9 8 7 6 5 4 3 2 1

PREFACE

Most students in introductory accounting will become users rather than preparers of accounting information. Many accounting programs, recognizing this reality, have altered the introductory course to stress the interpretation and application of accounting numbers and to deemphasize the mechanical, bookkeeping aspects of financial accounting. Understanding the conceptual issues from a user's perspective has become the focus of these programs, and some schools even teach little or no debits and credits.

This curriculum change does not imply that accounting students are free to ignore the mechanical aspects of accounting. Expectations for accounting preparers and for auditors differ from expectations for accounting users. Clearly, future employers of accounting graduates will expect them to understand bookkeeping; therefore, concerns about communication skills, computer skills, and general business skills are pleas for additional—not replacement—talents. Knowledge of debits and credits and all of the other "nuts and bolts" of accounting will remain part of the accountant's toolkit.

The question is not whether accounting programs should teach their majors bookkeeping; instead, the issue centers on determining the best place in the curriculum to teach these issues. Schools that adopt a user-friendly approach to Accounting 101 might attempt to push these topics into Intermediate Accounting. However, most Intermediate instructors whom I know would protest such a move because Intermediate Accounting already is loaded with many topics. An alternative approach is for schools to offer a course between Intro and Intermediate Accounting that covers these mechanical topics. This book is meant for such a course.

Besides the changing nature of the first accounting course, a second force is pushing on the accounting curriculum. Positions for accounting majors are evolving rapidly. No longer is it sufficient to know financial reporting, managerial accounting, taxes, and auditing. To succeed in practice, the student must also have a grasp of information systems and technology and must understand how accounting interfaces with the other business functions, such as marketing, finance, and logistics. Studying accounting information systems fills some of the computer technology gap. In addition, by organizing the accounting information system into parts dealing with like transactions, the student learns the major functions of the business and how they relate to accounting.

Presently, accounting information systems textbooks are being written for juniors and seniors who have taken a lot of accounting classes but few courses in information systems and computer technology. In my opinion, students would be better served by offering them several courses in accounting information systems. In addition, students need to understand the basics of accounting information systems before moving on to the more advanced topics of relational databases and data flow diagrams. This textbook assists students in this process. Unlike existing accounting information systems textbooks, the material in this book assumes only a rudimentary knowledge of accounting. It helps students "to walk before they run" by sticking to some basic notions of information systems. Of course, students should be exposed to additional courses in accounting information systems, and they can learn about relational databases, data flow diagrams, decision support systems, and expert systems in those classes.

Thus, the two purposes of this book are to provide the mechanics of bookkeeping and to introduce the reader to accounting information systems. The text also introduces the student to auditing, both its goals and its elementary principles and procedures. The idea is to break down some of the walls among accounting courses so that the student can get a better idea of how they fit together. The first half of the book deals with financial statements and the bookkeeping aspects necessary to prepare the financial report. The second half covers the basics of accounting information systems, with the focus on transactions processing. In each accounting cycle there is a discussion of the functions of the cycle, the source documents to the cycle, who processes what, and the outputs of the cycle. The two major purposes are linked via subsidiary ledgers and special journals. Initially, these topics are used to reinforce the students' learning of how to prepare journal entries and how and why to post them. Later, subsidiary ledgers and special journals are employed to explain accounting cycles and the organization of the firm from an accountant's perspective.

Since this book examines bookkeeping without apology, there is no need to move certain mechanical topics to appendices. For example, Principles of Accounting and Intermediate Accounting usually shunt subject matter such as special journals and subsidiary ledgers to appendices. In this book, such topics come to the forefront. Indeed, special journals and subsidiary ledgers play a central role in this book because accountants organize transactions into accounting cycles, and it is easy to explain these transaction cycles with their specific special journals and subsidiary ledgers.

The book is organized as follows. Chapter 1 provides an overview to the book by outlining the conceptual framework of the Financial Accounting Standard Board (FASB) and by introducing transactions processing, auditing, and the notion of internal controls. Chapter 2 reviews the balance sheet and income statement as well as the statement of changes in stockholders' equity for service organizations, merchandisers, and manufacturers. Chapter 3 covers the basics of the accounting cycle, with the accent on journal entries in the general journal and posting to the general ledger. These actions include adjusting and closing entries. Chapter 4 extends the discussion of the accounting cycle to subsidiary ledgers, special journals, worksheets, and reversing and correcting entries. Chapter 5 discusses the cash flow statement, both direct and indirect methods, and how to construct them with either the T-account method or worksheets.

Chapter 6 explains the concept of accounting information systems and organizes the firm's transactions into accounting cycles. It also defines files and explains the different types of files. Chapter 7 lays a foundation for internal control systems by discussing control objectives and some major control policies and procedures, illustrating the concepts with several cash examples. Chapter 8 describes setting up an accounting system and the general ledger cycle. Chapters 9 and 10 explore in depth the revenue cycle (sales and cash receipts) and the expenditure cycle (purchases and cash disbursements). Chapter 11 touches on the payroll, facilities, investments, financing, and production cycles.

Chapter 12 returns to the theme of financial reporting by discussing recognition, measurement, and disclosure issues in financial accounting. As such, it reminds the reader of the basic purpose of financial accounting and reporting—to provide information to investors and creditors and other interested parties about a particular firm.

This book originated from my class notes compiled while teaching this course at Penn State. The course itself arose out of a departmental strategic planning session and, later, a committee designed to flesh out the details. Penn State has required this course since 1996. Our experience has been positive. Not only does it free the Intermediate Accounting faculty from teaching bookkeeping details, but also the students obtain a solid command of the mechanics so that they can concentrate on the higher level concepts. It has also affected our auditing course because the auditing faculty can now assume some student background with transaction cycles and elementary concepts about the nature and purpose of auditing, relying primarily on the notion of internal controls. Serendipitously, more students have been able to obtain internships because they have some knowledge of auditing and accounting information systems, knowledge the recruiters earnestly desire in their interns.

When I teach the course, I dedicate about one week of class per chapter. This leaves me with time to give exams and projects. I typically assign two projects, one that augments the bookkeeping half of the course and one that focuses on accounting information systems. One of the projects I like using is the *Systems Understanding Aid for Financial Accounting* by Arens and Ward. Apparently, it is the only package that has the students work through the entire accounting cycle with the major business documents. It integrates such material very well. The other project generally consists of some computerized package, and there are a number of these packages on the market.

Some accounting information systems courses jump into relational databases and utilize entity-relation and data flow diagrams. We have considered such ideas but have rejected them as overpowering for students at this level. The objective is simpler—to equip the students with a basic vocabulary and an understanding of how the firm is organized into accounting cycles. This approach should help instructors in later accounting information systems courses.

Every chapter begins with a statement of learning objectives for the reader. These objectives act as a beacon to help the reader see what items are of vital importance in the chapter; they also serve as a means of organizing the chapter. The text of each chapter ends with a chapter summary in terms of these same learning objectives.

Another feature of the text is the section in each chapter named "Sights Along the Internet." Although this book covers a lot of material, academics realize that there is so much more. The Internet or the web contains many sites that are of interest to accountants, and students are encouraged to expand their horizons by looking at these sites. The most important sites are as follows.

American Institute of Certified Public Accountants	www.aicpa.org
Electronic Accountant	www.electronicaccountant.com
Financial Accounting Standards Board	www.rutgers.edu/Accounting/raw/fasb
Financial Executives Institute	www.fei.org
Independence Standards Board	www.cpaindependence.org
Institute of Internal Auditors	www.theiia.org
Institute of Management Accountants	www.imanet.org
Rutgers Accounting Web	www.rutgers.edu/Accounting
Securities Exchange Commission	www.sec.gov

Each chapter of the text also includes a glossary. This section helps the reader learn the vocabulary of accounting by highlighting the important words to know as well as providing definitions for the various terms that appear in the chapter.

The end-of-chapter material typically consists of review questions, discussion questions, exercises, and problems. Review questions ask readers to parrot back the material in the text and are appropriate when the chapter is first read. Discussion questions stretch the students by asking them to apply the concepts to other domains or to material from other chapters. This helps the student to think about the chapter's concepts in relation to all of the concepts in the text. In the first half of the text, exercises tend to be mechanical number crunching problems, designed to reinforce the information. Problems are either longer, harder, or less mechanical; the intention is to make sure the student thoroughly understands the chapter. In the second half of the book, some of the exercises and problems become essay questions rather than computations. This helps students grasp the ideas from the chapter, and it also forces them to think about the less structured and more ambiguous aspects of accounting.

Some questions or exercises raise ethical issues. Instead of formatting them in terms of ethics, most of these problems are written in terms of internal control issues. I have found students more willing to relate to these questions from a professional vantage point when they don't have to be defensive about their own ethical stances.

The first principle of my teaching philosophy is to ensure that students understand the concepts as they are enunciated in the chapter. After that, however, I push the students into topics and areas not directly covered by the material. If the students genuinely comprehend the topics, then this stretching helps them apply what they have learned to new areas. If they have problems, their understanding may not be very deep. For example, Chapter 6 gives COSO's model for internal controls. After discussing the model completely, I ask students to apply it to other areas, such as to a chemical company that wants to minimize the problem of explosions. Not only does it help them to apply the concept beyond the obvious areas, but it helps them to realize how broad some accounting and auditing concepts are. Those instructors who want the end-of-chapter material to cover only concepts that are presented and explained in the chapter should skip the discussion questions in the book.

This textbook was written primarily for a course that comes immediately after a user-oriented introductory class. The review in the early chapters, however, is thorough, so that this book could be employed in a first course for accounting majors. If it is used in this way, the early chapters need to be covered at a slower pace so that the student can have some "sink" time in learning the vocabulary and techniques.

I would like to thank Ken Pasch and Suzie Wright for reading various chapters in the book and commenting on them. I also thank my daughter Charity Ketz for reading portions of the book, especially for reading the exercises and problems and verifying the solutions.

In addition, I would like to thank the reviewers: Stanley Davis of Saint Joseph's University, PA, Corolyn Clark of St Joseph's University, PA, Jane Przybyla of Rhode Island College, RI, Florence Kirk of SUNY Oswego, NY, Gregory Bushong of Wright State University, OH, Mary Alice Seville of Oregon State University, OR, Linda Whitten of San Francisco State University, CA, Sherri Anderson of Sonoma State University, CA, Bradley Schwieger of Saint Cloud State University, MN, Tim Cairney of Florida Atlantic University, FL, Somnath Bhattacharya of Florida Atlantic University, FL, and Christine Haynes of University of Florida, FL.

Finally, I thank my wife Holly for her encouragement and support throughout this project. I especially thank her for the sacrifices during the last few months of the project when I was hobbled with a broken leg. For these reasons I dedicate this book to her.

J. Edward Ketz

CONTENTS

CHAPTER 1

AN OVERVIEW OF FINANCIAL ACCOUNTING AND AUDITING

The field of accounting encompasses a large range of activities and processes that deal with the capture, measurement, and communication of economic information to interested parties. Financial accounting focuses on providing information about the results of a company's activities to investors and creditors; management accounting concentrates on generating and communicating information to the managers of the enterprise; tax accounting emphasizes the information that a firm reports to tax authorities such as the Internal Revenue Service; accounting information systems center on how to gather and process data employed for financial, managerial, and tax purposes; and auditing is concerned with verification of management assertions about accounting.

In this text we focus on transactions and transactions processing. Transactions are the activities of the firm, and it is the accountant who tracks and records these transactions. At an appropriate time, the accountant summarizes the financial effects of the transactions and presents them to interested readers, typically in the form of financial statements or schedules. In addition to gathering data about transactions, the accountant also keeps the bookkeeping efforts free from error and misstatement. This means that the accountant will build controls into the accounting system so that errors, both intentional and unintentional, are discovered and corrected before the financial report is delivered to its audience.

Much of the subject matter of this book is part of financial accounting, though it also ventures into accounting information systems and auditing. It also touches on that part of management accounting that is based on transactions.

This chapter provides an overview of financial accounting and auditing. While the emphasis of the book is on transactions and transactions processing, it is important to keep in mind the objectives of financial accounting and auditing in order to consider how to construct a transactions processing system that meets those objectives. This requires study of the conceptual framework of financial accounting and the building blocks of auditing.

After reading and studying this chapter, you should be able to:

- Define accounting, financial accounting, and the conceptual framework of financial accounting;
- State the objective of financial accounting and reporting;
- Explain the qualitative characteristics of information;
- Define the elements of financial accounting;
- Define transaction and transactions processing;
- Discuss the nature of auditing and distinguish between external auditing and internal auditing;
- Identify management's assertions in the financial report and explain the importance of verifying these assertions;
- Define internal control and indicate its components;

- Discuss the contents of management's responsibility report and an unqualified audit report;
- Explain the most important ethical principle in financial accounting.

CONCEPTUAL FRAMEWORK OF FINANCIAL ACCOUNTING

Accounting is the process of capturing, measuring, and communicating economic information about a firm to interested parties. An *accountant* is one who engages in accounting. *Financial accounting* is the branch of accounting that focuses on issues of providing information about the results of a company's activities to users outside of the firm, notably investors and creditors. The corporation disseminates this information to present and potential investors and creditors through financial statements and press releases.

Financial reporting practices were mostly unregulated prior to the 1930s. Because of the 1929 stock market crash, Congress passed the Securities Act of 1933 and the Securities Exchange Act of 1934. These laws created the Securities Exchange Commission (SEC) and gave it the authority to govern the securities markets. Among other things, the SEC obtained the jurisdiction to create accounting and disclosure rules. Early in its history, the SEC decided to rely on the accounting profession to assist in the development of financial accounting standards.

The profession devised the Committee on Accounting Procedure in 1938, and it lasted until 1959. During its tenure, the Committee issued 51 Accounting Research Bulletins that established generally accepted accounting principles. Most of them have been superseded by more recent pronouncements.

The Accounting Principles Board replaced the Committee on Accounting Procedure in 1959. Continuing until 1973, the Board passed 31 Opinions, a few of which are still part of generally accepted accounting principles. The Accounting Principles Board was in turn supplanted by the Financial Accounting Standards Board.

Still operating today, the Financial Accounting Standards Board was established in 1973 to create financial accounting rules in the United States. One of its early actions, though it took several years to complete, was the construction of a conceptual framework of accounting and reporting. This conceptual framework is laid out in seven documents, which are called Statements of Financial Accounting Concepts, and they embrace such foundational issues as the objective of financial accounting, the qualitative characteristics of information, and the elements of financial accounting. In this chapter, we review some of these topics in order to obtain an overview of the financial accounting process. (The Financial Accounting Standards Board has also issued over 130 Statements of Financial Accounting Standards; they will constitute topics for discussion in later accounting courses.)

Objective of Financial Accounting and Reporting

Firms are instituted to provide goods or services to those who desire them in society. Corporations typically engage in these activities only when they can earn a profit. To carry out their activities, companies often obtain money from stock markets and credit markets. In similar fashion, investors and creditors usually supply these funds in order to earn a profit. Returns to investors are in the form of cash dividends and appreciation in the stock's value, which is a function, among other things, of the firm's earnings. Creditors desire a return of and a return on the borrowed amount, the principal plus cash interest on the principal.

Investors and creditors are concerned with such issues as how much profit they can make with a particular investment, how much risk is involved, and when they might expect to receive the returns. In their search of information to help answer these questions, they glean some of the needed information from corporate accounting reports.

The objective of financial accounting is to furnish investors and creditors with information that will help them make investment decisions. Other users also exist, such as managers, government officials, employees, and the press, but investors and creditors are considered the major users of accounting information. Managers are deemphasized in this context because they can obtain whatever information they want. The others have secondary status because they tend to use the information less frequently and because accounting information seems to play only a small role in the types of decisions they make.

What decisions would an investor or a creditor make? Essentially, the investor makes two types of decisions: whether to buy the stock and whether to sell it. If the investor buys the stock, he or she also needs to consider how many shares to acquire. The decision-making process gets complicated because the investor often tries to appraise the expected return on the stock, which is related to expected future cash flows and the risk underlying those cash flows. Similarly, a creditor considers whether to make a loan, how much interest to charge, whether to require collateral, and whether to sell the loan. This decision-making process leads to an assessment of how much cash will be received from the loan, when it will be received, and the risk that must be borne by the creditor.

From these brief characterizations, one can refine the basic objective of financial accounting and reporting. Accounting information is considered useful to investors and creditors if it helps them to determine how much cash will be received, when it will be received, and how much risk is involved concerning whether they will actually receive these cash flows.

The corporate accounting reports that are released to the public contain a balance sheet, an income statement, a statement of changes in stockholders' equity, and a cash flow statement. The *balance sheet* shows the economic resources of the firm (assets), its obligations (liabilities), and its residual owners' equity. The *income statement* publishes the revenues and the gains, the expenses and the losses, the earnings, and, if the entity is a corporation, the earnings per share. (For now, let's think of earnings per share as simply net income divided by the number of shares of common stock that is outstanding.) The *statement of changes in stockholders' equity* reveals the changes in the stockholders' equity accounts (such as retained earnings) during the period. The *cash flow statement* displays the cash flows of the corporation during the period. It shows that this change in cash comes from three sources: cash flows from operating, investing, and financing activities.

The information contained in these financial statements, along with the accompanying footnotes and schedules, give investors and creditors some of the information they need to make rational economic decisions. In this manner, financial accounting fulfills its mission in society.

Qualitative Characteristics of Information

Not everything that can be reported in accounting reports is useful to investors and creditors. For example, knowing the shoe size of the CEO of a firm likely won't help much when making investment decisions. So one should consider what makes information useful to decision makers.

Before addressing this matter, let's distinguish between data and information. *Data* are symbols that represent something. They include a book's library number, a license plate number, a team's win-loss record, and the amount of a firm's assets. *Information* is data that helps someone make a decision. Notice that what is useful to one person is not necessarily helpful to another. For example, a manager on the assembly line might like to know how many units of a product have been made by 10 A.M., but that fact is merely data to the CEO, who is more interested in how many units were made and sold during the month and in sales projections for the next few months.

Information is considered useful when it is relevant and reliable. *Relevance* indicates that the information is pertinent to a particular decision that needs to be made. As a practical matter, information is relevant if it might make a difference in the final decision. If a corporation is thinking about hiring a particular individual, for example, the recruiter might want to know the person's intelligence as measured, however imperfectly, by grades, SAT scores, or IQ tests. These data might be relevant to the hiring decision. On the other hand, the applicant's favorite ice cream flavor is irrelevant since one's taste does not affect the candidate's ability in most jobs.

Reliability is the property that the information represents what it is supposed to represent and that it is free from bias and measurement error. Grades are not necessarily a reliable index of intelligence because smart people might not study and receive poor grades, while average individuals might work hard and obtain excellent grades. IQ scores might not be a reliable measure of intelligence either since they contain racial biases and do not measure qualities like creativity.

Another aspect of reliability is *verifiability*, the ability of different measurers to obtain the same values when they employ the same measurement methods. To the extent that grades are useful to recruiters when assessing different applicants, the recruiters will look at a variety of grades. They realize that a particular teacher might be overly easy or very difficult, and so one grade might not reflect the candidate's ability. After throwing out a few extreme grades, the recruiter observes the grades to assess how a variety of graders rank the job seeker.

Accountants want to give the users relevant and reliable financial accounting information. In practice, however, there is often a tradeoff. Consider the problem of land valuation on a balance sheet. Market value data are frequently considered more relevant than original cost data, but market value may be less reliable because different appraisers might come up with vastly different estimates. Nonetheless, where possible, accountants strive for greater relevance and reliability in the information disseminated to the public.

Elements of Financial Accounting

The four financial statements are the balance sheet, the income statement, the statement of changes in stockholders' equity, and the cash flow statement. Each of these financial statements is made up of several components, and these components are referred to as the elements of financial accounting.

The balance sheet depicts the assets, liabilities, and stockholders' equity of the entity. *Assets* are resources owned or controlled by the firm that probably have future economic value. They include such items as cash, receivables, land, buildings, patents, and investments. To be an asset, the firm either must have legal title to the item, or it must possess property rights to the item that in effect yield the same benefits that ownership would confer. For example, airline companies sometimes acquire airplanes by leasing them from a bank instead of buying them. A leased airplane is an asset if the lessee (in this case, the airline company) has the privileges of ownership and is simply using the lease as a means of financing the "purchase." In addition, the future value of the item need not be guaranteed. An investment in XYZ stock is an asset, even though it is possible for XYZ to declare bankruptcy and for the stock to lose all its value. As long as the stock investment has probable future economic value, it is an asset.

Liabilities are obligations of the firm that can be discharged by disbursing assets, by providing services in the future, or by creating new obligations. Some typical liabilities are accounts payable, taxes payable, warranties payable, unearned subscription revenue, mortgages payable, and pension liability. The key feature of a liability is that, in general, the entity must pay out cash or some other asset in the future, or the company must provide a future service. For example, taxes payable, like most debts, are usually discharged by paying cash. In this case, the cash is paid to a governmental agency. Unearned subscription revenue arises when customers send cash to the company for a magazine subscription. The firm discharges this debt by mailing the magazine issues to the customers. Occasionally, the enterprise discharges an obligation by agreeing to another liability. For example, the firm might discharge an account payable with the creation of a note payable.

Stockholders' equity is the residual interest that stockholders have in the assets of the corporation. The definition employs the *accounting identity* (or *accounting equation*):

$$\text{Assets} = \text{Liabilities} + \text{Stockholders' Equity}$$

or

$$\text{Stockholders' Equity} = \text{Assets} - \text{Liabilities}$$

The second form of this identity emphasizes the legal fact that creditors' interests in the assets of the entity take precedence to the owners' interests. (The balance sheet gets its name because the left-hand side always equals or balances the right-hand side of the identity.)

A sole proprietorship is an unincorporated business with a single owner. In a sole proprietorship, the ownership is shown in a capital account that bears the owner's name, such as Ace, Capital. A partnership is an unincorporated business with several owners. In a partnership, the interest of each partner is given in separate capital accounts such as King, Capital and Queen, Capital and Jack, Capital. Instead of stockholders' equity, one would refer to the residual interest in a sole proprietorship or partnership as the owner's (or owners') equity.

A corporation is a business entity formed by application to a state government for its incorporation. The state grants this incorporated entity certain rights and responsibilities. A corporation has several stockholders' equity accounts such as common stock and retained earnings.

An income statement has five elements: revenues, gains, expenses, losses, and net income. A *revenue* is an inflow of assets (or outflow of liabilities) that arises because the firm sells a product or provides a service. A *gain* is an inflow of assets (or outflow of liabilities) that arises from some peripheral activity of the business. What discriminates a revenue from a gain is whether the inflow of *net assets* (assets minus liabilities) is a major part of the business or whether it is incidental. For our purposes, we will ignore the distinction between the two because the line differentiating major from incidental activity is ambiguous and because the effect on net income is the same. In practice, however, revenues are often stated at gross amounts while gains are measured at net amounts. Sales, service revenue, and interest revenue are some common revenues. Gains from the sale of land and gains from the sale of a stock investment are gains.

An *expense* is an outflow of assets (or inflow of liabilities) that arises from acquiring or manufacturing goods, providing services, or some other activity that is part of the major activities of the business. A *loss* is an outflow of assets (or inflow of liabilities) that arises from some peripheral activity of the business. Like the difference between revenues and gains, the distinction between expenses and losses is fuzzy, and in practice expenses are usually stated in gross amounts while losses are stated at net. Some common expenses are cost of goods sold, wages expense, advertising expense, utilities expense, and tax expense. Loss from sale of land and loss from sale of investments are two possible losses.

Net income is made up of revenues and gains minus expenses and losses. It is computed for a certain period of time such as one year. The income statement essentially indicates the firm's net income and the elements that go into income:

$$\text{Net Income} = \text{Revenues} + \text{Gains} - \text{Expenses} - \text{Losses}$$

The statement of changes in stockholders' equity relies on the elements of stockholders' equity and net income, both of which have already been discussed. It also needs two other elements, investments by owners and distributions to owners. *Investments by owners* are increases in stockholders' equity that result from an owner's transferring net assets or providing services to the business. Owners who transfer net assets or provide services increase their ownership interests in the entity. Issuance of common stock is an example of investments by owners. *Distributions to owners* are decreases in stockholders' equity that result from transferring net assets or providing services to owners. In a sole proprietorship or a partnership, such distributions are termed *drawings*, whereas in a corporation they are called *dividends*.

This statement utilizes the relationship that the ending balance of an account equals the beginning balance of the account plus its changes during the year. The primary changes in retained earnings are the increase due to earnings and the decrease due to dividends. Thus, the statement of changes of stockholders' equity would show this change by applying the relationship:

$$\text{Ending Retained Earnings} = \text{Beginning Retained Earnings} + \text{Net Income} - \text{Dividends}$$

The cash flow statement, as the name implies, displays the cash that comes into and flows out of the firm. A *cash flow* is any transaction that increases or decreases the cash of the entity. A *cash inflow* is any cash flow in which the cash is received by the firm. A *cash outflow* is any cash flow in which the cash is disbursed by the company. Cash sales, collections from accounts receivable, cash proceeds from selling land, and cash received from borrowing money are cash inflows. Cash paid to employees, cash paid to suppliers, cash paid to acquire equipment, and cash dividends are cash outflows.

These cash inflows and cash outflows are organized by the activity that generated them, such as operating, investing, and financing activities. Since the ending balance of cash equals the beginning balance of cash plus the cash inflows and outflows during the period, we have the relationship:

$$\text{Change in Cash} = \text{Cash from Operating Activities} + \text{Cash from Investing Activities} + \text{Cash from Financing Activities}$$

SUMMARY

We have sketched the fundamental points of financial accounting. Its major objective is to assist investors and creditors with their investment decision making, particularly helping them to assess the amounts, timing, and uncertainty of the investment cash flows. Accountants meet this objective by issuing financial reports that include the balance sheet, the income statement, the statement of changes in stockholders' equity, and the cash flow statement. These statements are accompanied by footnotes and schedules that give further data and explanations. Accountants try to make the information relevant to the users and the decisions they make, and they attempt to produce as reliable information as possible. We have also defined the elements of each of the four financial statements.

This portrait of financial accounting provides a foundation on which to discuss and elaborate financial accounting topics. Chapter 2 describes in greater detail the balance sheet, the income statement, and the statement of changes in stockholders' equity, while Chapter 5 does the same for the cash flow statement. As one might expect, the elements will be utilized when these statements are sketched in further detail. Chapter 12 discusses some recognition, measurement, and disclosure issues in financial accounting.

TRANSACTIONS AND TRANSACTIONS PROCESSING

Accountants gather data as exchanges and events take place so that they can process the data and eventually construct the financial statements. Corporations must design systems to capture these data and process them efficiently, for a large company can easily have thousands of transactions in a single day. Keep in mind that the purpose of gathering and processing the data is to publish a financial report and convey economic information about the firm to investors and creditors.

An *exchange* is the giving up of something of value to receive something of value. Sometimes an exchange is referred to as a reciprocal transfer. A cash sale is an exchange between the firm and a customer in which the firm gives up a product and receives cash. A *nonreciprocal transfer* is the giving up of something of value or the receiving of something of value, but not both. A charitable donation is an example of a nonreciprocal transfer. An *event* is an occurrence that has a financial consequence for the firm. Under certain conditions, some investments are measured at their market value, and gains and losses are calculated as changes in the market value. Changes in an investment's market value constitute an event for the corporation. In this definition we include internal events, such as the transformation of raw materials and labor into a product to be sold. The company would recognize that the raw materials inventory has been converted into the finished goods inventory. An *allocation* is the distribution of some cost to various departments, assets, expenses, or time periods. Depreciation of a long-term asset is an allocation because it distributes the cost of the asset over several years.

Usually, one does not have to be so meticulous about distinguishing among exchanges, nonreciprocal transfers, events, and allocations. We shall employ the term "transaction" to comprehend all of these situations. Therefore, a *transaction* is an exchange, a nonreciprocal transfer, an event, or an allocation of the entity. Transactions are important to accountants because they write a history of the firm with respect to these transactions and they utilize the transaction data for measuring economic consequences.

Accountants garner data concerning the transactions made by the firm. The purpose of obtaining these data is to employ them when preparing financial statements. *Transactions processing* comprises all of the activities that transform data about a firm's transactions into the firm's financial statements. The idea behind transactions processing is captured in Exhibit 1.1. First, a transaction takes place, and data concerning the transaction and its financial effects on the firm are recorded. These data include the date of the transaction, the participants in the transaction, and an explanation of what took place. Next, the accountant processes the data. This processing includes measuring the financial

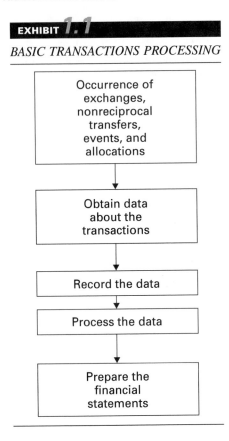

EXHIBIT 1.1

BASIC TRANSACTIONS PROCESSING

Occurrence of
exchanges,
nonreciprocal
transfers,
events, and
allocations

Obtain data
about the
transactions

Record the data

Process the data

Prepare the
financial
statements

effects of the transaction, aggregating like items, and summarizing the data in a manner useful to the readers. Finally, the accounting department prepares and distributes the financial report.

This textbook focuses primarily on transactions and transactions processing. Chapters 3 and 4 deal with simple transactions processing, which is referred to as the accounting cycle. Chapter 6 further develops the concept of transactions processing and lays a framework for what firms do to handle their transactions in an efficient and effective manner. Chapters 8–11 delve into the specifics of transactions processing and classify transactions into like categories such as sales transactions, cash receipts, purchase transactions, and cash disbursements.

EXTERNAL AND INTERNAL AUDITING

"Garbage in, garbage out" is a familiar adage that is applicable to accounting. Investors and creditors rely on the numbers in the financial report to make investment decisions. If the numbers are wrong, for whatever reason, then the investment decisions based on those numbers may be flawed. Similarly, managers utilize the numbers coming out of the accounting system for their own purposes, and they, too, want to maintain the integrity of the reporting system. Managers also want the resources of the firm protected from theft or other misuse.

Auditing is the process of examining and verifying information. Persons who perform auditing are called *auditors*. Although auditors can perform operational audits that assess the effectiveness and efficiency of some operating segment and compliance audits that determine whether the organization conforms to various regulations, we restrict the discussion to financial statement audits. In a financial statement audit, the auditor examines the underlying data—the transactions—to verify that the financial statements, taken as a whole, are properly prepared.

External auditors do not work for the firm. They are independent of the company, and so they are able to provide an objective, third-party review of the financial statements. Investors and creditors depend on external auditors to review the fairness with which the financial report has been assembled. On the other hand, *internal auditors* work for the firm in question. Corporations employ internal auditors to protect the assets of the firm and to build systems that will discover errors and correct them as soon as possible.

External Auditing

Suppose you want to purchase a car. You could go to an automobile dealer, listen to the sales rep, and make your decision based on what he or she says. One problem with listening solely to the sales rep is that the person is human and might make a mistake. The bigger issue is that the sales rep makes money on a commission basis; the more cars sold, the bigger the paycheck. This fact creates a conflict of interest: it is impossible for the sales rep to act in your best interest and at the same time optimize his or her commissions. Knowing this fact, you are not going to rely solely on the salesperson's information. You try to obtain some independent evidence about the car, its performance, its worth, and so on, and you get this information from an independent and reliable source such as *Consumer Reports*.

In the same way, investors and creditors realize that companies may make mistakes in their data preparation. And, more importantly, they understand that managers inherently are not objective in their preparation and dissemination of the financial report. Managers could lose their jobs if the financial statements revealed poor performance. Many companies offer bonuses to managers based on the accounting numbers, especially the net income figure. Managers oversee the accounting process in their companies, and they simultaneously are evaluated by those numbers. If this feature was not restrained in some fashion, one could expect some managers to "cook the books."

Firms hire someone to audit their books and provide an independent assessment of the trustworthiness of the financial report. The external auditors check and verify the financial statements; they do not examine whether the firm is a good investment. Just as *Consumer Reports* does not tell people which car to buy or what features to purchase, so external auditors do not indicate whether an investment in a particular firm is good or bad. *Consumer Reports* provides information so that consumers can make more informed judgments. In like manner, external auditors verify the information in the financial statements, so that users can make their own investment decisions.

When managers prepare a financial report, they basically are making a series of assertions that the external auditor will investigate. These assertions fall into five categories: assertions about existence or occurrence; assertions about completeness; assertions about valuation or allowance; assertions about rights and obligations; and assertions about presentation and disclosure. Assertions about existence or occurrence are statements that items on the balance sheet, such as assets, really existed on the balance sheet date and that transactions reported in the income statement, such as revenues, really took place during the year. Assertions about completeness deal with the issue of whether all accounts and all transactions have been properly accounted for. For example, are all liabilities included on the balance sheet? Are all expenses and losses contained in the income statement? Assertions about valuation or allowance pertain to measurement of the elements. Assertions about rights and obligations deal with the issue of whether the assets are really the rights of the company and whether the debts are really its obligations. Finally, assertions about presentation and disclosure essentially are assertions that everything that needs to be disclosed and explained has been.

The external auditor scrutinizes these assertions by management for their veracity and correctness. If there is any problem, the external auditor resolves the discrepancy with management. Once these difficulties are resolved, the firm publishes the financial statements along with a report by the external auditor. Usually, the external auditor issues a so-called unqualified opinion which states that the auditor believes that the financial statements, taken as a whole, are fairly stated. Other options exist if the auditor cannot issue an unqualified opinion.

Internal Auditing

Many companies have internal auditors who, among other things, investigate the financial statements. In ensuring the reliability of the corporation's financial reporting process, the internal auditors build transactions processing systems that will properly account for the transactions of the entity. Firms employ these individuals to make the auditing process more effective and more efficient. Internal auditors can provide managers valuable advice about accounting issues and give them information about how to protect the resources of the entity.

Internal auditors are not independent of the company economically, so they cannot write reports to the investing community. They cannot substitute for external auditors. Nonetheless, to do their job well, internal auditors must be free from any undue influence of the managers whom they are studying. This protection can be achieved by having internal auditors report directly to the board of directors. Thus, internal auditors need organizational independence to carry out their tasks.

One important aspect of internal auditing concerns the internal control system. Internal auditors build these controls and make sure that they are operating correctly. We turn to this topic in the next section.

INTERNAL CONTROLS

Internal control is the process of reasonably ensuring the realization of corporate goals. These goals can include effective and efficient operations and compliance with regulatory rules, but our primary interest here is in the goal of producing trustworthy financial statements.

As shown in Exhibit 1.2, internal control systems can be viewed as having five components. (This discussion relies on *Internal Control—Integrated Framework* by the Committee of Sponsoring Organizations of the Treadway Commission, the so-called COSO report, issued in 1992.) Internal control systems begin with a control environment that is concerned with the overall attitude toward ethics. A moral tone throughout the organization can help people understand their responsibilities within the firm. It establishes the concept that each person is accountable for his or her actions and the attitude that one must act in accordance with management's authority. Next, one should have a clear understanding of the risks that are faced in trying to achieve the corporate goals. These risks

EXHIBIT 1.2

COMPONENTS OF AN INTERNAL CONTROL SYSTEM

Component	Explanation of Component
1. Control environment	Ethical setting of firm
2. Risk assessment	Understanding of risks to corporate goals
3. Control procedures	Specific methods to carry out management goals
4. Information and communication	Production of reports to notify managers and directors of pertinent information
5. Monitoring	Assurance that the control system is working

include environmental factors such as price changes or expropriation as well as temptations to take corporate resources. With this understanding of the risks, the firm can develop control procedures to reduce the risks to acceptable levels.

Information should be sent to managers and directors to help them evaluate the firm's current position and determine what needs to be done to meet the corporate goals. Reports are prepared with the pertinent information and distributed to the appropriate managers and directors.

Designing an internal control system does not mean that it will work, nor does it mean that once it is operating, it will always do so. The internal control system therefore needs to be monitored to see that it is working the way it was designed to work.

In practice, internal auditors create the internal control system and assess its reliability. External auditors also test its effectiveness as a basis for their opinion on the financial report.

Chapters 7–11 provide expanded coverage of internal control systems. Chapter 7 fleshes out some basic internal control procedures, especially those dealing with cash. Then Chapters 8–11 explicate various transaction cycles, including the sales, purchases, cash receipts, and cash disbursements cycles. As these topics are developed, appropriate internal control mechanisms are also introduced and explained.

MANAGEMENT'S RESPONSIBILITY REPORT AND THE INDEPENDENT AUDITOR'S REPORT

When the financial report is published and distributed to the public, it sometimes includes management's statement about its responsibilities pertaining to the financial statements. At this time, management is not required to make such a statement in the annual report. An example of a *management responsibility report* is given in Exhibit 1.3.

The first paragraph of the report states that management prepares and is responsible for the financial statements. The purpose of this declaration is to inform the reader about the different responsibilities of management and the external auditor. The external auditor does not prepare the statements but is responsible for the opinion expressed about the statement's fairness. The second paragraph of the management responsibility report states that the firm has an internal control system and that management believes it is working properly. The third paragraph confirms that the board of directors is also involved through its audit committee. Only nonmanagement members of the board should serve on the audit committee. This committee interacts with the auditors and assures itself that the system is working.

EXHIBIT *1.3*

MANAGEMENT RESPONSIBILITY REPORT

The financial statements of Arthur, Inc. contained in this report are made by management, and responsibility for the reliability of its content rests with management. The financial statements have been audited by Rubinstein and Sons, independent auditors.

The corporation has a system of internal controls which is independently evaluated by a team of internal auditors. These controls encompass both organizational and accounting controls. We believe that this system of internal controls provides reasonable assurance that transactions are executed in accordance with management's authorization; that transactions are appropriately recorded to permit preparation of financial statements that are presented in conformity in all material respects with generally accepted accounting principles; and that assets are properly accounted for and safeguarded against loss from unauthorized use.

The Board of Directors has an Audit Committee made up solely of outside directors. The Audit Committee meets with the independent auditors, the internal auditors, and management to discuss internal control, auditing, and financial reporting issues.

Publicly issued financial statements contain a report by the independent auditor. Exhibit 1.4 illustrates an *unqualified audit opinion*, which basically affirms that the financial statements can be relied upon for the information they contain.

The first paragraph of the audit report says that the auditor has examined the financial statements. It also delineates the responsibilities of management and the public auditor by reporting that managers are responsible for the statements and the auditor is responsible for the opinion expressed about those financial statements. The second paragraph states that the auditor conducted the audit in accordance with professional standards. This includes a determination that the internal control system is indeed operating

EXHIBIT *1.4*

UNQUALIFIED AUDIT REPORT

We have audited the accompanying balance sheets of Arthur, Inc. as of December 31, 2001 and 2000, and the related statements of income, retained earnings, and cash flows for the years then ended. These financial statements are the responsibility of company's management. Our responsibility is to express an opinion on these financial statements based on our audits.

We conducted our audits in accordance with generally accepted auditing standards. Those standards require that we plan and perform the audit to obtain reasonable assurance about whether the financial statements are free of material misstatement. An audit includes examining, on a test basis, evidence supporting the amounts and disclosures in the financial statements. An audit also includes assessing the accounting principles used and significant estimates made by management, as well as evaluating the overall financial statement presentation. We believe that our audits provide a reasonable basis for our opinion.

In our opinion, the financial statements referred to above present fairly, in all material respects, the financial position of Arthur, Inc. as of December 31, 2001 and 2000 and the results of its operations and its cash flows for the years then ended in conformity with generally accepted accounting principles.

Rubinstein & Sons
March 1, 2002

properly. The third paragraph contains the opinion itself. In this case, the auditor claims that the financial statements present fairly what they are supposed to represent.

The purpose of management's responsibility report and the independent auditor's report is to enhance the credibility of the annual report and to assure investors and creditors that they can indeed make economic decisions based on the information in the financial statements. It accomplishes this purpose by exhibiting management's and the auditor's responsibility for the integrity of the data and by the audit opinion, which asserts that the financial statements fairly present the resources, obligations, residual interest, revenues, gains, expenses, losses, and cash flows of the enterprise.

PROFESSIONAL ETHICS

Accountants have a valued and responsible position in society, and so they should guard their status and meet their responsibilities by acting as ethically as possible. Through its long-time interest in ethics, the accounting profession has established a professional code of conduct. Rather than summarize the many points within this code here, it is more profitable to concentrate only on the most important ethical tenet in financial accounting, the disclosure principle.

As explained earlier in the chapter, the purpose of financial accounting is to provide information to the users of the financial report, primarily investors and creditors, so that they can make rational investment decisions. Accountants both communicate the financial results to the users and fulfill their obligations to them by providing all of the financial information that is relevant to the users. This duty is referred to as the *disclosure principle*. Hiding some of the information, whether good or bad, or distorting it, or outright lying about it, is morally wrong.

Financial accountants should follow a number of rules as they consider the proper accounting for transactions. Auditors who examine the financial statements need to make sure that these rules have been observed. The disclosure principle comes to the forefront when a manager wants to follow the letter of the law but not its spirit.

The 1969 Continental Vending case provides an illustration. The president of Continental Vending borrowed money from the corporation to buy Continental stock for himself, and Continental borrowed money from a subsidiary named Valley Commercial. Valley Commercial's payable to Continental Vending was collateralized by the president's investments. The president did not disclose all of the details about these arrangements in the financial report, nor did he reveal that Valley could not repay its debt to Continental. Although the auditors knew these facts, they issued an unqualified audit report anyway. Shortly thereafter, Continental went bankrupt. The Securities and Exchange Commission brought charges of criminal fraud against the auditors, asserting that all of the information should have been disclosed, not just part of it. The auditors defended their actions by stating that they had followed the rules. The court, however, ruled that they should have complied with the disclosure principle. Information important to the investors and creditors—namely, the loan to the president and Valley's inability to repay its loan—was omitted from the financial report, and so the report was inadequate and misleading. The three individuals in charge of the audit were found guilty of criminal fraud and were given prison sentences. They could have avoided all charges if they had kept in mind the accountant's duty to the public and had revealed the truth, the whole truth, and nothing but the truth.

SIGHTS ALONG THE INTERNET

While this book covers a lot of material, it cannot hope to be complete in this limited space. The Internet or the web contains many sites that are of interest to accountants, and students are encouraged to expand their horizons by looking at these sites.

To begin with, the reader is urged to check the web sites for the organizations that set rules for accounting. Some of the more important ones are:

Financial Accounting Standards Board (FASB)	www.rutgers.edu/Accounting/raw/fasb
Independence Standards Board (ISB)	www.cpaindependence.org
Internal Revenue Service (IRS)	www.irs.gov
Securities and Exchange Commission (SEC)	www.sec.gov

The reader should examine the mission statements of these bodies and determine their purposes.

In addition, the reader should consult the web sites for organizations that are associations of accountants. The chief associations are:

American Institute of Certified Public Accountants (AICPA)	www.aicpa.org
Financial Executives Institute (FEI)	www.fei.org
Institute of Internal Auditors	www.theiia.org
Institute of Management Accountants (IMA)	www.imanet.org

Finally, there is an honors fraternity for bright accounting students. It is:

Beta Alpha Psi	www.betaalphapsi.org

CHAPTER SUMMARY IN TERMS OF LEARNING OBJECTIVES

Define Accounting, Financial Accounting, and the Conceptual Framework of Financial Accounting Accounting is the process of capturing, measuring, and communicating economic information about a firm to interested parties. Financial accounting is the branch of accounting that focuses on issues of providing information about the results of a company's activities to users outside of the firm, especially investors and creditors.

The conceptual framework is a series of documents issued by the Financial Accounting Standards Board that discuss the foundations of financial accounting.

State the Objective of Financial Accounting and Reporting The objective of financial accounting is to furnish investors and creditors with information that will help them make investment decisions. More specifically, the objective of accounting is to help investors and creditors determine the amount of cash they are likely to receive, when it will be received, and how much risk is involved.

Explain the Qualitative Characteristics of Information

Information is most useful when it is relevant and reliable. Relevance refers to the pertinence of the information to a particular decision that needs to be made. Reliability is the property that the information represents what it is supposed to represent and that it is free from bias and measurement error.

Define the Elements of Financial Accounting

The balance sheet has three elements. Assets are resources owned or controlled by the firm that probably have future economic value. Liabilities are obligations of the firm that can be discharged by disbursing assets, by providing services in the future, or by creating new obligations. Stockholders' equity is the residual interest that stockholders have in the assets of the corporation.

The income statement has five elements: revenues—inflows of net assets that arise because the firm sells a product or provides a service; gains—inflows of net assets that arise from some peripheral activity of the business; expenses—outflows of net assets that arise from acquiring or manufacturing goods, providing services, or some other activity which is a part of the major activities of the business; losses—outflows of net assets that arise from some peripheral activity of the business; and net income—revenues and gains minus expenses and losses.

The statement of changes in stockholders' equity depends on stockholders' equity and net income and on two other elements. Investments by owners are increases in stockholders' equity that result from an owner's transferring net assets or providing services to the business. Distributions to owners are decreases in stockholders' equity that result from transferring net assets or providing services to owners.

The cash flow statement depends on the notion of cash flow, that is, any transaction that increases or decreases the cash of the entity. A cash inflow is any cash flow in which the cash is received by the firm; a cash outflow is a cash disbursement.

Define Transaction and Transactions Processing

A transaction is an exchange, a nonreciprocal transfer, an event, or an allocation of the entity. Transactions processing comprises all of the activities that transform data about a firm's transactions into the firm's financial statements.

Discuss the Nature of Auditing and Distinguish between External Auditing and Internal Auditing

Auditing is the process of examining and verifying information. Persons who perform auditing are called auditors. External auditors are independent of the company in order to provide an objective, third-party review of the financial statements. Internal auditors work for the company that they audit.

Identify Management's Assertions in the Financial Report and Explain the Importance of Verifying These Assertions

Managers make five types of assertions about the financial statements they issue. They make assertions about existence or occurrence; about completeness; about valuation or allowance; about rights and obligations; and about presentation and disclosure. These assertions are important because they form the basis of the external audit; that is, the external auditor needs to verify these assertions by management.

Define Internal Control and Indicate Its Components

Internal control is the process of reasonably ensuring the realization of corporate goals, including the goal of producing trustworthy financial statements. Internal control is comprised of the control environment, risk assessment, control procedures, information and communication, and monitoring.

Discuss the Contents of the Management's Responsibility Report and an Unqualified Audit Report
The management responsibility report basically states that management is responsible for preparation of the financial statements. It often also mentions that the firm has an internal control system and that management believes it is working as it should.

An unqualified audit report confirms that the external auditor has examined the financial statements and has conducted the audit according to professional requirements. This audit includes a determination that the internal control system is indeed operating properly. Most importantly, the auditor who issues an unqualified opinion asserts that the financial statements present fairly the information they are supposed to represent.

Explain the Most Important Ethical Principle in Financial Accounting
The disclosure principle is the fundamental ethical duty of financial accountants. This principle is the duty to communicate all of the information that is relevant to users of financial statements.

GLOSSARY

Accountant—one who engages in accounting.

Accounting—the process of capturing, measuring, and communicating economic information about a firm to interested parties.

Accounting identity (*accounting equation*)—the relationship in which assets equal liabilities plus stockholders' equity.

Allocation—the distribution of some cost to various departments, assets, expenses, or time periods.

Asset—a resource owned or controlled by the firm which probably has future economic value.

Auditing—the process of examining and verifying information.

Auditor—one who engages in auditing.

Balance sheet—a financial statement that shows the assets of the firm, its liabilities, and its stockholders' equity.

Cash flow—any transaction that increases or decreases the cash of the entity.

Cash flow statement—a financial statement that explains the change in cash as a sum of the cash flows from the operating, investing, and financing activities of the entity.

Cash inflow—a cash flow in which the cash is received by the firm.

Cash outflow—a cash flow in which the cash is disbursed by the company.

Data—symbols that represent something.

Disclosure principle—the ethical principle that accountants ought to reveal relevant accounting data to investors and creditors.

Distributions to owners—decreases in stockholders' equity that result from transferring net assets or providing services to owners.

Dividends—distributions to owners (stockholders) of a corporation.

Drawings—distributions to owners in a sole proprietorship or a partnership.

Event—the occurrence of something that has a financial consequence for the firm.

Exchange—the giving up of something of value to receive something of value.

Expense—an outflow of assets (or inflow of liabilities) that arises from acquiring or manufacturing goods, providing services, or some other activity that is part of the major activities of the business.

External auditor—an auditor who does not work for the firm being examined and who provides an independent review of the financial statements.

Financial accounting—the branch of accounting that focuses on issues of providing information about the results of a company's activities to investors and creditors.

Gain—an inflow of assets (or outflow of liabilities) that arises from some peripheral activity of the business.

Income statement—a financial statement that shows the revenues and the gains, the expenses and the losses, the earnings, and, if the entity is a corporation, the earnings per share.

Information—data that helps someone make a decision.

Internal auditor—an auditor who works for the firm being examined.

Internal control—the process of reasonably ensuring the realization of corporate goals.

Investments by owners—increases in stockholders' equity that result from an owner's transferring net assets or providing services to the business.

Liability—an obligation of the firm that can be discharged by disbursing assets, by providing services in the future, or by creating new obligations.

Loss—an outflow of assets (or inflow of liabilities) that arises from some peripheral activity of the business.

Management responsibility report—a statement by management that it is responsible for the financial statements issued by the firm.

Net assets—assets minus liabilities.

Net income—revenues and gains minus expenses and losses; sometimes called earnings.

Nonreciprocal transfer—the giving up of something of value or the receiving of something of value, but not both.

Relevance—the property that information is pertinent to a particular decision that needs to be made.

Reliability—the property that the information represents what it is supposed to represent and that it is free from bias and measurement error.

Revenue—an inflow of assets (or outflow of liabilities) that arises because the firm sells a product or provides a service.

Statement of changes in stockholders' equity—a financial statement that shows the changes in the stockholders' equity accounts during the period.

Stockholders' equity—the residual interest that stockholders have in the assets of the corporation.

Transaction—an exchange, a nonreciprocal transfer, an event, or an allocation of the entity.

Transactions processing—all of the activities that transform data about a firm's transactions into the firm's financial statements.

Unqualified audit opinion—an opinion by the firm's external auditors that they have examined the financial statements and that the financial statements present fairly what they are supposed to represent.

Verifiability—the ability of different measurers to obtain the same values when they employ the same measurement methods.

REVIEW QUESTIONS

1. What is accounting and what are its branches?

2. What is the conceptual framework of financial accounting?

3. Who are the users of financial reports?

4. What is the objective of financial accounting?

5. Name the four basic financial statements.

6. Distinguish between data and information.

7. What are the qualitative characteristics of information?

8. Explain what is meant by verifiability.

9. Define asset, liability, and stockholders' equity.

10. What is the accounting identity?

11. Define revenue, gain, expense, loss, and net income.

12. Define investments by owners and distributions to owners.

13. Relate ending retained earnings to beginning retained earnings. Also indicate the relationship between the ending retained earnings of one year with the beginning retained earnings of the next year.

14. What is meant by cash flow? cash inflow? cash outflow?

15. What is the sum of cash from operating activities, cash from investing activities, and cash from financing activities?

16. Give an example of an exchange, a nonreciprocal transfer, an event, and an allocation.

17. Define transaction and transactions processing.

18. What are the basic steps in transactions processing?

19. Define auditing, and differentiate an external auditor from an internal auditor.

20. What assertions do managers make when they prepare financial statements? What is important about these assertions?

21. What is internal control?

22. What components comprise internal control?

23. What is a management's responsibility report?

24. What is an unqualified audit report? What does it say?

25. What is the disclosure principle and why is it important?

DISCUSSION QUESTIONS

1. An objective of financial accounting might be to assist macroeconomic policy. For example, many economists think it is desirable to dampen the business cycle, that is, make the up and down cycles smaller, with the emphasis obviously on reducing the severity of a recession. Accounting could help accomplish this goal by tying the financial income number to taxable income, and then increase income, thereby increasing taxes, during the boom half of the cycle and decreasing income during a recession.

(a) Is this goal better or worse than the U.S. objective of financial accounting?

(b) What type of country might have this macroeconomic goal? What features does this country and the United States possess that explain why they adopt the objectives they do?

2. Finance theory informs us that investors and creditors need to assess the financial risk of potential firms in which to invest. Market value of debt/market value of common stock is one measure of financial risk.

(a) How might financial accounting assist investors and creditors in assessing financial risk? *Hint:* If the market value of either debt or common stock is not available, an investor won't be able to compute the above measure of financial risk.

(b) What are the qualitative characteristics of these accounting data?

3. Consider the following three cases involving assets and liabilities, and answer the questions.

(a) An executory contract is a promise for a promise. For example, I promise to give you $1 million one year from now, and you promise to give me 100,000 barrels of oil one year from now. An executory contract is not enforceable. If, however, one party fulfills its end of the bargain, then the contract is no longer executory and it is enforceable. Should an accountant record an executory contract? *Hint*: Consider the definitions of asset and liability.

(b) Tish Company has an accounts receivable from Posh, Inc. for $80,000. Tish also has an accounts payable of $65,000 to Posh. Is it permissible for Tish Company to offset this receivable and payable and report on the balance sheet a net receivable of $15,000? *Hint*: Could anything happen to make the net receivable misleading?

(c) A contingent asset is an economic resource that the entity might have, while a contingent liability is an obligation that the entity might acquire. If one is a plaintiff in a civil suit, one might prevail and obtain a receivable from the defendant. The possible judgment is a contingent asset. If one is the defendant, then it is possible to lose the case and be required to pay something to the plaintiff. The possible payment is a contingent liability for the defendant.

Should contingent assets be reported on the balance sheet? Should contingent liabilities be reported on the balance sheet? *Hint*: Consider the definitions of asset and liability and also consider the disclosure principle.

4. As stated in the text, management makes five assertions when it issues a financial report to the public. When an auditor audits the company's financial report, he or she tries to verify these management assertions. Some assertions by management are easier to believe than others since management has economic incentives to reveal truthfully some items and fewer incentives to reveal other items. Which assertions are more likely to be scrutinized by the auditor?

5. Flip 'n Flop is a greasy hamburger joint that handles cash sales only. List the likely transactions in which Flip 'n Flop will engage.

6. The president of Veritas University has read about a recent spate of cheating scandals at various institutions. She would like to ensure that Veritas University does not meet a similar fate, and she has hired you to help. Design an internal control system to curb cheating.

7. Though not a perfect analogy, financial accounting and auditing may be compared to news reporting because financial accounting reports what happened to the firm and auditing ensures that the news reports are accurate. What ethical principles do you think should be adhered to by news reporters?

EXERCISES

1. Determine the unknown variable in the following independent cases:

	Assets	Liabilities	Stockholders' Equity
a.	?	$ 600,000	$400,000
b.	$ 300,000	?	$200,000
c.	$1,500,000	$1,700,000	?

2. Solve for the unknown quantity in the following independent cases.

	Net Income	Revenues	Gains	Expenses	Losses
a.	?	$ 500,000	$100,000	$400,000	$ 0
b.	$ 0	?	$ 0	$500,000	$100,000
c.	$ 100,000	$1,000,000	$ 0	?	$ 0
d.	$ (100,000)	$1,000,000	$ 50,000	$650,000	?

Negative numbers are shown within parentheses.

3. Dr. Peppermint, a firm that makes a peppermint-tea cola, began operations in 2001. Data pertaining to its operations are given here for 2001–2004. Compute the missing values in this table.

Year	Ending Retained Earnings	Beginning Retained Earnings	Net Income	Dividends
2001	?	$0	$10,000	$ 5,000
2002	?	?	$15,000	$10,000
2003	$20,000	?	?	$ 5,000
2004	$25,000	?	$13,000	?

4. Calculate the unknown in each of the following independent cases.

	Change in Cash	Cash from Operating Activities	Cash from Investing Activities	Cash from Financing Activities
a.	?	$ 40,000	$(30,000)	$(5,000)
b.	$22,000	$ 20,000	?	$ 10,000
c.	$(8,000)	$(10,000)	$(4,000)	?

Negative numbers are shown within parentheses.

5. For each of the following accounts, indicate whether it is found on the balance sheet or the income statement. If it appears on the balance sheet, state whether the account is an asset, liability, or stockholders' equity. If found on the income statement, state whether it is a revenue, gain, expense, or loss.

(a) Accounts payable
(b) Accounts receivable
(c) Advertising expense
(d) Building
(e) Cash
(f) Common stock
(g) Cost of goods sold
(h) Gain on sale of land
(i) Interest revenue
(j) Investments
(k) Land
(l) Loss from sale of investments

(m) Mortgage payable
(n) Patents
(o) Pension liability
(p) Retained earnings
(q) Sales
(r) Service revenue
(s) Taxes
(t) Taxes payable
(u) Unearned subscription revenue
(v) Utilities
(w) Wages
(x) Warranties payable

6. Banks offer checking and savings accounts to customers, and typically refer to them as non–interest-bearing and interest-bearing deposits. Of course, the money belongs to the customers and the bank must repay them.

Banks earn profits by taking these deposits and creating loans such as mortgages. To the bank, these loans are receivables because the debtor is obligated to repay the bank the amount of the loan plus interest. Banks also buy securities to earn dividends and interest, and they also try to earn trading profits.

For each of the following accounts for a bank, indicate whether it is found on the balance sheet or the income statement. If it appears on the balance sheet, state whether the account is an asset, liability, or stockholders' equity. If found on the income statement, state whether it is a revenue, gain, expense, or loss.

(a) Gain on sale of investments
(b) Interest-bearing deposits
(c) Interest earned
(d) Interest expense
(e) Interest payable
(f) Interest receivable

(g) Investments
(h) Loans
(i) Mortgages
(j) Loss on sale of investment
(k) Non–interest-bearing deposits

7. An insurance company charges customers for the insurance policy, and the charges are termed insurance premiums. Besides premiums, insurance companies make money by investing the proceeds and earning dividends or interest or capital gains.

When the customer or the beneficiary is entitled to receive cash from the insurance company because of the insurance policy, then a payment is made. These are referred to as insurance claims.

For each of the following accounts for an insurance firm, indicate whether it is found on the balance sheet or the income statement. If it appears on the balance sheet, state whether the account is an asset, liability, or stockholders' equity. If found on the income statement, state whether it is a revenue, gain, expense, or loss.

(a) Claims outstanding
(b) Dividends earned
(c) Gains on sale of investments
(d) Insurance premiums

(e) Interest earned
(f) Investments
(g) Losses on sale of investments
(h) Policyholder benefits and claims

THE BALANCE SHEET, INCOME STATEMENT, AND STATEMENT OF CHANGES IN STOCKHOLDERS' EQUITY

The purpose of financial accounting is to provide information about the firm to outsiders, particularly to investors and creditors. Companies convey information about their economic status and their economic accomplishments during the past year (or quarter) by publishing accounting reports that contain the balance sheet, the income statement, the statement of changes in stockholders' equity, and the cash flow statement. In this chapter we describe the first three statements; the cash flow statement is addressed in Chapter 5. Building on the elements defined in Chapter 1, we construct these statements by explaining the line items within them.

Businesses fall into three broad categories: service companies, merchandisers, and manufacturers. *Service companies*, as the name implies, provide services to customers. Accountants, hair stylists, entertainers, lawyers, and sports teams are examples of service companies. *Merchandisers* buy goods from distributors and wholesalers and resell them. Clothing stores, gas stations, grocery stores, shoe stores, and sporting goods stores are merchandisers. *Manufacturers* make the goods and sell them, and include auto makers, home builders, and makers of photographic instruments and materials. Distinctions among these businesses lead to differences in the asset section of the balance sheet and the income statement.

One may also categorize firms by their organization. A *sole proprietorship* is an unincorporated business with a single owner. A *partnership* is an unincorporated business with more than one owner. A *corporation* is a business entity licensed by a state government, and it receives various rights and responsibilities. Accounting for these three types of organizations leads to differences in the owner's equity section of the balance sheet and to differences in the statement of changes in stockholders' (owner's) equity.

After reading and studying this chapter, you should be able to:

- Prepare a balance sheet;
- Construct an income statement;
- Compute net sales, cost of goods sold, and gross margin for a merchandiser;
- Calculate cost of raw materials used, cost of goods manufactured, and cost of goods sold for a manufacturer; and
- Prepare a statement of changes in stockholders' (owner's) equity.

BALANCE SHEET

A *balance sheet* is a financial statement that shows the assets of the firm, its liabilities, and its stockholders' (owner's) equity. More specifically, the balance sheet utilizes the *accounting identity*, which states that assets equal liabilities plus stockholders' equity. As defined in Chapter 1, *assets* are resources owned or controlled by the firm that probably have future economic value; *liabilities* are obligations of the firm that can be discharged by disbursing assets, by providing services in the future, or by creating new obligations; and *stockholders' equity* is the residual interest that stockholders have in the assets of the corporation. If the firm is not a corporation, stockholder's equity is simply called owner's equity.

Exhibit 2.1 depicts a balance sheet for Paul McGarry Tutoring, a service company and a sole proprietorship. The heading of a balance sheet has three lines. The first line names the company, the second identifies the statement, and the third gives the date of the balance sheet. Notice that this financial statement shows the elements of the balance sheet: assets, liabilities, and owner's equity. Also observe that total assets ($990) equal total liabilities ($630) plus owner's equity ($360).

Assets

As shown in Exhibit 2.1, assets and liabilities are broken down into subgroups. When this is done, the balance sheet is said to be classified. Most companies present classified balance sheets, the main exception being financial institutions. The assets are often subdivided into four categories: (1) current assets, (2) investments and funds, (3) property, plant, and equipment, and (4) intangible assets.

A *current asset* is an asset that can be converted into cash or be consumed within one year or the operating cycle, whichever is longer. The *operating cycle* is the time from the purchase or production of inventory until the time it is sold and the cash is collected from the customer. Entities with an operating cycle less than one year use the one-year cutoff to decide whether or not an asset is current. Industries with an operating cycle less than one year include service companies, the food industry, and the clothing industry. Firms with an operating cycle longer than one year will use the length of the operating cycle to distinguish current and noncurrent assets. Shipbuilding and the wine industries typically have operating cycles longer than one year.

The most common current assets are cash, short-term investments, accounts and notes receivable, inventory, and prepaid items. They are typically placed in order of liquidity, that is, how quickly they can be turned into cash.

Cash consists of currency, coins, checking accounts, and savings accounts if the funds can be withdrawn in a short amount of time. It also includes the dollar equivalent of foreign currency. It is assumed that there are no restrictions on the cash, such as the money must be spent on a particular purpose. If restrictions do exist, then the amount is designated as "Restricted cash" and placed in the investments-and-funds section.

Businesses sometimes buy stocks and bonds and other securities of other organizations. These investments are divided into trading securities, securities held to maturity, and available-for-sale securities. Trading securities are investments made with the intention of selling them in the near future; they are always current assets. Securities held to maturity are bonds (or other debt instruments) bought with the intention of holding them until they mature. Available-for-sale securities are all other investments. Securities held to maturity and available-for-sale securities are generally placed in investments and funds, though they may be placed in current assets if they will mature or if the firm expects to

EXHIBIT *2.1*

BALANCE SHEET

Paul McGarry Tutoring
Balance Sheet
April 30, 2000

ASSETS

CURRENT ASSETS

Cash		$ 45
Trading securities		25
Accounts receivable	$ 40	
Less: allowance for doubtful accounts	5	35
Supplies inventory		40
Prepaid rent		15
Current assets		$160

INVESTMENTS AND FUNDS

Securities available for sale		$ 40
Securities held to maturity		10
Restricted cash		5
Investments and funds		$ 55

PROPERTY, PLANT, AND EQUIPMENT

Land		$230
Building	$600	
Less: accumulated depreciation	150	450
Equipment	$100	
Less: accumulated depreciation	30	70
Property, plant, and equipment		$750

INTANGIBLE ASSETS

Goodwill		15
Patents		$ 5
Copyrights		5
Intangible assets		$ 25
TOTAL ASSETS		$990

LIABILITIES AND OWNER'S EQUITY

CURRENT LIABILITIES

Accounts payable	$ 30
Notes payable	20
Wages payable	10
Taxes payable	15
Interest payable	5
Current liabilities	$ 80

LONG-TERM LIABILITIES

Mortgage payable	$400
Long-term notes payable	150
Long-term liabilities	$550
Total liabilities	$630

OWNER'S EQUITY

Paul McGarry, Capital	$360
TOTAL LIABILITIES AND OWNER'S EQUITY	$990

sell them within one year or the operating cycle, whichever is longer. Trading securities and available-for-sale securities are measured at their fair market value, whereas securities held to maturity are measured at their historical or original cost.

Receivables are rights to receive cash. Accounts receivable often arise as the firm sells goods or services on credit. The customer is given a certain time period, such as one month, before the cash is due. Accounts receivable are always current assets. Notes receivable are also claims to cash, but they are effected by a formal note in which the debtor promises to pay the company the cash that is owed. Often interest is charged on these notes. Notes receivable are current assets if they become collectible within one year or the operating cycle, whichever is longer. If they are not current assets, the notes receivable are put in investments and funds.

Some of the receivables will likely never be collected. An estimate of this uncollectible amount is forecast and assigned to allowance for doubtful accounts. As in Exhibit 2.1, accounts receivable shows the total amount of the receivables, the allowance account reveals the uncollectible portion, and the difference (sometimes called net receivables) is the amount that is estimated to be collected.

Inventories come next on the balance sheet. A service company only has supplies inventory, which represents the cost of paper, pencils, pens, envelopes, and other supplies used in the business. A merchandiser has supplies inventory plus merchandise inventory. Merchandise inventory discloses the cost of the goods bought by the firm and held for sale to the customer. In addition to supplies inventory, a manufacturer has raw materials inventory, work-in-process inventory, and finished goods inventory. Raw materials inventory consists of items bought by the firm that will be included in the manufacturing process. Work-in-process represents goods started in the production process but are unfinished. Finished goods are goods that are completed and are awaiting sale to customers. As an illustration, consider an automobile manufacturer. Tires, radios, and engines are raw materials; autos started in production but not completed comprise work-in-process inventory; and autos ready to be shipped to dealerships and other customers make up finished goods inventory.

Prepaid items are rights to utilize certain things because the firm has already paid for the privilege. Prepaid rent, for example, represents the right to make use of some resource such as a building or equipment. Prepaid insurance shows the claim to insurance protection. Prepaid advertising indicates that the firm has the right to have itself or its products advertised.

After the current assets section comes *investments and funds*. This section displays noncurrent securities bought for the purpose of receiving dividends, interest, and earning a profit upon their sale. It also includes cash set aside for specific purposes or restricted in some other way and long-term receivables. Accounts found in this section include available-for-sale securities, securities held to maturity, long-term notes receivable, and restricted cash.

The third portion of the assets section of the balance sheet is *property, plant, and equipment* (sometimes called fixed assets). This section displays the physical assets used in the operations of the firm. It consists of land, buildings, machinery, equipment, automobiles, and furniture and fixtures.

Land is real estate used in operations. If land is bought for trading purposes, it is placed in the investments-and-funds section of the balance sheet.

Buildings include both administrative offices and factories. Equipment and machinery encompass the physical resources used to do work in the business, such as computer equipment, ovens, and jack hammers. Automobiles and other motor vehicles and furniture and fixtures are other assets found in property, plant, and equipment.

Whereas land is shown on the balance sheet at original cost, the rest of the assets in the property, plant, and equipment section are disclosed at their original cost less accumulated depreciation. Like the allowance for doubtful accounts, accumulated depreciation is a valuation account that reduces the gross amount to an appropriate net figure called the *book value*. This book value, however, is not a measure of the market value of the asset. Rather, the depreciation process allocates the cost of the asset less the salvage value (an estimate of the asset's value when it is retired or sold) over the asset's expected life. A fuller explanation of depreciation is given in the next chapter.

The last category is intangible assets. *Intangible assets* are assets that represent legal rights rather than physical resources. Intangible assets include goodwill, patents, copyrights, trademarks, and franchises.

Goodwill arises when one company purchases another. Accountants measure goodwill as the amount paid for the other entity less its book value (i.e., the excess paid for the firm). A patent gives the owner the exclusive right to make and sell an item. A copyright bestows the sole right to publish the item copyrighted (a book, a movie, a song, or some other creative work). A trademark is some symbol, usually of a company or a product. Upon registration with the government, the firm becomes the only one entitled to employ the trademark. A franchise gives the entity the exclusive right to sell a product or provide a service within a given area. For example, McDonald's sells franchises to individuals that allow them to own and operate a McDonald's store in a particular locale.

Like property, plant, and equipment, intangible assets are initially recorded at their original or historical cost. They are also depreciated, but the term used is amortization rather than depreciation. An accumulated amortization account, similar to an accumulated depreciation account, may be set up, but the more common practice is for firms merely to write down the intangible asset.

Liabilities

Exhibit 2.1 indicates that liabilities are partitioned into current and long-term liabilities. *Current liabilities* are liabilities that come due within one year or the operating cycle, whichever is longer. *Long-term liabilities* are any liabilities that are not current liabilities. Note that whatever time period is utilized to delineate current from noncurrent assets is the same time period employed by that firm to distinguish current from noncurrent liabilities.

Current liabilities have short maturities and include accounts payable, notes payable, wages payable, taxes payable, and interest payable. Accounts and notes payable are the counterparts of accounts and notes receivable. Accounts payable arise as the company buys products or obtains services from a vendor on credit. The payable is due within a relatively short time, say one month. Notes payable are borrowings usually formalized by a legal note in which the firm promises to repay the borrowed money, usually with interest. Notes payable may be current or long-term, depending on when the debt is due.

Wages payable, taxes payable, and interest payable arise when the enterprise recognizes unpaid wages expense, taxes expense, and interest expense. The liability is created to recognize this debt until the firm pays the employees, government agency, or funds provider.

Not all debts are repaid with cash. Some debts arise because the firm receives cash and it owes some goods or services to the other party. For example, a magazine company might receive cash for a one-year subscription. The firm owes the customer the magazines, and this is recognized in unearned subscription revenue. Similar situations are recorded as unearned revenues.

Long-term liabilities are essentially the same types of things, except that they are longer in duration. A mortgage, for example, is a liability in which the asset is pledged as collateral if the debtor defaults on a payment. This debt is called a mortgage payable.

Sometimes corporations issue securities called bonds. A bond typically has a principal or face amount, say $1,000 per bond. It will have a stated or nominal interest rate listed in the contract, and the company makes periodic interest payments, often every six months in the United States. It will also have a stated maturity or life at the end of which the principal must be paid. This principal amount, the amount that is owed, is shown as bonds payable.

Stockholders' Equity

The last section of the balance sheet is referred to as stockholders' equity if the firm is a corporation, as owner's equity if the firm is a sole proprietorship, or as owners' equity if it is a partnership. This equity is the residual interest that the proprietor or the partners or the stockholders have in the assets of the proprietorship or the partnership or the corporation.

Suppose the company is a sole proprietorship. Then the owner's equity section of the balance sheet is very simple: it consists only of the owner's capital account, depicted by the owner's name followed by the word capital. In Exhibit 2.1, we see this as "Paul McGarry, Capital." Later in the chapter we discuss the computation of the amount put in the capital account.

If the firm is a partnership, the owners' equity section has a capital account for each partner. If the number of partners is large, sometimes an aggregate account is placed in the balance sheet ("Partners' Capital") to recognize the total capital, and the individual partners' interests is divulged in a separate schedule.

The equity section for a corporation takes on a different look. An example is given in Exhibit 2.2. Stockholders' equity has three components: contributed capital, retained earnings, and treasury stock.

In Chapter 1 we defined *investments by owners* as increases in stockholders' equity that result from an owner's transferring *net assets* (assets minus liabilities) or providing services to the business. As the name suggests, *contributed capital* reflects investments by the owners in a corporation, the stockholders. Contributed capital in Exhibit 2.2 includes preferred stock, common stock, and additional paid-in capital.

EXHIBIT 2.2

STOCKHOLDERS' EQUITY SECTION

Blue Dolphin Restaurant
Balance Sheet—Stockholders' Equity
April 30, 2000

Preferred stock, par value $5 per share, 10,000 shares authorized, 4,000 shares issued and outstanding	$ 20,000
Common stock, par value $1 per share, 200,000 shares authorized, 50,000 shares issued, 40,000 shares outstanding	50,000
Additional paid-in capital	375,000
Retained earnings	180,000
Treasury stock, 10,000 shares of common stock	(25,000)
Stockholders' equity	$600,000

Preferred stockholders or shareholders typically have preference over the common stockholders in terms of dividends and liquidation. In other words, common stockholders cannot receive any dividends until preferred stockholders receive theirs. If the firm liquidates, then preferred shareholders recover their investments before common stockholders receive anything back (but creditors receive their funds first). Preferred stockholders are usually limited in the amount of dividends they receive, whereas common shareholders are not.

Preferred stock has a par value, which is an arbitrarily assigned number by the board of directors. When the stock is issued, the amount of par value is reported in preferred stock. Any extra value that is received is recorded in additional paid-in capital or premium on preferred stock. Firms often report not only the par value of the preferred stock, but also how many shares are authorized to be issued (legally permissible to be sold), how many have been issued, and how many are outstanding (as opposed to those shares issued and repurchased by the firm).

If common stock has a par value, then it is accounted for in the same way, substituting common stock for preferred stock. Sometimes common stock does not have a par value for legal purposes but has a stated value for accounting purposes. The accounting is the same as if it had a par value by simply substituting the stated value for the par value. Occasionally, common stock is distributed that has neither par value nor stated value. In this case, the entire amount of the equity is reported in common stock.

After contributed capital, the second component of stockholders' equity, as can be seen in Exhibit 2.2, is retained earnings. *Retained earnings* reflects net income earned by the corporation that has not been distributed as dividends. (Some other items can affect retained earnings, but they are beyond the scope of this text.)

The third and last component of stockholders' equity is treasury stock. *Treasury stock* represents stock that has been issued by the firm, has been reacquired by the company, and has not been canceled. This implies that the firm can reissue the stock sometime in the future. The most common way of accounting for treasury stock is to measure it at cost. Then the amount is shown as a negative amount on the statement of stockholders' equity since it is a disinvestment by the owners. Negative amounts are often shown as numbers in parentheses.

Summary

The balance sheet states the resources, obligations, and owner's residual interest of the enterprise as of a particular date. The balance sheet embodies the accounting identity:

$$\text{Assets} = \text{Liabilities} + \text{Stockholders' equity}$$

We have expanded each of these elements into various subdivisions so that the expanded accounting identity for a sole proprietorship and partnership is

$$CA + IF + PPE + IA = CL + LTD + OC$$

For a corporation the expanded accounting identity becomes

$$CA + IF + PPE + IA = CL + LTD + CC + RE - TS$$

where

CA = current assets

IF = investments and funds

PPE = property, plant, and equipment

IA = intangible assets

CL = current liabilities

LTD = long-term liabilities

OC = owner's (owners') capital

CC = contributed capital

RE = retained earnings

TS = treasury stock

INCOME STATEMENT

An *income statement* is a financial statement that shows the revenues and gains, the expenses and losses, the net income, and, if the entity is a corporation, the earnings per share. A *revenue* is an inflow of net assets that arises because the firm sells a product or provides a service. A *gain* is an inflow of net assets that arises from some peripheral activity of the business. An *expense* is an outflow of net assets that arises from acquiring or manufacturing goods, providing services, or some other activity that is part of the major activities of the business. A *loss* is an outflow of net assets that arises from some peripheral activity of the business. *Net income* is revenues and gains minus expenses and losses.

Service Company

The income statement for a service company simply lists the revenues, gains, expenses, and losses of the firm. An illustration may be found in Exhibit 2.3. The heading of an income statement has three lines. The first line names the company, the second identifies

---

EXHIBIT 2.3

INCOME STATEMENT—SERVICE COMPANY

Matt Pliskin Consulting
Income Statement
For the year ended December 31, 2001

Revenues:	
Consulting fees	$1,000
Speaking fees	500
Gain on sale of equipment	200
Total revenues	$1,700
Expenses:	
Wages and salaries	$ 250
Rent expense	300
Supplies expense	150
Bad debts expense	25
Utilities expense	40
Interest expense	55
Loss on sale of investments	40
Taxes expense	320
Total expense	$1,180
Net income	$ 520

the statement, and the third gives the time period for the income statement. The reader should notice that a balance sheet is prepared as of a particular date, whereas an income statement is made for a certain time period. This difference is also reflected in the definitions of their elements. The elements of the balance sheet are defined as "stocks," amounts of resources or obligations or residual interest on a given date. The elements of the income statement are defined as "flows," amounts of net assets flowing in or out of the firm during a specific period.

Exhibit 2.3 gives the income statement for Matt Pliskin Consulting, a service company and a sole proprietorship. The format is a single-step format, which means that all of the revenues and gains are listed first, followed by all of the expenses and losses. Many firms will call the two sections "revenues" and "expenses," and will fold gains into revenues and losses into the expense section.

The revenues in Exhibit 2.3 consist of consulting fees and speaking fees. They represent the inflow of net assets, such as cash and accounts receivable, because of the services the firm provides to its customers. The gain is a gain on sale of equipment, which represents an inflow of net assets because the firm is selling its equipment at an amount greater than the book value of the equipment.

The income statement shows several expenses. Wages and salaries represents the outflow of net assets, such as cash and wages payable, to the employees of the business. Rent expense is the outflow of net assets to obtain the right to utilize an economic resource that belongs to someone else. Supplies expense characterizes the consumption of supplies inventory during the period. Bad debts expense reflects the uncollectibility of accounts and notes receivable. Utilities expense depicts the outflow of net assets, usually cash, for the use of electricity, natural gas, and telephones. Interest expense is the outflow of net assets, probably cash and interest payable, to obtain the use of somebody else's money. The loss on sale of investments represents an outflow of net assets because the company sold the investments for an amount less than their book value. Taxes expense portrays the outflow of net assets to government agencies.

The bottom line is net income. Net income is calculated as revenues plus gains minus expenses minus losses.

Merchandiser

The income statement for a merchandiser is like the service company's, except that it introduces sales discounts, sales returns and allowances, and cost of goods sold. A corporation's income statement also discloses earnings per share. Exhibit 2.4 depicts these differences, and it also illustrates a multistep format.

Suppose Lori Ann Miller sets up a cookie store and the firm is organized as a corporation. She buys cookies and other sweets from distributors and other suppliers and resells them. The income statement for 2001 is given in Exhibit 2.4. As usual, the heading identifies the company, the financial statement, and the time period it covers.

This income statement, as already noted, has a multistep format. This means that net sales are listed first, and then cost of goods sold is subtracted from net sales to arrive at gross margin or gross profit. Operating expenses are enumerated next. Then other revenues and other expenses are added and subtracted, which yields income before taxes. Subtracting the income tax expense gives you net income. Of course, the single-step and multistep formats produce the same net income; they merely arrange the data differently.

Sales indicates the net assets, probably cash and accounts receivable, that flow into the Miller corporation during the year as a result of selling cookies to customers.

EXHIBIT 2.4

INCOME STATEMENT—MERCHANDISER

Lori Ann Miller Cookies
Income Statement
For the year ended June 30, 2001

Sales			$200,000
Sales discounts		$ 10,000	
Sales returns and allowances		25,000	35,000
Net Sales			$165,000
Cost of goods sold			
Beginning merchandise inventory		$ 50,000	
Purchases	$90,000		
Freight in	5,000		
Purchase discounts	$3,000		
Purchase returns and allowances	7,000	(10,000)	
Net purchases		85,000	
Cost of goods available for sale		$135,000	
Ending merchandise inventory		65,000	
Cost of goods sold			70,000
Gross margin			$ 95,000
Selling and administrative expenses			
Wages and salaries		$ 40,000	
Utilities		15,000	
Depreciation		10,000	
Freight out		5,000	70,000
			$ 25,000
Other revenues			
Interest earned		$ 7,000	
Other expenses			
Loss on sale of land		2,000	5,000
Income before taxes			$ 30,000
Income taxes			20,000
Net income			$ 10,000
Earnings per share			$ 1.60

Sometimes a corporation that makes credit sales will offer cash discounts if the customer pays early. Terms of 2/10, n/30 means that if the customer pays within 10 days, a 2% discount may be taken; otherwise, the net amount is payable in 30 days. Suppose Miller sells $1,000 of cookies on credit to a fraternity. If the fraternity pays after the 10-day discount period, it must pay the full $1,000. If the fraternity pays within the discount period, however, it only pays $980. Miller accounts for this transaction by showing sales of $1,000 and sales discounts of $20; the net amount is $980.

Occasionally, customers will return the goods because the products are damaged or because they really wanted something else. If cash is given to the customer or if the customer's balance is reduced, then this exchange is shown as a sales returns. Sometimes, for example, if the goods are only slightly damaged, the firm will offer the customer a lower price. In this case, the reduction is referred to as a sales allowance. In practice, returns and allowances are often combined, so one has sales returns and allowances.

Net sales are equal to sales minus sales discounts and sales returns and allowances. This computation correctly shows the amount of net assets that has flowed into the corporation because of the selling activities.

Miller, of course, must pay the distributors and other vendors for the cookies. The expense cost of goods sold shows the outflow of net assets, typically cash and accounts payable, for these goods. As shown in Exhibit 2.4, cost of goods sold is a calculation: beginning merchandise inventory plus net purchases minus ending merchandise inventory.

The number of units of beginning merchandise inventory plus the number of units of net purchases equals the number of units available for sale to the customers. The firm either sells these items, or they are still in ending inventory at year-end; therefore, the number of units available for sale to the customers minus the number of units in ending inventory yields the number of units sold during the time period.

Instead of number of units, the income statement reveals a similar calculation in terms of cost. Beginning merchandise inventory shows the cost of the goods that can be sold to the customer but have not been sold as of the beginning of the fiscal year. Net purchases reflects the net cost of buying new merchandise from the distributors and other suppliers. Adding the two together produces the cost of goods available for sale. Subtracting the cost of ending merchandise inventory—the cost of the units unsold during the year—gives the cost of goods sold.

Let's look at net purchases more closely. Purchases reflect the outflow of net assets to obtain new merchandise. Shipping and handling charges are reported as freight in and are sometimes called transportation in. Just as customers could enjoy sales discounts and return unwanted or damaged goods or receive an allowance, Miller Cookies may take advantage of cash discounts or return merchandise to the suppliers or obtain an allowance. In this context, the cash discounts and merchandise returns are called purchase discounts and purchase returns and allowances. Putting these factors together, we have net purchases equals purchases plus freight in minus purchase discounts minus purchase returns and allowances.

Gross profit or gross margin equals net sales minus cost of goods sold. This is an important statistic since the merchandiser must have a large enough markup over cost to pay for other expenses and to generate profits.

The operating expenses come next on the income statement. Although not shown in Exhibit 2.4, they are sometimes divided into administrative and selling expenses. Administrative expenses cover the nonselling activities of the firm, such as the costs of secretaries, janitors, and accountants. Selling expenses include wages of the sales staff, advertising costs, and use of cars by the sales staff. The new operating expenses in Exhibit 2.4 are depreciation and freight out. Depreciation is an outflow of net assets, specifically some long-term assets, such as a building or equipment, because of its use during the period. In other words, depreciation is a cost allocation technique since it takes the cost of the long-term asset and parcels it out over the time period in which the entity is expected to hold the asset. Freight out, also called transportation out, discloses the shipping and handling costs when the corporation is the seller and bears explicitly the transportation charges. Note that both freight in and freight out are costs of transportation; the costs go to freight in if the firm is the purchaser and to freight out if it is the seller.

Other revenues are interest earned, an inflow of net assets, cash, or interest receivable, because the company allowed somebody to use its money. Other expenses is loss on sale of land. These items are added and subtracted to obtain income before taxes. Income taxes are subtracted, and net income is determined.

Finally, earnings per share must be disclosed if the company is a corporation. Doubtless, earnings per share (sometimes abbreviated as eps) is one of the most used accounting statistics by investors and creditors. The financial press, stock brokers, and financial analysts often quote company earnings per share in their reports.

In Chapter 1 we defined earnings per share as net income divided by the number of common shares. Since we have discussed preferred stock, this definition can now be expanded. Earnings per share shows the earnings available to common shareholders, so the numerator is net income minus preferred dividends. The denominator is the number of common shares issued and outstanding; in other words, treasury shares are omitted. If Lori Ann Miller Cookies has $2,000 preferred dividends and 5,000 outstanding shares of common stock, then earnings per share equals $1.60 (($10,000 − $2,000) / 5,000).

Manufacturing Concern

The income statement for manufacturers is essentially the same as the one for merchandisers. The only difference is in the computation of cost of goods sold, so our discussion of this document will focus on that calculation.

There are three types of manufacturing costs: direct materials, direct labor, and factory overhead (also called manufacturing overhead or simply overhead). *Direct materials* are the raw materials that are used in the production of a good and become an integral part of the product. If the product is a car, the direct materials include engines, power trains, frames, and tires. Direct materials are distinguished from *indirect materials*, which are raw materials too small to keep track of—such as nails and nuts and bolts and screws.

Direct labor is labor performed during the production process which can be traced to the products. For an auto maker, direct labor means the people on the assembly line who are putting the car together. *Indirect labor* is other labor during the production process that cannot be easily traced to the products. For an auto maker, indirect labor includes the supervisors and the technicians who keep the equipment running.

Factory overhead refers to any resources employed in the production process except for direct materials and direct labor. Factory overhead encompasses indirect materials, indirect labor, maintenance costs, rent, depreciation of factory buildings or equipment, factory supplies, and factory utilities.

The accountant keeps track of the cost of direct materials, direct labor, and factory overhead. At the end of the period, these resources are listed either in one of the inventories or in cost of goods sold. Recall from the earlier discussion of the balance sheet that raw materials inventory are items bought by the firm to be included in the manufacturing process, work-in-process inventory represents goods started but unfinished in the production process, and finished goods inventory includes completed goods that are awaiting sale to customers.

Although the determination of cost of goods sold could be displayed in one table or one formula, it would be unwieldy, so we will obtain cost of goods sold with three successive schedules. The first is the *cost-of-raw-materials schedule*, which figures out the cost of the direct materials employed in the production process during the period. The second schedule is the *cost-of-goods-manufactured schedule*, and it gauges the manufacturing costs of those goods finished during the period. The *cost-of-goods-sold schedule* shows the manufacturing costs of those items sold during the period.

Exhibit 2.5 displays a cost-of-raw-materials-used schedule. Notice that structurally this schedule is the same as the merchandiser's cost-of-goods-sold schedule (compare Exhibits 2.4 and 2.5), with raw materials inventory substituting for merchandise inventory. This makes sense because a merchandiser purchases the goods it plans to sell, whereas a manufacturer purchases the goods it plans to utilize in the production process. Instead of

EXHIBIT 2.5

COST OF RAW MATERIALS USED

Stan Anderson and Company
Cost of Raw Materials Used
For the year ended February 28, 2001

Beginning raw materials inventory			$ 50,000
Purchases		$90,000	
Freight in		5,000	
Purchase discounts	$3,000		
Purchase returns and allowances	7,000	(10,000)	
Net purchases			85,000
Cost of raw materials available			$135,000
Ending raw materials inventory			65,000
Cost of raw materials used in production			$ 70,000

arriving at cost of goods sold, however, this formula now yields the cost of raw materials used during production. This too is logical since a merchandiser sells the purchased units as they are, but a manufacturer introduces the purchased items into a production process that transforms them into different products.

Exhibit 2.6 illustrates a cost-of-goods-manufactured schedule. Beginning work-in-process inventory shows the manufacturing cost of goods started in the production process last period but unfinished as of the end of last period. The manufacturing costs—direct materials, direct labor, and factory overhead—of the current period are then registered in the schedule. Beginning work-in-process plus the manufacturing costs gives the cost of goods started in the production process. These items are either complete or incomplete at

EXHIBIT 2.6

COST OF GOODS MANUFACTURED

Stan Anderson and Company
Cost of Goods Manufactured
For the year ended February 28, 2001

Beginning work-in-process inventory			$ 50,000
Direct materials		$ 70,000	
Direct labor		45,000	
Factory overhead			
Indirect materials	$35,000		
Indirect labor	65,000		
Factory rent	20,000		
Factory depreciation	10,000		
Factory supplies	12,000		
Factory utilities	7,000		
Factory overhead		149,000	
Manufacturing costs			264,000
Cost of goods started in production			$314,000
Ending work-in-process inventory			34,000
Cost of goods manufactured			$280,000

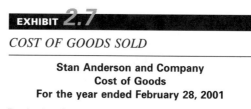

COST OF GOODS SOLD

Stan Anderson and Company
Cost of Goods
For the year ended February 28, 2001

Beginning finished goods inventory	$ 90,000
Cost of goods manufactured	280,000
Cost of goods available for sale	$370,000
Ending finished goods inventory	80,000
Cost of goods sold	$290,000

the end of the period. Thus, the cost of goods started in production minus the cost of ending work-in-process inventory (i.e., not finished) equals the cost of goods manufactured (i.e., finished) for the period.

The third and last schedule is the cost-of-goods-sold schedule, as illustrated in Exhibit 2.7. The cost of beginning finished goods inventory is added to the cost of goods manufactured to obtain the cost of goods available for sale. Since the goods are either sold or not sold, the cost of goods available for sale minus the cost of ending finished goods inventory (unsold items) equals the cost of goods sold.

This cost of goods sold is an expense of a manufacturing concern, the same as it is an expense for a merchandiser. The rest of the income statement is similar to that for other firms.

Summary

The income statement discloses the net income of the entity as the revenues plus the gains minus the expenses and the losses during a particular period such as one year. Thus, the income statement employs the formula:

$$\text{Net income} = \text{Revenues} + \text{Gains} - \text{Expenses} - \text{Losses}$$

In addition, if the firm is a corporation, it will report the earnings per share which equals the net income minus the preferred dividends, all divided by the number of common shares outstanding.

Service companies do not have net sales or cost of goods sold; merchandisers and manufacturers do. Net sales is computed as

$$\text{Net Sales} = \text{Sales} - \text{SD} - \text{SRA}$$

where

$\quad$ SD = sales discounts

$\quad$ SRA = sales returns and allowances

Merchandisers and manufacturers have cost of goods as one of their expenses. Merchandisers determine cost of goods sold with the formula:

$$\text{COGS} = \text{BI} + \text{NP} - \text{EI}$$

where

$\quad$ COGS = cost of goods sold

$\quad\quad$ BI = beginning merchandise inventory

$\quad\quad$ NP = net purchases

$\quad\quad$ EI = ending merchandise inventory

The formula for net purchases is

$$NP = P + FI - PD - PRA$$

where

$\quad\quad$ P = purchases

$\quad\quad$ FI = freight in

$\quad\quad$ PD = purchase discounts

$\quad\quad$ PRA = purchase returns and allowances

Manufacturers determine cost of goods sold in a three-step process. They calculate first the cost of raw materials used, then the cost of goods manufactured, and finally the cost of goods sold. The formulas are

$$CORMU = BRM + NP - ERM = BRM + P + FI - PD - PRA - ERM$$
$$COGM = BWIP + CORMU + DL + FOH - EWIP$$
$$COGS = BFG + COGM - EFG$$

where

$\quad$ CORMU = cost of raw materials used

$\quad\quad$ BRM = beginning raw materials inventory

$\quad\quad$ ERM = ending raw materials inventory

$\quad$ COGM = cost of goods manufactured

$\quad\quad$ BWIP = beginning work-in-process inventory

$\quad\quad$ DL = direct labor

$\quad\quad$ FOH = factory overhead

$\quad\quad$ EWIP = ending work-in-process inventory

$\quad\quad$ BFG = beginning finished goods inventory

$\quad\quad$ EFG = ending finished goods inventory

and the other symbols retain their previous definitions.

STATEMENT OF CHANGES IN STOCKHOLDERS' EQUITY

The third statement we will unravel in this chapter is the statement of changes in stock-holders' equity, if the entity is a corporation. If the firm is a sole proprietorship or partnership, it is known as the statement of changes in owner's or owners' capital.

Let's assume that we are talking about a corporation. Then, the *statement of changes in stockholders' equity* shows the changes in the stockholders' equity accounts during the period. These changes include *investments by owners* (increases in stockholders' equity that result from an owner's transferring net assets or providing services to the business)

EXHIBIT **2.8**

STATEMENT OF OWNER'S CAPITAL

Suzanne Wright Tax Services
Statement of Owner's Capital
December 31, 2001

Suzanne Wright, Capital, January 1, 2001	$ 1,000
Investments by owner	30,000
	$ 31,000
Net income	188,000
	$219,000
Withdrawals	29,000
Suzanne Wright, Capital, December 31, 2001	$190,000

---

and *distributions to owners* (decreases in stockholders' equity that result from transferring net assets or providing services to owners). In a sole proprietorship or a partnership, distributions to owners are called *drawings*, but in a corporation they are labeled *dividend*. The changes also focus on net income that is not distributed as drawings or dividends. Finally, if the company has the corporate form, it must deal with changes in treasury stock.

Sole Proprietorship and Partnership

Exhibit 2.8 demonstrates a statement of owner's capital for a sole proprietor. The beginning capital balance is increased by earnings (decreased if earnings are negative) and by additional investments by the proprietor, and it is decreased by withdrawals. If the firm is a partnership, then each partner has a capital account, and the change in each capital account is computed as it is in Exhibit 2.8. A statement of owners' capital would show these changes for all the partners.

Corporation

Exhibit 2.9 displays a statement of retained earnings for a corporation. Retained earnings basically represent earnings that have not yet been distributed to the stockholders as dividends. The account is increased by net income and decreased by dividends. This statement, however, concerns only one stockholders' equity account, namely, retained earnings.

EXHIBIT **2.9**

STATEMENT OF RETAINED EARNINGS

Mdlrus Manufacturing
Statement of Retained Earnings
October 31, 2001

Retained earnings, November 1, 2000	$100,000
Net income	500,000
	$600,000
Dividends	250,000
Retained earnings, October 31, 2001	$350,000

Exhibit 2.10 shows a statement of changes in stockholders' equity. It has a heading similar to the other statements that identifies the company, statement, and time period which the statement covers. The statement lists each stockholders' equity account and reveals the changes that have taken place over the three-year period. All accounts indicate the change in the dollar amount, and common stock and treasury stock also show the change in the number of shares involved.

Unique Captions issued 2,000 shares of common stock for $54,000 in 2002. Since the par value is $2 per share, $4,000 (2,000 shares times $2 per share) is added to common stock. The rest ($54,000 − $4,000 = $50,000) is added to additional paid-in capital in 2002.

The retained earnings portion of the statement is straightforward. Consistent with earlier statements, ending retained earnings is the beginning balance plus net income (though there is a loss in 2004) minus dividends.

During 2003 Unique Captions bought 1,000 shares of its own common stock for $22,000, or $22 per share. Notice that the $22,000 cost is entered as a negative number since treasury stock reduces stockholders' equity. In 2004 the enterprise sold 400 treasury shares for $10,000, and stockholders' equity was increased by this amount. The cost of these 400 treasury shares is $8,800 (400 shares times $22 per share). The difference is $10,000 − $8,800 or $1,200, and it represents additional contributed capital. It is placed in the additional paid-in capital account.

Of course, the last line in the statement of changes in stockholders' equity gives the account balances for the current year. These numbers should match those in the stockholders' equity section of the balance sheet.

EXHIBIT 2.10

STATEMENT OF CHANGES IN STOCKHOLDERS' EQUITY

Unique Captions
Statement of Changes in Stockholders' Equity
For the years ended December 31, 2002, 2003, and 2004

	Common Stock		*Additional Paid-in Capital*	*Retained Earnings*	*Treasury Stock*	
	Shares	*Amount*			*Shares*	*Amount*
Balance, December 31, 2001	10,000	$20,000	$240,000	$420,000	0	$ 0
Issue common stock	2,000	4,000	50,000			
Net income				75,000		
Dividends				(14,000)		
Balance, December 31, 2002	12,000	$24,000	$290,000	$481,000	0	$ 0
Repurchase common stock					1,000	$(22,000)
Net income				30,000		
Dividends				(5,000)		
Balance, December 31, 2003	12,000	$24,000	$290,000	$506,000	1,000	$(22,000)
Issue treasury stock			1,200		(400)	8,800
Net loss				(5,000)		
Balance, December 31, 2004	12,000	$24,000	$291,200	$501,000	600	$(13,200)

Summary

The statement of owner's equity for a sole proprietor utilizes the relationship

$$ENDCAP = BEGCAP + INVEST + NI - Drawings$$

where

> ENDCAP = ending owner's capital
>
> BEGCAP = beginning owner's capital
>
> INVEST = additional investments by the owner
>
> NI = net income

A statement of owners' equity for a partnership would employ the same relationship for each and every partner.

A statement of changes in stockholders' equity also tries to reconcile the beginning and ending balances in stockholders' equity. For retained earnings, the following relationship is applied:

$$ERE = BRE + NI - D$$

where

> ERE = ending retained earnings
>
> BRE = beginning retained earnings
>
> NI = net income
>
> D = dividends

Ending common stock (or preferred stock) equals the beginning balance plus new issuances.

Ending additional paid-in capital is the beginning additional paid-in capital plus or minus the changes that occurred during the year.

Finally, ending treasury stock equals beginning treasury stock plus additional purchases of treasury stock minus the cost of treasury stock sold.

SIGHTS ALONG THE INTERNET

The reader ought to apply the knowledge gained from this chapter by looking at some balance sheets and income statements of real-world companies. Several firms that display their annual reports on the Internet are (the ticker symbols are contained in parentheses; these are abbreviations used by Wall Street when giving market quotations):

Apple Computer (AAPL)	www.apple.com
Banc One Corporation (ONE)	www.bankone.com
Chevron Corporation (CHV)	www.chevron.com
GATX Corporation (GMT)	www.gatx.com
General Motors (GM)	www.gm.com
J. C. Penney Company (JCP)	www.jcpenney.com
Mellon Bank (MEL)	www.mellon.com
Tribune Company (TRB)	www.tribune.com
Wendy's International (WEN)	www.wendys.com

Large firms that sell securities publicly must file reports with the SEC. Copies of these reports can be obtained from the EDGAR database. They can be accessed at:

SEC (then click on EDGAR)	www.sec.gov
EDGAR database (directly)	www.sec.gov.edgarhp.htm

Some important documents on EDGAR are termed forms 10-K, 10-Q, and 8-K. What data can be found in these reports? Using the nine firms listed above, compare and contrast the annual report with the company's 10-K.

CHAPTER SUMMARY IN TERMS OF LEARNING OBJECTIVES

Prepare a Balance Sheet. A balance sheet shows the assets, liabilities, and stockholders' equity of the firm. Assets—resources owned or controlled by the company that probably have future economic value—are divided into current assets, investments and funds, property, plant, and equipment, and intangible assets. A current asset is an asset that can be converted into cash or be consumed within one year or the operating cycle, whichever is longer. The operating cycle is the time from the purchase or production of inventory until the time it is sold and the cash is collected from the customer. Investments and funds are noncurrent investments, cash set aside for specific purposes or restricted in some other way, and long-term receivables. Property, plant, and equipment are noncurrent, physical assets used in the operations of the firm. Intangible assets are assets that represent legal rights rather than physical resources.

Liabilities—obligations of the firm that can be discharged by disbursing assets, by providing services in the future, or by creating new obligations—are partitioned into current and long-term liabilities. Current liabilities are liabilities that come due within one year or the operating cycle, whichever is longer. Long-term liabilities are any liabilities that are not current liabilities.

Stockholders (or owner's) equity is the residual interest that stockholders have in the assets of the corporation. A sole proprietorship or a partnership shows only the owner's capital account(s). The equity section for a corporation consists of contributed capital, retained earnings, and treasury stock. Contributed capital reflects investments made by the stockholders. Retained earnings indicates net income earned by the corporation that has not been distributed as dividends. Treasury stock represents stock that had been issued by the firm, has been reacquired by the company, and has not been canceled.

The format of the balance sheet is as follows: current assets plus investments and funds plus property, plant, and equipment plus intangible assets equal current liabilities plus long-term liabilities plus contributed capital plus retained earnings minus treasury stock.

Construct an Income Statement. The income statement shows the revenues and gains, the expenses and losses, the net income, and, if the entity is a corporation, the earnings per share. Revenues are inflows of net assets that arise because the firm sells a product or provides a service. Gains are inflows of net assets that arise from some peripheral activity of the business. Expenses are outflows of net assets that arise from acquiring or manufacturing goods, providing services, or some other activity that is a part of the major activities of the business. Losses are outflows of net assets that arise from some peripheral activity of the business. Net income equals revenues plus gains minus expenses minus losses. Earnings per share equals net income minus preferred dividends, all divided by the number of common shares outstanding.

Compute Net Sales, Cost of Goods Sold, and Gross Margin for a Merchandiser.
Net sales are sales minus sales discounts and sales returns and allowances. Cost of goods sold for a merchandiser is beginning merchandise inventory plus net purchases minus ending merchandise inventory. Net purchases equals purchases plus freight in minus purchase discounts minus purchase returns and allowances. Gross margin, also called gross profit, is net sales less cost of goods sold.

Calculate Cost of Raw Materials Used, Cost of Goods Manufactured, and Cost of Goods Sold for a Manufacturer.
Cost of goods sold for a manufacturer is determined by three schedules. Cost of raw materials used equals beginning raw materials inventory plus net purchases minus ending raw materials inventory. (Net purchases is computed as above for a merchandiser.)

Cost of goods manufactured depends on the manufacturing costs of the entity: direct materials, direct labor, and factory overhead. Direct materials are the raw materials that are used in the production of a product and become an integral part of the product. Direct labor is the labor performed during the production process which can be traced to the products. Factory overhead is the resources employed in the production process except for direct materials and direct labor. Cost of goods manufactured equals beginning work-in-process inventory plus direct materials (cost of raw materials used) plus direct labor plus factory overhead minus ending work-in-process inventory.

Cost of goods sold equals beginning finished goods inventory plus cost of goods manufactured minus ending finished goods inventory.

Prepare a Statement of Changes in Stockholders' (Owner's) Equity.
If the firm is a sole proprietorship or partnership, then this statement simply displays the changes in the capital account(s). Ending capital is equal to beginning capital plus additional investments by the owner plus net income minus drawings.

If the company has a corporate organization, then the changes are shown for contributed capital, retained earnings, and treasury stock. Ending contributed capital (such as common stock, preferred stock, and additional paid-in capital) is the beginning balance plus whatever changes have occurred, typically for the issuance of new stock. Ending retained earnings is obtained as beginning retained earnings plus net income minus dividends. Beginning treasury stock plus additional purchases of treasury stock minus sales of treasury stock yields ending treasury stock.

GLOSSARY

Accounting identity—the relationship that assets equal liabilities plus stockholders' equity.

Asset—a resource owned or controlled by the firm that probably has future economic value.

Balance sheet—a financial statement that shows the assets of the firm, its liabilities, and its stockholders' equity.

Book value—original cost minus accumulated depreciation.

Contributed capital—investments by the stockholders.

Corporation—a business entity licensed by the government that receives various rights and has certain responsibilities.

Cost-of-goods-manufactured schedule—a table that gauges the manufacturing costs of those goods finished during the period.

Cost-of-goods-sold schedule—a table that shows the costs of items sold during the period.

Cost-of-raw-materials-schedule—a table that shows the cost of the direct materials employed in the production process during the period.

Current assets—assets that can be converted into cash or be consumed within one year or the operating cycle, whichever is longer.

Current liabilities—liabilities that come due within one year or the operating cycle, whichever is longer.

Direct labor—labor performed during the production process which can be traced to the products.

Direct materials—the raw materials that are used in the production of a product and become an integral part of the product.

Distributions to owners—decreases in stockholders' equity that result from transferring net assets or providing services to owners.

Dividends—distributions to owners (stockholders) of a corporation.

Drawings—distributions to owners in a sole proprietorship or a partnership.

Expense—an outflow of assets (or inflow of liabilities) that arises from acquiring or manufacturing goods, providing services, or some other activity that is part of the major activities of the business.

Factory overhead—resources employed in the production process except for direct materials and direct labor.

Gain—an inflow of assets (or outflow of liabilities) that arises from some peripheral activity of the business.

Income statement—a financial statement that shows the revenues and gains, the expenses and losses, the earnings, and, if the entity is a corporation, the earnings per share.

Indirect labor—labor during the production process that cannot be easily traced to the products.

Indirect materials—the raw materials that are used in production but are too small to keep track of.

Intangible assets—assets that represent legal rights rather than physical resources.

Investments and funds—noncurrent investments, cash set aside for specific purposes or restricted in some other way, and long-term receivables.

Investments by owners—increases in stockholders' equity that result from an owner's transferring net assets or providing services to the business.

Liability—an obligation of the firm that can be discharged by disbursing assets, by providing services in the future, or by creating new obligations.

Long-term liabilities—liabilities that are not current liabilities.

Loss—an outflow of assets (or inflow of liabilities) that arises from some peripheral activity of the business.

Manufacturers—firms that make and sell goods.

Merchandisers—firms that buy goods from distributors and wholesalers and resell them.

Net assets—assets minus liabilities.

Net income—revenues and gains minus expenses and losses.

Operating cycle—the time from the purchase or production of inventory until the time it is sold and the cash is collected from the customer.

Partnership—an unincorporated business with more than one owner.

Property, plant, and equipment—noncurrent, physical assets used in the operations of the firm.

Retained earnings—net income earned by the corporation that has not been distributed as dividends.

Revenue—an inflow of assets (or outflow of liabilities) that arises because the firm sells a product or provides a service.

Service companies—firms that provide services to customers.

Sole proprietorship—an unincorporated business with a single owner.

Statement of changes in stockholders' equity—a financial statement that shows the changes in the stockholders' equity accounts during the period.

Stockholders' equity—the residual interest that stockholders have in the assets of the corporation.

Treasury stock—stock that has been issued by the firm, has been reacquired by the company, and has not been canceled.

REVIEW QUESTIONS

1. Differentiate among service companies, merchandisers, and manufacturers.

2. Distinguish among sole proprietorships, partnerships, and corporations.

3. What is a balance sheet?

4. What are assets, liabilities, and stockholders' equity?

5. What is meant by operating cycle, and what is its significance?

6. What are current assets? Name some current assets.

7. Companies can buy stocks and bonds and other securities of other firms. What are the three types of investment accounts?

8. What inventories exist for a service company, a merchandiser, and a manufacturer?

9. What are investments and funds? Name some assets found in the section labeled investments and funds.

10. What is property, plant, and equipment? Name some assets that are typically categorized as property, plant, and equipment.

11. What is the book value of an asset?

12. What are intangible assets? Name some intangible assets.

13. What are current liabilities? What are long-term liabilities? Give examples of each.

14. What accounts comprise the owner's equity section of a sole proprietorship and a partnership?

15. What is contributed capital? What accounts are usually found in this section?

16. What is retained earnings?

17. What is treasury stock?

18. What is an income statement?

19. Define revenue, gain, expense, loss, and net income.

20. What are sales, sales discounts, and sales returns and allowances?

21. What are purchases, purchase discounts, and purchase returns and allowances?

22. Indicate the difference between freight in and freight out.

23. What is earnings per share?

24. There are three manufacturing costs. Name them.

25. What is the difference between direct materials and indirect materials?

26. What is the difference between direct labor and indirect labor?

27. What is a statement of changes in stockholders' equity?

28. What makes up the statement of changes in owner's equity in a sole proprietorship? in a partnership?

29. What comprises the statement of changes in stockholders' equity in a corporation?

DISCUSSION QUESTIONS

1. Recall the discussion in Chapter 1 about relevance—the property that information is pertinent to a particular decision that needs to be made. The Financial Accounting Standards Board claims that relevance has three components: predictive value, feedback value, and timeliness. Predictive value means that the variable can be used to predict things important to the decision maker. Feedback value refers to the variable's confirming beliefs about things important to the decision maker. Timeliness implies that the information is released in time to assist individuals in making decisions.

Investors and creditors probably feel that the two most important statistics produced by accountants are net income and earnings per share. Discuss the relevance of these two accounting numbers.

2. Reliability was defined in Chapter 1 as the property that the information represents what it is supposed to represent and that it is free from bias and measurement error. The Financial Accounting Standards Board asserts that reliability is made up of verifiability, representational faithfulness, and neutrality. We defined verifiability as the ability of different measurers to obtain the same values when they employ the same measurement methods. Representational faithfulness means that the variable and its measurement represent accurately what it is meant to represent. Neutrality implies that the accountant has not biased the numbers in any particular way.

Most assets are valued at their original cost, that is, the amount the firm paid to obtain or make them. The usual reason for adhering to this principle is that it increases reliability. But consider the reliability of market value. What is the reliability of measuring (a) inventory, (b) investments, and (c) buildings at their market value?

3. Land may appear on the balance sheet either as a current asset, property, plant, and equipment, or investments and funds. Explain.

4. As presented in this chapter, accountants measure cost of goods sold implicitly. If the company is a merchandiser, this method, called the periodic method, measures net purchases and counts inventory and computes cost of goods sold as beginning inventory plus net purchases minus ending inventory. A manufacturer determines cost of goods sold as beginning finished goods inventory plus cost of goods manufactured minus ending finished goods inventory.

Suppose the entity incurs breakage of the inventory or spoilage or theft. How does this company account for these events?

5. Part A. Accountants are required to place the current portion of long-term debt in the current liabilities section of the balance sheet. Consider Heidi Company which borrows $1 million on January 2, 2000 and repays $200,000 of the loan every January 2 for the next five years. Assume that Heidi's operating cycle is less than one year and that its fiscal year is the calendar year, and ignore interest. How should the balance sheet display this debt on December 31, 2000–2004? Ignore interest on the loan.

Part B. As current portions of long-term debt are reclassified as current liabilities, accountants also reclassify current portions of long-term receivables and investments as current assets. Accountants, however, typically do not reclassify current portions of plant and equipment. Why not?

6. Jodi Manufacturing incurs rent of $100,000. Where will the cost be shown in the financial report?

EXERCISES

1. Prepare the assets section of the balance, given the following accounts and their balances.

Accounts receivable	$ 50
Accumulated depreciation	14
Allowance for doubtful accounts	8
Cash	13

Copyrights	110
Cost of goods sold	320
Land	80
Securities available for sale	27
Securities held to maturity	33
Supplies inventory	38
Taxes	21
Tools	89
Trading securities	22
Treasury stock	9

2. Prepare the liabilities section of the balance sheet, given the following accounts and their balances.

Accounts payable	$ 600
Bonds payable	1,000
Interest expense	42
Interest payable	8
Loss from sale of equipment	14
Mortgage payable	425
Notes payable	280
Notes payable—long term	155
Pension debt—current portion	27
Pension debt—long term	323
Taxes payable	17
Warranties payable	8

3. Prepare the stockholders' equity section of the balance, given the following accounts and their balances.

Additional paid-in capital	$800
Cash	75
Common stock	250
Cost of goods sold	320
Preferred stock	200
Retained earnings	560
Sales	645
Treasury stock	50

4. Pat Thomas has started a typing service, specializing in graduate theses. Prepare the balance sheet for Thomas Typing, given the following accounts:

Accounts payable	$ 2,000
Accounts receivable	5,000
Accumulated depreciation	14,000
Cash	1,000
Notes payable	4,000
Office equipment	35,000
Prepaid insurance	1,000
Prepaid rent	12,000
Supplies inventory	11,000
Thomas, Capital	45,000

5. Thomas Typing provides typing services. Prepare an income statement for Thomas Typing, given the following income statement accounts.

Depreciation	$ 7,000
Insurance expense	3,000
Miscellaneous revenue	2,000

Proofreading revenue	15,000
Rent expense	6,000
Supplies expense	5,000
Taxes	14,000
Typing revenue	62,000
Utilities expense	5,000

6. Reno Ranchero sells western toys, cowboy and cowgirl outfits, and boots. From the following data, compute the cost of goods sold for Reno Ranchero.

Freight in	$ 5,000
Merchandise inventory, January 1	2,000
Merchandise inventory, December 31	15,000
Purchase discounts	4,000
Purchase returns and allowances	5,000
Purchases	514,000

7. Justine Smith is trying to assess the earnings per share of her company Justine Junction. Net income is $246,000 and preferred dividends is $30,000. There are 100,000 shares of common stock issued, but 20,000 have been reacquired as treasury shares. Compute the earnings per share of Justine Junction.

8. Dial L Computers takes computer parts and manufactures computer systems. Determine the cost of raw materials used from these data for Dial L Computers.

Purchase discounts	$ 14,000
Purchase returns and allowances	22,000
Purchases	896,000
Transportation in	23,000
Raw materials inventory, January 1	9,000
Raw materials inventory, December 31	12,000

9. Dial L Computers is trying to understand its manufacturing costs. Help the accounting department of Dial L Computers by calculating the cost of goods manufactured.

Direct labor	$200,000
Direct materials	500,000
Factory depreciation	74,000
Factory insurance	23,000
Factory utilities	82,500
Indirect labor	300,200
Indirect materials	45,000
Work-in-process inventory, January 1	1,000
Work-in-process inventory, December 31	2,000

10. Dial L Computers is rushing hard to finish its financial report, and the managers need your help in figuring out cost of goods sold. Help them by using the following data.

Cost of goods manufactured	$1,287,000
Finished goods inventory, January 1	93,000
Finished goods inventory, December 31	102,000

11. Linda Roan, CFO for Roan Manufacturing, is preparing year-end financial statements, but her computer is on the fritz. From the accounts below, help her by constructing the cost of goods sold for Roan Manufacturing.

Administrative expenses	$ 780
Cash	310
Depreciation—factory equipment	50

Depreciation—office equipment	20
Direct labor	600
Direct materials	4,000
Factory rent	170
Factory utilities	900
Finished goods, beginning	500
Finished goods, ending	420
Indirect labor	1,100
Indirect materials	620
Retained earnings	3,600
Sales	6,000
Selling expenses	850
Taxes expense	1,300
Work-in-process, beginning	100
Work-in-process, ending	210

12. Jack and Jill have established a partnership in water fetching. The beginning balances in their capital accounts are $137,000 and $165,000, respectively. The partnership earned $200,000 during 2001, and, according to their partnership agreement, Jill gets 60% of the profits while Jack gets 40%. During 2001 Jack withdrew $50,000 and Jill withdrew $55,000. Prepare a statement of owners' equity for the Jack and Jill partnership.

13. Nittany Lion Bank offers checking and savings accounts to customers. Banks earn profits by taking these deposits and creating loans such as mortgages. To the bank, these deposits are payables and these loans are receivables. Banks also buy securities to earn dividends and interest, and they also try to earn trading profits. Prepare an income statement and an unclassified balance sheet for Nittany Lion Bank, given these data.

Additional paid in capital	$1,290,000
Buildings (net of accumulated depreciation)	400,000
Cash	20,000
Checking deposits	900,000
Common stock	100,000
Consumer loans	1,000,000
Gain on sale of investments	125,000
Interest expense	120,000
Interest revenue	200,000
Loss on sale of investments	30,000
Mortgages	1,000,000
Retained earnings	930,000
Savings deposits	600,000
Securities available for sale	900,000
Securities held to maturity	300,000
Trading securities	200,000

PROBLEMS

1. For each account listed in the following chart, indicate on which financial statement (BS = balance sheet and IS = income statement) the account appears. (One item goes on both the balance sheet and the income statement.) In the last column provide details. If the account is found on the balance sheet, tell whether it typically belongs to current assets (CA), property, plant, and equipment (PPE), intangible assets (IA), investments and funds (IF), current liabilities (CL), long-term debt (LTD), or stockholders' equity (SE). If the account is found on the income statement, state whether it is a revenue (REV), part of the calculation of cost of goods sold (COGS), or some other expense (EXP). An example is given to you in the second row of the table.

Accounts	*BS/IS*	*Details*
	Financial Statements	
Example: Accumulated depreciation	BS	PPE
1. Accounts payable		
2. Accounts receivable		
3. Additional paid-in capital		
4. Allowance for doubtful accounts		
5. Building		
6. Cash		
7. Common stock		
8. Freight out		
9. Income taxes		
10. Insurance expense		
11. Interest expense		
12. Interest receivable		
13. Interest revenue		
14. Land		
15. Merchandise inventory		
16. Notes payable (90 days)		
17. Patents		
18. Preferred stock		
19. Prepaid rent		
20. Purchases		
21. Purchases discounts		
22. Retained earnings		
23. Sales		
24. Sales returns and allowances		
25. Treasury stock		

2. Following is a list of accounts for the Jennifer Parkes Recreational Center. From these accounts, prepare a classified balance sheet.

Accounts payable	$ 20
Accounts receivable	35
Accumulated depreciation—building	160
Accumulated depreciation—equipment	25
Additional paid-in capital	240
Building	400
Cash	5
Common stock	50
Depreciation	30

Dividends	10
Equipment	90
Interest expense	75
Investments held to maturity	200
Land	80
Merchandise inventory	110
Mortgage payable	85
Prepaid rent	5
Purchases	450
Retained earnings	?
Sales	600
Tax expense	50
Transportation in	25
Wages payable	3

3. Following is a list of accounts for the Kandy Korner. From these accounts, prepare an income statement for the year ended December 31, 2001, showing the cost of goods sold. Ignore the earnings per share disclosure.

Accounts payable	$ 45
Accounts receivable	60
Accumulated depreciation	235
Advertising	20
Bonds payable	400
Cash	115
Depreciation	30
Dividends	50
Furniture	190
Freight in	25
Freight out	20
Insurance expense	15
Interest revenue	25
Inventory, January 1	75
Inventory, December 31	100
Land	555
Purchases	600
Purchase discounts	30
Purchase returns and allowances	15
Rent expense	50
Retained earnings	?
Salaries expense	100
Sales	1500
Sales discounts	20
Sales returns and allowances	35
Supplies expense	60
Taxes expense	100
Utilities expense	80
Wages	150

4. Ralph Arditti started his own hairstyling business during 2000, though he continues to act as a real estate broker in his spare time. His firm Heads Up just finished fiscal year 2001 ending on December 31, and Ralph has hired you to prepare the financial statements. Given the following accounts and their balances, prepare the income statement, the statement of owner's equity, and the balance sheet for Heads Up.

Accounts payable	$ 3,000
Accumulated amortization—leased auto	4,500

Accumulated depreciation—building	12,500
Arditti, capital, January 1	(10,000)
Arditti, drawings	22,000
Building	250,000
Cash	25,000
Depreciation	3,000
Electricity expense	6,500
Gains on sale of securities	8,900
Hair styling fees	400,000
Income tax expense	180,000
Income taxes payable	80,000
Interest earned	5,700
Interest expense	6,200
Interest payable	2,000
Land	81,800
Lease amortization expense	4,500
Leased auto	45,000
Manicure fees	46,000
Mortgage payable	150,000
Payroll taxes	12,900
Payroll taxes payable	3,800
Pension expense	8,300
Real estate broker commissions	124,500
Supplies	22,500
Supplies expense	12,400
Telephone expense	800
Trading securities	75,000
Wages and salaries	75,000

5. Suzie's Music Store is located downtown, and it sells popular CDs and other musical items. Accounts are listed below along with their amounts. Prepare an income statement, a statement of retained earnings, and a balance sheet for Suzie's Music Store for the year ended December 31, 2001.

Accounts payable	$ 47,000
Accounts receivable	34,000
Accumulated depreciation—building	30,000
Accumulated depreciation—furniture and fixtures	9,000
Additional paid-in capital	333,000
Advertising	3,000
Building	580,000
Cash	63,000
Common stock, $10 par	200,000
Depreciation	11,000
Dividends—common	40,000
Dividends—preferred	25,000
Electricity	4,000
Freight in	5,000
Freight out	2,000
Furniture and fixtures	120,000
Income taxes	96,000
Land	1,200,000
Merchandise inventory, December 31, 2000	42,000
Merchandise inventory, December 31, 2001	44,000
Mortgage payable	440,000
Notes payable	23,000

Notes payable—long term	100,000
Phone expense	6,000
Preferred stock, $100 par	100,000
Prepaid insurance	2,000
Purchase discounts	5,000
Purchase returns and allowances	6,000
Purchases	475,000
Retained earnings, December 31, 2000	717,000
Sales	823,000
Sales discounts	6,000
Sales returns and allowances	11,000
Securities available for sale	30,000
Securities held to maturity	25,000
Supplies expense	5,000
Supplies inventory	2,000
Taxes payable	36,000
Trading securities	22,000
Wages and salaries	60,000

6. Upon graduation, Dan Winsor starts his own business producing widgets with a technique that he invented. Winsor's Widgets has just completed its fiscal year on December 31, 2001, and the company needs your accounting expertise. Prepare the income statement, the statement of retained earnings, and the balance sheet for Winsor's Widgets using the following data.

Accounts payable	$ 199,000
Accounts receivable	173,000
Accumulated depreciation—building	700,000
Accumulated depreciation—furniture and fixtures	5,000
Accumulated depreciation—robotic equipment	50,000
Additional paid-in capital	1,273,000
Advertising	19,000
Allowance for bad debts	23,000
Bad debts expense	18,000
Bonds payable	516,000
Building	1,400,000
Cash	45,000
Common stock, $1 par	100,000
Depreciation	34,000
Direct labor	300,000
Dividends, common stock	500,000
Dividends, preferred stock	100,000
Factory depreciation	50,000
Factory insurance	30,000
Factory utilities	60,000
Finished goods, December 31, 2000	142,000
Finished goods, December 31, 2001	98,000
Freight in	35,000
Freight out	38,000
Furniture and fixtures	100,000
Income taxes	426,000
Indirect labor	80,000
Indirect materials	25,000
Insurance	28,000
Interest earned	20,000
Interest expense	215,000

Interest payable	5,000
Land	1,750,000
Loss on sale of investments	60,000
Loss on sale of robotic equipment	220,000
Mortgage payable	1,216,000
Notes payable	45,000
Notes payable—long term	79,000
Patents (net)	400,000
Preferred stock, $100 par	300,000
Purchase discounts	15,000
Purchase returns and allowances	8,000
Purchases	800,000
Raw materials, December 31, 2000	75,000
Raw materials, December 31, 2001	80,000
Retained earnings, December 31, 2000	210,000
Robotic equipment	500,000
Sales	3,977,000
Sales discounts	30,000
Sales returns and allowances	59,000
Securities available for sale	190,000
Securities held to maturity	65,000
Supplies expense	22,000
Supplies, December 31, 2001	25,000
Taxes payable	64,000
Trademarks	60,000
Trading securities	98,000
Treasury stock	60,000
Utilities	85,000
Wages and salaries	400,000
Wages payable	2,000
Work-in-process, December 31, 2000	90,000
Work-in-process, December 31, 2001	120,000

7. Chris Ore opened his own mining company which he called Ore's Ores. The firm started on January 2, 2001 by issuing 20,000 shares of $1 par value common stock for $6 each. Late in December 2001, Ore's Ores issued 2,000 shares of $100 par value preferred stock for $102. The dividend rate of this preferred stock is $3 per share per year. During 2001 the corporation generated an income of $5,000.

In 2002 Ore's Ores enjoyed income of $80,000, paid the preferred dividends, and paid common dividends of $2 per share.

The firm issued 1,000 additional shares of preferred stock on January 3, 2003 at $103 per share. Unfortunately, the firm lost $10,000 that year; however, it still paid the preferred dividends.

2004 was a banner year for Chris. Early in the year the firm issued 5,000 additional shares of common stock at $10 per share. Net income was $150,000. Preferred stockholders received dividends of $3 per share, while common shareholders receive dividends of $5 per share.

Required: Prepare a statement of changes in stockholders' equity for Ore's Ores, depicting the changes in stockholders' equity from 2001 through 2004.

CHAPTER **3**

THE ACCOUNTING CYCLE

Financial accounting provides information about the firm through the balance sheet, the income statement, the statement of changes in stockholders' equity, and the cash flow statement. In the last chapter we examined the first three statements, and in Chapter 5 we will describe the cash flow statement.

The accounting information system must capture the relevant data about the firm's transactions, categorize them, and store them in such a way that one can retrieve the information and prepare the financial statements of the entity. This process is called the accounting cycle. The present chapter discusses journal entries, posting entries to a ledger, trial balances, adjusting entries, and closing entries, whereas Chapter 4 describes subsidiary ledgers, worksheets, special journals, reversing entries, and correcting entries. Throughout these two chapters, the reader should not overlook the purpose of financial reporting—to help readers of the financial statements make better economic decisions. Journals and ledgers and so on are merely tools to achieve this end. At this stage of the book, we also assume that the accountant already has the relevant data to prepare the journal entries. Chapters 6–11 will indicate how the data are captured, and Chapter 12 will focus on measurement and disclosure of these items.

After reading and studying this chapter, you should be able to:

- Describe the accounting cycle;
- Prepare journal entries;
- Describe the general journal;
- Post journal entries;
- Describe the general ledger;
- Construct a trial balance;
- Make adjusting entries; and
- Make closing entries.

OVERVIEW OF THE ACCOUNTING CYCLE

Accountants gather data as transactions occur so that they can process the data and convert the data into financial statements. The *periodicity principle* states that accounting reports should be prepared on a periodic basis such as once per year, quarter, or month. Unless stated otherwise, one should assume that the report is annual. It should also be assumed, unless otherwise stated, that the fiscal year is the calendar year; that is, the last day of the fiscal year is December 31. These are assumptions held in the present text, especially in the exercises and problems. The purpose of the accounting cycle is to publish the financial statements for the period.

As explained in Chapter 1, a *transaction* is an exchange (the giving up of something of value to receive something of value), a nonreciprocal transfer (the giving up of something of value or the receiving of something of value but not both), an event (the occurrence of something that has a financial consequence for the firm), or an allocation of

53

the entity (the distribution of some cost to various departments, assets, expenses, or time periods). In a sense, these transactions are the activities of the business enterprise, and the financial reports are historical narratives of what took place during a particular period.

Transactions may be classified as either internal or external. *Internal transactions* are transactions that do not involve another entity. They include adjusting entries and closing entries, which are described later in the chapter. *External transactions* are transactions that do involve other entities. Examples of such transactions include sales to customers and purchases from vendors.

Financial accountants concern themselves with how to record these transactions and their economic consequences in financial statements. We use the term transactions processing to describe this recording and converting of data into financial information. In other words, *transactions processing* comprises all of the activities that transform data about a firm's transactions into the firm's financial statements.

One records a transaction through *accounts*, which are specific assets, liabilities, stockholders' equities, revenues, or expenses. For example, land may be an asset of the firm. An account is set up called "land," and its balance is initially set at zero. When the enterprise purchases land for (say) $1 million, we increase the balance to that amount. Accountants continue to record the increases and decreases to the account as land is acquired or disposed. An ending balance may be obtained by adding the increases to and subtracting the decreases from the beginning balance.

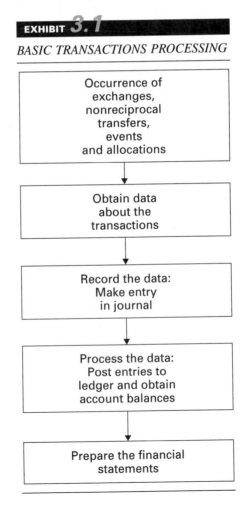

EXHIBIT 3.1

BASIC TRANSACTIONS PROCESSING

Occurrence of
exchanges,
nonreciprocal
transfers,
events
and allocations

Obtain data
about the
transactions

Record the data:
Make entry
in journal

Process the data:
Post entries to
ledger and obtain
account balances

Prepare the financial
statements

EXHIBIT 3.2

THE ACCOUNTING CYCLE

1. Prepare a journal entry for the transaction.
2. Post the journal entry to a ledger.
3. Prepare a trial balance.
4. Make the adjusting entries in the general journal.
5. Post the adjusting entries to the general ledger.
6. Prepare an adjusted trial balance.
7. Prepare the financial statements:
   (a) balance sheet;
   (b) income statement;
   (c) statement of changes in stockholders' equity; and
   (d) cash flow statement.
8. Enter the closing entries in the general journal.
9. Post the closing entries to the general ledger.
10. Prepare a post-closing trial balance.

Exhibit 3.1, which is an extension of Exhibit 1.1 from Chapter 1, illustrates this basic transactions processing. First, some transaction takes place. Then the bookkeeper obtains data about the transaction, such as what took place, when it occurred, and who participated in it. The bookkeeper records the data by making a journal entry in what is called a journal. A *journal* is a chronological record of the economic effects of an entity's transactions. A *journal entry* is the recording of the economic effects of a particular transaction. The data are placed in a more useful form by categorizing the data into accounts. This process, called *posting*, involves the transfer of account data from a journal to a ledger. A *ledger* lists the accounts and their balances. The income statement, the statement of changes in retained earnings, and the balance sheet can then be prepared directly from the data in the ledger.

Another, more traditional way of considering what accountants do is called the accounting cycle. The *accounting cycle* lists the steps in transactions processing, as shown in Exhibit 3.2. First, the bookkeeper prepares a journal entry for the transaction and writes this journal entry in a journal. Second, the journal entry is posted to a ledger. Third, the accountant makes a *trial balance*, which is a listing of all of the accounts and their balances to ensure against certain kinds of errors. Fourth, the accountant enters adjusting entries into the general journal, and, fifth, he or she posts the adjusting entries to the general ledger. These *adjusting entries* are journal entries prepared at the end of the accounting cycle to update a revenue or an expense account to its correct balance. (The general journal and general ledger are defined and explained later in the chapter.) Sixth, another trial balance is taken, again to guard against errors. Seventh, the accountant constructs the financial statements. Eighth and ninth, he or she enters the closing entries into the general journal and posts them to the general ledger. *Closing entries* are journal entries prepared at the end of the accounting cycle so that revenues and expenses and dividends have zero balances. Finally, another trial balance is prepared.

The rest of this chapter fleshes out details about the accounting cycle. We focus on (1) journal entries, (2) posting entries to a ledger, (3) trial balances, (4) adjusting entries, and (5) closing entries. Some additional steps and details are provided in the next chapter as well.

JOURNAL ENTRIES

The first step in the accounting cycle is to prepare journal entries that show the economic effects of the company's transactions. These entries are written in a journal in chronological order. There are two types of journals: a general journal and various special journals. A *general journal* is a journal that records all transactions not entered in a special journal. A *special journal* is a journal that records only certain types of transactions, such as sales, cash receipts, purchases, and cash disbursements. Special journals are discussed in the next chapter.

Accounting Identity

Before describing what a general journal looks like, we need to discuss how to record a particular entry. To motivate this discussion, let us begin with the *accounting identity* (also called the accounting equation). Recall that this identity states that assets equal liabilities plus stockholders' equity. This identity will always hold as long as no error has been made.

For example, consider the transactions for Oakley Drive, Inc. given in Exhibit 3.3. The company begins with cash of $1,000, accounts receivable of $20,000, tools of $25,000, and land of $50,000, thus having total assets of $96,000. It also has accounts payable of $5,000 and mortgage payable of $20,000 to yield total liabilities of $25,000. The firm's common stock is $43,000, and its retained earnings is $28,000, giving total stockholders'

EXHIBIT 3.3

TRANSACTIONS AND THE ACCOUNTING IDENTITY

Oakley Drive, Inc.
Successive Balance Sheets

ASSETS = LIABILITIES + STOCKHOLDERS' EQUITY

Cash	+ Accounts receivable	+ Tools	+ Land	= Accounts payable	+ Mortgage payable	+ Common stock	+ Retained earnings
$ 1,000	+ $20,000	+ $25,000	+ $50,000	= $ 5,000	+ $20,000	+ $43,000	+ $28,000
			25,000 =		25,000		
$ 1,000	+ $20,000	+ $25,000	+ $75,000	= $ 5,000	+ $45,000	+ $43,000	+ $28,000
20,000				=		20,000	
$21,000	+ $20,000	+ $25,000	+ $75,000	= $ 5,000	+ $45,000	+ $63,000	+ $28,000
		8,000		= 8,000			
$21,000	+ $20,000	+ $33,000	+ $75,000	= $13,000	+ $45,000	+ $63,000	+ $28,000
9,000	+ (9,000)			=			0
$30,000	+ $11,000	+ $33,000	+ $75,000	= $13,000	+ $45,000	+ $63,000	+ $28,000
(7,000)			=	(7,000)			
$23,000	+ $11,000	+ $33,000	+ $75,000	= $ 6,000	+ $45,000	+ $63,000	+ $28,000

equity of $71,000. Liabilities plus stockholders' equity equals $25,000 plus $71,000, or $96,000. Assets equal liabilities plus stockholders' equity.

Oakley Drive, Inc. purchases land of $25,000 by obtaining a mortgage. The balance in the land account goes from $50,000 to $75,000. The balance in the mortgage payable account increases from $20,000 to $45,000. Notice that one asset increases by $25,000, so that total assets increase by $25,000, from $96,000 to $121,000. One liability increases by $25,000, so that total liabilities increase by $25,000, going from the initial amount of $25,000 to $50,000. The transaction does not affect stockholders' equity, and so it stands at $71,000. Notice that after the transaction is accounted for, assets ($121,000) still equal liabilities ($50,000) plus stockholders' equity ($71,000).

The second transaction for Oakley is issuing common stock for $20,000. The cash and common stock accounts increase by $20,000. Total assets now are $141,000, total liabilities are $50,000, and stockholders' equity becomes $91,000. The accounting identity remains valid.

Oakley's third transaction is obtaining $8,000 worth of tools on credit. The effect is to increase tools and accounts payable by $8,000. Total assets are $149,000 and total liabilities equal $58,000, while stockholders' equity is $91,000. Again, the accounting identity holds.

Oakley's fourth transaction is to receive $9,000 from customers who pay off their balances. The transaction increases cash by $9,000 and decreases accounts receivable by the same amount. The transaction does not change total assets, total liabilities, or stockholders' equity. They remain at $149,000, $58,000, and $91,000, respectively.

The last transaction is the corporation's paying $7,000 of its debts to suppliers. Cash and accounts payable decline by $7,000. Total assets are $142,000: cash, $23,000; accounts receivable, $11,000; tools, $33,000; and land, $75,000. Total liabilities are $51,000: accounts payable, $6,000, and mortgage payable, $45,000. Stockholders' equity is $91,000: common stock, $63,000, and retained earnings, $28,000. Yet again, total assets equal total liabilities plus stockholders' equity.

What is happening is straightforward. A new firm begins with no assets, liabilities, or stockholders' equity, and so the accounting identity is true ($0 = 0 + 0$). As transactions take place, each transaction will have the specific asset (or assets) that is involved equaling the specific liability (or liabilities) and the specific stockholders' equity. It follows that total assets will still equal total liabilities plus stockholders' equity. The accounting identity always holds—providing that the accountant has made no errors.

Although transactions could be recorded as presented in Exhibit 3.3, in practice they are not, for this method would be cumbersome and inefficient. Several centuries ago, Italian merchants developed another method, one that depends on debits and credits. This technique of debits and credits remains closely aligned with the method shown in Exhibit 3.3 because if debits equal credits, the accounting identity will hold.

Debits and Credits

Accounts can be written in a T-format, thus the name *T-account*. The name of the account is written above the T. *Debits* are written on the left-hand side of the account, and *credits* are placed on the right-hand side. Consequently, a T-account would be written as

ACCOUNT TITLE

debits	credits

The power of debits and credits derives from their implementation. Debits reflect increases to assets and expenses and decreases to liabilities, stockholders' equity, and revenues. Credits reflect decreases to assets and expenses and increases to liabilities, stockholders' equity, and revenues. Any transaction is recorded so that debits equal credits. As long as debits equal credits for all transactions, the accounting identity will be true. We refer to this system of accounting as *double-entry bookkeeping*.

Specific assets, liabilities, and stockholders' equity accounts are known as *balance sheet accounts*. Revenues and expenses constitute net income. Since net income is transferred into retained earnings (recall that ending retained earnings equals beginning retained earnings plus net income minus dividends), revenues and expenses are *nominal or temporary accounts*. Revenues increase net income, which in turn increases stockholders' equity. Increases and decreases to revenues are represented in the same way as increases and decreases to stockholders' equity. On the other hand, expenses decrease net income and stockholders' equity. Notice that increases and decreases to expenses are represented in the opposite manner as increases and decreases to stockholders' equity.

Dividends (drawings) is also a nominal account because it gets transferred into retained earnings (owner's capital) at the end of the year. Increases in dividends imply a reduction in stockholders' equity. Thus, increases in dividends are shown with debits, whereas decreases to the dividends account are depicted by credits.

These rules for debits and credits are summarized in Exhibit 3.4. Debits, or the left-hand side of an account, increase assets, expenses, and dividends or drawings. The left-hand side is also used to decrease liabilities, owner's equity, and revenues. Credits, or the right-hand side of an account, accomplishes the opposite effects.

To have an asset implies that the firm at some time increased its asset account, thereby debiting the asset account. This fact implies that assets normally possess debit balances. In similar fashion, liabilities usually have credit balances, and stockholders' equities usually have credit balances. Revenue accounts typically have credit balances, and expenses typically have debit balances. Dividends normally has a debit balance.

In a few accounts, normal balances are opposite of what is typical, and so they are referred to as *contra accounts*. Thus, we can speak of contra-assets which have credit balances and are illustrated by allowance for doubtful accounts and accumulated depreciation; contra-liabilities and contra-stockholders' equities, which have debit balances and include treasury stock as a contra-stockholders' equity; contra-revenues, which also have debit balances and include sales discounts and sales returns and allowances; and contra-expenses which have credit balances and they include purchase discounts and purchase returns and allowances.

EXHIBIT 3.4

CONSEQUENCES OF DEBITS AND CREDITS

ACCOUNT	
DEBITS (left-hand side):	CREDITS (right-hand side):
Increase assets	Decrease assets
Decrease liabilities	Increase liabilities
Decrease owners' equity	Increase owners' equity
Decrease revenues	Increase revenues
Increase expenses	Decrease expenses
Increase drawings	Decrease drawings
(dividends)	(dividends)

When writing a journal entry, you enter the debit first and the credit second. You write the account name and the dollar amount with which the account is increased or decreased. It is also traditional to indent the credit in order to show clearly which accounts are being debited and which are being credited. Hence, one would write

Debit account	$XXX	
Credit account		$XXX

All debit accounts are placed before any credit account. And, for any transaction, the total debits should equal the total credits.

Consider the five transactions for Oakley Drive, Inc. In the first transaction, the firm bought land for $25,000 using a mortgage. Land, an asset, increases by $25,000, and we show an increase to an asset with a debit, so we debit land for $25,000. Mortgage payable is a liability, and it increases $25,000; accountants depict an increase to a liability with a credit, so we credit mortgage payable $25,000. The entry is

Land	$25,000	
Mortgage payable		$25,000

Next, the company issued common stock for $20,000 cash. Cash increases; it is an asset, so debit cash $20,000. Common stock increases; it is a stockholders' equity account, and increases to stockholders' equity are shown with a credit. Therefore, the entry is

Cash	$20,000	
Common stock		$20,000

The third transaction was the acquisition of tools on credit for $8,000. The asset tools increase; debit tools for $8,000. The liability accounts payable increases; credit accounts payable for $8,000.

Tools	$8,000	
Accounts payable		$8,000

The fourth transaction is the collection of $9,000 of accounts receivable. Debit cash for $9,000 since the asset cash increases by that amount. Accounts receivable decreases by $9,000. Decreases to an asset account are shown with credits, so the bookkeeper credits accounts receivable for $9,000.

Cash	$9,000	
Accounts receivable		$9,000

Oakley's fifth transaction is the payment of $7,000 of the corporation's accounts payable. Cash decreases by $7,000; it is an asset, so credit cash $7,000. Accounts payable decreases by $7,000; it is a liability, and since decreases to a liability are represented by debits, we debit accounts payable $7,000. The entry is

Accounts payable	$7,000	
Cash		$7,000

General Journal

The journal entries that are prepared for a corporation are written into a general journal. Although many variations exist, a typical general journal contains five columns. The first column records the date of the transaction. The second column entitled "Description" or "Accounts" gives the names of the accounts that are affected by the transaction. As already indicated, debits are entered before the credits, and the bookkeeper indents the accounts that are credited. The third column is called a folio ("F") column or a reference ("Ref") column. (Its purpose is explained later in this chapter when we describe posting.) Debits constitute the fourth column, and credits make up the fifth.

Exhibit 3.5 illustrates a general journal. Dates of transactions are placed in column 1. Notice that the entries are recorded in chronological order. The accounts that are debited and credited are placed in the second column, and credits are appropriately indented. The dollar amounts are placed in the last two columns. You might also recognize that debits equal credits for all journal entries.

If desired, the accountant can write an explanation of the transaction. This is especially helpful if the transaction is unusual or rare. If an explanation is given, it is shown in the description column immediately after the entry.

EXHIBIT 3.5

MAKING ENTRIES IN THE GENERAL JOURNAL

General Journal   **PAGE 1**

Date	Description	F	Debit	Credit
1-2	Cash	100	$200,000	
	Cleat, Capital	300		$200,000
1-3	Cash	100	$100,000	
	Notes payable	220		$100,000
1-3	Prepaid rent	140	$ 30,000	
	Cash	100		$ 30,000
1-3	Furniture and fixtures	170	$ 46,000	
	Cash	100		$ 46,000
2-7	Trading securities	110	$ 50,000	
	Cash	100		$ 50,000
3-9	Purchases	500	$200,000	
	Accounts payable	210		$200,000
3-12	Accounts payable	210	$100,000	
	Purchase discounts	505		$ 2,000
	Cash	100		$ 98,000

(continued)

EXHIBIT 3.5

MAKING ENTRIES IN THE GENERAL JOURNAL (continued)

General Journal   PAGE 2

Date	Description	F	Debit	Credit
3-13	Freight in	520	$ 3,000	
	Cash	100		$ 3,000
6-9	Cash	100	$150,000	
	Sales	400		$150,000
6-13	Accounts payable	210	$ 60,000	
	Cash	100		$ 60,000
7-3	Cash	100	$ 13,000	
	Trading securities	110		$ 10,000
	Gain—sale of securities	450		$ 3,000
7-20	Accounts receivable	120	$180,000	
	Sales	400		$180,000
7-23	Cash	100	$107,800	
	Sales discounts	410	$ 2,200	
	Accounts receivable	120		$110,000

(continued)

Illustration

Let's suppose that Jimmy Cleat starts a shoe business called Soleful Strut. His business has the following transactions in its first year. Your mission is to record these transactions in the general journal. The solution is given in Exhibit 3.5, and the reader should verify the journal entries made for these transactions.

> January 2. Cleat invests $200,000 cash into the firm.
> January 3. Soleful Strut borrows $100,000 and signs a note. Due in one year, the note carries an interest rate of 9%.
> January 3. The company pays $30,000 for one year's rent of office space.
> January 3. Soleful Strut purchases furniture and fixtures for $46,000.
> February 7. The firm buys trading securities for $50,000.

EXHIBIT **3.5**

MAKING ENTRIES IN THE GENERAL JOURNAL (continued)

General Journal   PAGE 3

Date	Description	F	Debit	Credit
11-3	Sales returns and allowances	420	$ 5,000	
	Accounts receivable	120		$ 5,000
12-14	Operating expenses	570	$100,000	
	Cash	100		$100,000
12-30	Accounts payable	210	$ 2,000	
	Purchase returns and allowances	510		$ 2,000

March 9. Soleful Strut purchases on account $200,000 of inventory. A 2% discount is allowed if payment is made in 10 days.

March 12. Soleful pays off half of the debt incurred on March 9 and takes the cash discount for that amount.

March 13. The company pays freight charges on the inventory purchase. The transportation bill is $3,000.

June 9. Cash sales are made for $150,000.

June 13. A cash disbursement is made for $60,000 of the remaining accounts payable.

July 3. One-fifth of the trading securities acquired on February 7 are sold for $13,000. The cost of these securities is $\frac{1}{5}$ of $50,000 or $10,000.

July 20. Credit sales are made for $180,000. Cleat allows a 2% discount if payment is received within 10 days.

July 23. Customers pay $110,000 of the accounts receivable originating from July 20, and they take the cash discount.

November 3. Customers return items that sold for $5,000.
December 14. Operating expenses cost $100,000.
December 30. Soleful Strut returned items to suppliers that were purchased for $2,000.

Although Exhibit 3.5 presents the solution to this demonstration problem, we give some additional comments here. Let's begin with sales. Notice that both cash sales (June 9) and credit sales (July 20) are shown with credits made to the sales account. Sales is a revenue, and increases to a revenue account are revealed with a credit.

On July 23 customers paid off $110,000 of their accounts receivable and claimed their cash discount of $2,200 (2% of $110,000). The amount of cash collected is $110,000 − $2,200 = $107,800. The cash received is shown via a debit to the cash account. Accounts receivable is reduced by $110,000—since the customers have paid what they owed—and this is shown by a credit to the accounts receivable account. The difference is debited to sales discounts for $2,200. Sales discounts is a contra-revenue, so an increase to the account is displayed with a debit.

On November 3, customers returned $5,000 of goods. We reduce accounts receivable for that amount since the customers discharged their debt by returning the goods. The return is reflected by debiting sales returns and allowances. Like sales discounts, sales returns and allowances is a contra-revenue, and increases are shown by debits to the account.

Let us now consider the components of cost of goods sold: purchases, purchase discounts, purchase returns and allowances, and freight in. Increases to purchases and freight in are shown by debits, whereas increases to purchase discounts and purchase returns and allowances are given by credits. We consider beginning and ending inventory later in the chapter. (This method of accounting for the purchase of inventory is called the periodic method. This and the perpetual method are discussed further in Chapter 10.)

The purchases on March 9 are shown by debiting purchases for $200,000 and crediting accounts payable for $200,000.

On March 12 Soleful Strut paid off $100,000 of its accounts payable. This payment entitles the firm to the discount of 2% of $100,000 or $2,000. This transaction is journalized by debiting accounts payable for $100,000, crediting purchase discounts for $2,000, and crediting cash for $98,000.

Freight in, incurred on March 13, is handled in a direct manner—simply debit freight in and credit cash.

The return of purchased goods on December 30 is journalized by reducing the debt, that is, debiting accounts payable for $2,000, and by increasing purchase returns and allowances for $2,000.

One more transaction requires some additional explanation, and that is the selling of trading securities for $13,000. The extra wrinkle is that the accountant must determine the gain or loss on the sale of the securities. This gain or loss is equal to the cash proceeds minus the carrying value of the securities. If the number is positive, then it is a gain and is shown as a credit. If the number is negative, it is a loss and is written as a debit. In this example, the carrying value is $10,000, so there is a gain of $3,000. The entry is therefore a debit to cash for the amount of the proceeds, $13,000, a credit to trading securities for their carrying value, $10,000, and a credit to gain on sale of securities for the difference, $3,000.

Summary

Each transaction affects two or more accounts so that the accounting identity—assets equal liabilities plus stockholders' equity—is always true. The actual journal entries involve making debits and credits to the affected accounts. Debits reflect increases to assets and expenses and decreases to liabilities, stockholders' equity, and revenues. Credits reflect decreases to assets and expenses and increases to liabilities, stockholders' equity, and revenues. (Debits and credits to contra accounts are exactly opposite.) For every transaction debits equal credits. As long as debits equal credits for all transactions, the accounting identity also will persist.

POSTING ENTRIES TO THE GENERAL LEDGER

The general journal contains the written narrative about the company's transactions in chronological order. The data are not very useful in this form because they cannot answer such questions as how much cash does the firm have on hand or how much income did the company earn. To respond to such queries, accountants copy the data to the various accounts of the firm contained in the ledger. This process is referred to as *posting*. Thus, the second step in the accounting cycle is to post the journal entries to a ledger.

The *general ledger* is a listing of the accounts of the entity and their balances. The firm may also have a subsidiary ledger for certain accounts. A *subsidiary ledger* lists the components of some accounts, such as customer balances that constitute accounts receivable. Subsidiary ledgers are described more fully in the next chapter.

The idea is to transcribe all entries, both debits and credits, that are made to a particular account. This process is repeated for all accounts. Debits, of course, are placed on the left-hand side while credits are put on the right-hand side. Let's return to the Oakley Drive, Inc. illustration. After posting all of the journal entries involving cash, the cash account would appear as

CASH

$ 1,000	$ 7,000
$20,000	
$ 9,000	
$23,000	

This T-account shows not only the cash balance at the end of the year ($23,000), but also the various increases and decreases in the cash account. The process can be carried out for all accounts, and the results can be seen in Exhibit 3.6. The reader should verify the posting for each of the accounts.

This depiction of the cash account is rather informal. A more formal way is shown in Exhibit 3.7. This general ledger includes all of the accounts of Soleful Strut. (The reader is invited to make T-accounts for Soleful Strut and a general ledger for Oakley Drive, Inc.) The title of each account is given at the top of the account, along with an account number. The account number comes from the firm's *chart of accounts*, a list of all accounts used by the entity and the numbers used to code the accounts. Although these numbers are arbitrary, the firm can assign numbers that will be meaningful in the posting process. For example, assets may be assigned 100–199, liabilities may be designated by the 200s, stockholders' equity by 300s, revenues by 400s, and expenses by 500s. This is the scheme employed for the Soleful Strut example.

Each account in the general ledger has six columns. (Obviously, there can be variations in practice.) The first column states the date of the transaction. The second column is a description column in which the bookkeeper may write a short explanation of the

EXHIBIT *3.6*

POSTING ENTRIES TO T-ACCOUNTS
(OAKLEY DRIVE EXAMPLE)

Cash			Accounts receivable			Tools	
$ 1,000	$7,000		$20,000	$9,000		$25,000	
20,000						8,000	
9,000							
$23,000			$11,000			$33,000	

Land			Accounts payable			Mortgage payable	
$50,000			$ 7,000	$5,000			$20,000
25,000				8,000			25,000
$75,000				$6,000			$45,000

Common stock			Retained earnings	
	$43,000			$28,000
	20,000			
	$63,000			$28,000

Notice: Total debits equal total credits ($142,000).

transaction. The third column is a folio or reference column. (Again we will explain it shortly.) The fourth and fifth columns are debit and credit columns, respectively. The amount of the transaction is placed in the appropriate column, depending on whether the account increases or decreases. The last column gives the balance of the account. Increases are added to the previous total, and decreases are subtracted from the previous total. In this way, an individual can take a glance at the account and observe its balance.

Consider Soleful Strut's first transaction on January 2:

Cash $200,000
        Cleat, Capital $200,000

The cash portion of the entry is transcribed to the general ledger cash account. (The accountant also posts the second half of the entry to the Cleat, capital account, though we do not discuss that posting here.) In the general ledger cash account, the accountant enters the date (January 2), describes the transaction as the owner's initial investment in the firm, and states that the amount is $200,000. This transaction increases cash, so it is a debit, and the cash balance becomes $200,000.

The folio or reference column in the general journal and the general ledger serve to cross-reference the two books. It also helps show the bookkeeper whether the entry in the general journal has been posted. The folio column in the general journal indicates the account number of the account; the folio column in the general ledger displays the page

EXHIBIT **3.7**

POSTING ENTRIES TO THE GENERAL LEDGER

General Ledger
Cash

Account No. 100

Date	Description	F	Debits	Credits	Balance
	Balance				$ 0
1-2	Initial investment	1	$200,000		$200,000
1-3	Borrowing	1	$100,000		$300,000
1-3	Rent	1		$ 30,000	$270,000
1-3	Furniture & fixtures	1		$ 46,000	$224,000
2-7	Buy securities	1		$ 50,000	$174,000
3-12	Accounts payable	1		$ 98,000	$ 76,000
3-13	Freight	2		$ 3,000	$ 73,000
6-9	Cash sales	2	$150,000		$223,000
6-13	Accounts payable	2		$ 60,000	$163,000
7-3	Sell securities	2	$ 13,000		$176,000
7-23	Cash collections	2	$107,800		$283,800
12-14	Operating expenses	3		$100,000	$183,800

Trading Securities

Account No. 110

Date	Description	F	Debits	Credits	Balance
	Balance				$ 0
2-7	Purchase	1	$ 50,000		$ 50,000
7-3	Sale	2		$ 10,000	$ 40,000

Accounts Receivable

Account No. 120

Date	Description	F	Debits	Credits	Balance
	Balance				$ 0
7-20	Credit sales	2	$180,000		$180,000
7-23	Collections	2		$110,000	$ 70,000
11-3	Returns	3		$ 5,000	$ 65,000

(continued)

EXHIBIT 3.7

POSTING ENTRIES TO THE GENERAL LEDGER (continued)

Prepaid Rent

Account No. 140

Date	Description	F	Debits	Credits	Balance
	Balance				$ 0
1-3	Payment	1	$ 30,000		$ 30,000

Furniture and Fixtures

Account No. 170

Date	Description	F	Debits	Credits	Balance
	Balance				$ 0
1-3	Purchase	1	$ 46,000		$ 46,000

Accounts Payable

Account No. 210

Date	Description	F	Debits	Credits	Balance
	Balance				$ 0
3-9	Purchases	1		$200,000	$200,000
3-12	Payment	1	$100,000		$100,000
6-13	Payment	2	$ 60,000		$ 40,000
12-30	Returns	3	$ 2,000		$ 38,000

Notes Payable

Account No. 220

Date	Description	F	Debits	Credits	Balance
	Balance				$ 0
1-3	Borrowing	1		$100,000	$100,000

Cleat, Capital

Account No. 300

Date	Description	F	Debits	Credits	Balance
	Balance				$ 0
1-2	Investment	1		$200,000	$200,000

EXHIBIT 3.7

POSTING ENTRIES TO THE GENERAL LEDGER (continued)

Sales

Account No. 400

Date	Description	F	Debits	Credits	Balance
	Balance				$ 0
6-9	Sales	2		$150,000	$150,000
7-20	Sales	2		$180,000	$330,000

Sales Discounts

Account No. 410

Date	Description	F	Debits	Credits	Balance
	Balance				$ 0
7-23	Payment	2	$ 2,200		$ 2,200

Sales Returns and Allowances

Account No. 420

Date	Description	F	Debits	Credits	Balance
	Balance				$ 0
11-3	Return	3	$ 5,000		$ 5,000

Gain on Sale of Securities

Account No. 450

Date	Description	F	Debits	Credits	Balance
	Balance				$ 0
7-3	Sale	2		$ 3,000	$ 3,000

Purchases

Account No. 500

Date	Description	F	Debits	Credits	Balance
	Balance				$ 0
3-9	Purchases	1	$200,000		$200,000

(continued)

EXHIBIT 3.7

POSTING ENTRIES TO THE GENERAL LEDGER (continued)

Purchase Discounts

Account No. 505

Date	Description	F	Debits	Credits	Balance
	Balance				$ 0
3-12	Payment	1		$ 2,000	$ 2,000

Purchase Returns and Allowances

Account No. 510

Date	Description	F	Debits	Credits	Balance
	Balance				$ 0
12-30	Return	3		$ 2,000	$ 2,000

Freight In

Account No. 520

Date	Description	F	Debits	Credits	Balance
	Balance				$ 0
3-13	Freight	2	$ 3,000		$ 3,000

Operating Expenses

Account No. 570

Date	Description	F	Debits	Credits	Balance
	Balance				$ 0
12-14	Various expenses	3	$100,000		$100,000

number of the general journal in which the entry is recorded. Bookkeepers should not enter the data into the folio columns until all of the other data for the entry are posted to the ledger. Then, if any entries in the general journal have blank folio columns, the bookkeeper will recognize that the entry still needs to be posted.

All of the journal entries given in Exhibit 3.5 have been posted into Exhibit 3.7's general ledger. The reader should verify the postings, including the cross-referencing given in the folio columns of both the general journal and general ledger.

TRIAL BALANCES

The third step in the accounting cycle is to prepare the unadjusted trial balance. A *trial balance* is a listing of all the accounts and their balances to ensure that total debits equal total credits. Obviously, if total debits do not equal total credits, an error has occurred, and the accountant has to track down the error and correct it.

An example of a trial balance appears in Exhibit 3.8. The accounts and their balances for Soleful Strut are found in the general ledger in Exhibit 3.7. The accounts and their balances are written in the trial balance, the bookkeeper being careful to place the amount in the proper column. He or she then adds the debit column to find that total debits sum to $675,000. Adding the credit column, the accountant observes that total credits are $675,000. Total debits equal total credits, so the ledger indeed is in balance.

Note that the trial balance does not catch all mistakes. For example, if a cash sale for $200 takes place, but the accountant records it as a debit to cash for $2,000 and a credit to sales for $2,000, then debits will equal credits, even though an error exists. The trial balance detects only those errors that lead to an imbalance between debits and credits.

The accounting cycle has three trial balances. The first is called the *unadjusted trial balance* because it is prepared prior to making the adjusting entries. The second, the *adjusted trial balance*, is drafted after the adjusting entries are made but before the closing entries are registered. The third is the *post-closing trial balance*, and it is composed after both adjusting and closing entries are recorded and posted. The idea is the same for all three trial balances—you want to ascertain whether total debits equal total credits.

EXHIBIT 3.8

TRIAL BALANCE

Soleful Strut
Trial Balance
December 31, 2001

Account	*Debits*	*Credits*
Cash	$183,000	
Trading securities	40,000	
Accounts receivable	65,000	
Prepaid rent	30,000	
Furniture and fixtures	46,000	
Accounts payable		$ 38,000
Notes payable		100,000
Cleat, capital		200,000
Sales		330,000
Sales discounts	2,200	
Sales returns and allowances	5,000	
Gain on sale of securities		3,000
Purchases	200,000	
Purchase discounts		2,000
Purchase returns and allowances		2,000
Freight in	3,000	
Operating expenses	100,000	
Totals	$675,000	$675,000

ADJUSTING ENTRIES

When accountants publish the financial reports, they want the financial statements to be up-to-date and accurate. Some things may change between the initial recording of a transaction and the status of the revenues and expenses and assets and liabilities by year-end. The accountant deals with these changes by creating *adjusting entries*—journal entries prepared at the end of the accounting cycle to update a revenue or an expense account to its correct balance.

The *realization principle* states that a revenue is recorded when the firm has provided the goods or services to the customer. At the end of the fiscal year, the accountant determines whether an item is a revenue and how much should be recorded as a revenue. The accountant makes adjustments to the accounts as necessary to ensure adherence to the realization principle. The *matching principle* states that an expense is recorded in the same period that its associated revenue is recorded. At the end of the fiscal year, the accountant examines transactions to determine whether adjustments need to be made concerning the recognition of expenses. These two principles, the realization principle and the matching principle, form the conceptual rationale for adjusting entries.

There are five types of adjusting entries: (1) asset-expense deferrals, (2) liability-revenue deferrals, (3) asset-revenue accruals, (4) liability-expense accruals, and (5) valuation adjustments. Let's discuss each of these entries, giving an example of each.

Asset-Expense Deferrals

Suppose a firm pays $2,400 for a one-year insurance policy on April 1, 2001. At December 31, 2001, how much of an asset and how much of an expense are there? Nine months of insurance coverage have elapsed, and the firm will receive three months of coverage in 2002. Since the insurance costs $200 per month ($2,400/12), the firm should recognize as insurance expense $1,800 ($200 * 9 months) and as prepaid insurance $600 ($200 * 3 months).

If the original entry is

| Prepaid insurance | $2,400 | |
| Cash | | $2,400 |

then the adjusting entry on December 31, 2001 is

| Insurance expense | $1,800 | |
| Prepaid insurance | | $1,800 |

After this entry is recorded, prepaid insurance has a debit balance of $600 ($2,400 − $1,800) and insurance expense has a debit balance of $1,800—precisely what they should be.

The original entry may have had a debit to insurance expense. This is okay as long as the proper adjusting entry is made. If the original entry is

| Insurance expense | $2,400 | |
| Cash | | $2,400 |

then the adjusting entry on December 31, 2001 must be

| Prepaid insurance | $600 | |
| Insurance expense | | $600 |

Afterward, prepaid insurance has a balance of $600, as it should. Insurance expense has the correct balance of $1,800 ($2,400 − $600). The end result is the same in either case.

Sometimes students wonder why the second possibility is allowed since theoretically the cash payment for insurance is an asset. The answer is that no harm is done since financial statements are not prepared at that date. As long as adjusting entries are executed prior to the release of financial reports, there is no problem in using a conceptually inferior entry. The gain is practical. If the company pays for six months of insurance on April 1 and debits insurance expense, it does not have to make any adjusting entry later. If prepaid insurance is debited, then an adjusting entry will be required to indicate that the asset has expired.

Other asset-expense deferrals involve supplies-supplies expense and prepaid rent-rent expense.

Liability-Revenue Deferrals

Suppose a magazine publisher sells one-year subscriptions to customers for $1,200 starting with the August issue. At December 31 the company has released five issues and so has earned $\frac{5}{12}$ of the revenue. The company still owes seven issues to these customers and must show this as unearned revenue. At December 31 the accountant wants $500 ($\frac{5}{12}$ of $1,200) on the income statement as subscription revenue and $700 ($\frac{7}{12}$ of $1,200) on the balance sheet as unearned subscription revenue.

If the original entry is recorded as

Cash	$1,200	
Subscription revenue		$1,200

then the adjusting entry is

Subscription revenue	$700	
Unearned subscription revenue		$700

On the other hand, if the original entry is

Cash	$1,200	
Unearned subscription revenue		$1,200

then the adjusting entry is

Unearned subscription revenue	$500	
Subscription revenue		$500

Notice that both pairs of transactions lead to the correct reporting of a $500 revenue and a liability for $700.

Asset-Revenue Accruals

Sometimes revenues are unrecorded at year-end, and an adjusting entry is needed to recognize them. For example, if a company issues a one-year $10,000 note on June 1 for 12% interest, then it journalizes the entry as

Notes receivable	$10,000	
Cash		$10,000

At December 31 the firm earns interest because it has provided services to the borrower, namely, the use of its money. Interest is computed with the simple interest formula

$$\text{Interest} = \text{Principal} * \text{rate} * \text{time}$$

where the principal is the amount borrowed, rate is the interest rate, and time is the amount of time for which interest is earned. It is critical that the rate and the time be measured in the same units. If the rate is an annual rate, then time is number of years.

In this example, interest equals $10,000 * .12 * 7/12 or $700. The adjusting entry is

Interest receivable	$700	
Interest revenue		$700

On June 1 of the following year, the company collects the money, both principal ($10,000) and interest ($10,000 * 12% * 1 year = $1,200). The firm records this receipt of cash and chronicles the amount of interest earned during the second year. The entry is

Cash	$11,200	
Notes receivable		$10,000
Interest receivable		$ 700
Interest revenue		$ 500

Liability-Expense Accruals

If expenses are also unrecorded at year-end, adjustments must be made to rectify this situation. One example involves wages. Suppose that an enterprise pays wages every two weeks, ending on Friday. In most years the last payday in a year will not coincide with the last day in the fiscal year. Employees will work some days past this last payday of the fiscal year. Since the cost has been incurred, the firm needs to accrue the amount of the wages earned. If the amount of wages is $950, then the company makes the adjusting entry

Wages expense	$950	
Wages payable		$950

If the company pays $2,500 at the next payday, only $2,500 − $950 or $1,550 is an expense of the second fiscal year. The journal entry at that time is

Wages expense	$1,550	
Wages payable	$ 950	
Cash		$2,500

Valuation Adjustments

The last type of adjusting entry is valuation adjustments. Included in this group are depreciation, depletion, amortization, and recognition of bad debts expense. Depreciation is an attempt to spread a cost of a long-term asset, such as a building, over the years of the asset's life. Assuming that the building contributes to the revenues of the firm evenly over its life, it is appropriate to employ straight-line depreciation. The yearly portion of the depreciation is computed by the straight-line formula:

$$\text{Depreciation} = (\text{Cost} - \text{Salvage value})/\text{ Life}$$

The cost is the amount paid for the asset. The salvage value is the estimated amount of proceeds that will be collected upon disposal of the asset. The life is the number of years that the firm expects to utilize the asset.

Suppose a firm buys an automobile for $18,000 with a four-year life and a salvage value of $2,000. The annual depreciation charge is ($18,000 − $2,000)/4 = $4,000. The journal entry is

Depreciation	$4,000	
Accumulated depreciation		$4,000

Depreciation is an expense account that goes on the income statement account. Accumulated depreciation is a contra-asset, specifically contra to the automobile account. These accounts are shown on the balance sheet as

Automobile	$18,000
Less: accumulated depreciation	4,000
	$14,000

Natural resources, such as gold or bauxite or coal, are depreciated in the same manner, except that it is called depletion. Intangible assets, including patents and copyrights, are depreciated usually with zero salvage value, but the process is referred to as amortization.

Another valuation adjustment focuses on uncollectible accounts receivable. Suppose a company has $59,000 accounts receivable, but some of the receivables will prove to be uncollectible in the future. The firm recognizes an expense for these bad debts and creates a valuation adjustment called allowance for doubtful accounts. If the firm determines that it should recognize bad debts expense of $1,300, then it enters the following adjusting entry

Bad debts expense	$1,300	
Allowance for doubtful accounts		$1,300

The allowance account is a contra-asset, specifically contra to accounts receivable, and it is shown on the balance sheet as follows:

Accounts receivable	$59,000
Less: allowance for doubtful accounts	1,300
	$57,700

Illustration

Returning to the continuing saga of Soleful Strut, we need to record its adjusting entries. First, the company has a note outstanding with a principal value of $100,000 and an interest rate of 9%. The interest expense is $100,000 * .09 * 1 year = $9,000. The enterprise paid $30,000 for rent for two years. An entry is needed to partition this cost into $15,000 rent expense for 2001 and $15,000 for 2002. Third, Soleful Strut bought furniture and fixtures at $46,000. The salvage value is $6,000, and the life is eight years. Accordingly, the depreciation is $5,000 per year. Fourth, the company needs to record bad debts expense of $1,000.

The journal entries for these adjustments are displayed in Exhibit 3.9. The reader should check them for accuracy. Exhibit 3.9 also discloses the accounts in the general ledger that are affected by the adjusting entries. The reader ought to verify the postings to the general ledger.

After the adjusting entries are recorded and posted, the firm produces an adjusted trial balance. This is left as an exercise for the reader, and you should obtain total debits and credits equaling $690,000.

ENTERING ADJUSTING ENTRIES IN THE GENERAL JOURNAL
AND POSTING THEM TO THE GENERAL LEDGER

General Journal   **PAGE 4**

Date	Description	F	Debits	Credits
	ADJUSTING ENTRIES			
12-31	Interest expense	585	$ 9,000	
	Interest payable	240		$ 9,000
12-31	Rent expense	580	$15,000	
	Prepaid rent	140		$15,000
12-31	Depreciation	590	$ 5,000	
	Accumulated depreciation	175		$ 5,000
12-31	Bad debts expense	595	$ 1,000	
	Allowance for uncollectible accounts	125		$ 1,000

Allowance for Doubtful Accounts

Account No. 125

Date	Description	F	Debits	Credits	Balance
	Balance				$ 0
12-31	Adjustment	4		$ 1,000	$ 1,000

Prepaid Rent

Account No. 140

Date	Description	F	Debits	Credits	Balance
	Balance				$ 0
1-3	Payment	1	$30,000		$30,000
12-31	Adjustment	4		$15,000	$15,000

(continued)

EXHIBIT **3.9**

ENTERING ADJUSTING ENTRIES IN THE GENERAL JOURNAL
AND POSTING THEM TO THE GENERAL LEDGER (continued)

Accumulated Depreciation

Account No. 175

Date	Description	F	Debits	Credits	Balance
	Balance				$ 0
12-31	Adjustment	4		$ 5,000	$ 5,000

Interest Payable

Account No. 240

Date	Description	F	Debits	Credits	Balance
	Balance				$ 0
12-31	Adjustment	4		$ 9,000	$ 9,000

Rent Expense

Account No. 580

Date	Description	F	Debits	Credits	Balance
	Balance				$ 0
12-31	Adjustment	4	$15,000		$15,000

Interest Expense

Account No. 585

Date	Description	F	Debits	Credits	Balance
	Balance				$ 0
12-31	Adjustment	4	$ 9,000		$ 9,000

Depreciation

Account No. 590

Date	Description	F	Debits	Credits	Balance
	Balance				$ 0
12-31	Adjustment	4	$ 5,000		$ 5,000

Bad Debts Expense

Account No. 595

Date	Description	F	Debits	Credits	Balance
	Balance				$ 0
12-31	Adjustment	4	$ 1,000		$ 1,000

Next the accountant prepares the financial statements. Jimmy Cleat counts his merchandise inventory and determines that the ending balance is $40,000. Recall that this is the first year of operations, so beginning inventory is $0. With this information and the account balances in Exhibits 3.7 and 3.9, one can manufacture the financial statements. The income statement, the statement of owner's equity, and the balance sheet for Soleful Strut are given in Exhibit 3.10. Again, the reader is asked to verify the presentation.

EXHIBIT 3.10

FINANCIAL STATEMENTS

Soleful Strut
Income Statement
For the year ended December 31, 2001

Sales				$330,000
Sales discounts			$ 2,200	
Sales returns and allowances			5,000	7,200
Net sales				$322,800
Cost of goods sold:				
Beginning merchandise inventory			$ 0	
Purchases		$200,000		
Freight in		3,000		
Purchase discounts	$2,000			
Purchase returns and allowances	2,000	(4,000)		
Net purchases			199,000	
Cost of goods available for sale			$199,000	
Ending merchandise inventory			40,000	
Cost of goods sold				159,000
Gross profit				$163,800
Selling and administrative expenses:				
Operating expenses (except for others)			$100,000	
Rent expense			15,000	
Depreciation			5,000	
Bad debts expense			1,000	
Selling and administrative expenses				121,000
Income before taxes				$ 42,800
Other revenues				
Gain on sale of securities				3,000
				$ 45,800
Other expenses				
Interest expense				9,000
Net income				$ 36,800

Soleful Strut
Statement of Owner's Equity
For the year December 31, 2001

Jimmy Cleat, Capital, January 1, 2001	$ 0
Investment by owner	200,000
	$200,000
Net income	36,800
Jimmy Cleat, Capital, December 31, 2001	$236,800

(continued)

EXHIBIT **3.10**

FINANCIAL STATEMENTS (continued)

Soleful Strut
Balance Sheet
December 31, 2001

ASSETS

Current assets		
Cash		$183,800
Trading securities		40,000
Accounts receivable	$ 65,000	
Less: allowance for doubtful accounts	1,000	64,000
Prepaid rent		15,000
Merchandise inventory		40,000
Current assets		$342,800
Property, plant, and equipment		
Furniture and fixtures	$ 46,000	
Less:accumulated depreciation	5,000	
Property, plant, and equipment		$ 41,000
Total assets		$383,800

LIABILITIES AND OWNER'S EQUITY

Current liabilities		
Accounts payable		$ 38,000
Notes payable		100,000
Interest payable		9,000
Current liabilities		$147,000
Cleat, Capital		236,800
Total liabilities and owner's equity		$383,000

CLOSING ENTRIES

Basics

Suppose the hometown football team wins its game 24–10. Next week they are at home and playing their chief rival. The game is ready to start, but the scoreboard reads 24–10. The visitors likely will protest, saying that the 24 points for the home team were earned in a different game. The referees obviously agree and change the score to 0–0. The scoreboard should disclose only those points obtained in the current game.

Revenue and expense accounts, as well as dividends (or drawings), are like the scoreboard. These accounts should proclaim the revenues and expenses and dividends for the current year and the current year only. The balances of these accounts need to be reset to zero before the new year begins. This goal is achieved through closing entries. *Closing entries* are journal entries prepared at the end of the accounting cycle that make revenues and expenses and dividends (or drawings) have zero balances.

Suppose a service company has the following accounts: service revenue, $100,000; wages expense, $25,000; rent expense, $20,000; taxes, $15,000; and dividends, $17,000. The closing entries are

Service revenue		$100,000	
	Income summary		$100,000
Income summary		$ 60,000	
	Wages expense		$ 25,000
	Rent expense		$ 20,000
	Taxes		$ 15,000
Income summary		$ 40,000	
	Retained earnings		$ 40,000
Retained earnings		$ 17,000	
	Dividends		$ 17,000

The debit to service revenue decreases the account by $100,000. Since it previously had a balance of $100,000, it now has a balance of zero. Credits to wages expense, rent expense, and taxes decrease these accounts to zero as well. The offsetting account is income summary, which is merely a temporary account used in the closing entry process.

After the first two closing entries, income summary has a credit balance of $40,000. This number is the net income of the firm. If income summary had a debit balance at this stage, it would indicate that the firm incurred a net loss. The third closing entry transfers net income to retained earnings. Income summary is debited for $40,000, giving it a zero balance, and retained earnings is increased by that amount.

The last closing entry gives the dividends account a zero balance, as desired, and reduces retained earnings by the amount of the dividends declared during the period. The astute reader should discern that the last two closing entries are a debit-and-credit enactment of a familiar formula—ending retained earnings equals beginning retained earnings plus net income minus dividends.

The mission is accomplished. Revenues and expenses and dividends have zero balances, and the accountant is ready to record the transactions of the next year. And, as just noted, the retained earnings account is updated from its beginning balance to its proper ending balance.

The Merchandiser's Sales and COGS

A merchandiser has sales, sales discounts, and sales returns and allowances. Sales has a credit balance, so it is closed with a debit. Sales discounts and sales returns and allowances are contra-revenues; they typically have debit balances. Sales discounts and sales returns and allowances are closed with credits. For example, if sales is $250,000, sales discounts $5,000, and sales returns and allowances $4,000, the following entry closes the three accounts to zero.

Sales	$250,000	
Sales discounts		$ 5,000
Sales returns and allowances		$ 4,000
Income summary		$241,000

The credit to income summary reflects the net sales of the firm.

Suppose the merchandiser has purchases, $180,000; freight in, $10,000; purchase discounts, $3,000; purchase returns and allowances, $2,000; and inventory, $11,000. Keep in mind that the balance in the inventory account reflects the balance at the beginning of the period. The firm needs to ascertain the ending inventory; let's assume it is $13,000. The following entry will force purchases, freight in, purchase discounts, and purchase returns and allowances to zero balances. It also will update inventory to the proper ending amount. Finally, notice that the income summary reflects cost of goods sold. In other words, this closing entry is a debit-and-credit enactment of the cost-of-goods-sold formula: cost of goods sold equals beginning inventory plus purchases plus freight in minus purchase discounts minus purchase returns and allowances minus ending inventory.

Income summary	$183,000	
Purchase discounts	$ 3,000	
Purchase returns & allowances	$ 2,000	
Inventory (ending)	$ 13,000	
Purchases		$180,000
Freight in		$ 10,000
Inventory (beginning)		$ 11,000

Some firms will debit cost of goods sold instead of income summary and later close out the cost-of-goods-sold account to income summary. They do this to show explicitly that cost of goods sold equals $183,000. A further variation is to include this entry in the adjusting entry process and then close out cost of goods sold in the closing entry step. These variations lead to exactly the same results, so it does not matter which variation is carried out in practice.

The Manufacturer's COGS

The manufacturer's cost of goods sold is more complex. In this case, it is recommended that three closing entries be made—one for cost of raw materials used, one for cost of goods manufactured, and one for cost of goods sold. These entries will be debit-and-credit enactments of the formulas presented in Chapter 2 for their calculation, and it may be a good idea to review these formulas.

The accounts dealing with the purchase of raw materials is closed out in similar fashion to the merchandiser. Using the above numbers, but assuming that the inventory is raw materials, we obtain

Cost of raw materials used	$183,000	
Purchase discounts	$ 3,000	
Purchase returns & allowances	$ 2,000	
Raw materials (ending)	$ 13,000	
Purchases		$180,000
Freight in		$ 10,000
Raw materials (beginning)		$ 11,000

We close out purchases, freight in, purchase discounts, purchase returns, and allowances, we update raw materials inventory to its correct ending balance, and we create a cost-of-raw-materials-used account. The last-named is closed out in the very next step.

The second stage involves closing out raw materials used, direct labor, and overhead, and updating the work-in-process inventory account. In practice, there may be lots of overhead accounts, but we will assume only one account. Suppose that direct labor is $20,000, overhead is $200,000, and the work-in-process account has a balance of $15,000. This balance is the beginning balance. The accountant counts the ending work-in-process and determines that it is $21,000. The closing entry is

Cost of goods manufactured	$397,000	
Work-in-process (ending)	$ 21,000	
Cost of raw materials used		$183,000
Direct labor		$ 20,000
Overhead		$200,000
Work-in-process (beginning)		$ 15,000

As desired, cost of raw materials used, direct labor, and overhead are closed out. In addition, the work-in-process inventory is updated to its ending balance. We have also created cost of goods manufactured, but it is closed out in the third step.

The finished goods inventory account has a balance of $32,000. Consistent with the other inventories, this balance is the beginning balance. The accountant checks the inventory and finds that ending finished goods equals $28,000. The closing entry is

Cost of goods sold		$401,000	
Finished goods (ending)		$ 28,000	
	Cost of goods manufactured		$397,000
	Finished goods (beginning)		$ 32,000

Cost of goods sold is then closed out, as is every other expense.

EXHIBIT *3.11*

ENTERING CLOSING ENTRIES IN THE GENERAL JOURNAL

General Journal   **PAGE 5**

Date	Description	F	Debit	Credit
12-31	Sales	400	$330,000	
	Sales discounts	410		$ 2,200
	Sales returns and allowance	420		$ 5,000
	Income summary	900		$322,800
12-31	Income summary	900	$159,000	
	Merchandise inventory	140	$ 40,000	
	Purchase discounts	505	$ 2,000	
	Purchase returns and allowance	510	$ 2,000	
	Purchases	500		$200,000
	Freight in	520		$ 3,000
12-31	Income summary	900	$130,000	
	Operating expense	570		$100,000
	Rent expense	580		$ 15,000
	Interest expense	585		$ 9,000
	Depreciation	590		$ 5,000
	Bad debts expense	595		$ 1,000
12-31	Gain on sale of securities	450	$ 3,000	
	Income summary	900		$ 3,000
12-31	Income summary	900	$ 36,800	
	Cleat, capital	300		$ 36,800

Although this closing out process is somewhat tedious for the manufacturer, it only requires the application of the formulas for cost of raw materials used, cost of goods manufactured, and cost of goods sold. One should close out the relevant accounts and update the appropriate inventory account in each step. Together, these three steps close out all of the cost-of-goods-sold accounts.

Illustration

Soleful Strut's closing entries are displayed in Exhibit 3.11. Assume that the ending merchandise inventory is $40,000. Only the entries in the general journal are shown; in practice, the accountant would also post these closing entries to the general ledger.

After the closing entries are recorded and posted, the firm produces the post-closing trial balance. This is left as an exercise for the reader, and you should obtain total debits and credits equaling $389,800.

This completes the accounting cycle. Time to celebrate—perhaps with a new pair of shoes.

SIGHTS ALONG THE INTERNET

If the student is interested in the origins of the accounting conventions, several sites give the historical details. They are:

Academy of Accounting Historians	weatherhead.cwru.edu/Accounting
ACAUS—"Why study accounting history?"	www.acaus.org/history
Luca Pacioli—father of accounting	acct.tamu.edu/smith/ethics/pacioli.htm
Luca Paciloli—father of accounting	members.tripod.com/~FlynF/pacioli.htm

Also, the focus of this text is U.S. accounting. Despite this emphasis, the reader needs to acknowledge that we live in a global economy. A couple of international sites are:

Accounting Web (United Kingdom)	www.accountingweb.co.uk
International Accounting Standards Committee (IASC)	www.iasc.org.uk
International Federation of Accountants	www.ifac.org

CHAPTER SUMMARY IN TERMS OF LEARNING OBJECTIVES

Describe the Accounting Cycle. The accounting cycle lists the steps in transactions processing. First, the bookkeeper prepares a journal entry for the transaction and writes this journal entry in a journal. Second, the journal entry is posted to a ledger. Third, the accountant makes the unadjusted trial balance. Fourth and fifth, the accountant enters adjusting entries and posts them. These adjusting entries are journal entries prepared at the end of the accounting cycle to update a revenue or an expense account to its correct balance. Sixth, the adjusted trial balance is prepared. Seventh, the accountant constructs the financial statements. Eighth and ninth, the accountant makes closing entries and posts them. Closing entries are journal entries prepared at the end of the accounting cycle so that revenues and expenses and dividends have zero balances. Tenth, the post-closing trial balance is constructed.

Prepare Journal Entries. An account is a specific asset, liability, stockholders' equity, revenue, or expense. Debits are written on the left-hand side of the account; credits are placed on the right-hand side. Debits reflect increases to assets and expenses and decreases to liabilities, stockholders' equity, and revenues. Credits reflect decreases to assets and expenses and increases to liabilities, stockholders' equity, and revenues. Debits and credits to contra accounts have the opposite effects. A transaction is recorded so that debits equal credits. As long as debits equal credits for all transactions, the accounting identity (assets = liabilities + stockholders' equity) will remain true.

Describe the General Journal. Journal entries are written into a general journal. A typical general journal has five columns. The first column records the date of the transaction. The second column, entitled "Description" or "Accounts," gives the names of the accounts that are affected by the transaction. Debits are entered before the credits, and the credits are indented. The third column is called a folio column or a reference column, and account numbers are placed in the column after the data are posted to the ledger. Debits constitute the fourth column, while credits make up the fifth column.

Post Journal Entries. Posting entails the transfer of account data from a journal to a ledger. The debits and credits to the accounts are transformed from the journal's chronological arrangement to organizing the data into accounts. After the posting is completed, the account balance may be obtained by adding increases to and subtracting decreases from the beginning balance.

Describe the General Ledger. The general ledger is a listing of the accounts of the entity and their balances. Each account in the general ledger has six columns. The first column states the date of the transaction. The second column is a description column in which the bookkeeper may write a short explanation of the transaction. The third column is a folio or reference column that provides a cross-reference with the journal. After the entries are posted to the ledger, the numbers in this column are the page numbers of the journal where the entry is recorded. The fourth and fifth columns are debit and credit columns, and the amount is placed in one of these columns, depending on whether the account increases or decreases. The last column gives the balance of the account. Increases are added to the previous total, and decreases are subtracted from the previous total.

Construct a Trial Balance. A trial balance is a listing of all the accounts and their balances to ensure that total debits equal total credits. If total debits do not equal total credits, an error has occurred, and the accountant has to track down the error and correct it. The accounting cycle has three trial balances: the unadjusted trial balance is prepared prior to making the adjusting entries; the adjusted trial balance is drawn up after the adjusting entries are made but before the closing entries are registered; and the post-closing trial balance is created after both adjusting and closing entries are recorded and posted.

Make Adjusting Entries. Adjusting entries are journal entries that are tabulated to update a revenue or an expense account to its correct balance. Conceptually, adjusting entries are founded on the realization and matching principles. The realization principle states that a revenue is recorded when the firm has provided the goods or services to the customer. The matching principle states that an expense is recorded in the same period that its associated revenue is recorded. There are five types of adjusting entries: (1) asset-expense deferrals, (2) liability-revenue deferrals, (3) asset-revenue accruals, (4) liability-expense accruals, and (5) valuation adjustments. In every adjusting entry there is a debit or credit to an income statement account, and there is a debit or credit to a balance sheet account.

Make Closing Entries. Closing entries are journal entries prepared at the end of the accounting cycle that make revenues and expenses and dividends have zero balances. The balances of these accounts are reset to zero before the new year begins so that a year's revenues and expenses and dividends reflect the activities of the year and no other year. All nominal accounts are closed out at year-end, but no balance sheet account is ever closed out.

GLOSSARY

Account—a specific asset, liability, stockholders' equities, revenue, or expense.

Accounting cycle—the steps in transactions processing.

Accounting identity—the relationship that assets equal liabilities plus stockholders' equity.

Adjusted trial balance—a trial balance prepared after the adjusting entries are made, but before the closing entries are made.

Adjusting entry—a journal entry prepared at the end of the accounting cycle to update a revenue or an expense account to its correct balance.

Balance sheet account—an account that represents an asset, a liability, or stockholders' equity.

Chart of accounts—a list of all accounts used by an entity and the numbers used to code the accounts.

Closing entry—a journal entry prepared at the end of the accounting cycle that makes a revenue or an expense or dividends (or drawings) have a zero balance.

Contra account—an account that does not have the normal balance for that type of account.

Credit—right side of an account. Credits reflect decreases to assets and expenses and increases to liabilities, stockholders' equity, and revenues. They also reflect increases to contra-assets and contra-expenses and decreases to contra-liabilities, contra-stockholders' equity, and contra-revenues.

Debit—left side of an account. Debits reflect increases to assets and expenses and decreases to liabilities, stockholders' equity, and revenues. They also reflect decreases to contra-assets and contra-expenses and increases to contra-liabilities, contra-stockholders' equity, and contra-revenues.

Double-entry bookkeeping—a system of accounting based on the premise that debits equal credits.

External transactions—transactions that involve other entities.

General journal—a journal that records all transactions not entered in a special journal.

General ledger—a listing of the accounts of an entity and their balances.

Internal transactions—transactions that do not involve another entity.

Journal—a chronological record of the economic effects of an entity's transactions.

Journal entry—the recording of the economic effects of a particular transaction.

Ledger—a listing of the accounts of an entity and their balances, which is called a general ledger, or a listing of the components of some account, which is called a subsidiary ledger.

Matching principle—an expense is recorded in the same period that its associated revenue is recorded.

Nominal account—an account other than a balance sheet account; also called a temporary account.

Periodicity principle—accounting reports should be prepared on a periodic basis.

Post-closing trial balance—a trial balance prepared after the closing entries are made.

Posting—the transfer of account data from a journal to a ledger.

Realization principle—a revenue is recorded when the firm has provided the goods or services to the customer.

Special journal—a journal that records only certain types of transactions, such as sales, cash receipts, purchases, and cash disbursements.

Subsidiary ledger—a listing of the components of some account.

T-account—an account written in the shape of a T.

Temporary account—an account other than a balance sheet account; also called a nominal account.

Transaction—an exchange, a nonreciprocal transfer, an event, or an allocation of the entity.

Transactions processing—all of the activities that transform data about a firm's transactions into the firm's financial statements.

Trial balance—a listing of all of the accounts and their balances to ensure that total debits equal total credits.

Unadjusted trial balance—a trial balance prepared before the adjusting entries are made.

REVIEW QUESTIONS

1. What is the periodicity principle?

2. What are transactions and transactions processing?

3. Describe the accounting cycle.

4. What is a journal? What is a journal entry? Distinguish between a general journal and a special journal.

5. State the accounting identity.

6. What is an account? Differentiate between balance sheet accounts and nominal accounts.

7. Define debits and credits. What do they show about changes in accounts?

8. What is the normal balance for assets, liabilities, stockholders' equities, revenues, expenses, and dividends?

9. What is a contra account, and how does it differ from a normal account?

10. How does one write a journal entry?

11. Describe a general journal.

12. What is posting, and why is it done?

13. Distinguish between a general ledger and a subsidiary ledger.

14. Define chart of accounts.

15. Describe the general ledger.

16. What is a trial balance? What are the three trial balances, and what is different about them?

17. What is an adjusting entry, and what is its purpose?

18. What is the realization principle?

19. What is the matching principle?

20. What are the five types of adjusting entries? What distinguishes deferrals from accruals from valuation adjustments?

21. What is the formula for straight-line depreciation?

22. What are closing entries, and what is their purpose?

DISCUSSION QUESTIONS

1. We have asserted that if a transaction is recorded so that debits equal credits, then the accounting identity holds true. Let's simplify the proposition in two ways. First, let's define equities to be liabilities (creditors' equities) plus stockholders' equities, so that the accounting identity becomes

assets equal equities. Second, let's restrict the set of transactions to those with only one debit and one credit. With these simplifications, prove that if a transaction is recorded so that the debit equals the credit, then assets equal equities.

Hint: The proof should assume initially that assets equal equities. Then a transaction occurs and is recorded. You need to show that assets equal equities after this transaction is recorded. Note that there are only four types of transactions; consider each of these four cases separately.

2. One benefit of the periodicity principle is that it increases comparability. How does periodicity accomplish this?

3. Some accounting theorists have stated that there are two types of matching: product matching and period matching. Product matching implies that product costs, including transportation, are put into an inventory account until the product is sold, when the costs are transferred from inventory to cost of goods sold. Period matching says that costs other than product costs are to be expensed in the period in which they occur. Given that the matching principle claims that an expense ought to be recorded in the same period that its associated revenue is recorded, how well is this objective met by product matching and by period matching?

4. Substance over form is the doctrine that the accountant should account for a transaction in accordance with its economic substance rather than its legal form. This principle supports the disclosure principle discussed in Chapter 1. Consider the following two independent cases and indicate how the accountant should record the transaction.

(a) A real estate firm owns a large subdivision. It divides this subdivision into 300 lots and offers them for sale at $140,000 each. The offer requires no down payment and may be rescinded by the buyer up until three years after the buyer signs the contract. During the first year, the real estate firm sells all of the lots, with no buyer paying any cash up front. How much revenues should the real estate put into its income statement?

(b) A chemical company issues $500 million preferred stock at par. The issue pays dividends of $25 million every six months; the dividends are cumulative, meaning that if the firm skips a dividend payment, it must pay all back dividends before any dividends can be paid to the common stockholders; and the issue has a five-year life—that is, the company will buy back the preferred stock at par five years later. Is the preferred stock debt or equity?

5. What does depreciation measure? How reliable is the depreciation calculation?

EXERCISES

1. Prepare journal entries for Kendel's Kennels, which had the following transactions during the month of January.

January 2. Obtained $5,000 from a bank by signing a note.
January 5. Paid electric bill for $300.
January 7. Obtained $3,000 worth of dog food on account.
January 10. Charged customers $20,000 for kenneling services.
January 14. Paid employees $1,000.
January 16. Customers paid $16,000 on their accounts.
January 20. Paid rent of $2,000.
January 24. Obtained paper supplies on account for $1,000.
January 26. Paid insurance bill of $3,000.
January 28. Paid employees $1,000.
January 30. Kendel withdraws $2,500 for personal use.
January 31. Paid the January 7 bill.

2. Fred Nester sets up shop as Nester's Nostrums, and he sells all sort of knickknacks. His transactions during February are given below. Prepare journal entries for these transactions.

February 1. Purchased goods for $60,000 on account. A 2% discount is allowed if the bill is paid within 10 days.

February 2. Nester pays the transportation charges of $500.

February 4. Nester sent back $5,000 worth of the goods purchased because they were damaged.

February 5. Nester has cash sales of $6,500.

February 7. The February 1 bill is paid in full.

February 10. Nester has credit sales of $40,000. A 2% discount is allowed if the bill is paid within 10 days.

February 15. Nester purchases $1,000 of trading securities.

February 16. Customers return $3,500 of goods because they have the wrong color.

February 17. Nester has credit sales of $30,000. A 2% discount is allowed if the bill is paid within 10 days.

February 20. Customers pay off their bills from the February 10 sales.

February 25. The securities acquired on the fifteenth are sold for $1,700.

February 28. Operating expenses of $10,000 are paid.

3. Billy Bob Kerplunker just incorporated his business of selling hot peppers and barbecue sauce. Prepare journal entries for the following transactions.

March 1: Billy Bob Kerplunker, Inc. issues 10,000 shares of common stock at $43 per share. The stock has a par value of $5 per share.

March 5: Billy Bob Kerplunker transferred land with a fair value of $100,000 and a mortgage with a balance of $60,000 to the corporation in exchange for 1,000 shares of common stock.

March 8: Billy Bob Kerplunker, Inc. has credit sales of $50,000.

March 15: Billy Bob Kerplunker, Inc. has operating expenses of $25,000.

March 20: Billy Bob Kerplunker, Inc. declares dividends of $1 per share payable to shareholders who own the stock on March 22. Dividends will be paid on March 27.

March 22: Billy Bob Kerplunker determines who owns the stock on this day and is entitled to receive the dividends. (*Hint:* Has a transaction occurred?)

March 27: Billy Bob Kerplunker pays the dividends.

4. Paula McCartney runs Alae, Inc., which has the following stockholders' equity section as of March 31, 2001.

Preferred stock (100,000 shares authorized, issued, and outstanding)	$10,000,000
Common stock (3,000,000 shares authorized and 2,000,000 shares issued)	2,000,000
Additional paid in capital	43,000,000
Retained earnings	26,000,000
Stockholders' equity	$81,000,000

Alae, Inc. engaged in the following transactions during April, 2001.

April 1. The firm buys 50,000 shares of its own common stock at $19 each.

April 6. The company declares dividends of $2 per share on preferred stock and dividends of $1 per share on common stock, both payable to shareholders of record (those who own the stock) on April 16. Both dividends will be paid on April 21. (*Hint:* Does it make any sense to pay dividends on treasury stock?)

April 16. The corporation determines who owns the stock on this date.

April 21. The dividends are paid.

April 28. The firm sells 40,000 treasury shares for $23 each. (*Hint:* Put the additional amount into additional paid-in capital.)

You are hired as a consultant to tell management how it should record these transactions. *Required:* Prepare journal entries for Alae's April transactions, and prepare the stockholder's equity section of the balance sheet as of April 30, 2001. Assume April's net income equals $3,100,000.

5. Dewey Decimal owns a book franchise. His accounts are as follows:

Cash		Accounts receivable		Land	
10,000		20,000		100,000	

Building		Accounts payable		Mortgage payable	
250,000			8,000		260,000

D.D., Capital		Sales		Operating expenses	
	82,000		200,000	170,000	

Dewey Decimal's general journal contains the following journal entries:

		Debit	Credit
Accounts receivable		$40,000	
	Sales		$40,000
Cash		$43,000	
	Accounts receivable		$43,000
Operating expenses		$33,000	
	Cash		$33,000
Accounts payable		$ 5,000	
	Cash		$ 5,000
Mortgage payable		$10,000	
	Cash		$10,000
Dewey Decimal, drawings		$ 2,000	
	Cash		$ 2,000

Required: Post these entries to the T-accounts and prepare a trial balance.

6. The bookkeeper for Quarantine Anonymous prepared all of the journal entries correctly except for one. When making the adjusting entries, the bookkeeper should have debited depreciation expense and credited accumulated depreciation for $10,000; instead, he debited depreciation expense and debited accumulated depreciation for $10,000. Except for this entry, debits and credits in the trial balance equal $856,000. Also, prior to this adjusting entry, the balance in the accumulated depreciation account is $43,000.

Required: Answer the following questions pertaining to the trial balance, including the effects from the erroneous entry.

(a) What is the balance in depreciation expense? Indicate whether it is a debit or credit balance. Is this balance correct? If not, what should it be?

(b) What is the balance in accumulated depreciation? Indicate whether it is a debit or credit balance. Is this balance correct? If not, what should it be?

(c) What is the total of the debits column of the trial balance?

(d) What is the total of the credits column of the trial balance?

(e) How will the error be detected?

7. As an accountant for Lisztless in Lisbon, you are looking at the following three trial balances. Can you determine which trial balance is which?

Lisztless in Lisbon
Trial Balance #1
December 31, 2001

Accounts	*Debits*	*Credits*
Cash	$ 2	
Accounts receivable	6	
Allowance for doubtful accounts		$ 4
Building	20	
Accumulated depreciation		6
Accounts payable		5
Retained earnings		6
Sales		20
Wages expense	7	
Rent expense	1	
Bad debts expense	3	
Depreciation expense	2	
Totals	$41	$41

Lisztless in Lisbon
Trial Balance #2
December 31, 2001

Accounts	*Debits*	*Credits*
Cash	$ 2	
Accounts receivable	6	
Allowance for doubtful accounts		$ 4
Building	20	
Accumulated depreciation		6
Accounts payable		5
Retained earnings		13
Totals	$28	$28

Lisztless in Lisbon
Trial Balance #3
December 31, 2001

Accounts	*Debits*	*Credits*
Cash	$ 2	
Accounts receivable	6	
Allowance for doubtful accounts		$ 1
Building	20	
Accumulated depreciation		4
Accounts payable		5
Retained earnings		6
Sales		20
Wages expense	7	
Rent expense	1	
Totals	$36	$36

8. Lisa Herr is the bookkeeper for HerrLooks, an upbeat fashion boutique. She is in the midst of her work, but the only adjustments on her mind concern the length of her hair. A partial trial balance is given below:

Cash	3,000
Insurance expense	600
Notes receivable	10,000
Prepaid rent	3,600
Supplies expense	5,250
Wages expense	8,750

Required: Prepare the following adjusting entries.

(a) HerrLooks paid $600 for a one-year insurance policy on May 31.

(b) On September 30 HerrLooks extended a six-month $10,000 loan to one of its favorite customers, Dennis Rodman. The loan carries an interest rate of 8%, and no interest needs to be paid until maturity.

(c) The firm paid one year's rent for its building beginning on February 28.

(d) Lisa counted inventory for the firm and determined that HerrLooks had an office supplies inventory at December 31 of $520.

(e) HerrLooks last paid its employees on December 19 and will not pay them again until January 2 of next year. The employees earned $575 during the December 19–31 period.

9. A manager at Carrolton, Inc. is looking at the adjusting entries at December 31, 2002, and she is trying to reconstruct some data. Please help her with the following questions.

(a) On May 31 Carrolton purchased one year's insurance. On December 31 the firm made the adjusting entry:

Prepaid insurance	$300	
Insurance expense		$300

What was the original entry on May 31?

(b) Carrolton had supplies inventory of $500 at January 1 and $850 at the end of the year. If supplies expense is $2,100, how much did the company pay for supplies?

(c) Carrolton signed a one-year note on June 1. The note carried an interest rate of 8%. Determine the entry on June 1 if the adjusting entry on December 31 is

Interest expense	$700	
Interest payable		$700

(d) Carrolton purchased an automobile on January 1, 2001. At December 31, 2003 the accumulated depreciation account has a balance of $7,500. If the auto is considered fully depreciated on December 31, 2004 and if it has a salvage value of $2,000, what is the original cost of the automobile?

(e) One day Carrolton sold one-year magazine subscriptions. At the end of the year, after adjusting entries and before closing entries are prepared, unearned subscription revenue has a balance of $400 and subscription revenue has a balance of $2,000. On what date did the original transaction occur?

10. Scienter, Ltd. acquired some equipment for $570,000 on January 2, 2001. This equipment has an economic life of five years and a salvage value of $20,000.

Required:

(a) Prepare a depreciation schedule for this asset, using straight-line depreciation. This schedule will have five rows, one for each year of the equipment's life. It will have a column for the year, the depreciation expense, the accumulated depreciation, and the book value.

(b) Is depreciation closed out at the end of the year? How is this fact shown in the depreciation table?

(c) Is accumulated depreciation closed out at the end of the year? How is this fact shown in the depreciation schedule?

(d) Scienter sells the asset on December 30, 2004. Prepare the journal entry if the asset is sold for (i) $110,00, (ii) $130,000, and (iii) $150,000. Assume that the entry recognizing depreciation expense during 2004 has been made in all three cases.

11. Judy Pressler will soon be retiring from her position as administrative assistant. Before doing so, she must prepare closing entries for the company. Having learned no accounting, she is having difficulty. Below is the list of accounts. Assist Judy by making the closing entries for her. The ending balance in merchandise inventory should be $14,000.

Accumulated depreciation	8,000	Land	100,000
Advertising expense	9,000	Merchandise inventory	12,000
Building	400,000	Purchase discounts	3,000
Cash	10,000	Purchase returns	1,000
Common stock	200,000	Purchases	180,000
Depreciation	10,500	Retained earnings	500,000
Dividends	2,000	Sales discounts	4,000
Flood loss	50,000	Sales returns	2,000
Interest expense	7,300	Sales	300,000
Investment revenue	10,000	Supplies expense	6,000
		Transportation in	1,000
		Utilities expense	11,000
		Wages expense	75,000

12. Clearance Company is having a close-out sale early January, 2003. But at December 31, 2002 management needs someone to close their books. Prepare closing entries for them given the following accounts. Clearance employs the periodic method of accounting for inventories.

Direct labor	300	Raw materials, Jan. 1	20
Dividends	100	Raw materials, Dec. 31	30
Finished goods, Jan. 1	80	Sales	3,000
Finished goods, Dec. 31	100	Selling expenses	200
Overhead	500	Taxes	250
Purchases	800	Transportation in	35
Purchase discounts	15	Work-in-process, Jan. 1	30
Purchase returns & allow	10	Work-in-process, Dec. 31	10

PROBLEMS

1. In the following chart a number of accounts are listed for a manufacturing concern. *Required:* In column 2 indicate whether the account typically has a debit or credit or zero balance. In column 3 state in which financial statement the account would be found (BS = balance sheet; IS = income statement; SCSE = statement of changes in stockholders' equity). Some accounts may be found on more than one statement; some may be found on none. In the last column provide details. If the item is found on the balance sheet, tell whether it is a current asset (CA), property, plant, and equipment (PPE), intangible asset (IA), investments (INV), current liability (CL), long-term debt (LTD), or stockholders' equity (SHE). If the account is found on the income statement, state whether it is a revenue (REV) or expense (EXP) or part of cost of goods sold (COGS). Finally, if the account is a contra account, place a minus sign in front of the designation.

An example is given to you in the second row of the table.

Accounts	DR or CR or 0	Financial Statements	
		BS/IS/SCSE	Details
Example: Accumulated depreciation	CR	BS	-PPE
1. Accounts payable	CR	BS	CL
2. Accounts receivable	DR	BS	CA
3. Additional paid-in capital	CR	SCSE	
4. Allowance for doubtful accounts	CR	BS	—
5. Building	DR	BS	PPE
6. Cash	DR	BS	CA
7. Common stock	DR	SCSE	
8. Direct labor	DR	IS	CogS
9. Dividends	DR	SCSE	
10. Finished goods	DR	BS	
11. Freight in	DR	IS	COGS
12. Goodwill	DR	BS	
13. Income summary	0	none	
14. Income taxes	CR	BS	
15. Insurance expense	CR	IS	EXP
16. Interest expense	CR	IS	EXP
17. Interest receivable	DR	BS	
18. Interest revenue	DR	IS	Rev
19. Land	DR	BS	
20. Notes payable (90 days)	CR	BS	CL
21. Overhead	DR	BS	
22. Patents	DR	BS	
23. Prepaid rent	DR	BS	
24. Purchases	DR	IS	COGS
25. Purchase discounts	CR	IS	COGS
26. Purchase returns	CR	IS	COGS
27. Raw materials	DR	BS	
28. Retained earnings	CR	SCSE	
29. Sales	CR	IS	Rev
30. Sales discounts	DR	IS	— Rev
31. Sales returns and allowances	DR	IS	— Rev
32. Treasury stock	DR	SCSE	IA
33. Work-in-process	DR	BS	CogS

2. Karen Jenkins starts her own consulting company on January 2, 2001. During 2001 Jenkins Consulting engages in the following transactions:

(a) January 2: Jenkins invests $50,000 cash, a building valued at $200,000, and land worth $100,000.

(b) January 2: Jenkins buys equipment costing $100,000 by signing a three-year note payable. The note carries an 8% interest rate, and the first payment is due January 2, 2002.

(c) April 1: Jenkins charges $300,000 on a consulting contract.

(d) June 1: Customers pay $250,000 on their accounts.

(e) September 1: Jenkins incurs the following expenses: wages, $100,000; utilities, $50,000; and office supplies, $30,000. → ALL INTO A.P.

(f) November 3: Jenkins pays $160,000 of the bills received on September 1.

(g) December 5: Karen Jenkins withdraws $10,000 for personal use.

Additional information: The building has a life of 20 years and a salvage value of $50,000. The equipment has a life of five years and no salvage value. Bad debts expense is $1,000. The ending supplies inventory is $4,000.

Required: Go through the accounting cycle for Jenkins Consulting for 2001. Enter journal entries in the general journal: put entries (a)–(f) on page 1, entry (g) and the adjusting entries on page 2, and the closing entries on page 3. Post them to the general ledger. Make all three trial balances. Prepare the income statement, the statement of owner's equity, and the balance sheet in good form. Use the following chart of accounts.

Jenkins Consulting
Chart of Accounts

Cash	100
Accounts receivable	120
Allowance for bad debts	130
Office supplies	140
Land	170
Building	180
Accumulated depreciation—building	185
Equipment	190
Accumulated depreciation—equipment	195
Accounts payable	210
Interest payable	230
Notes payable	280
Jenkins, capital	300
Service revenue	400
Wages expense	500
Utilities expense	510
Office supplies expense	520
Depreciation expense	530
Interest expense	540
Bad debts expense	550
Jenkins, drawings	600
Income summary	900

3. Chris and Dave Stevens set up a paint store on January 2, 2001, and they name it Stevens' Stains. During 2001 Stevens' Stains has the following transactions.

(a) January 2: The firm issues 100,000 shares of stock for $10 per share. The stock has a par value of $1 per share.

(b) January 3: Stevens' Stains buys land and a building and paid cash. The land is valued at $200,000 and the building at $300,000.

(c) March 1: The company purchases $500,000 of merchandise on account.

(d) March 5: The company sells merchandise on account for $800,000.
COGS $320,000

(e) March 11: Stevens' Stains pays its suppliers $400,000 less a 1% cash discount.
(f) March 15: Customers pay $600,000 on their accounts less a 2% cash discount.
(g) July 17: Wages of $50,000 are paid.

Additional information: The building has a life of 25 years and a salvage value of $50,000. Bad debts expense is estimated as $2,000. Ending merchandise inventory is counted at $10,000.

Required: Go through the accounting cycle for Stevens' Stains for 2001. Enter journal entries in the general journal: put entries (a)–(e) on page 1, entries (f) and (g) and the adjusting entries on page 2, and the closing entries on page 3. Post them to the general ledger. Make all three trial balances. Prepare the income statement, the statement of owner's equity, and the balance sheet in good form. Use the following chart of accounts.

Stevens' Stains
Chart of Accounts

Cash	100
Accounts receivable	120
Allowance for bad debts	130
Merchandise inventory	140
Land	170
Building	180
Accumulated depreciation	185
Accounts payable	210
Common stock	300
Additional paid-in capital	310
Retained earnings	360
Sales	400
Sales discounts	420
Purchases COGS	500
Purchase discounts	520
Wages expense	600
Depreciation expense	610
Bad debts expense	620
Income summary	999

4. Lou Kearse starts a hardware store in 2001 which she calls Hardly Working. The post-closing trial balance at December 31, 2003 is

Hardly Working, Inc.
Post-Closing Trial Balance
December 31, 2003

Account	Debits	Credits
Cash	$ 40,000	
Accounts receivable	50,000	
Allowance for bad debts		$ 5,000
Merchandise inventory	30,000	
Land	400,000	
Building	310,000	
Accumulated depreciation		90,000
Accounts payable		50,000
Common stock (par $5 per share)		200,000
Additional paid-in capital		400,000
Retained earnings		85,000
Totals	$830,000	$830,000

During 2004 Hardly Working, Inc. conducts the following transactions.

(a) January 15: Collects $30,000 from customers. (These customers are not entitled to a cash discount.)
(b) February 15: Purchases $500,000 worth of goods on account.
(c) February 25: Pays freight charges of $15,000 on the goods purchased.
(d) March 15: Makes credit sales of $800,000. COGS 360,000
(e) April 15: Collects $500,000 from customers less a 2% cash discount.
(f) May 15: Pays $400,000 to suppliers less a 2% cash discount.
(g) June 15: Declares dividends of $20,000 to those on record June 25.
(h) July 15: Pays the dividends.
(i) August 15: Customers have returns and allowances amounting to $25,000. COGS 11250
(j) September 15: Returns and allowances to suppliers amounts to $15,000.
(k) October 15: Pay workers $120,000.

Additional information: Depreciation on the building is $15,000, and bad debts expense for 2004 is $1,000.
~~Ending merchandise inventory is $35,000.~~

Required: Go through the accounting cycle for Hardly Working, Inc. for 2004. Enter journal entries in the general journal: put entries (a)–(f) on page 1, entries (g)–(k) and the adjusting entries on page 2, and the closing entries on page 3. Post them to the general ledger. Make all three trial balances. Prepare the income statement, the statement of retained earnings, and the balance sheet in good form. Use the following chart of accounts.

Hardly Working, Inc.
Chart of Accounts

Cash	100
Accounts receivable	120
Allowance for bad debts	130
Merchandise inventory	140
Land	170
Building	180
Accumulated depreciation	185
Accounts payable	210
Dividends payable	220
Common stock	300
Additional paid-in capital	310
Retained earnings	360
Sales	400
Sales discounts	420
Sales returns and allowances	440
~~Purchases~~ COGS	500
Purchase discounts	520
~~Purchase returns and allowances~~	~~540~~
Freight in	560
Wages expense	600
Depreciation expense	610
Bad debts expense	620
Dividends	700
Income summary	999

CHAPTER **4**

FURTHER ASPECTS OF THE ACCOUNTING CYCLE

As has been stated several times, financial accounting provides information about the firm through the financial statements—the balance sheet, income statement, statement of changes in stockholders' equity, and cash flow statement. Chapter 2 describes the balance sheet, income statement, and statement of changes in stockholders' equity, while the next chapter elucidates the cash flow statement.

To prepare and publish these statements, the firm needs an accounting information system that can capture the relevant data about the firm's transactions, categorize them, store them, and retrieve them in appropriate ways. This process of gathering and storing transaction data is known as the financial accounting cycle, or simply, the accounting cycle. The previous chapter explains and clarifies journal entries, posting entries to a ledger, trial balances, adjusting entries, and closing entries. This chapter completes the accounting portrait by sketching subsidiary ledgers, special journals, worksheets, reversing entries, and correcting entries. Strictly speaking, accountants do not need subsidiary ledgers, worksheets, special journals, or reversing entries, but they employ them to make their work easier and quicker. Reversing entries, however, are dying out because computers have virtually eliminated whatever benefit they used to provide. We discuss them because some firms still employ reversing entries.

It is appropriate to repeat the caution stated in Chapter 3. As the reader delves into the mechanics of bookkeeping, there is a tendency to think of the mechanics as an end in itself. The student should always keep in mind the purpose of financial reporting—to assist readers of the financial statements in making better economic decisions. Subsidiary ledgers, worksheets, and so on are merely tools to achieve this end.

We will still assume that the accountant already has the relevant data to prepare the journal entries, ledgers, and other bookkeeping steps. Chapters 6–11 will indicate how the data are captured.

After reading and studying this chapter, you should be able to:

- Describe the accounting cycle;
- Define a subsidiary ledger and post entries to a subsidiary ledger;
- Describe the purpose of special journals;
- Utilize a sales journal;
- Employ a purchases journal;
- Use a cash receipts journal;
- Utilize a cash disbursements journal;
- Prepare a worksheet;
- Make reversing entries; and
- Make correcting entries.

96

OVERVIEW OF THE ACCOUNTING CYCLE

Chapter 3 discusses the fundamentals of the financial accounting cycle. To review, *transactions processing* encompasses all the activities that transform data about a firm's transactions into the firm's financial statements. The *accounting cycle* lists the steps in transactions processing. The cycle, as presented in Chapter 3, consists of 10 steps. First, the bookkeeper prepares a journal entry for the transaction and writes this journal entry in a journal. Second, the journal entry is posted to a ledger. Third, the accountant constructs the unadjusted trial balance. Fourth, the accountant enters adjusting entries. Fifth, he or she posts them. Sixth, the adjusted trial balance is prepared. Seventh, the accountant constructs the financial statements. Eighth, the accountant makes closing entries and, ninth, posts them. Tenth, the post-closing trial balance is constructed.

In this chapter, we expand the mechanics of bookkeeping to include subsidiary ledgers, worksheets, special journals, reversing entries, and correcting entries. This expansion modifies the accounting cycle somewhat. The steps in the new accounting cycle are shown in Exhibit 4.1.

EXHIBIT 4.1

THE ACCOUNTING CYCLE

---

1. Make a journal entry for the transaction either in the general journal or in a special journal.

2. Post the journal entry to the general ledger and, when appropriate, to a subsidiary ledger.

3. Construct the worksheet.

   (a) Prepare the unadjusted trial balance.

   (b) Make the adjustments.

   (c) Prepare the adjusted trial balance.

   (d) Assemble the preliminary balance sheet and the preliminary income statement.

4. Prepare the financial statements:

   (a) balance sheet;

   (b) income statement;

   (c) statement of changes in stockholders' equity; and

   (d) cash flow statement.

5. Enter the adjusting entries into the general journal.

6. Post the adjusting entries into the general ledger.

7. Enter the closing entries into the general journal.

8. Post the closing entries into the general ledger.

9. Prepare a post-closing trial balance.

10. Enter the reversing entries into the general journal.

11. Post the reversing entries into the general ledger.

Note: When errors are discovered, correcting entries are entered into the general journal and posted to the general ledger and, when appropriate, to a subsidiary ledger. Subsidiary schedules can be prepared as management desires for any subsidiary ledger.

Before exploring this modified series of steps in the accounting cycle, let's review some terms. A *journal* is a chronological record of the economic effects of an entity's transactions. In Chapter 3 all journal entries are entered into the general journal. We define a *general journal* to be a journal that records all transactions not entered in a special journal. A *special journal*, on the other hand, is a journal that records only certain types of transactions, such as credit sales, credit purchases, cash receipts, and cash disbursements. As explained later, special journals are employed to garner like transactions together and record them in one place. Four special journals are illustrated later in this chapter: the sales journal, the purchases journal, the cash receipts journal, and the cash disbursements journal. For now, notice that we amend the first step of the previous accounting cycle to indicate that the transaction is recorded either in the general journal or in a special journal.

A *ledger* is a listing of the accounts of an entity and their balances or a listing of the components of some account. In Chapter 3 we concerned ourselves only with general ledgers; a *general ledger* is a listing of the accounts of an entity and their balances. Managers sometimes need to know the balance of a particular customer's account, and peering into the accounts receivable account of the general ledger won't reveal that balance. To obtain the balance of some specific customer, accountants create subsidiary ledgers. A *subsidiary ledger* is just a listing of the components of some account. To operate a subsidiary ledger requires an amendment of the posting process—the second step of the accounting cycle—so that journal entries are posted both to the general ledger and to the subsidiary ledger. This is discussed further in the next section of the chapter.

Companies often employ worksheets to harness the data that will be utilized in manufacturing the balance sheet and the income statement. These *worksheets*, elaborated on and illustrated later in the chapter, contain the unadjusted trial balance, adjustments (which are the adjusting entries informally entered on the worksheet), the adjusted trial balance, and the preliminary income statement and preliminary balance sheet. We modify the accounting cycle to make the third step the construction of the worksheet. Notice that this step includes the production of the unadjusted and adjusted trial balances. Also recognize that it does not replace the step of making the adjusting entries since the adjustments are worksheet entries only.

The fourth step becomes the preparation of the financial statements. The worksheet shows the balance sheet and the income statement and, at least implicitly, the statement of retained earnings. The rest of the data necessary to put together the statement of stockholders' equity and the cash flow statement does not depend on any of the remaining steps, and so these statements can be prepared and disseminated to the public.

The fifth and sixth steps of the accounting cycle are to make and post the adjusting entries. The seventh and eighth steps are to make and post the closing entries. The ninth step is to prepare the post-closing trial balance. Special journals, subsidiary ledgers, worksheets, reversing entries, and correcting entries do not affect these steps.

The last two steps concern the journalizing and posting of reversing entries. These entries, entered on the first day of the new fiscal year, reverse some of the adjusting entries made at the end of the previous year. These reversing entries are designed to increase the efficiency of the bookkeeping work.

Correcting entries, the last topic of this chapter, are recorded in step one. Whenever the error is discovered, the appropriate correction is carried out.

Exhibit 4.1 summarizes the accounting cycle steps. There really is no substantive difference between these steps and those listed in Exhibit 3.2 in Chapter 3. We have merely modified the original list for the new bookkeeping tools that will be presented in this chapter.

The rest of this chapter fleshes out details about these new aspects of the accounting cycle. We focus on (1) subsidiary ledgers, (2) special journals, (3) worksheets, (4) reversing entries, and (5) correcting entries.

SUBSIDIARY LEDGERS

Accounts are specific assets, liabilities, stockholders' equities, revenues, or expenses. The general ledger contains these accounts and their balances. Whenever a manager desires to know the balance of some account, such as buildings, he or she can ask the accountant who can consult the general ledger and ascertain that the balance in the buildings account is so many dollars. One of the main purposes of the general ledger is to provide the current balances of the accounts.

Sometimes, however, the manager wants to ask a different question. For example, the accounts receivable account displays the balance of the total accounts receivable, but the manager often wants to know about specific customers and their balances. What does Mr. Brown or Ms. Redd owe us? The question may even become poignant when the firm starts thinking about a particular customer's ability to repay the debt. For example, managers often consider whether to extend further credit to customers. The first move in making this decision is knowing how much the customers already owe the company. Subsidiary ledgers yield this information.

A *subsidiary ledger*, as noted earlier, is a listing of the components of some account. The accounts receivable subsidiary ledger and the accounts payable subsidiary ledger are two very important subsidiary ledgers of the business enterprise. The *accounts receivable subsidiary ledger* lists the customers and their balances owed to the firm, whereas the *accounts payable subsidiary ledger* lists the suppliers and the balance owed them by the corporation. We also define a *controlling account* as an account whose balance is the sum of the related subsidiary accounts. A *subsidiary account* is a component of the subsidiary ledger for some controlling account.

Suppose a company has three customers. Mary owes $100, Sherry $300, and Terry $400. Accounts receivable has a debit balance of $800. The general ledger accounts receivable is referred to as a controlling account because the sum of the customer balances is indeed $800, as it should be. The accounts receivable subsidiary ledger has three accounts: accounts receivable—Mary; accounts receivable—Sherry; and accounts receivable— Terry. These latter three accounts are referred to as subsidiary accounts. Note that they do not go on the balance sheet; placing them on the balance sheet would double count them, for the controlling account already is found on the balance sheet. The purpose of the subsidiary accounts is to allow a manager to find out the balance in any of these accounts. If the accountant or the manager examines accounts receivable—Sherry, he or she will discover that Sherry owes the company $300.

Business enterprises frequently prepare a report for managers that lists the customers and their balances. This report is called a *subsidiary schedule*. For this example, the accounts receivable subsidiary schedule would appear as

Some Funky Firm
Schedule of Accounts Receivable
July 31, 2002

Mary	$100
Sherry	300
Terry	400
Total	$800

The title of the schedule indicates the name of the company, the name of the schedule, and the date of the report.

Let's consider the following example of an accounts receivable subsidiary ledger. Gamma Gophers is a sporting goods store. Gamma Gophers has five customers. They, and their account balances on September 1, 2001, are

Joan Coraor	$ 5,000
Bruce Johnson	60,000
Stephanie Ling	7,000
Roosevelt Smith	1,000
Zachary Unitas	2,600
Total	$75,600

This, of course, implies that accounts receivable has a balance of $75,600. At all times, unless a mistake has been made, the controlling account equals the sum of the related subsidiary accounts. Cash has a balance of $20,790 while sales and sales returns and allowances have zero balances. (Gamma closes its nominal accounts every month.) Other accounts will be ignored.

Gamma Gophers (GG) sells sporting goods on credit. Terms are net/30. GG has the following transactions in September:

September 13: GG sold $2,000 of goods to Stephanie Ling.
September 14: GG sold $5,000 of goods to Roosevelt Smith.
September 15: Stephanie Ling complains about the ice skates sold to her. GG agrees to give her an allowance of $500.
September 23: GG receives $5,000 from Stephanie Ling.
September 29: GG sold $3,000 of goods to Zachary Unitas.

You are asked to make the appropriate journal entries in the general journal, post them to the general ledger and to the accounts receivable subsidiary ledger, and compose an accounts receivable schedule as of September 30, 2001. Exhibit 4.2 shows the solution to this problem. Panel A gives the journal entries, panel B shows the affected accounts of the general ledger, panel C reveals the subsidiary ledger and all of the subsidiary accounts, and panel D divulges the schedule of accounts receivable at the end of September.

The journal entries contained in panel A of Exhibit 4.2 involve no new concepts. They are written according to the usual debit and credit rules of bookkeeping and the conventions about indentation. Posting to cash, sales, sales returns and allowances, and the controlling account accounts receivable is performed as it was in Chapter 3. The amount is carried from the general journal to the general ledger and placed in the debit or credit column, whichever is appropriate. The account number is placed in the folio column of the general journal, as it always is.

The new item in panel A is the recording of the customer's name. We have placed this name after the entry; some bookkeepers, however, put it on the line immediately following accounts receivable, whereas others set it on the same line if there is room. Once the item is posted to the accounts receivable subsidiary ledger, some notation is used to indicate this fact. We place an asterisk ("*") in the folio column to show that the posting has been accomplished, although variations exist in practice.

The general ledger can be viewed in panel B. Note that the postings and balancings are performed as presented in Chapter 3. This panel contains no new concepts.

The student should carefully examine panel C of Exhibit 4.2 in which the accounts receivable subsidiary ledger is displayed. Postings to the subsidiary ledger look remarkably similar to that in the general ledger. The date is placed in the first column, and a

EXHIBIT 4.2

EXAMPLE OF AN ACCOUNTS RECEIVABLE SUBSIDIARY LEDGER

Panel A: Journal entries in the general journal

General Journal

PAGE 27

Date	Description	F	Debit	Credit
9-13	Accounts receivable	120	$2,000	
	Sales	600		$2,000
	Stephanie Ling	*		
9-14	Accounts receivable	120	$5,000	
	Sales	600		$5,000
	Roosevelt Smith	*		

General Journal

PAGE 28

Date	Description	F	Debit	Credit
9-15	Sales returns and allowances	630	$ 500	
	Accounts receivable	120		$ 500
	Stephanie Ling	*		
9-23	Cash	100	$5,000	
	Accounts receivable	120		$5,000
	Stephanie Ling	*		
9-29	Accounts receivable	120	$3,000	
	Sales	600		$3,000
	Zachary Unitas	*		

Panel B: General ledger (partial)

General Ledger
Cash

Account No. 100

Date	Description	F	Debits	Credits	Balance
	Opening Bal				$20,790
9-23	Collection	28	$5,000		$25,790

(continued)

EXHIBIT *4.2*

EXAMPLE OF AN ACCOUNTS RECEIVABLE SUBSIDIARY LEDGER (continued)

Accounts Receivable

Account No. 120

Date	Description	F	Debits	Credits	Balance
	Opening Bal				$75,600
9-13	Sale	27	$2,000		$77,600
9-14	Sale	27	$5,000		$82,600
9-15	Allowance	28		$ 500	$82,100
9-23	Collection	28		$5,000	$77,100
9-29	Sale	28	$3,000		$80,100

Sales

Account No. 600

Date	Description	F	Debits	Credits	Balance
9-13		27		$2,000	$ 2,000
9-14		27		$5,000	$ 7,000
9-29		28		$3,000	$10,000

Sales Returns and Allowances

Account No. 630

Date	Description	F	Debits	Credits	Balance
9-15		28	$ 500		$ 500

Panel C: Subsidiary Ledger

Accounts Receivable Subsidiary Ledger
Joan Coraor

Date	Description	F	Debits	Credits	Balance
	Opening Bal				$ 5,000

Bruce Johnson

Date	Description	F	Debits	Credits	Balance
	Opening Bal				$60,000

(continued)

EXHIBIT 4.2

EXAMPLE OF AN ACCOUNTS RECEIVABLE SUBSIDIARY LEDGER *(continued)*

Stephanie Ling

Date	Description	F	Debits	Credits	Balance
	Opening Bal				$ 7,000
9-13	Sale	27	$2,000		$ 9,000
9-15	Return	28		$ 500	$ 8,500
9-23	Collection	28		$5,000	$ 3,500

Roosevelt Smith

Date	Description	F	Debits	Credits	Balance
	Opening Bal				$ 1,000
9-14	Sale	27	$5,000		$ 6,000

Zachary Unitas

Date	Description	F	Debits	Credits	Balance
	Opening Bal				$ 2,600
9-29	Sale	28	$3,000		$ 5,600

Panel D: Schedule of accounts receivable

Gamma Gophers
Schedule of Accounts Receivable
September 30, 2001

Customer	Amount
Joan Coraor	$ 5,000
Bruce Johnson	60,000
Stephanie Ling	3,500
Roosevelt Smith	6,000
Zachary Unitas	5,600
Total	$80,100

description of the transaction may be written in the second column if desired. The page number of the general journal is inscribed in the folio column once the posting has been finished. This number provides a cross-reference if an accountant or auditor wants to check the transaction's recording. The amount is placed in the debit column if the account receivable increases and in the credit column if it decreases. The last column shows the customer's balance.

At all times, the amount of the controlling account ought to equal the sum of the balances of the subsidiary accounts. Accounts receivable at the end of September shows a balance of $80,100; see the accounts receivable account in panel B. Note that the sum of the subsidiary accounts in panel C equals $80,100 ($5,000 + $60,000 + $3,500 + $6,000 + $5,600) as well.

Managers do not want to spend so much of their time poring over journals and ledgers, and so accountants periodically prepare an accounts receivable schedule. Many businesses publish this schedule internally on a monthly basis. Panel D of Exhibit 4.2 demonstrates an accounts receivable schedule for this illustration. The schedule merely places the data in the subsidiary ledger in a more readable document.

In summary, usage of a subsidiary ledger allows the firms to look at details of the account. Although we have employed an accounts receivable example, other accounts could have subsidiary accounts. An accounts payable subsidiary ledger could show how much is owed to individual suppliers; an inventory subsidiary ledger might reveal the amounts of individual inventory items; or an additional paid-in capital subsidiary ledger could indicate the different sources of additional paid-in capital (such as common stock, preferred stock, and treasury stock transactions).

SPECIAL JOURNALS

Some transactions, such as credit sales and the purchase of merchandise inventory, are repetitive. Many years ago accountants discovered that streamlining the recording of these repetitive transactions in special journals could lead to many efficiencies. At this time, we introduce four special journals: the sales journal, the purchases journal, the cash receipts journal, and the cash disbursements journal. These special journals, together with the general journal, contain the journal entries of the company's transactions in chronological order.

Credit sales are recorded in the *sales journal;* credit purchases are registered in the *purchases journal;* all cash receipts, including cash sales, are entered into the *cash receipts journal;* and all cash disbursements, including cash purchases of inventory, are chronicled in the *cash disbursements journal*, also called the *cash payments journal*. All other transactions are recorded in the general journal. (In practice other special journals are possible, and variations to the special journals are sometimes introduced.)

Accountants employ special journals for two reasons. First, special journals reduce the amount of posting time, and so they are more efficient than a general journal for all transactions. This advantage virtually disappears in a computerized system, however, because the postings are performed automatically. Second, accounting systems are often designed around transaction cycles for internal control purposes. We will defer discussion of this topic until our discussion of transaction cycles in later chapters.

The introduction of special journals requires a modification to the posting procedures. Once posting is completed, the reference or folio column in the general ledger and any subsidiary ledgers shows the page number of the journal in which the journal entry is recorded. If only the page number was given in the ledgers, then an ambiguity would arise as to which journal contains the journal entry. Bookkeepers eliminate this ambiguity by indicating the journal as well as the page number in the reference or folio column. The general journal is referred to as "J" (sometimes "GJ"), the sales journal as "S," the purchases journal as "P," the cash receipts journal as "CR," and the cash disbursements or cash payments journal as either "CD" or "CP." Thus, J23 in the ledger's folio column means that the journal entry can be found on page 23 of the general journal. If the column shows P21, you can find the entry on page 21 of the purchases journal.

Sales Journal

The sales journal contains data about the credit sales of merchandise. Cash sales go into the cash receipts journal. Credit sales of items other than merchandise—for example, the sale of property, plant, or equipment—should be recorded in the general journal.

All credit sales of merchandise are put into the sales journal, and only such transactions are recorded here. This means that all of the transactions found in the sales journal are recorded as a debit to accounts receivable and a credit to sales. Given this fact, the accounts are usually omitted from the journal. The knowledgeable reader of the sales journal understands the debit and credit by implication.

Exhibit 4.3 presents an example of a sales journal with five columns. The first column reveals the date of the transaction. The second column tells the invoice number (which we will discuss shortly). Column 3 gives the customer's name. The reference or folio column in the fourth column is employed when posting to the accounts receivable subsidiary ledger. Once the bookkeeper posts the transaction to the accounts receivable subsidiary ledger, he or she notes that the posting is complete with an asterisk in the fourth column. The fifth column discloses the amount of the sale.

Periodically, the accountant posts the total to the general ledger. This task is achieved by summing the last column. In Exhibit 4.3 the total is $5,500. Since all transactions are credit sales, the accountant posts one summary entry to the general ledger:

Accounts receivable	$5,500	
Sales		$5,500

Once the posting is concluded, the bookkeeper jots down the account numbers. Efficiency is obtained by posting only this one entry instead of each of the many sales transactions a firm would have in practice. Instead of placing the account numbers in a folio column, the account numbers are written below the totaled amount, the debit account first. The example assumes that the firm's chart of accounts assigns 120 to accounts receivable and 600 to sales.

Let's return to the invoice number. An *invoice* is a bill, a document sent to a customer that indicates the price for goods or services provided by the seller and the terms for settlement. The document serves as evidence that a legitimate transaction has occurred, and it requests payment by the customer. Each sales transaction is assigned a unique invoice number so that it can be more easily researched later if necessary. Enumerating the invoice number in the sales journal cross-references the transaction with the invoice that

EXHIBIT 4.3

SALES JOURNAL

Sales Journal

Page S7

Date	Invoice Number	Customer	F	Amount
12-1	1302	Karpov	*	$1,000
12-3	1303	Kasparov	*	850
12-4	1304	Short	*	3,450
12-4	1305	Kamsky	*	200
	TOTAL			$5,500
				(120) (600)

authorizes the transaction. Including this information in the sales journal increases the internal control over sales transactions. We expand this discussion in Chapter 9 when we examine the sales cycle and the various documents and controls associated with the sales cycle.

Purchases Journal

The purchases journal is the mirror image of the sales journal, and so they are very similar. The purchases journal includes data about credit purchases of inventory. Cash purchases are recorded in the cash disbursements journal. Purchases of other items, such as investments or equipment, should be recorded in the general journal.

All credit purchases of inventory are placed in the purchases journal, and only such transactions are recorded here. All of the transactions detected in the purchases journal are recorded as a debit to purchases (assuming a periodic system of inventory; discussed in a later chapter) and a credit to accounts payable. Similar to the sales journal, the accounts are often omitted from the purchases journal, but the accountant is cognizant of the implied entry.

Exhibit 4.4 demonstrates the purchases journal. It has five columns: the first column reveals the date of the transaction; the second recounts the purchase order number; the third contains the supplier's or vendor's name; the fourth is the reference or folio column to indicate that the posting to the accounts payable subsidiary ledger has already taken place; and the fifth cites the amount of the purchase.

From time to time, the accountant posts the total amount to the general ledger. The implied summary entry in Exhibit 4.4 is

Purchases	$2,540	
Accounts payable		$2,540

Once the posting is concluded, the bookkeeper jots down the account numbers of purchases (500) and accounts payable (200).

EXHIBIT 4.4

PURCHASES JOURNAL

Purchases Journal

Page P13

Date	Purchase Order Number	Vendor	F	Amount
12-2	2516	Morphy	*	$ 800
12-7	2517	Steinitz	*	1,200
12-9	2518	Lasker	*	240
12-14	2519	Alekhine	*	300
	TOTAL			$2,540
				(500) (200)

The purchase order is the flip side of the invoice. Specifically, the *purchase order* is a document sent by the entity to commence a purchase. Each purchase transaction has a unique purchase order number, and that number is set down in the purchases journal to provide a cross-reference for the transaction and to increase internal control. Chapter 10 describes the purchases cycle and examines the various documents and controls allied with the purchases cycle.

Cash Receipts Journal

Exhibit 4.5 contains an example of the cash receipts journal. This particular special journal archives all of the transactions in which the entity has received cash. Unlike the previous two special journals, more than one type of journal entry can be recorded in the cash receipts journal. The accountant thinks of which transactions are going to be repetitive for the particular company and creates columns to handle these transactions. The most common form of the cash receipts journal includes columns for cash sales and for the collection of customer accounts. In addition, a "miscellaneous" or "other" column is added to deal with other cash inflow transactions.

If the transaction is a cash sale, then the entry is

Cash	$XXX
Sales	$XXX

If the transaction is a collection of a customer's account, the journal entry is either

Cash	$XXX
Accounts receivable	$XXX

EXHIBIT 4.5

CASH RECEIPTS JOURNAL

Cash Receipts Journal

Page CR5

Date	Cash (DR)	Sales Discount (DR)	Accounts Receivable Customer	F	(CR)	Sales (CR)	Other Account	F	(DR)	(CR)
12-1	$ 800					$800				
12-2	$ 980	$ 20	Fischer	*	$1,000					
12-5	$5,000						Common Stock	320		$5,000
12-8	$ 500		Timman	*	$ 500					
TOTAL	$7,280	$ 20			$1,500	$800				
	(100)	(620)			(120)	(600)				

or

Cash	$XXX	
Sales discount	$XXX	
Accounts receivable		$XXX

depending on whether the customer pays within the discount period, assuming that a sales discount is available. The other transactions have a debit to cash but unknown credits.

Column 1 of the cash receipts journal shown in Exhibit 4.5 gives the date of the transaction. By definition, every transaction included in this special journal has a debit to cash. Column 2 indicates how much cash is received. Column 3 displays sales discounts. If the firm offers a cash discount for early receipt, and if the firm receives the cash from the customer within the discount period, then the amount debited to sales discount is recorded in this column. Column 4 is for accounts receivable, and it is subdivided into three more columns for the customer's name, a folio column, and a credit column. The folio column is employed to announce that the posting to the accounts receivable subsidiary ledger has been made, and the amount is recorded in the credit column. The fifth column in the cash receipts journal is sales; any cash sales have a credit to sales, and they are recorded in this column. The last column is for other cash receipts. This column is subdivided into four columns: the account that is being debited or credited; a folio column to show that the posting to this account has been carried out; and debits and credits, whichever is appropriate.

The first transaction in Exhibit 4.5 is a cash sale; the second is a collection of a customer's account receivable and includes a sales discount; the third is the issuance of common stock at par; and the fourth is a collection of a customer's account that is not entitled to a sales discount.

Periodically, the columns are totaled, and the sum is posted to the appropriate account. The cash account (in column 2) totals to $7,280 and is posted to cash. Once the posting is finished, the account number is written below the sum. The same thing is done for sales discounts, accounts receivable (this posting is to the controlling account), and sales. Once the miscellaneous accounts are posted, a notation is made such as an asterisk or an "X."

Cash Disbursements Journal

The cash disbursements journal contains the transactions in which cash is paid out, and it is the flip side of the cash receipts journal. We assume that there are two repetitive transactions: buying inventory for cash and paying off an accounts payable, with or without a discount. Recall that a cash purchase is recorded as

Purchases	$XXX	
Cash		$XXX

The entry for a cash disbursement made to settle an account with a vendor is either

Accounts payable	$XXX	
Cash		$XXX

or

Accounts payable	$XXX	
Purchases discount	$XXX	
Cash		$XXX

depending on whether the company is entitled to take a purchase discount.

A cash disbursements or cash payments journal is illustrated in Exhibit 4.6. Column 1 gives the date of the transaction, column 2 the credit to cash, and column 3 the purchase discounts taken. Column 4 connotes activity in accounts payable and is subdivided into three other columns: the vendor's name, a folio column to indicate posting to the accounts payable subsidiary ledger, and the amount of the debit to accounts payable. The fifth column displays debits to purchases. The last column in the journal is for other cash outflows and is further partitioned into the account, the folio for posting, and debits or credits, whichever is appropriate.

Exhibit 4.6 records four transactions: a cash purchase; a payment to a supplier, including taking the purchase discount; the purchase of a car; and the payment to a vendor, but with no discount.

Periodically, the account columns are totaled and posted to the general ledger. Notice that the "TOTAL" row exhibits these sums and the next row contains the account numbers after the sum is posted to the general ledger. Once the postings are made for the miscellaneous accounts, an asterisk (or some other notation) is written to show that the posting process has been completed.

To summarize, accountants make use of special journals to increase efficiency and to organize the accounting of repetitive transactions. The traditional special journals are the sales journal, purchases journal, cash receipts journal, and cash disbursements or cash payments journal. Credit sales are recorded in the sales journal, credit purchases in the purchases journal, cash receipts in the cash receipts journal, and cash disbursements in the cash disbursements journal. All other transactions are chronicled in the general journal. Variations exist, and the accountant must be flexible to adapt to these modifications.

EXHIBIT 4.6

CASH DISBURSEMENTS OR PAYMENTS JOURNAL

Cash Payments Journal

Page CP30

Date	Cash (CR)	Purchase Discount (CR)	Accounts Payable Vendor	F	(DR)	Purchases (DR)	Other Account	F	(DR)	(CR)
12-1	$ 150					$150				
12-4	$ 98	$ 2	Rubinstein	*	$ 100					
12-6	$ 9,000						Auto	161	$9,000	
12-14	$ 1,000		Capablanca	*	$1,000					
TOTAL	$10,248	$ 2				$1,100	$150			*
	(100)	(510)			(200)	(500)				

WORKSHEETS

A *worksheet* is a document that is used to facilitate the preparation of some financial statement; in this context, it helps in constructing the income statement and the balance sheet. In the next chapter, a worksheet is used to help create the cash flow statement. Accountants use worksheets when carrying out other tasks as well.

Here we explore a worksheet that is prepared manually. In practice, they are created with a computer, often using a spreadsheet package such as Lotus 123 or Excel.

Accountants are not required to make worksheets, for they provide no new information; nonetheless, most companies use them because they are a convenient document in which to store relevant data. The typical worksheet has six columns, as illustrated in Exhibit 4.7. The first column is a listing of the general ledger accounts; the second is simply the unadjusted trial balance; adjusting entries are placed in the third column; and the fourth holds the adjusted trial balance. The last two columns are the income statement and the balance sheet.

If the firm produces a worksheet, then it does not have to make either an adjusted or unadjusted trial balance, for the simple reason that the trial balances are embedded within the worksheet. On the other hand, placing adjusting entries in the worksheet does not eliminate the need to enter them into the general journal. The worksheet does not replace any journal; thus, the adjusting entries are copied from the worksheet into the general journal, and they are posted in the usual fashion. Finally, the worksheet does not replace either the income statement or the balance sheet since the worksheet is not going to be issued to the public. The worksheet may be thought of as a rough draft of the financial statements.

Worksheet for a Service Organization

Let's assume that the firm is a service organization and construct a worksheet for it. The first step in building a worksheet is to list the balances of the accounts at the end of the period in the unadjusted trial balance column. The accountant places each account either as a debit or as a credit, depending on its balance. An example is shown in panel A of Exhibit 4.7. The process is exactly the same as preparing the unadjusted trial balance.

The second step is to write down the adjusting entries in the adjustments column. These entries are the same as the adjusting entries that a firm makes later in the general journal. Often they are cross-referenced either with numbers or letters to ease the readability of the document. An example is given in panel B of Exhibit 4.7. The two adjusting entries are

(1)	Insurance expense	$400	
	Prepaid insurance		$400

and

(2)	Depreciation expense	$1,000	
	Accumulated depreciation		$1,000

The debit and credit columns are added up to ensure equality; in this case, we get $1,400. (We remind the reader that the accountant still needs to record the adjusting entries in the general journal.)

For the third step, we add the accounts across the page in order to obtain the adjusted trial balance, for example, Exhibit 4.7 panel B. Follow the usual rules of debits and

EXHIBIT 4.7

WORKSHEET FOR A SERVICE COMPANY

Panel A: Unadjusted trial balance

Account	Unadjusted Trial Balance		Adjustments		Adjusted Trial Balance		Income Statement		Balance Sheet	
	Debit	Credit	Debit	Credit	Debit	Credit	Debit	Credit	Debit	Credit
Cash	100									
Prepaid insurance	1,200									
Building	10,000									
Accumulated depreciation		2,000								
Accounts payable		500								
Mortgage payable		5,000								
Waldron, capital		2,800								
Waldron, drawings	2,000									
Service revenue		10,000								
Wages expense	7,000									
TOTALS	20,300	20,300								

(continued)

EXHIBIT 4.7

WORKSHEET FOR A SERVICE COMPANY (continued)

Panel B: Adjustments and the adjusted trial balance

Account	Unadjusted Trial Balance Debit	Unadjusted Trial Balance Credit	Adjustments Debit	Adjustments Credit	Adjusted Trial Balance Debit	Adjusted Trial Balance Credit	Income Statement Debit	Income Statement Credit	Balance Sheet Debit	Balance Sheet Credit
Cash	100				100					
Prepaid insurance	1,200			(1) 400	800					
Building	10,000				10,000					
Accumulated depreciation		2,000		(2)1,000		3,000				
Accounts payable		500				500				
Mortgage payable		5,000				5,000				
Waldron, capital		2,800				2,800				
Waldron, drawings	2,000				2,000					
Service revenue		10,000				10,000				
Wages expense	7,000				7,000					
TOTALS	20,300	20,300								
Insurance expense			(1) 400		400					
Depreciation			(2)1,000		1,000					
TOTALS			1,400	1,400	21,300	21,300				

(continued)

EXHIBIT 4.7

WORKSHEET FOR A SERVICE COMPANY (continued)

Panel C: Income statement and balance sheet columns

Account	Unadjusted Trial Balance		Adjustments		Adjusted Trial Balance		Income Statement		Balance Sheet	
	Debit	Credit	Debit	Credit	Debit	Credit	Debit	Credit	Debit	Credit
Cash	100				100				100	
Prepaid insurance	1,200			(1) 400	800				800	
Building	10,000				10,000				10,000	
Accumulated depreciation		2,000		(2)1,000		3,000				3,000
Accounts payable		500				500				500
Mortgage payable		5,000				5,000				5,000
Waldron, capital		2,800				2,800				2,800
Waldron, drawings	2,000				2,000				2,000	
Service revenue		10,000				10,000		10,000		
Wages expense	7,000				7,000		7,000			
TOTALS	20,300	20,300								
Insurance expense			(1) 400		400		400			
Depreciation			(2)1,000		1,000		1,000			
TOTALS			1,400	1,400	21,300	21,300	8,400	10,000	12,900	11,300
NET INCOME							1,600			1,600
TOTALS							10,000	10,000	12,900	12,900

credits to add and subtract the numbers. Cash has no adjustments, so the balance in the adjusted trial balance is the same as it is in the unadjusted trial balance ($100). Prepaid insurance goes from $1,200 to $800 ($1,200 − $400), thus reflecting the credit in the adjusting entry. The balance in accumulated depreciation is $2,000 + $1,000 = $3,000, and it has a credit balance. And so on for the other accounts. If we need new accounts, we simply place them at the end of the list of accounts in column 1. For example, we add depreciation expense because we debit the account for $1,000 and carry that number into the adjusted trial balance.

The fourth step is to copy the numbers in the adjusted trial balance to the income statement column or the balance sheet column, whichever is appropriate. Cash is a balance sheet account with a debit balance, so copy the $100 into the balance sheet debit column. Accumulated depreciation is a balance sheet account with a credit balance, so copy the $3,000 in the adjusted trial balance to the balance sheet credit column. Service revenue is an income statement account with a credit balance. Thus, the bookkeeper copies the $10,000 in the adjusted trial balance into the income statement credit column. This transcription process continues until all of the general ledger accounts are placed in either the income statement or the balance sheet column. Panel C illustrates this process. The only account that is a bit unusual is Waldron, drawings. If the accountant publishes formal financial statements, then drawings will show up in the statement of owner's capital. Here we place it in the balance sheet as one stage in obtaining the correct ending owner's capital.

The fifth step is to add up the debit and credit columns of the income statement and to add up the debit and credit columns of the balance sheet. Unlike the previous three columns, these debits and credits need not equal. However, the difference between the total debits and the total credits of the income statement column must equal the difference between the total debits and the total credits of the balance sheet column. Moreover, if the income statement column has debits greater than credits, then the balance sheet column has credits greater than debits, and vice versa.

The reason for this requirement is that the difference in the income statement debits and credits is net income. The net income is positive if credits exceed debits in the income statement column; if debits are bigger than credits, then there is a net loss. The difference on the balance sheet side is also net income because the net income needs to be transferred into owner's equity. Note how this is handled in panel C in Exhibit 4.7. Net income equals $1,600. This number is placed in the debit side of the income statement column as well as in the credit side of the balance sheet column. Add the debits and credits, and you should obtain equality for both statement columns. This process is akin to closing out the income summary account to the owner's capital account.

Let's look deeper into the adding of net income to the balance sheet credit side. Why does this make the process work? The answer is easy once you notice that the owner's capital account shows the beginning balance. Accountants, of course, want to place the ending balance on the balance sheet. This ending balance is indeed there, but it is implicit. The reader can acknowledge this fact by recalling that ending owner's equity is equal to beginning owner's equity plus net income minus drawings. Look again at panel C, and you will recognize beginning owner's capital ($2,800 credit), owner's drawings ($2,000 debit), and net income ($1,600 credit). Although the ending balance of owner's capital is not shown explicitly (it is $2,400), the three components are listed there and together they yield the correct number. In other words, the worksheet folds the statement of changes in owner's equity into the balance sheet.

Worksheet for a Merchandiser

When making a worksheet for a merchandising organization, one follows the same steps as above. The only thing that requires comment is how to handle the net sales and the cost of goods sold accounts. One key fact to remember when preparing the worksheet is that the accounts sales, sales discounts, sales returns and allowances, purchases, purchase discounts, purchase returns and allowances, and freight in are income statement accounts. In addition, it is critical to understand that inventory, though a balance sheet account, is also a component in the measurement of cost of goods sold. Recall from Chapter 2 that cost of goods sold is equal to beginning inventory plus net purchases minus ending inventory.

Notice in Exhibit 4.8, in either panel A or B, that sales, sales discounts, and sales returns and allowances are transferred from the adjusted trial balance to the income statement column. Sales goes into the credit column, while sales discounts and sales returns and allowances go into the debit column. This makes sense, for net sales equals sales minus sales discounts and sales returns and allowances.

Cost of goods sold, however, can be handled in either of two ways. Panel A of Exhibit 4.8 shows cost of goods sold handled by transferring the accounts to the income statement columns. Note that purchases and freight in are transferred from the debit column of the adjusted trial balance to the debit column of the income statement. In addition, purchase discounts and purchase returns and allowances are carried from the credit column of the adjusted trial balance to the credit column of the income statement. Inventory is dealt with in a slightly more complicated manner. Beginning inventory is found in the debit columns of the unadjusted and adjusted trial balances and is copied into the debit column of the income statement. Then the ending inventory is placed into the credit column of the income statement and into the debit column of the balance sheet. The reader should understand two things from this process. First, inventory is updated in the balance sheet from the beginning to the ending balance, as is desired. Second, even though there is no cost of goods sold account, it implicitly is part of the income statement column. Cost of goods sold equals beginning inventory plus purchases plus freight in minus purchase discounts minus purchase returns and allowances minus ending inventory. The plus numbers are found on the debit side of the worksheet's income statement column, and the numbers being subtracted are found on the credit side of the worksheet's income statement column. This procedure works because it implicitly calculates cost of goods sold and places it as an expense in the income statement column of the worksheet.

Panel B is an alternative way of manipulating the cost of goods sold accounts. This approach handles them explicitly by making an adjusting entry (analogous to the closing entry discussed in Chapter 3). This entry is found in Exhibit 4.8, panel B, in the adjustments column. Entry #2 is:

Cost of goods sold	$6,350	
Inventory (ending)	$1,750	
Purchase discounts	$ 500	
Purchase returns	$ 300	
Inventory (beginning)		$1,000
Purchases		$7,000
Freight in		$ 900

Purchases, purchase discounts, purchase returns and allowances, and freight in are closed out (on the worksheet; remember that worksheet entries do not replace journal entries), and inventory is updated from its beginning to its ending balance, while cost of goods

EXHIBIT 4.8

PARTIAL WORKSHEET FOR A MERCHANDISER

Panel A: Handling COGS accounts by transfer to the income statement column

Account	Unadjusted Trial Balance Debit	Credit	Adjustments Debit	Credit	Adjusted Trial Balance Debit	Credit	Income Statement Debit	Credit	Balance Sheet Debit	Credit
Cash	1,100				1,100				1,100	
Prepaid advertising	800			(1) 350	450				450	
Inventory	1,000				1,000		1,000	1,750	1,750	
Bartges, capital		1,000				1,000				1,000
Sales		10,000				10,000		10,000		
Sales discounts	600				600		600			
Sales returns	400				400		400			
Purchases	7,000				7,000		7,000			
Purchase discounts		500				500		500		
Purchase returns		300				300		300		
Freight in	900				900		900			
TOTALS	11,800	11,800								
Advertising expense			(1) 350		350		350			
TOTALS			350	350	11,800	11,800	10,250	12,550	3,300	1,000
NET INCOME							2,300			2,300
TOTALS							12,550	12,550	3,300	3,300

(continued)

EXHIBIT 4.8

PARTIAL WORKSHEET FOR A MERCHANDISER (continued)

Panel B: Handling COGS accounts as an adjusting entry

Account	Unadjusted Trial Balance		Adjustments		Adjusted Trial Balance		Income Statement		Balance Sheet	
	Debit	Credit	Debit	Credit	Debit	Credit	Debit	Credit	Debit	Credit
Cash	1,100				1,100				1,100	
Prepaid advertising	800			(1) 350	450				450	
Inventory	1,000		(2)1,750	(2)1,000	1,750				1,750	
Bartges, capital		1,000				1,000				1,000
Sales		10,000				10,000		10,000		
Sales discounts	600				600		600			
Sales returns	400				400		400			
Purchases	7,000			(2)7,000						
Purchase discounts		500	(2) 500							
Purchase returns		300	(2) 300							
Freight in	900			(2) 900						
TOTALS	11,800	11,800								
Advertising expense			(1) 350		350		350			
Cost of goods sold			(2)6,350		6,350		6,350			
TOTALS			9,250	9,250	11,000	11,000	7,700	10,000	3,300	1,000
NET INCOME							2,300			2,300
TOTALS							10,000	10,000	3,300	3,300

sold is established. Then in the worksheet the accountant carries cost of goods sold from the adjusted trial balance to the debit side of the income statement column, as one would do with any expense.

A similar process would be conducted for a manufacturer's worksheet. The bookkeeper could handle the cost of goods sold accounts either by copying the relevant accounts to the income statement column or by making adjustments to a cost of goods sold account and carrying the cost of goods sold account to the income statement column.

Once the worksheet is completed, the accountant can prepare the income statement, the statement of retained earnings, and the balance sheet. He or she is also in a position to enter the adjusting entries and closing entries into the general journal.

REVERSING ENTRIES

A *reversing entry* is a journal entry made at the beginning of an accounting cycle that reverses the effects of an adjusting entry made at the end of the previous accounting cycle. Its purpose is to increase the efficiency of performing bookkeeping tasks, but this rationale is diminished in today's computerized world.

Suppose a firm pays $1,200 for one year's worth of rent on May 1, 2001. The journal entry on May 1, 2001 is

Rent expense	$1,200	
Cash		$1,200

while the adjusting entry on December 31, 2001 is

Prepaid rent	$500	
Rent expense		$500

If the organization does not employ reversing entries, then it makes the following entry on April 30, 2002.

Rent expense	$500	
Prepaid Rent		$500

Notice that this accounting results in rent expense of $700 in 2001 and $500 in 2002. It shows prepaid rent of $500 at year-end 2001 but zero at year-end 2002.

Now suppose that the firm does use reversing entries, so that on January 1, 2002 it flip-flops the adjusting entry. The reversing entry is

Rent expense	$500	
Prepaid rent		$500

What entry does it make on April 30, 2002? The answer is that no entry is needed because the financial effects are already displayed in the accounts. The reader should verify that the use of reversing entries in this manner leads to showing rent expense of $700 in 2001 and $500 in 2002. It also leads to a balance in prepaid rent of $500 at December 31, 2001 and $0 at April 30, 2002. These effects are exactly the same as the case when the firm does not employ reversing entries.

So what is gained by utilizing reversing entries? Basically, the bookkeeper's task is eased because he or she need not worry about how to make the entry on April 30. This is perhaps a small gain in time, but if the company has thousands of adjusting entries, the savings might become substantial, especially in a manual system.

These gains are not available with all adjusting entries. Reversing entries are helpful when the adjusting entry is an accrual or when it is a deferral, if the original entry involves an expense or a revenue account. Reversing entries do not simplify the bookkeeping whenever the adjusting entry is a deferral, if the original entry involves an asset or liability account, or if the adjusting entry concerns depreciation.

CORRECTING ENTRIES

Sometimes the accountant makes mistakes in journalizing transactions. When errors occur, the accountant makes *correcting entries* to undo the mistakes and restore the accounts to their proper balances. In this text, we assume that the error is caught in the year it was made. If caught later, the accountant must make a prior period adjustment, a topic found in Intermediate Accounting textbooks.

To correct an error, the accountant should determine the entry that should have been made and the entry that was actually made. The accountant then must choose the entry to get the accounts from their current balances to their proper balances.

Consider the following example. Land was acquired at January 2 for $100,000 cash. The correct journal entry that reflects this transaction is

Land	$100,000	
Cash		$100,000

But let's assume that the bookkeeper somehow thought that this was store equipment. Not only that, but the bookkeeper depreciates this store equipment at year-end. The actual entries are

Jan. 2	Store equipment	$100,000	
	Cash		$100,000
Dec. 31	Depreciation	$ 10,000	
	Accumulated depreciation		$ 10,000

To correct this error, the accountant analyzes the two sets of entries, the correct and the incorrect ones, to assess how to correct the mistakes. Cash is the same under both scenarios, so it does not need to be changed; land must be put on the books, while store equipment, depreciation, and accumulated depreciation must be removed. Therefore, the correcting entry is

Land	$100,000	
Accumulated depreciation	$ 10,000	
Store equipment		$100,000
Depreciation		$ 10,000

Notice that all accounts are returned to their proper balances after this entry is made.

The above correcting entry assumes that closing entries have not yet been made. If they have, the accountant could make the correcting entry as above and then reclose the affected income statement accounts. In practice, however, usually the accountant simply debits or credits balance sheet accounts and uses retained earnings instead of any revenue or expense account. This leaves the revenues and expenses at zero (which is correct after closing entries are made) and changes retained earnings to the correct number. When the income statement is prepared, the accountant enters the correct numbers for all of the revenues and expenses.

SIGHTS ALONG THE INTERNET

A number of Internet sites provide a wealth of information about accounting and what accountants do. These general-purpose sites are quite useful in finding additional data and facts about the profession. (Actually, the CEO Express site is a general management site, but it has lots of useful information for anybody in business.) The most helpful sites are:

Accountants World	www.accountantsworld.com
American Institute of Certified Public Accountants (AICPA)	www.aicpa.org
CEO Express	www.ceoexpress.com
CPA Net	www.cpanet.com/index.asp
Electronic Accountant	www.electronicaccountant.com
Rutgers Accounting Web	www.rutgers.edu/Accounting

An important topic on the AICPA site concerns the CPA Vision Project. Once you find the site, click on "CPA Vision Project" and see how the AICPA forecasts the future for the profession. The AICPA vision imagines accountants performing very broad consulting assignments.

CHAPTER SUMMARY IN TERMS OF LEARNING OBJECTIVES

Describe the Accounting Cycle.   The accounting cycle lists the steps in transactions processing. First, the bookkeeper prepares a journal entry for the transaction. Credit sales are entered in the sales journal; credit purchases are recorded in the purchases journal; cash receipts are placed in the cash receipts journal; cash payments are registered in the cash disbursements journal; and all other transactions are written in the general journal.

Second, the journal entry is posted to the general ledger. In addition, some accounts (such as accounts receivable and accounts payable) have subsidiary ledgers. Debits and credits to these accounts are posted to both the general ledger and to the appropriate subsidiary ledger.

Third, the accountant prepares the worksheet. This worksheet contains the unadjusted trial balance, adjustments, the adjusted trial balance, and the preliminary income statement and balance sheet.

Fourth, the accountant constructs the financial statements.

Fifth and sixth, the accountant makes the adjusting entries and posts them.

Seventh and eighth, the accountant makes closing entries and posts them.

Ninth, the post-closing trial balance is constructed.

Tenth and eleventh, the accountant enters the reversing entries and posts them.

Define a Subsidiary Ledger and Post Entries to a Subsidiary Ledger.
The purpose of subsidiary accounts and subsidiary ledgers is to allow a manager to find out the balance in any of the components (e.g., customer or supplier balances) of the account. A subsidiary ledger is a listing of the components of some account. A controlling account is an account whose balance is the sum of the related subsidiary accounts. A subsidiary account is one of the components of the subsidiary ledger for some controlling account. Business enterprises frequently prepare a report for managers that lists the components and their balances; this report is called a subsidiary schedule.

Each subsidiary account in the subsidiary ledger has six columns. The first column states the date of the transaction. The second column is a description column in which the bookkeeper may write a short explanation of the transaction. The third is a folio or reference column that provides a cross-reference with the journal. After the entries are posted to the subsidiary ledger, the numbers in this column are the page numbers of the journal where the entry is recorded. (An asterisk is placed in the folio column of the journal to indicate that the posting is finished.) The fourth and fifth columns are debit and credit columns, and the amount is placed in one of these columns, depending on whether the account increases or decreases. The last column gives the balance of the subsidiary account. Increases are added to the previous total, and decreases are subtracted from the previous total.

Describe the Purpose of Special Journals.   Since some transactions are repetitive, special journals can increase the efficiency of the bookkeeping process. These special journals are efficient in a manual system because they reduce the number of postings that must be made. Even in computerized systems, accounting information systems are often organized around transactions cycles and the special journals used to record them because internal controls are most easily designed and implemented around repetitive transactions.

Utilize a Sales Journal.   The sales journal contains data about credit sales of merchandise. The typical sales journal consists of five columns. The first column reveals the date of the transaction, the second column the invoice number, the third the customer's name, the fourth the reference or folio column (to show posting to the accounts receivable subsidiary ledger), and the fifth the amount of the sale. Total accounts receivable and total sales are posted to the general ledger.

Employ a Purchases Journal.   The purchases journal includes data about the credit purchases of inventory. The typical purchases journal has five columns. The first column reveals the date of the transaction, the second the purchase order number, the third the vendor's name, the fourth the folio column (to indicate postings to the accounts payable subsidiary ledger), and the fifth the amount of the purchase. Total purchases and total accounts payable are posted to the general ledger.

Use a Cash Receipts Journal.   The cash receipts journal holds the data for all transactions in which cash is received. The typical cash receipts journal has six main columns. The first column contains the date of the transaction, the second the debit to cash, the third the debit to sales discounts, the fourth the credit to accounts receivable, the fifth the credit to sales, and the sixth debits or credits to other accounts.

The fourth column, the credit to accounts receivable, is subdivided into three more columns. The first subcolumn gives the customer's name, the second the posting reference to the accounts receivable subsidiary ledger, and the third the amount to credit.

The sixth column, the miscellaneous column, is divided into four subcolumns. The first is used to write the account that is being debited or credited; the second shows the posting to this account in the general ledger; and the third and fourth columns are the debits and credits, whichever is appropriate.

Utilize a Cash Disbursements Journal.   The cash disbursements journal incorporates the data for all transactions in which cash is paid. The typical cash disbursements journal has six main columns, showing, respectively, the date of the transaction, the credit to cash, the credit to purchase discounts, the debit to accounts payable, the debits to purchases, and the debits or credits to other accounts.

The fourth column, the debit to accounts payable, is separated into three subcolumns: the vendor's name, a posting reference to the accounts payable subsidiary ledger, and the amount of the debit to accounts payable.

Similarly, the sixth column is subdivided into four subcolumns. The first is used to write the account that is being debited or credited; the second shows the posting to this account in the general ledger; and the third and fourth columns are the debits and credits, whichever is appropriate.

Prepare a Worksheet. A worksheet is a document that is used to facilitate the preparation of some financial statement. Most companies use them because they are a convenient document in which to store relevant data. A typical worksheet designed to prepare the income statement and the balance sheet has six columns: a listing of the general ledger accounts, the unadjusted trial balance, the adjusting entries, the adjusted trial balance, the income statement, and the balance sheet.

There are six steps in making a worksheet. First, list the balances of the accounts at the end of the period in the unadjusted trial balance column. Second, write down the adjusting entries in the adjustments column. Third, add the accounts across the page to obtain the adjusted trial balance. Fourth, copy the numbers in the adjusted trial balance to the income statement column or the balance sheet column, whichever is appropriate. Fifth, add up the debit and credit columns of the income statement and add up the debit and credit columns of the balance sheet. Sixth, obtain the difference between the debits and credits—it should be the same for both columns—and add it to the smaller number. Add debits and credits; they ought to be equal for both columns.

Make Reversing Entries. A reversing entry is a journal entry made at the beginning of an accounting cycle that reverses the effects of an adjusting entry made at the end of the previous accounting cycle. Reversing entries can be helpful, especially in a manual system, when the adjusting entry is an accrual or when it is a deferral, if the original entry involves an expense or a revenue account.

Make Correcting Entries. Sometimes the accountant makes mistakes when journalizing transactions. As errors occur, the accountant makes correcting entries to undo the mistakes and restore the accounts to their proper balances.

GLOSSARY

Accounting cycle—the steps in transactions processing.

Accounts payable subsidiary ledger—a subsidiary ledger that lists the suppliers and the balance owed them by the corporation.

Accounts receivable subsidiary ledger—a subsidiary ledger that lists the customers and their balances owed to the firm.

Cash disbursements journal—a special journal that records the cash disbursements of the entity.

Cash payments journal—a cash disbursements journal.

Cash receipts journal—a special journal that records the cash receipts of the entity.

Controlling account—an account whose balance is the sum of the related subsidiary accounts.

Correcting entry—a journal entry to undo some error in a previous journal entry. The correcting entry restores the accounts to their proper balances.

General journal—a journal that records all transactions not entered in a special journal.

General ledger—a listing of the accounts of an entity and their balances.

Invoice—a document sent to a customer indicating the price for goods or services provided by the seller and the terms for settlement.

Journal—a chronological record of the economic effects of an entity's transactions.

Ledger—a listing of the accounts of an entity and their balances, which is called a general ledger, or a listing of the components of some account, which is a subsidiary ledger.

Purchase order—a document sent by the entity to purchase goods from the vendor.

Purchases journal—a special journal that records the credit purchases of the entity.

Reversing entry—a journal entry made at the beginning of an accounting cycle that reverses the effects of an adjusting entry made at the end of the previous accounting cycle.

Sales journal—a special journal that records the credit sales of the entity.

Special journal—a journal that records only certain types of transactions, such as sales, cash receipts, purchases, and cash disbursements.

Subsidiary account—one of the components of the subsidiary ledger for some controlling account.

Subsidiary ledger—a listing of the components of some account.

Subsidiary schedule—a report that enumerates the details of some account.

Transactions processing—all of the activities that transform data about a firm's transactions into the firm's financial statements.

Worksheet—a document that is used to facilitate the preparation of some financial statement, such as the income statement and the balance sheet.

REVIEW QUESTIONS

1. Describe the accounting cycle.

2. Distinguish between the general ledger and subsidiary ledgers.

3. What is a controlling account? What is a subsidiary account?

4. Define a subsidiary schedule? For whom is a subsidiary schedule prepared?

5. For what purpose do special journals exist?

6. When posting, how does the bookkeeper distinguish among the various journals?

7. Describe the sales journal.

8. What is an invoice, and why is the invoice number recorded in the sales journal?

9. Explain the purpose of the purchases journal and how it is used.

10. Why is the purchase order number recorded in the purchases journal?

11. What is the cash receipts journal, and how is it employed?

12. Discuss the nature and usage of the cash disbursements journal.

13. What is a worksheet? Why does it replace an unadjusted and an adjusted trial balance, but not replace journalizing adjusting entries?

14. Discuss the process of filling out a worksheet.

15. What is a reversing entry, and what is its purpose?

16. What are correcting entries?

DISCUSSION QUESTIONS

1. Subsidiary ledgers exist to help managers understand the components of an account, and they are not restricted to accounts receivable and accounts payable.

Part a. Show how one can have a subsidiary ledger for cash.

Part b. Subsidiary ledgers are not restricted to balance sheet accounts, and it is possible to partition some ledger account along two attributes. Consider the following example.

Victor Bryan owns his own motorcycle shop and has a sales staff of three individuals: Tom, Dick, and Harry. Victor Bryan wants to examine sales by salesperson and by region (east coast and west coast). The following transactions occur.

April 1: Tom sells $50,000 goods to customers in the east. Dick sells $40,000 goods to customers in the west.

April 5. Harry sells $60,000 goods to customers in the west, and Dick sells $25,000 goods to customers in the east.

April 15. Tom sells $15,000 goods to customers in the east, while Harry sells $23,000 goods to customers in the west. Dick sells $5,000 goods to customers in the east and $6,000 to customers in the west.

Required: Journalize these transactions and post them into the appropriate ledgers to achieve Victor Bryan's goals.

2. As discussed in the text, accounts receivable is a general ledger account, and it often has a subsidiary ledger with such subsidiary accounts as accounts receivable-Mensah and accounts receivable-Wessner. It is possible, however, to design an accounting system with the account assets and the subsidiary accounts cash, accounts receivable, inventory, and so on. In one case accounts receivable is the general ledger account, and in the other it is one of the subsidiary accounts. How does one decide whether to make an account such as accounts receivable a general ledger account or a subsidiary account?

3. One repetitive transaction is the payment of wages (workers, after all, like to be paid). How might a payroll journal look? To keep things simple, let's assume that the only payroll deductions are federal income taxes and FICA (social security) taxes.

4. The worksheet presented in this chapter focuses on the preparation of the income statement and the balance sheet, and this is handled directly in the income statement and balance sheet columns of the worksheet. Ending retained earnings (or owner's capital) is manipulated indirectly by placing the beginning balance and net income and dividends (or drawings) in the balance sheet column. The worksheet can be modified to compute the ending retained earnings (or owner's capital) explicitly by adding a retained earnings (or owner's capital) column.

Required: Modify Exhibit 4.7 by adding a retained earnings column. You may omit the unadjusted trial balance and the adjustments column.

5. Suppose that a firm buys $4,000 of goods on account. Of course, the entry ought to be recorded as a debit to purchases for $4,000 and a credit to accounts payable for $4,000. Suppose that the entry is actually recorded as a debit to purchases for $4,000 and a debit to accounts payable for $4,000. What is the correcting entry? What does this imply about the rule that debits equal credits?

EXERCISES

1. Jason Lights, Inc. has $24,000 in accounts receivable, as seen in the following subsidiary T-accounts.

AR-Anderson		AR-Campolo		AR-Clark	
10,000	2,000	1,000		3,000	2,000
3,000	5,000	3,000		5,000	6,000
				1,000	
6000		4000		1000	

AR-Larsen		AR-Smith		AR-Warren	
2,000	8,000	4,000	9,000	10,000	9,000
10,000	5,000	6,000			
12,000					
11000		1000		1000	

Required: Prepare an accounts receivable subsidiary schedule for Jason Lights, Inc.

2. The accounts payable ledger account for Galway, Inc. and the accounts payable subsidiary ledger are as follows.

Accounts Payable
Account no. 220

Date	Debits	Credits	Balance
Beginning bal.			$100,000
9- 4	$10,000		90,000
9- 5		$ 4,000	94,000
9- 6		19,000	113,000
9- 7		7,000	120,000
9- 8	10,000		110,000
9- 9		5,000	115,000
9-10	20,000		95,000
9-14		8,000	103,000
9-15		6,000	109,000

Subsidiary Accounts Payable Ledger
Jones, Inc.

Date	Debits	Credits	Balance
Beginning bal.			$ 50,000
9- 5		$ 4,000	54,000
9- 7		7,000	61,000
9-10	20,000		41,000

Klasker and Company

Date	Debits	Credits	Balance
Beginning bal.			$ 30,000
9- 4	$10,000		20,000
9- 9	5,000		15,000
9-14		8,000	23,000

Smith Supplies

Date	Debits	Credits	Balance
Beginning bal.			$ 20,000
9- 6		19,000	39,000
9- 8	10,000		29,000
9-15		6,000	35,000

Required: Notice that the sum of the accounts in the subsidiary ledger adds to $99,000 ($41,000 + $23,000 + $35,000), which is not the balance in the controlling account, $109,000. Explain why not.

3. Dewey Evans has set up an accounting system with a general journal, a sales journal, a purchases journal, a cash receipts journal, and a cash disbursements journal. For each of the following transactions, tell Dewey Evans in which journal it should be recorded.

a. Pay rent
b. Adjusting entries
c. Credit sales
d. Purchase land on account
e. Issue stock for cash
f. Pay employees their wages
g. Cash sales
h. Closing entries
i. Purchase inventory for cash
j. Reversing entries
k. Purchase inventory on account

4. Posting from the four special journals involves either (a) posting the column total to the general ledger, (b) posting the line item to the general ledger, and/or (c) posting the line item to the subsidiary ledger. Assuming that the corporation has an accounts receivable subsidiary ledger as well as an accounts payable subsidiary ledger, indicate how the following accounts are posted from the special journals.

Sales journal

1. Accounts receivable
2. Sales

Purchases journal

3. Purchases
4. Accounts payable

Cash receipts journal

5. Cash
6. Sales discounts
7. Accounts receivable
8. Sales
9. Other accounts

Cash disbursements journal

10. Cash
11. Purchase discounts
12. Accounts payable
13. Purchases
14. Other accounts

5. On the next page is a worksheet for Shawna Enterprise. Your mission is to complete the worksheet.

6. The following table presents eight adjusting entries. *Required:* Indicate in the second column whether the entry should be reversed. For those that should be reversed, give the reversing entry in the last column.

Adjusting Entries		Should It Be Reversed?	What Is the Reversing Entry?
Interest expense	10		
Interest payable	10		
Prepaid rent	15		
Rent expense	15		
Depreciation	20		
Accumulated dep.	20		
Wages expense	25		
Wages payable	25		
Insurance expense	30		
Prepaid insurance	30		
Amortization expense	35		
Patents	35		
Interest receivable	40		
Interest earned	40		
Subscription revenue	45		
Unearned subscript	45		

WORKSHEET—SHAWNA ENTERPRISE

Account	Unadjusted Trial Balance		Adjustments		Adjusted Trial Balance		Income Statement		Balance Sheet	
	Debit	Credit	Debit	Credit	Debit	Credit	Debit	Credit	Debit	Credit
Cash	2,000									
Accounts receivable	7,000									
Land	30,000									
Building	20,000									
Acc.Dep.-Bldg.		1,000		1,000						
Accounts payable		10,000								
Mortgage payable		20,000								
Common stock		20,000								
Retained earnings		10,000								
Service revenue		8,000								
Wages expense	5,000		500							
Utilities expense	4,000									
Taxes expense	1,000									
TOTALS	69,000	69,000								
Depreciation			1,000							
Wages payable				500						
TOTALS			1,500	1,500						

7. Henrietta Johnson is an internal auditor for Kantar, Inc., and she discovers an incorrect entry. The bookkeeper recorded a credit sale as

Accounts payable	$8,000	
Sales		$8,000

(a) What entry should Henrietta Johnson suggest to correct the error?

(b) If Henrietta Johnson had not discovered the error, what is the most likely way it would have been detected?

8. On January 1, 2001 Audrey Root and Company purchases a building for $200,000 cash. It has a salvage value of $20,000 and a 20-year life. It was recorded as a debit to purchases and a credit to cash. The error is discovered on December 31, 2001. *Required:* Prepare the journal entry that corrects the mistake.

PROBLEMS

1. Yarns and Fables is a book distributor. Below you will find a general journal, a general ledger, and the accounts receivable subsidiary ledger. Yarns and Fables has the following transactions in June:

(a) June 6: Sales to C. Dickens on account for $200.
(b) June 9: J. Austen pays $1,000 on her account.
(c) June 18: Sales to N. Hawthorne on account for $400.
(d) June 28: Sales to G. Elliott on account for $100.
(e) June 29: N. Hawthorne pays $150 on his account.

Required: Make the journal entry for each transaction in the general journal and post each entry.

Yarns and Fables
General Journal

J29

Date	Account Titles	F	Debits	Credits

Yarns and Fables
General Ledger

Cash

Account No. 100

Date	Description	F	Debits	Credits	Balance
	Opening Bal				$19,000

Accounts Receivable

Account No. 110

Date	Description	F	Debits	Credits	Balance
	Opening Bal				$2,100

Sales

Account No. 600

Date	Description	F	Debits	Credits	Balance
	Opening Bal				$86,000

Yarns and Fables
Accounts Receivable Subsidiary Ledger

Charles Dickens

Date	Description	F	Debits	Credits	Balance
	Opening Bal				$500

Jane Austen

Date	Description	F	Debits	Credits	Balance
	Opening Bal				$1,200

Nathaniel Hawthorne

Date	Description	F	Debits	Credits	Balance
	Opening Bal				$300

George Elliott

Date	Description	F	Debits	Credits	Balance
	Opening Bal				$100

2. Epstein Furniture has the purchases journal depicted below. Finish the work for Epstein Furniture by posting the entries to the general and subsidiary ledgers.

Epstein Furniture
Purchases Journal

PJ 11

Date	Account Credited	Purchase Order No.	Ref	Amount
10-2	Bontrager's Woods	1206		$1,905
10-5	Hackman's Carpentry	1207		$ 800
10-8	Linda's Luxuries	1208		$ 450
10-15	Bontrager's Woods	1209		$ 675
10-23	Hackman's Carpentry	1210		$1,800
				$5630

Epstein Furniture Act 720
General Ledger

Act 200

Cash

Account No. 100

Date	Description	F	Debits	Credits	Balance
	Opening Bal				$238,000

Accounts Receivable

Account No. 110

Date	Description	F	Debits	Credits	Balance
	Opening Bal				$ 46,900

Accounts Payable

Account No. 200

Date	Description	F	Debits	Credits	Balance
	Opening Bal				$ 35,000

Sales

Account No. 600

Date	Description	F	Debits	Credits	Balance
	Opening Bal				$622,000

Purchases

Account No. 720

Date	Description	F	Debits	Credits	Balance
	Opening Bal				$321,000

Epstein Furniture
Account Subsidiary Ledger

Bontrager's Woods

Date	Description	F	Debits	Credits	Balance
	Opening Bal				$ 15,000

Hackman's Carpentry

Date	Description	F	Debits	Credits	Balance
	Opening Bal				$ 5,000

Jacoby's Transfer

Date	Description	F	Debits	Credits	Balance
	Opening Bal				$ 9,000

Linda's Luxuries

Date	Description	F	Debits	Credits	Balance
	Opening Bal				$ 6,000

3. Hatteras, Inc. employs a sales journal. From the following list of transactions, record those that belong in the sales journal. Then post the total to the general ledger accounts that are affected. Make the notation to indicate posting to the subsidiary ledger, but do not make any postings to the relevant subsidiary ledger.

October 5: Sold an unused computer to John Joseph for $2,000.
October 11: Sold merchandise to Kathleen Bird on account for $3,000, sales invoice no. 295.
October 12: Sold merchandise to Karen Lee for cash for $4,210, sales invoice no. 296.
October 19: Sold merchandise to Samuel David on account for $950, sales invoice no. 297.
October 23: Issued 200 shares of preferred stock to Joseph Patrick at $105 per share. The par value is $100 per share.
October 24: Sold merchandise to David Lee on account for $700, sales invoice no. 298.
October 29: Sold merchandise to Janet Richardson on account for $1,150, sales invoice no. 299.

4. Dan Nold, Inc., a grocery store, uses a purchases journal. For the following list of transactions, record only those that belong in the purchases journal and post them to the general ledger. Record these transactions at gross amounts. Make the notation to indicate posting to the subsidiary ledger, but do not make any postings to the relevant subsidiary ledger.

October 6: Purchased caramel popcorn from Fisher's Popcorn for $3,000. Issued check no. 502 in payment. The purchase order number is 237.
October 12: Purchased land as an investment for $100,000. Atlantic Credit Bank financed the purchase with a 12% mortgage.
October 15: Purchased $1,000 pastry from Meister's Donuts on credit, terms 2/10, n/30. The purchase order number is 238.
October 20: Purchased T-shirts from Dimensions for $10,000. Credit terms are 1/10, n/30. The purchase order number is 239.
October 24: Purchased a company car for $20,000. This transaction was financed by an auto loan from Mellon Bank at 9%. The purchase order number is 240.

PROBLEMS **133**

5. Holly Parker Company keeps a cash receipts journal. From the following list of transactions, record those that belong in the cash receipts journal. Ignore posting to the ledgers.

   November 3: Sold merchandise to Daleen Purdie for $1,400 cash.

   November 5: Sold merchandise to David & Son, Inc. on credit for $2,000.

   November 10: Collected rent revenue of $3,000 from Eileen Stramel.

   November 12: Received interest from its investment in Megastar bonds of $1,500.

   November 16: Paid its utilities bill of $750.

   November 22: Collected $882 cash from Phyllis Company for a sale made on November 13. Terms were 2/10, n/30.

   November 27: Sold merchandise to Uncle Robert's Boutique for $200 cash.

   November 30: Collected $1,800 from Elaine's Room in payment for a sale made on November 3. The terms were 2/10, n/30.

6. Jay Viscount uses a cash disbursements journal. For the following transactions, record only those that belong in the cash disbursements journal. Ignore posting to the ledgers.

   August 1: Viscount sells $5,000 merchandise on credit to Rocking Chair, Inc.

   August 3: Viscount pays $500 to Greenbrier Electric Company for its use of electricity.

   August 4: Viscount has $2,000 cash sales to Cowboy, Inc.

   August 15: Viscount issues a $4,000 check for merchandise from Atherton Company.

   August 18: Viscount pays $800 rent to Paul Bartges.

   August 24: Viscount pays $4,000 to Park Lane Company less the 1% discount.

   August 30: Viscount borrows $10,000 from First National Bank and signed a two-year note with a 12% interest rate.

   August 31: Viscount pays its employees $4,800.

7. Samuel Sproul starts his own merchandising business on January 2, 2001. On December 31, 2001 he finds the following totals in the special journals.

Sales journal	$200,000
Purchases journal	$120,000
Cash receipts journal	
Cash	$300,000
Sales discounts	$ 5,000
Accounts receivable	$175,000
Sales	$ 30,000
Other accounts:	
Common stock	$100,000
Cash disbursements journal	
Cash	$162,000
Purchase discounts	$ 3,000
Accounts payable	$100,000
Purchases	$ 20,000
Other accounts:	
Building	$100,000
Land	$200,000
Mortgage payable	$270,000
Dividends	$ 5,000
Freight in	$ 10,000

The general journal contained only three journal entries. They are:

Sales returns and allowances	$4,000	
Accounts receivable		$4,000
Accounts payable	$3,000	
Purchase returns and allowances		$3,000
Depreciation	$5,000	
Accumulated depreciation		$5,000

Required: Armed with these data and with the fact that ending inventory is $10,000, prepare the income statement, the statement of retained earnings, and the balance sheet.

8. The Rip-em-off Campus Bookstore has hired you as their ace consultant. Three days of sales data are listed below. All sales are cash sales.

Monday

Cash	$105,100
Sales—textbooks	75,000
Sales—other books	23,100
Sales—miscellaneous	7,000

Tuesday

Cash	$210,000
Sales returns	12,000
Sales—textbooks	195,000
Sales—other books	18,000
Sales—miscellaneous	9,000

Wednesday

Cash	$200,000
Sales returns	8,000
Sales—textbooks	189,000
Sales—other books	16,000
Sales—miscellaneous	3,000

Required: Design a cash sales journal for Rip-em-off Campus Bookstore that will meet its managerial needs for accounting for repetitive transactions. Then enter the three days' transactions into the cash sales journal, and indicate how the postings would appear in your special journal. Do not show the postings in the general ledger.

9. Mark Dirsmith Enterprises has started working on its worksheet, which is given on the next page. Additional data are:

(a) At the end of the year, there are accrued wages of $800.

(b) Ending inventory is $12,000.

Required: Complete the worksheet.

Account	Unadjusted Trial Balance Debit	Unadjusted Trial Balance Credit	Adjustments Debit	Adjustments Credit	Adjusted Trial Balance Debit	Adjusted Trial Balance Credit	Income Statement Debit	Income Statement Credit	Balance Sheet Debit	Balance Sheet Credit
Cash	10,600				10,600				10,600	
Inventory	25,800				25,800		25,800		12,000	
Common stock		15,000				15,000				15,000
Retained earnings		23,000				23,000				23,000
Sales		32,000				32,000		32,000		
Sales discounts	1,900				1,900		1,900			
Sales returns	700				700		700			
Purchases	17,300				17,300		17,300			
Purchase discounts		1,900				1,900		1,900		
Purchase returns		1,100				1,100		1,100		
Freight in	1,700				1,700		1,700			
Wages expense	15,000		800		15,800		15,800			
TOTALS	73,000	73,000								
Wages Payable				800		800				800
Totals			800	800	73,800	73,800	63,200	47,600	28,600	38,800
Net Loss								16,800	16,200	
Totals							63,200	63,200	38,800	38,800

CHAPTER 5

THE CASH FLOW STATEMENT

Up to this point we have focused almost exclusively on the balance sheet, the income statement, and the statement of retained earnings, as well as the mechanics of dealing with balance sheet and income statement accounts. The fourth and last major financial statement is the cash flow statement. It augments the other statements, especially the income statement, by explaining how the cash account changed during a certain period of time.

This chapter introduces the cash flow statement and the mechanics of its preparation. The statement contains information useful to readers of financial reports because it indicates the firm's ability to generate cash through its operations and by other means and it also shows how the firm is spending its cash.

After reading and studying this chapter, you should be able to:

- Indicate the purpose of the cash flow statement;
- State the components of the cash flow statement;
- Explain changes in cash in terms of operating, investing, and financing activities;
- Reconcile revenues with cash received from revenue activities and expenses with cash expenditures;
- Employ the T-account method to determine cash flow from operating, investing, and financing activities;
- Use the worksheet method to measure cash flow from operating, investing, and financing activities; and
- Prepare a statement of cash flows using either the indirect or direct method for calculating operating cash flows.

PURPOSE OF THE CASH FLOW STATEMENT

The cash flow statement explains the change in cash in terms of cash flows from the operating, investing, and financing activities of the firm. Although the cash flow statement has been required only since 1987 (FASB's Statement of Financial Accounting Standards No. 95), it is a very important financial statement because it helps investors and creditors understand the liquidity and solvency of the firm. *Liquidity* is the ability to generate cash, and *solvency* refers to the ability to pay debts as they come due. If the firm is unable to pay its liabilities, then it becomes subject to various penalties such as higher interest rates, extra charges in terms of late fees, and—at the limit—corporate bankruptcy. Since investors and creditors can lose some or all of their money if a bankruptcy materializes, they want advance warning of the likelihood that a firm will be unable to pay off its debts. One source of information is the cash flow statement.

Another purpose of the statement deals with quality of earnings. As the student should know, the determination of accounting earnings involves a number of estimates (such as the life of an asset being depreciated) and a choice among various accounting conventions. When investors analyze a corporation's income statement, they want to know how the number was computed. Did the managers employ conservative methods and estimates (e.g., short lives for depreciation), or did they make aggressive choices (e.g., long lives for depreciation)?

Quality of earnings refers to the informativeness of the net income number in making investment decisions. The quality of earnings is usually high when management uses conservative estimates and procedures and low when managers are more liberal. The cash flow statement can be used to help assess the quality of earnings because a high quality of earnings implies that cash is coming into the firm. A low quality of earnings is often associated with a relatively small cash flow from operating activities.

In addition to the accounting purposes, studying the cash flow statement also has some pedagogical advantages. To prepare a cash flow statement requires one to integrate the many transactions and obtain a picture of the whole. Beginning accounting students often focus on the immediate transaction under consideration and miss the big picture. For example, what causes changes to the accumulated depreciation account? Of course, recognition of depreciation expense will lead to increases in accumulated depreciation, but the accountant also needs to remember that sales of long-term depreciable assets will cause their associated accumulated depreciation to be reduced. In addition, preparing a cash flow statement provides more practice in mechanics, as will be seen when the T-account and the worksheet methods are discussed.

COMPONENTS OF THE CASH FLOW STATEMENT

A *cash flow* is any transaction that increases or decreases the cash of the entity. If the cash is received by the firm, it is a *cash inflow*. If the cash is disbursed by the company, it is a *cash outflow*.

The *cash flow statement* is a financial statement that explains the change in cash as a sum of the cash flows from the operating, investing, and financing activities of the entity. Although the cash flow statement has a recent origin, it can be useful to investors and creditors and managers because it displays changes in the cash account and explains what caused the fluctuation in cash. The statement registers how much cash was generated, or expended, by the operating activities of the business, how much cash was produced through financing decisions, and how much cash was created via the firm's investments.

One example of a cash flow statement is shown in Exhibit 5.1. The heading is similar to those for other financial statements. The first line states the name of the firm, the second line indicates that the statement is the cash flow statement, and the third line tells the time period for which the statement is prepared. Note that, like the income statement, the cash flow statement covers a certain period of time—it is not made as of a particular date.

Next notice the bottom line. In this illustration, there is a net increase in cash of $5. The last line indicates the change in cash, and so it reflects whether there has been an increase or a decrease in cash and by how much. This change can always be verified by looking at the balance sheets as of the beginning of the period and the end of the period. (Some firms display this verification on the cash flow statement.) The bottom line of the cash flow statement merely reflects the difference between those two balance sheet cash balances.

Let's now turn our attention to the middle of the statement. This middle section has three parts, each showing the amount of cash generated or utilized by the company's operating, investing, or financing activities. Within each category further detail is given. Cash

<table>
<tr><td>EXHIBIT 5.1</td></tr>
</table>

CASH FLOW STATEMENT—INDIRECT METHOD

Richard France, Inc.
Statement of Cash Flows
For the year ended June 30, 2001

Cash flows from operating activities		
Net income	$ 45	
Depreciation	55	
Gain on sale of land	(40)	
Increase in accounts receivable	(15)	
Increase in inventory	(20)	
Decrease in prepaid rent	5	
Increase in accounts payable	5	
Increase in wages payable	10	
Increase in interest payable	5	
Net cash from operating activities		$ 50
Cash flows from investing activities		
Proceeds from selling land	$100	
Purchase of building	(300)	
Net cash from investing activities		(200)
Cash flows from financing activities		
Proceeds from mortgage	$ 55	
Proceeds from issuing common stock	130	
Payment of dividends	(30)	
Net cash from financing activities		155
Net increase in cash		$ 5

flowing into the firm is denoted by a positive number, but cash flowing out of the company is shown by a negative number—a number usually displayed with parentheses.

Operating activities refers to the profit-making transactions and events of the firm. A practical definition is that an operating activity is any transaction or event except for investing and financing activities. Accordingly, cash flows from operating activities are the amounts of cash received from sales of goods or services less the amounts of cash disbursed for materials, labor, and other goods and services, assuming that all of these transactions and events refer to profit-making activities.

Exhibit 5.1 calculates the cash flow from operating activities using the indirect method. In the *indirect method*, cash flow from operating activities equals net income plus or minus any noncash expenses and revenues and plus or minus changes in current assets (except cash and notes receivable) and current liabilities (except short-term notes payable). The latter remark assumes that all changes in current assets (except cash and notes receivable) and current liabilities (except short-term notes payable) reflect operating activities, an assumption that will be maintained in this textbook. On the other hand, transactions with notes receivable and notes payable are financing activities. The formula will be explained in detail in the next section of the chapter.

Investing activities refers to transactions and events that pertain to the making of loans, such as notes receivable, and to the long-term assets of the firm, such as land, buildings, equipment, patents, copyrights, goodwill, bond investments, and stock investments. The idea is to invest money in assets and hope for a return on the investment either from a gain in its value or from use of the asset. Cash given as a loan, cash purchases of long-term assets, cash proceeds from any loans, and cash proceeds from selling loans and long-term assets are depicted as cash flows from investing activities.

The context of the firm determines whether some cash flows are for operating or investing activities. The making of loans is a natural part of the bank's everyday business, so these cash flows are part of a bank's operating activities. Making loans is not the main business for most other firms, and so the cash flows from making loans is part of investing activities for these companies.

Financing activities refers to transactions and events that pertain to borrowing money and to common and preferred stock. These activities include receiving cash by borrowing money with a note payable or a mortgage payable or by issuing stocks or bonds. They also include paying off the liabilities with cash, paying cash dividends, and redeeming stock (i.e., buying back the stock either as treasury shares or canceling them).

The FASB, the organization that makes accounting rules, has declared that cash interest payments are part of operating activities. We will follow that dictate in this book, though many accountants and financial analysts believe it is more logical to consider cash interest payments a part of cash outflows for financing activities.

Exhibit 5.2 shows the cash flow statement for the same example utilizing the direct method instead of the indirect method. Before focusing on this point, the reader should recognize several things. The headings are the same in the two illustrations. The cash-flows-from-investing-activities section and the cash-flows-from-financing-activities section are identical for both exhibits. Even though the calculations for cash flows from operating activities are different, the amount of the net cash from operating activities is

---

EXHIBIT 5.2

CASH FLOW STATEMENT—DIRECT METHOD

Richard France, Inc.
Statement of Cash Flows
For the year ended June 30, 2001

Cash flows from operating activities		
Cash from selling activities	$385	
Cash paid for inventory	(265)	
Rent payments	(15)	
Wage payments	(15)	
Interest payments	(15)	
Tax payments	(25)	
Net cash from operating activities		$ 50
Cash flows from investing activities		
Proceeds from selling land	$100	
Purchase of building	(300)	
Net cash from investing activities		(200)
Cash flows from financing activities		
Proceeds from mortgage	$ 55	
Proceeds from issuing common stock	130	
Payment of dividends	(30)	
Net cash from financing activities		155
Net increase in cash		$ 5

the same under both methods. Since the cash flows from the three activities are the same, the net increase or decrease in cash is the same under the two methods.

In the *direct method*, cash flow from operating activities equals revenues converted from an accrual basis to a cash basis minus expenses converted from an accrual basis to a cash basis. For example, in place of sales, we want to substitute cash from sales. This conversion process involves removing sales made on account for which the customers have not paid off their bills and including customer receipts this year for sales made in previous periods. This conversion from the accrual basis to the cash basis will be explained further later in the chapter.

The FASB requires that firms employing the direct method also provide a reconciliation schedule. This schedule reconciles net income with cash from operating activities, and it replicates the indirect method for obtaining cash from operating activities. In other words, a corporation that uses the direct method, as illustrated in Exhibit 5.2, must also disclose the indirect method of computing cash from operating activities, as seen in the top section of Exhibit 5.1. Given that this disclosure does not provide anything new conceptually, we will ignore this detail in the remainder of the chapter.

Cash flow statements thus display the cash flows from operating, investing, and financing activities. Cash flows from operating activities are obtained with either the indirect or direct method, and firms may choose whichever method they want.

THE CHANGE-IN-CASH FORMULA

Derivation of the Change-in-Cash Formula

This section derives the formula: change in cash is equal to the cash flows from operating, investing, and financing activities. It requires only high school algebra, but if your algebraic skills are rusty, then you may omit this section and advance to the discussion on applying the formula. This justification is given to explain why the formula works and is unnecessary for actually using it when preparing the cash flow statement.

To keep the number of variables to a manageable level, we presume no notes receivable or payable. This assumption allows us to state that changes in current assets (other than cash) and current liabilities relate to operating activities. Let's also suppose that there is no preferred stock and that changes in retained earnings are due only to earnings and cash dividends. Finally, we will ignore the selling of notes receivable and long-term assets and thereby assume that there are no gains and losses from their sale. None of these assumptions affects our conclusion—they merely minimize the number of terms one has to deal with.

To obtain the change-in-cash formula, start with the fundamental accounting equation—assets equal liabilities plus stockholders' equity. This fundamental accounting identity is always true, and we will use the identity at the beginning of the accounting period and at the end. The subscript "b" refers to the beginning, while "e" denotes the ending of the accounting period.

Assets equal liabilities plus stockholders' equity. Expanding each of these groups, we have cash plus other current assets plus long-term assets equal current liabilities plus long-term debts plus common stock plus retained earnings. In symbols, this relationship at the beginning and end of the period is

$$C_e + CA_e + LTA_e = CL_e + LTD_e + CS_e + RE_e \tag{5.1}$$

$$C_b + CA_b + LTA_b = CL_b + LTD_b + CS_b + RE_b \tag{5.2}$$

where

$$C = \text{cash}$$
$$CA = \text{current assets (other than cash)}$$
$$LTA = \text{long-term assets}$$
$$CL = \text{current liabilities}$$
$$LTD = \text{long-term debts}$$
$$CS = \text{common stock}$$
$$RE = \text{retained earnings}$$

Next, subtract Eq. (5.2) from Eq. (5.1) and group like terms together. The symbol Δ means difference. Thus, ΔC means change in cash, and ΔRE means change in retained earnings. Also note that the Δ operator is always the ending balance minus the beginning balance—be careful not to subtract the ending from the beginning balance. So ΔC equals ending cash minus beginning cash. Subtract Eq. (5.2) from Eq. (5.1) to obtain Eq. (5.3).

$$\Delta C + \Delta CA + \Delta LTA = \Delta CL + \Delta LTD + \Delta CS + \Delta RE \tag{5.3}$$

The next step is to rearrange Eq. (5.3) so that change in cash is on the left-hand side and everything else is on the other side of the equation. By assumption, the change in retained earnings is equal to net income (NI) minus cash dividends (DIV), which allows us to substitute NI $-$ DIV for ΔRE. Thus,

$$\Delta C = -\Delta CA - \Delta LTA + \Delta CL + \Delta LTD + \Delta CS + NI - DIV \tag{5.4}$$

One last thing must be handled before the final solution is reached—namely, depreciation. Depreciation (denoted by DEP) is a noncash expense that is subtracted when calculating net income. It is also added to accumulated depreciation, which is a contra-long-term asset. To undo its effects—because it is not associated with any cash flow—add depreciation back to net income and to long-term assets. Consequently, add and subtract depreciation to the right-hand side of Eq. (5.4) and then simplify until the desired formula is achieved.

$$\Delta C = -\Delta CA - \Delta LTA - DEP + \Delta CL + \Delta LTD + \Delta CS + NI + DEP - DIV \tag{5.5}$$
$$\Delta C = (NI + DEP - \Delta CA + \Delta CL) - (\Delta LTA + DEP) + (\Delta LTD + \Delta CS - DIV) \tag{5.6}$$
$$\Delta C = CFO + CFI + CFF \tag{5.7}$$

As advertised, the change in cash for a particular period is equal to the cash flow from operating activities (NI + DEP $-$ ΔCA + ΔCL) plus the cash flow from investing activities $[-(\Delta LTA + DEP)]$ plus the cash flow from financing activities (ΔLTD + $\Delta CS - DIV$).

Application of the Change-in-Cash Formula

The formula just derived is an identity; it is always true. We have taken pains to derive the formula because it provides information about how to compute each of the three components of the cash flow statement.

The first component on the right-hand side of Eqs. (5.6) and (5.7) is cash flow from operating activities computed under the indirect method. It reveals that cash flows from operating activities equals net income plus depreciation minus changes in current assets (other than cash) plus changes in current liabilities.

In practice, the current assets and the current liabilities are enumerated separately in terms of their increases or decreases. If the current account has increased, we can leave the sign as is. However, if the current account has decreased, it is useful to restate the formula by changing the sign. (Remember that minus times a minus is a plus.) Restating the formula: the cash flow from operating activities is equal to net income plus depreciation minus increases in current asset accounts (or plus decreases in current asset accounts) plus increases in current liability accounts (or minus decreases in current liability accounts).

Take another look at Exhibit 5.1. To arrive at cash flow from operating activities, begin with net income $45. Add back depreciation $55 since it involved no cash flow. Subtract increases in current asset accounts: accounts receivable $40 and inventory $15. Add decreases in current asset accounts: prepaid rent $5. Add increases in current liability accounts: accounts payable $5, wages payable $10, and interest payable $5. Subtract decreases in current liability accounts: none in Exhibit 5.1.

Because of the simplifying assumptions in the derivation of the formula, one item in Exhibit 5.1 was omitted: gain on sale of land. Gains and losses from the sales of notes receivable and long-term assets are handled like depreciation since the gain or loss does not reflect any cash flow. Suppose that the original cost of the land is $60 and it is sold for $100. The journal entry for the transaction is

Cash	$100	
Land		$60
Gain		$40

The gain is added back to net income because it does not reflect cash flow. There is a cash inflow, but it is due to the investment in the land so that it properly goes into cash flow from investing activities.

If the long-term asset had been a depreciable asset, such as buildings or equipment, then the related accumulated depreciation account would affect the gain or loss. For example, suppose that we have a building with a historical cost of $200,000 and accumulated depreciation of $75,000 and suppose that it is sold for $150,000. The gain is the cash proceeds less the book value (cost minus accumulated depreciation) of the building: $150,000 − $125,000 = $25,000. When the indirect method is employed, the cash flow from operating activities is the net income minus the gain of $25,000 plus or minus the other items. The cash proceeds of $150,000 are shown in the investing section. If there had been a loss, it would be added to net income.

The second component on the right-hand side of (5.6) and (5.7) is cash flow from investing activities. The formula reveals that it is equal to changes in long-term assets other than accumulated depreciation. It has a minus sign because increases in long-term assets represent acquisitions which require cash outflows. Cash inflows arise when the long-term assets are sold.

Glance at the cash flows from investing activities in Exhibit 5.1 or Exhibit 5.2. The cash inflow arises from selling land for $100. The cash outflow occurs because the corporation paid $300 for a building.

The third and last component of Eqs. (5.6) and (5.7) is cash flow from financing activities. As the equations demonstrate, it is equal to increases in long-term debt plus increases in common stock minus cash dividends. Decreases in long-term debt or common stock would be subtracted.

In Exhibit 5.1 or Exhibit 5.2, cash flows from financing activities have two inflows and one outflow. The cash inflows come from an increase in mortgage payable (i.e., the firm borrowed $55) and from issuing common stock for $130. There is one cash outflow; namely, cash dividends of $30 were paid.

The change-in-cash formula has assisted in the understanding of the cash flow statement, and it has presented us with the way to manufacture the statement, as long as the indirect method is chosen. Firms may employ the direct method, so we need to consider how to measure the cash flows from operating activities under the direct method.

CASH FLOWS FROM OPERATING ACTIVITIES: THE DIRECT METHOD

The previous section developed a formula that utilized the indirect method. Managers may, however, choose the direct method, so we need to discuss how to obtain cash flow from operating activities under the direct method. The approach is to look at revenue and expense accounts and observe how they can be transformed from an accrual basis to a cash basis. Once this modification is made, cash flow from operating activities equals the cash-based revenues minus the cash-based expenses.

Under *cash-based accounting*, revenues are reported when cash is received and expenses are reported when cash is paid. Accrual accounting deemphasizes the timing of cash receipts and disbursements and focuses on when the entity performs the revenue-generating acts or experiences an outflow of net assets. *Accrual accounting* is a system of accounting in which revenues are reported when earned and expenses are reported when incurred. The primary difference between cash-based accounting and accrual accounting is the timing of the revenues and expenses. In other words, cash-based accounting has the same amounts of revenues and expenses as accrual accounting, but the cash-based system reports them in different time periods. These differences are contained in the current asset and current liability accounts. To obtain the cash-based revenues and expenses, start with the accrual-based revenues and expenses and adjust them for changes in these current accounts. Exhibit 5.3 indicates how to do this.

Revenues and Cash Received from Revenues

As defined in Chapter 1, a revenue is an inflow of net assets that derives from a firm's selling goods or services to a customer. The accounting profession feels that the revenue should be recognized in the income statement when the company has provided the goods or the services it promises and when the firm can reasonably estimate the amounts of the revenues.

To convert from accrual to cash accounting, the associated current asset or liability must be known. The easiest way to think of this is to consider when cash is received relative to when the revenue is recognized. Exhibit 5.3 shows this situation as two cases when converting revenues into cash from revenues. In the first instance, a revenue is recognized prior to the cash inflow. When this occurs, there is an associated current asset such as accounts receivable. In the second instance, cash is received prior to the recognition of revenue. A current liability is booked when the firm obtains the cash since the company owes the customer a good or service. Let's examine each of these cases in depth.

Case 1: Cash Received After Revenue Recognition. If a corporation does not receive cash but has earned revenue, it typically reflects this by debiting a receivable such as accounts receivable or interest receivable. Later when it receives the cash, the firm debits cash and credits the receivable. Thus, an increase in a receivable account reveals that a revenue has been recognized without the cash flow, while a decrease in a receivable account indicates that a cash inflow has been received. From this reasoning the conversion formula is obtained:

$$\text{Cash from revenue} = \text{Revenue} \begin{cases} - \text{ Increase in related current asset} \\ \text{or} \\ + \text{ Decrease in related current asset} \end{cases}$$

As an illustration, consider a company with sales of $100,000 in 2001 and $140,000 in 2002. The firm's accounts receivable balances as of December 31, 2000, 2001, and

---

EXHIBIT 5.3

CONVERTING ACCRUALS INTO CASH-BASED MEASURES

Converting Revenues into Cash from Revenues

Case 1: Cash received after revenue recognition

Formula: Cash from revenue = Revenue − Δ Current asset

Example: Cash from sales = Sales − Δ Accounts receivable

Case 2: Cash received before revenue recognition

Formula: Cash from revenue = Revenue + Δ Current liability

Example: Cash from subscriptions = Subscription revenue + Δ Unearned subscription revenue

Converting Expenses into Cash Expenditures

Case 1: Cash paid after expense recognition

Formula: Cash expenditure = Expense − Δ Current liability

Example: Interest expenditure = Interest expense − Δ Interest payable

Case 2: Cash paid before expense recognition

Formula: Cash expenditure = Expense + Δ Current asset

Example: Rent expenditure = Rent expense + Δ Prepaid rent

Case 3: Cash paid before and/or after expense recognition

Formula: Cash expenditure = Expense + Δ Current asset − Δ Current liability

Example: COGS (cash) = COGS + Δ Inventory − Δ Accounts payable

Case 4: No cash involved though an expense is recognized

Formula: Cash expenditure = 0

Example: Depreciation expenditure = 0

2002, respectively, are $20,000, $30,000, and $25,000. Notice that there is an increase in accounts receivable of $10,000 in 2001 and a decrease of $5,000 in 2002. What is the cash generated from sales in 2001 and 2002? In 2001 it is $100,000 − $10,000 or $90,000. In 2002 the amount is $140,000 + $5,000 or $145,000.

Case 2: Cash Received Before Revenue Recognition. Sometimes a firm receives cash before it is appropriate to recognize it as revenue. Generally, recognition in the income statement is delayed because the business has not sent the goods sold or has not provided the services contracted. In this circumstance, the typical way to account for the event is to record the receipt of cash and to recognize a liability for the debt owed to the other party.

Similar to the previous case, the data needed to transform the accrual number to the cash flow number are found in the current accounts. In the previous case, you would look for the related current asset. In this situation, you look at the change in the related current liability. If the current liability increases, then cash has been received, but the revenue has not yet been recorded. A decrease in the current liability demonstrates that revenue has been recognized for some cash flow that occurred in a previous period. The conversion formula is

$$\text{Cash from revenue} = \text{Revenue} \begin{cases} + \text{ Increase in related current asset} \\ \quad\quad\quad\quad \text{or} \\ - \text{ Decrease in related current asset} \end{cases}$$

A magazine company sells subscriptions to customers who must pay first. Subscription revenues are $80,000 in 2001 and $90,000 in 2002. Unearned subscription revenue has balances of $15,000, $25,000, and $10,000 at December 31, 2000, 2001, and 2002, respectively. What is the cash flow from the customers during 2001 and 2002? The answer for 2001 is the revenue of $80,000 plus the increase in unearned subscription revenue of $10,000—a cash flow of $90,000. In 2002 it is $90,000 minus the decrease of $15,000—a cash flow of $75,000.

Expenses and Cash Disbursed for Expenses

An expense is an outflow of net assets because of the use or production of goods or the rendering of services. Recognition of expenses is determined by the matching principle that states, where possible, that expenses should be recognized in the same period as the revenues that they bring in. The cost of buying or manufacturing goods to be sold to customers is held as an asset—inventory—until the items are sold. At that time the expense—cost of goods sold—is recognized. The cost of using a building or equipment is usually allocated across time according to a formula such as the straight-line method. Depreciation expense is recognized by this matching of the cost of the asset across its economic life. Most other costs are simply recognized as expenses in the period in which they occur.

To convert from accrual to cash accounting, one generally adjusts the expense for changes in the associated current account. One exception is mentioned later in this chapter. The formulas are summarized in Exhibit 5.3 under four different cases. These rules are quite similar to those for revenues except that some expenses have two related current accounts and some have no cash flow consequences.

Case 1: Cash Paid After Expense Recognition.   When an enterprise books an expense prior to the cash disbursement, it often recognizes a liability. In effect, the reason for the expense entry is that the firm has received some good or service and it owes the third party for those goods or services. The firm later pays off the debt. This consideration leads to the following observation. An increase in this current liability indicates an expense recognition without cash disbursement. A decrease in the current liability discloses that a cash payment was made for some expense recognized in a previous period. The conversion rule is

$$\text{Cash expenditure} = \text{Expense} \begin{cases} - \text{ Increase in related current liability} \\ \quad\quad\quad\quad \text{or} \\ + \text{ Decrease in related current liability} \end{cases}$$

The relationship between interest expense and interest payable will serve as an example. ABC, Inc. has interest expense of $10,000 in 2001 and $18,000 in 2002. From its balance sheets you learn that interest payable at December 31, 2000, 2001, and 2002 is $3,000, $5,000, and $2,000, respectively. How much did ABC, Inc. disburse for interest? Note the increase in interest payable in 2001 of $2,000 and the decrease in 2002 of $3,000. Utilizing the formula, we find the expenditure for interest in 2001 is $8,000 ($10,000 − $2,000); in 2002 it is $21,000 ($18,000 + $3,000).

Case 2: Cash Paid Before Expense Recognition. Some items such as rent and insurance require cash to be paid prior to receiving the services. Because it is not yet proper to reflect the item as an expense, and because the item indicates an economic resource that will be utilized in the future, it is booked as an asset such as prepaid rent or prepaid insurance. As the current asset increases, the company pays out cash for future services, and as the current asset decreases, those services are used up and therefore expensed. The conversion rule is straightforward:

$$\text{Cash expenditure} = \text{Expense} \begin{cases} + \text{ Increase in related current asset} \\ \text{or} \\ - \text{ Decrease in related current asset} \end{cases}$$

Let's have a variation on the examples provided thus far by transforming the cash flow number into the accrual number. A company pays $60,000 in 2001 and $80,000 in 2002 for rent. If prepaid rent is $5,000 at December 31, 2000, $10,000 at December 31, 2001, and $8,000 at December 31, 2002, how much is the rent expense in 2001 and 2002? One sees that there is an increase in prepaid rent in 2001 of $5,000 and a decrease in 2002 of $2,000. Working backwards, rent expense in 2001 is equal to the rent expenditure of $60,000 minus the increase in prepaid rent of $5,000 or $55,000. In like manner, rent expense in 2002 is $80,000 + $2,000 or $82,000.

Case 3: Cash Paid Before and/or After Expense Recognition. A few income statement accounts have more than one related current account. In this textbook, the only one we shall consider is cost of goods sold. Cost of goods sold is associated with inventory purchases and with accounts payable. The logic is the same as expense cases 1 and 2; we just combine them.

Assume that accounts payable is unchanged. If inventory increases, then the firm has paid out cash but has not yet recognized the expense. If inventory decreases, then the firm recognizes the expense even though the cash was disbursed during a previous period. This observation implies that expense case 2 holds when comparing cost of goods sold and inventory.

Now keep inventory constant. If accounts payable increases, the firm has obtained and sold more goods and so has expensed them for this period even though the cash will be paid later. If accounts payable decreases, the firm pays its suppliers but shows no expense in that period. This fact suggests that expense case 1 is operative when comparing cost of goods sold and accounts payable.

Putting the two together, one gets the following formula:

$$\text{COGS (cash)} = \text{COGS} \begin{cases} + \text{ Increase in} \\ \text{inventory} \\ \text{or} \\ - \text{ Decrease in} \\ \text{inventory} \end{cases} \text{ and } \begin{cases} - \text{ Increase in accounts} \\ \text{payable} \\ \text{or} \\ + \text{ Decrease in accounts} \\ \text{payable} \end{cases}$$

Now let us consider an example. Alpha Company has inventory of $40,000 in 2001 and $53,000 in 2002. It has accounts payable of $32,000 in 2001 and $19,000 in 2002. If it incurred cost of goods sold of $123,000 in 2002, what is its cash expenditure for these goods? According to the formula, it is equal to $123,000 plus the increase in inventory of $13,000 plus the decrease in accounts payable of $13,000 for $149,000.

Case 4: No Cash Involved Though an Expense Is Recognized. A variety of expenses exist that are not associated with any operating cash flow, such as depreciation, depletion, amortization, and bad debt expense. In this case, the rule is simple: the cash expenditure is zero.

Before leaving this case, however, we should explain why this statement is true. Depreciation on a building, for example, is related to the building itself. The firm has to pay cash to receive the building and will receive cash upon its sale. So what is meant by the statement that there is no cash flow? The answer is that there is no operating cash flow. Cash paid out for a building and cash proceeds received upon sale are cash flows from investing activities.

Exhibit 5.3, as stated already, contains the formulas for converting accruals into cash-based measures, for both revenues and expenses. The reader should not only become familiar with these relationships, but also understand why they work.

PREPARING THE CASH FLOW STATEMENT WITH THE T-ACCOUNT METHOD

To prepare a cash flow statement in practice, one typically garners the data with either the T-account method or the worksheet method. As the names suggest, the T-account method sets up temporary T-accounts for the relevant accounts and manipulates them to produce the line items for a cash flow statement, whereas the worksheet method operates in a similar manner except that it uses a worksheet. The former method is explained in this section and the latter in the next.

Let's assume the data in Exhibit 5.4 for Richard France, Inc. That exhibit contains two balance sheets and the intervening income statement along with a statement of retained earnings. Notice that cash is $10 in 2000 and $15 in 2001. This increase in cash of $5 will be explained by the cash flows from the three activities.

The essence of the T-account method is to construct temporary T-accounts for all of the balance sheet accounts and several special accounts dealing with the activity cash flows. Which accounts are created depends on whether one employs the indirect or direct method. Entries are then made to these accounts. The before-closing balances in each activity account yields the cash flow from that activity. Keep in mind that these entries are only for the purpose of making the cash flow statement; they are not real entries. The accountant is not entering these data into any journal or any ledger.

Indirect Method

If the indirect method is used when computing cash flows from operating activities, the T-account method consists of five steps.

- Step 1: Prepare a T-account for each balance sheet account, cash from operating (CFO) activities, cash from investing (CFI) activities, and cash from financing (CFF) activities.

- Step 2: Calculate the change in each balance sheet account and enter the change on the debit or credit side of the account, depending on the type of account and whether there is an increase or decrease. When doing this, apply the usual definitions of debits and credits. For example, a decrease in an asset is placed on the credit side of the account.

- Step 3: Make entries in these T-accounts that explain the changes in the balance sheet accounts. When cash is part of the entry, decide to which activity the trans-

EXHIBIT **5.4**

DATA TO PREPARE THE CASH FLOW STATEMENT

Richard France, Inc.
Comparative Balance Sheets
June 30, 2000 and 2001

		2000		2001
CURRENT ASSETS				
Cash		$ 10		$ 15
Accounts receivable		25		40
Inventory		30		50
Prepaid rent		10		5
Current assets		$ 75		$110
PROPERTY PLANT AND EQUIPMENT				
Land		$110		$ 50
Building	$500		$800	
Less: accumulated depreciation	150	350	200	600
Equipment	$ 75		$ 75	
Less: accumulated depreciation	45	30	50	25
Property plant and equipment		$490		$675
TOTAL ASSETS		$565		$785
LIABILITIES AND SHAREHOLDERS' EQUITY				
CURRENT LIABILITIES				
Accounts payable		$ 55		$ 60
Wages payable		5		15
Interest payable		10		15
Current liabilities		$ 70		$ 90
LONG-TERM LIABILITIES				
Mortgage payable		$100		$155
Total liabilities		$170		$245
SHAREHOLDERS' EQUITY				
Common stock		$ 50		$ 80
Premium on common stock		150		250
Retained earnings		195		210
Shareholders' equity		$395		$540
TOTAL LIABILITIES AND				
SHAREHOLDERS' EQUITY		$565		$785

(continued)

action belongs and replace the cash account with the appropriate activity cash flow account. When earnings is accounted for or any revenue or expense is involved, substitute the account cash from operating activities. Continue this process until all balance sheet accounts are explained.

- Step 4: Close out CFO, CFI, and CFF to the cash account.
- Step 5: Obtain the balance in cash after the closings and verify that the balance equals the change in cash for the period. If it doesn't, an error has been made.

EXHIBIT 5.4

DATA TO PREPARE THE CASH FLOW STATEMENT (continued)

Richard France, Inc.
Income Statement
For the year ended June 30, 2001

Sales		$400
Cost of goods sold		250
Gross margin		$150
Operating expenses:		
Wages expense	$25	
Rent expense	20	
Depreciation expense	55	
Interest expense	20	120
		$ 30
Other revenue:		
Gain on sale of land		40
Income before taxes		$ 70
Tax expense		25
Net income		$ 45

Richard France, Inc.
Statement of Retained Earnings
June 30, 2001

Retained earnings, June 30, 2000	$195
Net income	45
	$240
Dividends	30
Retained earnings, June 30, 2001	$210

You are now ready to produce the cash flow statement with the data in the CFO, CFI, and CFF accounts. Debits in these three accounts reflect cash inflows from those activities; credits show cash outlays.

Taking the financial statements given in Exhibit 5.4, we will illustrate the T-account method. After implementing the first two steps, you should have the T-accounts displayed in Exhibit 5.5. Each balance sheet account is given along with the change in the account. For example, accumulated depreciation on the building increases from $150 to $200. Increases in a contra-asset account are shown with a credit, so enter a credit of $50 in that account. Underline these amounts so that you do not confuse the change in the account with the entries that explain the change in the account.

One might prepare a trial balance, at least mentally, to ensure that no arithmetic mistake has been made. Doing this with the data in Exhibit 5.5, one discovers that debits equal credits equal $340.

The heart of the T-account method is step three. Prepare T-account entries so that these changes are accounted for. Although any order is acceptable—as long as you know what you are doing—it is easiest to start with earnings, dividends, and then adjust for noncash revenues and expenses. These entries are assembled in Exhibit 5.6. The entries are cross-referenced with numbers (letters could be used) to allow one to understand what has been done and to trace for errors. Following is an explanation of each entry to justify the work.

EXHIBIT **5.5**

PREPARING THE CASH FLOW STATEMENT WITH T-ACCOUNTS:
SETUP FOR THE INDIRECT METHOD

Cash		CFO		CFI		CFF	
5							

Acct receivable		Inventory		Prepaid rent		Land	
15		20			5		60

Building		Acc. Dep.-Bldg.		Equipment		Acc. Dep.-Equip.	
300			50	0			5

Acct payable		Wages payable		Interest payable		Mortgage payable	
	5		10		5		55

Common stock		Premium on CS		Retained Earnings	
	30		100		15

EXHIBIT 5.6

PREPARING THE CASH FLOW STATEMENT WITH T-ACCOUNTS:
COMPLETION OF THE INDIRECT METHOD

Cash		CFO		CFI		CFF	
5		(1) 45	40 (4)	(4) 100	300 (8)	(12) 55	30 (2)
(14) 5		(3) 55	15 (5)			(13) 130	
		(7) 5	20 (6)				
		(9) 5					
		(10) 10					
		(11) 5					
			50(14)	(14) 200			155 (14)

Acct receivable		Inventory		Prepaid rent		Land	
15		20			5		60
(5) 15		(6) 20			5 (7)		60 (4)

Building		Acc. Dep.-Bldg.		Equipment		Acc. Dep.-Equip.	
300			50	0			5
(8) 300			50 (3)				5 (3)

Acct payable		Wages payable		Interest payable		Mortgage payable	
	5		10		5		55
	5 (9)		10 (10)		5 (11)		55 (12)

Common stock		Premium on CS		Retained Earnings	
	30		100		15
	30 (13)		100 (13)	(2) 30	45 (1)

Net income is $45. It is an initial indication of cash flow, though it requires adjustment, and when closing entries are made, net income is transferred to retained earnings. (The numbers in parentheses correspond to the numbers in Exhibit 5.6.) Thus, the entry is

(1)	Cash from operating activities	$45	
	Retained earnings		$45

The enterprise disbursed cash dividends of $30. This type of transaction is a financing one, so the entry is

(2)	Retained earnings	$30	
	Cash from financing activities		$30

The student should realize that the retained earnings account is now "explained." Entry (1) increases retained earnings by $45, entry (2) decreases it by $30, and there is a net increase of $15. Since that is the amount by which retained earnings increases, as shown by the $15 credit above the line, we are finished with the account. If you want to keep track of when an account is "explained," you might indicate it with a check mark.

The third entry is for depreciation. Accumulated depreciation on the building increased by $50, and accumulated depreciation on the equipment increased by $5. These facts imply that depreciation expense is $55. Show the entry to depreciation expense, an income statement item, by making the entry to cash from operating activities.

(3)	Cash from operating activities	$55	
	Accumulated depreciation—building		$50
	Accumulated depreciation—equipment		$ 5

Next account for the sale of the land. Land decreased by $60, and there was a gain on the sale of the land of $40, so the cash proceeds were $100. Make the usual entry, replacing cash with cash from investing activities (since that is the type of cash flow) and replacing the gain account with cash from operating activities.

(4)	Cash from investing activities	$100	
	Cash from operating activities		$40
	Land		$60

Though not illustrated here, one could have a sale of buildings or equipment. Those entries would be handled in a similar fashion, except that one would also have to remove the associated accumulated depreciation. If such a transaction occurred, one would deal with it before backing out the amount of depreciation as in entry (3). This helps to obtain the correct amount of depreciation expense.

The next three entries concern the current assets other than cash. Show the increases or decreases in these accounts with an offsetting entry to cash from operating activities. In essence, you are adjusting net income for these increases or decreases as part of the process in determining cash from operating activities.

(5)	Accounts receivable	$15	
	Cash from operating activities		$15
(6)	Inventory	$20	
	Cash from operating activities		$20
(7)	Cash from operating activities	$ 5	
	Prepaid rent		$ 5

Entry (8) is for the increase in the building account. What can account for the change? The obvious response is that the firm acquired a new building, a transaction that is an investing activity.

| (8) Building | $300 | |
| Cash from investing activities | | $300 |

The next three entries pertain to the current liabilities that are associated with income statement accounts. Thus, the changes are paired with the cash-from-operating-activities account.

(9) Cash from operating activities	$ 5	
Accounts payable		$ 5
(10) Cash from operating activities	$10	
Wages payable		$10
(11) Cash from operating activities	$ 5	
Interest payable		$ 5

Mortgage payable has increased by $55. The most likely reason for an increase is that the firm has borrowed money. The entry is

| (12) Cash from financing activities | $55 | |
| Mortgage payable | | $55 |

The final changes in the balance sheet accounts concern common stock and premium on common stock. The best explanation for their increases is that common stock has been issued. This is a financing transaction, so the entry is

(13) Cash from financing activities	$130	
Common stock		$ 30
Premium on common stock		$100

All balance sheet accounts have been explained, so step 3 is finished.

Step 4 in the T-account method is to close out the activity accounts. They began with zero balances, and they must end with zero balances. The balances before closing are: cash from operating activities has a debit balance of $50, cash from investing activities has a credit balance of $200, and cash from financing activities has a debit balance of $155. Closing them out leads to entry (14):

(14) Cash	$ 5	
Cash from investing activities	$200	
Cash from operating activities		$ 50
Cash from financing activities		$155

The fifth and last step in the T-account method is to verify that the entry to cash is what is desired. Since cash increases by $5 from one balance sheet to the next and the closing entry provides a debit of $5, the T-account method balances.

What is left to do is prepare the cash flow statement itself. The critical thing to recognize from all this work is that all the line items in a cash flow statement are provided in the three activity accounts. Note that debits in the activity accounts refer to cash inflows and that credits depict cash outflows. Also recognize that the cash from operating activities account is measured as the net income (entry 1) plus or minus noncash revenues and expenses (entries 3 and 4) plus or minus increases or decreases in the current accounts (entries 5–7 and 9–11). In other words, the T-account CFO implicitly is measuring cash from operating activities exactly as the change-in-cash formula told us to do. Cash from investing activities consists of two cash flows, and they are given in the T-account. Similarly, cash from financing activities includes three activities that are contained in that T-account.

From these numbers, one can construct the cash flow statement originally displayed in Exhibit 5.1. The reader should verify each of the line items in Exhibit 5.1 with each of the activity accounts listed in Exhibit 5.6.

Direct Method

There are also five steps in applying the T-account method to the direct computation of cash from operating activities. In step 1, in addition to T-accounts for each balance sheet account, CFO, CFI, and CFF, we create T-accounts for cash from sales, inventory payments, rent payments, and so on. In other words, T-accounts are also set up for the individual cash inflows and outflows within the operating activities component. The other steps are the same, though we implement step 3 slightly differently. Under the indirect method, one adjusts for net income as a total. With the direct method, however, one adjusts for each revenue and expense by debiting or crediting retained earnings. The offsetting debit or credit will be to the cash inflow or outflow related to the revenue or expense. In this way we create the various line items within cash from operating activities. Otherwise, the T-account method is the same for both indirect and direct methods.

Let's employ the data in Exhibit 5.4 for Richard France, Inc. to make a cash flow statement with the direct method. Exhibit 5.7 gives the solution.

Notice that in Exhibit 5.7 the additional T-accounts are cash from sales, inventory payments, rent payments, wage payments, interest payments, and tax payments. These accounts change from situation to situation. Simply observe what revenues and expenses the firm has, and consider cash inflows and outflows related to those accounts. Also notice that there is no new account for depreciation or for gain on sale of land. This makes sense, for those items do not affect cash from operating activities.

With the direct method, it is easiest to begin with the income statement and adjust each revenue and each expense separately. One simultaneously adjusts for the related current asset or current liability and thereby directly obtains the cash flow for that item. The astute student should observe that in effect the T-account method is utilizing the formulas developed in the section "Cash Flows from Operating Activities: The Direct Method" and summarized in Exhibit 5.3. The only difference is that the formula is solved with a T-account instead of an algebraic formula. (The numbers in parentheses correspond to those in Exhibit 5.7.) For cash from sales, one enters

(1)	Cash from sales	$400	
	Retained earnings		$400
(2)	Accounts receivable	$ 15	
	Cash from sales		$ 15

Thus, cash from sales is $385.

Now determine that inventory expenditures are $265. This is calculated in the usual fashion: cost of goods sold plus the increase in inventory minus the increase in accounts payable.

(3)	Retained earnings	$250	
	Inventory payments		$250
(4)	Inventory	$ 20	
	Inventory payments		$ 20
(5)	Inventory payments	$ 5	
	Accounts payable		$ 5

Wage payments equal wages expense minus the increase in wages payable.

(6)	Retained earnings	$25	
	Wage payments		$25
(7)	Wage payments	$10	
	Wages payable		$10

EXHIBIT 5.7

PREPARING THE CASH FLOW STATEMENT WITH T-ACCOUNTS:
THE DIRECT METHOD

Cash		CFO		CFI		CFF	
5		(19) 50		(13) 100	300 (16)	(17) 55	30 (15)
(20) 5						(18) 130	
			50 (20)	(20) 200			155 (20)

Cash from sales		Inventory payments		Rent payments	
(1) 400	15 (2)	(5) 5	250 (3)	(9) 5	20 (8)
			20 (4)		
	385 (19)			(19) 15	

Wage payments		Interest payments		Tax payments	
(7) 10	25 (6)	(12) 5	20 (11)	(19) 25	25 (14)
(19) 15		(19) 15			

Acct receivable		Inventory		Prepaid rent		Land	
15		20		5		60	
(2) 15		(4) 20			5 (9)		60 (13)

Building		Acc.Dep.-Bldg.		Equipment		Acc.Dep.-Equip.	
300			50	0			5
(16) 300			50 (10)				5 (10)

Acct payable		Wages payable		Interest payable		Mortgage payable	
	5		10		5		55
	5 (5)		10 (7)		5 (12)		55 (17)

Common stock		Premium on CS		Retained Earnings	
	30		100		15
	(30) 18		100 (18)	(3) 250	400 (1)
				(6) 25	40 (13)
				(8) 20	
				(10) 55	
				(11) 20	
				(14) 25	
				(15) 30	

Rent payments equal rent expense minus the decrease in prepaid rent.

(8)	Retained earnings	$20	
	Rent payments		$20
(9)	Rent payments	$ 5	
	Prepaid rent		$ 5

The next expense on the income statement is depreciation. The entry is

(10)	Retained earnings	$55	
	Accumulated depreciation-building		$50
	Accumulated depreciation-equipment		$ 5

The expense portion is debited to retained earnings, reducing it as any expense does. The offsetting accounts are the two accumulated depreciations. Recognize that no cash flow account is debited or credited, as is desired since depreciation involves no cash flow.

Interest payments equal interest expense minus the increase in interest payable.

(11)	Retained earnings	$ 20	
	Interest payments		$ 20
(12)	Interest payments	$ 5	
	Interest payable		$ 5

The gain on sale of the land is adjusted with a credit of $40, the amount of the gain, but the credit is made to retained earnings. The cash proceeds are placed in the investing activities section, as it should be.

(13)	Cash from investing activities	$100	
	Land		$60
	Retained earnings		$40

The last income statement account is tax expense, and tax payments are the same as tax expense. If there had been a prepaid tax account or a taxes payable account, then tax expense would be adjusted for changes in the related current accounts.

(14)	Retained earnings	$25	
	Tax payments		$25

Entry (15) concerns dividends, entry (16) deals with the purchase of a building, entry (17) handles the mortgage payable, and entry (18) focuses on the issuance of common stock. They are unchanged from the indirect method: they are entries (2), (8), (12), and (13), respectively, in Exhibit 5.6. They are repeated here for the sake of completeness.

(15)	Retained earnings	$ 30	
	Cash from financing activities		$ 30
(16)	Building	$300	
	Cash from investing activities		$300
(17)	Cash from financing activities	$ 55	
	Mortgage payable		$ 55
(18)	Cash from financing activities	$130	
	Common stock		$ 30
	Premium on common stock		$100

Entry (19) is a closing entry; it closes out the cash inflow and outflow accounts to cash from operating activities. The net effect of this is to obtain the amount of cash from operating activities, $50.

(19) Cash from operating activities $ 50
       Inventory payments $265
       Rent payments $ 15
       Wage payments $ 15
       Interest payments $ 15
       Tax payments $ 25
         Cash from sales $385

Finally, close out the three activity accounts. This entry (20) corresponds with entry (14) with the indirect method.

(20) Cash $ 5
    Cash from investing activities $200
       Cash from operating activities $ 50
       Cash from financing activities $155

After this T-account method is followed, one needs to prepare the cash flow statement itself. As with the indirect method, the main thing to recognize is that all the line items in a cash flow statement are provided in the three activity accounts. Debits in the activity accounts refer to cash inflows, and credits involve cash outflows. The cash from operating activities account is measured as the cash inflows (e.g., cash from sales) less cash outflows (inventory payments, rent payments, etc.). Cash from investing activities and cash from financing activities are exactly the same as before.

From these data, you can construct the cash flow statement originally tabulated in Exhibit 5.2. The student should confirm that each of the line items in Exhibit 5.2 comes from the activity accounts listed in Exhibit 5.7.

PREPARING THE CASH FLOW STATEMENT WITH A WORKSHEET

An alternative to the T-account method is the usage of worksheets. Fortunately, the worksheet approach operates in a manner very similar to the T-account method, so there is little new to learn.

Indirect Method

For the indirect method, the accountant sets up a worksheet with the balance sheet accounts listed in the first column. This column also contains the three activity cash flows, and space is provided to add details as the worksheet is completed. Column 2 contains the balance sheet account balances for the first year, while column 5 shows the balances for the second year. Summary journal entries are prepared to explain the changes in these account balances, and they are entered in the third and fourth columns. As with the T-account method, these entries are for the worksheet only; they are not put into any journal or ledger.

With one exception, the summary entries operate exactly as they did with the T-account method. Indeed, the entries are the same. This fact is illustrated in Exhibit 5.8 which displays a worksheet for Richard France, Inc. under the indirect method. Notice that the entries are the same in Exhibit 5.6 and Exhibit 5.8. The exception is closing entry (14). In the worksheet method, you do not accumulate the totals of the activities accounts. Instead, you add the debits and credits for the activity accounts. In Exhibit 5.8 you get $410 as the total debits and $405 as the total credits. (Be careful not to include the debits and credits for the balance sheet accounts.) The closing entry now simply debits cash

EXHIBIT **5.8**

PREPARING THE CASH FLOW STATEMENT WITH A WORKSHEET: INDIRECT METHOD

Richard France, Inc.
Worksheet for the Cash Flow Statement
For the year ended June 30, 2001

	2000	Summary entries Debits	Summary entries Credits	2001
ASSETS				
Cash	10	(14) 5		15
Accounts receivable	25	(5) 15		40
Inventory	30	(6) 20		50
Prepaid rent	10		(7) 5	5
Land	110		(4) 60	50
Building	500	(8) 300		800
Less: accumulated depreciation	(150)		(3) 50	(200)
Equipment	75			75
Less: accumulated depreciation	(45)		(3) 5	(50)
TOTAL ASSETS	565			785
EQUITIES				
Accounts payable	55		(9) 5	60
Wages payable	5		(10) 10	15
Interest payable	10		(11) 5	15
Mortgage payable	100		(12) 55	155
Common stock	50		(13) 30	80
Premium on common stock	150		(13) 100	250
Retained earnings	195	(2) 30	(1) 45	210
TOTAL EQUITIES	565			785
CASH FROM OPERATING ACTIVITIES				
Net income		(1) 45		
Depreciation		(3) 55		
Gain on sale of land			(4) 40	
Increase in accounts receivable			(5) 15	
Increase in inventory			(6) 20	
Decrease in prepaid rent		(7) 5		
Increase in accounts payable		(9) 5		
Increase in wages payable		(10) 10		
Increase in interest payable		(11) 5		
CASH FROM INVESTING ACTIVITIES				
Proceeds from sale of land		(4) 100		
Purchase of a building			(8) 300	
CASH FROM FINANCING ACTIVITIES				
Cash dividends			(2) 30	
Proceeds from mortgage		(12) 55		
Issuance of common stock		(13) 130		
		410	405	
Net increase in cash			(14) 5	
		410	410	

for the increase of $5 and notes that a credit of $5 is needed to make the cash flow debits and credits equal. The main point, however, is that all of the other entries in Exhibit 5.8 are the same as in Exhibit 5.6; the student is encouraged to verify this statement.

Direct Method

For the direct method, set up columns 1, 2, and 5 the same way as before, except for the line items within cash from operating activities. Under the indirect method, the line items for cash from operating activities are net income adjusted for depreciation and other non-cash revenues and expenses and are adjusted for increases and decreases of current assets and liabilities. Under the direct method, the line items are the various cash inflows from revenue activities and the cash expenditures for expense activities.

Except for the closing entry, the entries are the same for the worksheet method and the T-account method. See the example in Exhibit 5.9. Entries (1)–(18) in Exhibits 5.7 and 5.9 are identical. The reader should corroborate this statement. What is different is that the closing entries in Exhibit 5.7—entries (19) and (20)—are replaced with entry (19) in Exhibit 5.9.

(19) Cash $5
           Net increase in cash $5

The "net increase in cash" is the difference between the debits and credits tallied in the third and fourth columns for the activity accounts only.

As with the T-account method, the accountant can prepare the cash flow statement with the data contained in the worksheet. The numbers that are needed are shown in the activity accounts in the worksheet. From Exhibit 5.8, the cash flow statement displayed in Exhibit 5.1 can be generated. Similarly, with the data from the worksheet in Exhibit 5.9, the accountant can prepare the cash flow statement given in Exhibit 5.2.

SIGHTS ALONG THE INTERNET

The reader can now apply the knowledge gained from this chapter by looking at some cash flow statements of real-world companies. Several firms that display their annual reports on the Internet are (the ticker symbols are contained in parentheses):

Apple Computer (AAPL)	www.apple.com
Banc One Corporation (ONE)	www.bankone.com
Chevron Corporation (CHV)	www.chevron.com
GATX Corporation (GMT)	www.gatx.com
General Motors (GM)	www.gm.com
J. C. Penney Company (JCP)	w.ww.jcpenney.com
Mellon Bank (MEL)	www.mellon.com
Tribune Company (TRB)	www.tribune.com
Wendy's International (WEN)	www.wendys.com

How do they display the cash flow statement? Do they use the direct or the indirect format? How does the cash from operations compare to the income from operations?

Unfortunately, when firms report their financial statements electronically, they sometimes exclude items found in the annual report itself. The FASB discusses this problem on its site: www.rutgers.edu/Accounting/raw/fasb. Go to the site and click on "Business Reporting Research Project."

EXHIBIT *5.9*

PREPARING THE CASH FLOW STATEMENT WITH A WORKSHEET: DIRECT METHOD

Richard France, Inc.
Worksheet for the Cash Flow Statement
For the year ended June 30, 2001

	2000	*Debits*	*Credits*	*2001*
ASSETS				
Cash	10	(19) 5		15
Accounts receivable	25	(2) 15		40
Inventory	30	(4) 20		50
Prepaid rent	10		(9) 5	5
Land	110		(13) 60	50
Building	500	(16) 300		800
Less: accumulated depreciation	(150)		(10) 50	(200)
Equipment	75			75
Less: accumulated depreciation	(45)		(10) 5	(50)
TOTAL ASSETS	565			785
EQUITIES				
Accounts payable	55		(5) 5	60
Wages payable	5		(7) 10	15
Interest payable	10		(12) 5	15
Mortgage payable	100		(17) 55	155
Common stock	50		(18) 30	80
Premium on common stock	150		(18) 100	250
Retained earnings	195	(3) 250	(1) 400	210
		(6) 25	(13) 40	
		(8) 20		
		(10) 55		
		(11) 20		
		(14) 25		
		(15) 30		
TOTAL EQUITIES	565			785
CASH FROM OPERATING ACTIVITIES				
Cash from sales		(1) 400	(2) 15	
Inventory payments		(5) 5	(3) 250	
			(4) 20	
Rent payments		(9) 5	(8) 20	
Wage payments		(7) 10	(6) 25	
Interest payments		(12) 5	(11) 20	
Tax payments			(14) 25	
CASH FROM INVESTING ACTIVITIES				
Proceeds from sale of land		(13) 100		
Purchase of a building			(16) 300	
CASH FROM FINANCING ACTIVITIES				
Cash dividends			(15) 30	
Proceeds from mortgage		(17) 55		
Issuance of common stock		(18) 130		
		710	705	
Net increase in cash			(19) 5	
		710	710	

CHAPTER SUMMARY IN TERMS OF LEARNING OBJECTIVES

Indicate the Purpose of the Cash Flow Statement. The first purpose is to help investors and creditors to understand the liquidity and solvency of the firm. Liquidity is the ability to generate cash, and solvency is the ability to pay debts as they come due. The second purpose is to assist in evaluating a firm's quality of earnings, that is, the informativeness of the net income number in making investment decisions.

State the Components of the Cash Flow Statement. There are three sections of the cash flow statement: cash from operating activities, cash from investing activities, and cash from financing activities. Operating activities are the profit-making transactions and events of the firm. Investing activities are transactions and events that pertain to the making of loans and to the long-term assets of the firm. Financing activities are transactions and events that pertain to borrowing money and to common and preferred stock.

Explain Changes in Cash in Terms of Operating, Investing, and Financing Activities. Change in cash is equal to the cash from operating activities plus the cash from investing activities plus the cash from financing activities. In the indirect method, cash from operating activities is equal to net income plus or minus any noncash expenses and revenues and plus or minus changes in current assets (except cash and notes receivable) and current liabilities (except short-term notes payable).

Reconcile Revenues with Cash Received from Revenue Activities and Expenses with Cash Expenditures. In the direct method, cash from operating activities is equal to revenues converted from an accrual basis to a cash basis minus expenses converted from an accrual basis to a cash basis. The rules for converting from the accrual basis to the cash basis are listed in Exhibit 5.3. Briefly, cash from revenue equals the revenue minus the change in the related current asset or plus the change in the related liability. Cash expenditure equals the expense minus the change in the related current liability or plus the change in the related current asset. Some expenses, such as depreciation, have no cash expenditure.

Employ the T-account Method to Determine Cash Flow from Operating, Investing, and Financing Activities. The T-account method has five steps. First, prepare a T-account for each balance sheet account, cash from operating activities, cash from investing activities, and cash from financing activities. With the direct method, also create T-accounts for cash from sales, inventory payments, and other cash flows relating to operating activities. Second, calculate the change in each balance sheet account and enter the change in the T-account. Third, make entries in the T-accounts to explain the changes in the balance sheet accounts. With the indirect method, adjust for net income as a total, for depreciation and other noncash revenues and expenses, and for changes in relevant current asset and current liability accounts. With the direct method, account separately for the cash flow from each revenue and each expense. Fourth, close out cash from operating activities, cash from investing activities, and cash from financing activities. Fifth, obtain the balance in cash after the closing entries and verify that the balance equals the change in cash for the period.

Use the Worksheet Method to Measure Cash Flow from Operating, Investing, and Financing Activities. The worksheet method has five steps that roughly correspond to the five steps of the T-account method. First, set up a worksheet with the first column having the balance sheet accounts, cash from operating activities, cash from investing activities, and cash from financing activities. In the indirect method, the items within cash from operating activities are net income, depreciation and other noncash revenues and expenses, and increases or decreases in the current accounts. In the direct method, the items within cash from operating activities are the individual cash revenues and cash expenses. Second, put the balance sheet account balances for the beginning of the year in the second column and the balances for the end of the year in the fifth column. Third, make entries to explain the changes in the balance sheet accounts. For the most part, these entries are the same as those under the T-account method. Fourth, add the debits and credits of the entries for the cash flow accounts in columns 3 and 4. Fifth, the difference in the total debits and total credits should be the change in cash.

Prepare a Statement of Cash Flows Using Either the Indirect or Direct Method for Calculating Operating Cash Flows. Take the data in the cash flow accounts from either the T-account method or the worksheet method and transcribe them into statement form. Keep in mind that debits in the three cash flow accounts reflect cash inflows and credits are cash outflows.

GLOSSARY

Accrual accounting—a system of accounting in which revenues are reported when earned and expenses are reported when incurred.

Cash flow—any transaction that increases or decreases the cash of the entity.

Cash flow statement—a financial statement that explains the change in cash as a sum of the cash flows from the operating, investing, and financing activities of the entity.

Cash inflow—a cash flow in which the cash is received by the firm.

Cash outflow—a cash flow in which the cash is disbursed by the company.

Cash-based accounting—a system of accounting in which revenues are reported when cash is received and expenses are reported when cash is paid.

Direct method—the method of computing cash flow from operating activities as revenues converted from an accrual basis to a cash basis minus expenses converted from an accrual basis to a cash basis.

Financing activities—transactions and events that pertain to borrowing money and to common and preferred stock.

Indirect method—the method of computing cash flow from operating activities as net income plus or minus any noncash expenses and revenues and plus or minus changes in current assets (except cash and notes receivable) and current liabilities (except short-term notes payable).

Investing activities—transactions and events that pertain to the making of loans and to the long-term assets of the firm.

Liquidity—the ability to generate cash.

Operating activities—the profit-making transactions and events of the firm. A practical definition is that an operating activity is any transaction or event except for investing and financing activities.

Quality of earnings—the informativeness of the net income number in making investment decisions.

Solvency—the ability to pay debts as they come due.

REVIEW QUESTIONS

1. What are the purposes of the cash flow statement?
2. Define cash flow, cash inflow, and cash outflow.
3. What is the cash flow statement, and what are its components?
4. What is meant by operating, investing, and financing activities?
5. One way of computing cash flows from operating activities is with the indirect method. What is the indirect method?
6. Why is depreciation added to net income in the indirect method?
7. Why are gains (losses) from the sale of assets such as land, buildings, and equipment subtracted from (added to) net income in the indirect method?
8. Contrast accrual accounting and cash accounting.
9. What is the direct method?
10. Explain how to convert a revenue from the accrual to a cash basis.

11. Explain how to convert an expense from the accrual to a cash basis.

12. What are the five steps in the T-account method?

13. When applying the T-account method, one makes entries that explain the changes in the balance sheet accounts. Explain how you handle income statement accounts and how you handle cash when you carry out this step.

14. How can one prepare the cash flow statement from the T-account indirect method?

15. Indicate how the T-account method for the indirect method corresponds with the change-in-cash formula for the indirect method.

16. How does one prepare the cash flow statement from the T-account direct method?

17. Discuss the formation of the cash flow statement with the worksheet for the indirect method. for the direct method.

DISCUSSION QUESTIONS

1. How can a firm have positive earnings and yet go bankrupt?

2. Why might a growth firm have a strain on its cash flow? Does a negative cash flow automatically imply that a firm is in financial trouble?

3. The most common way of preparing the cash flow statement, as discussed in the chapter, is to use the accounts to generate the balance sheet and the income statement and then adjust these statements via the T-account or the worksheet method. It is possible, however, to employ subsidiary cash accounts that enable the preparation of the cash flow statement, as long as the direct method is used. The subsidiary cash accounts are beginning cash balance, cash from operating activities, cash from investing activities, and cash from financing activities. These accounts could be refined even further (for example, replacing cash from operating activities by cash from sales, cash expended for inventory, cash expended for wages, etc.).

Kendel's Kennels employs a subsidiary ledger for cash that indicates the cash flow activity. The beginning cash balance is $3,500. Kendel's Kennels had the following transactions during the month of January.

> January 2. Obtained $5,000 from a bank by signing a note.
> January 5. Paid electric bill for $300.
> January 7. Obtained $3,000 worth of dog food on account.
> January 10. Charged customers $20,000 for kenneling services.
> January 14. Paid employees $1,000.
> January 16. Customers paid $16,000 on their accounts.
> January 20. Paid rent of $2,000.
> January 24. Obtained paper supplies on account for $1,000.
> January 26. Paid insurance bill of $3,000.
> January 28. Paid employees $1,000.
> January 30. Kendel withdraws $2,500 for personal use.
> January 31. Paid the January 7 bill.

> Part A: prepare journal entries for Kendel's Kennels' transactions, including the entry to the cash subsidiary account.
> Part B: show the cash account and the cash subsidiary ledger at the beginning of January.
> Part C: show the cash account and the cash subsidiary ledger at the end of January.
> Part D: prepare the cash flow statement for Kendel's Kennels.

4. Some analysts believe that the cash flow statement is most informative when it is placed next to the income statement, and the reader can observe the contrast between the cash-based numbers and the accrual numbers. This combined statement may be termed the statement of operations. Notice that this statement utilizes only the cash-from-operating-activities section of the cash flow statement and that it necessitates that the direct method be employed.

Required: Prepare a statement of operations for Richard France, Inc., using the data shown in the exhibits of the chapter. Then comment on the pros and cons of this presentation.

EXERCISES

1. For each of the following transactions, indicate whether it is a cash flow from operating activities, a cash flow from investing activities, a cash flow from financing activities, or none of the above.

(a) Cash sales

(b) Credit sales

(c) Cash receipts from accounts receivable

(d) Cash purchases of inventory

(e) Credit purchases of inventory

(f) Cash payments of accounts payable

(g) Purchases of equipment for cash

(h) Purchases of equipment on credit

(i) Depreciation of equipment

(j) Sale of used equipment

(k) Issuance of common stock

(l) Declaration of dividends

(m) Payment of cash dividends

(n) Cash from a mortgage

(o) Payment on a mortgage loan (the payment includes a portion of principal and interest)

2. The following data of Michael Fedyna Company shows the operating activities for the year. Compute the cash flow from operating activities.

Cash sales	$20,000	Cash payment of accounts payable	$35,000
Credit sales	80,000	Cash payment of wages	20,000
Cash collection of accounts receivable	65,000	Depreciation	4,000
Cash purchases of inventory	5,000	Taxes payable	6,000
Credit purchases of inventory	45,000		

3. Lisa Mittelman and Company earns interest of $40,000 in 2001, for which it receives $25,000 in 2001 and the rest in 2002. Lisa Mittelman then earns interest of $50,000 in 2002, for which it receives $30,000 in 2002 and the rest in 2003. Assume that interest receivable is zero on January 1, 2001.

a. Prepare the journal entries for these transactions in 2001 and 2002.

b. How much interest revenue is there in 2001 and 2002?

c. What is the balance of interest receivable on December 31, 2001 and 2002?

d. Show how cash from interest is computed from interest revenue and interest receivable in 2001 and 2002.

4. For the following independent cases, compute the unknown amounts. Assume that no accounts are written off as uncollectible and that no sales discounts are offered. Then verify the formula: cash from sales equals sales minus the increase in accounts receivable.

Beginning Accounts Receivable	Ending Accounts Receivable	Increase in Accounts Receivable	Cash Sales	Credit Sales	Total Sales	Collection of Cash from Credit Customers	Cash from Selling Activities
a. $12,000	$22,000	$?	$20,000	$ 80,000	$?	$?	$?
b. 20,000	?	15,000	?	100,000	110,000	?	?
c. ?	18,000	9,000	?	120,000	155,000	?	?
d. 25,000	?	(10,000)	22,000	?	?	?	75,000
e. 23,000	23,000	?	15,000	?	?	120,000	?

5. Charles Dennis receives $24,000 cash on August 1, 2001 for the one-year rental of office space it owns. The rental runs from August 1, 2001 to July 31, 2002. The company also receives $36,000 on May 1, 2002 for the one-year rental of another office complex. This second rental extends from May 1, 2002 to April 30, 2003. Assume that unearned rent revenue is zero on January 1, 2001.

a. Prepare the journal entries for these transactions in 2001 and 2002.

b. How much rent revenue is there in 2001 and 2002?

c. What is the balance of unearned rent revenue on December 31, 2001 and 2002?

d. Show how cash from rentals is computed from rent revenue and unearned rent revenue in 2001 and 2002.

6. Jerrod Zipparo starts a family-run business on January 1, 2001. During 2001 Zipparo Consulting pays $25,000 in federal income taxes. At the end of the year, it estimates that it will have to pay an additional $8,000 in federal income taxes; this payment is made in 2002. During 2002 the firm also pays $32,000 in taxes on 2002 earnings. At the end of 2002, Zipparo Consulting estimates that it will have to pay an additional $10,000 in federal income taxes, payment to be made in 2003.

a. Prepare the journal entries for these transactions in 2001 and 2002.

b. How much income tax expense is there in 2001 and 2002?

c. What is the balance of income taxes payable on December 31, 2001 and 2002?

d. Show how cash payments for taxes is computed from income tax expense and income taxes payable in 2001 and 2002.

7. Stephanie Sanderson, Inc. opens for business on May 1, 2001. On this date, a one-year insurance policy is obtained for $12,000. On May 1, 2002 the policy is renewed for one year at a cost of $18,000.

a. Prepare the journal entries for these transactions in 2001 and 2002.

b. How much insurance expense is there in 2001 and 2002?

c. What is the balance of prepaid insurance on December 31, 2001 and 2002?

d. Show how cash payments for insurance is computed from insurance expense and prepaid insurance expense in 2001 and 2002.

8. Jeff Russell Company has the following account balances at December 31:

	2001	*2002*	*2003*
Merchandise inventory	$10,000	$13,000	$19,000
Accounts payable	4,000	29,000	23,000
Cost of goods sold	50,000	55,000	60,000

Compute the cash paid for inventory in 2002 and 2003. Why can't cash paid for inventory in 2001 be determined?

9. For the following independent cases, compute the unknown amounts. Assume that there are no purchase discounts. Then verify the formula: cash for inventory equals cost of goods sold plus the increase in inventory minus the decrease in accounts payable.

Beginning Inventory	*Ending Inventory*	*Increase in Inventory*	*Beginning Accounts Payable*	*Ending Accounts Payable*	*Increase in Accounts Payable*
a. $19,000	$22,000	$?	$15,000	$16,000	$?
b. 10,000	?	2,000	?	21,000	4,000
c. ?	14,000	?	21,000	?	4,000
d. 9,000	?	4,000	?	17,000	?
e. 11,000	?	?	24,000	?	?

Cash Purchases	*Credit Purchases*	*Total Purchases*	*Payment on Accounts Payable*	*Cost of Goods Sold*	*Cash payments for inventory*
a. $ 5,000	$90,000	$?	$?	$?	$?
b. 8,000	?	105,000	?	?	?
c. ?	96,000	100,000	?	101,000	?
d. 10,000	?	103,000	?	?	100,000
e. ?	?	90,000	104,000	95,000	107,000

10. Jessica Martinez and Company is a broadcasting corporation. From the data gathered below, create the cash-from-investing-activities section of the cash flow statement for this firm.

Purchase of land	$100,000	Depreciation expense	$27,000
Construction of a building	200,000	Proceeds from sell of equipment	18,000
Purchase of inventory	110,000	Cash dividends	5,000

11. Dev Desai, Ltd. sells for cash two assets, a building and some equipment. The building has a cost of $250,000, accumulated depreciation of $100,000, and is sold for a gain of $50,000. The equipment has a cost of $90,000, accumulated depreciation of $60,000, and is sold for a loss of $17,000.

(a) Prepare the journal entries for these two transactions.

(b) What are the effects from these transactions on the income statement?

(c) What are the effects from these transactions on the cash flow statement?

12. ZYX Inc. manufactures cosmetics. From the data below, prepare the cash-from-financing-activities section of the cash flow statement for ZYX Inc.

Borrow money with a mortgage	$800,000	Pay interest on the mortgage	$ 80,000
Issue common stock	300,000	Redeem (i.e., buy back) bonds payable	200,000
Pay dividends	25,000		

PROBLEMS

1. Oneoaka Hendricks, Inc. manufactures cosmetics. Using the following list of cash flows, compose the cash flow statement for the year ended December 31, 2005, direct method, for Oneoaka Hendricks, Inc.

Cash dividends	$ 4,000	Purchase of land	$20,000
Collections from customers	100,000	Sale of equipment	3,000
Construction of buildings	60,000	Sale of investments	1,000
Issuance of notes payable	23,000		
Issuance of preferred stock	45,000		
Payments for interest	2,000		
Payments for other operating expenses	11,000		
Payments to employees	24,000		
Payments to suppliers	45,000		
Purchase of equipment	6,000		

2. Lisa Myers and Company sells water beds. Using the following data, create the cash flow statement for the year ended March 15, 2007, indirect method, for Lisa Myers and Company.

Decrease in accounts payable	$ 9,000	Purchase of furniture and fixtures	$35,000
Decrease in accrued liabilities	10,000	Purchase of truck	19,000
Depreciation expense	6,000	Retirement of long-term debt	9,000
Gain on sale of investments	2,000	Sale of investments	27,000
Increase in accounts receivable	12,000		
Increase in inventory	22,000		
Issuance of long-term notes payable	28,000		
Issuance of short-term notes payable	17,000		
Net income	100,000		
Payment of dividends	8,000		

3. Carol Reitz Enterprises owns and operates several radio stations. The income statement and the cash flow statement (indirect method) for 2002 are

Carol Reitz Enterprises
Income Statement
For the year ended December 31, 2002

Sales		$65,000
Cost of goods sold	$25,000	
Wages expense	13,000	
Insurance expense	1,000	
Depreciation expense	6,000	45,000
Operating income		$20,000
Gain on sale of equipment		4,000
Net income		$24,000

Carol Reitz Enterprises
Cash Flow Statement (indirect method)
For the year ended December 31, 2002

Cash from operating activities		
Net income	$24,000	
Depreciation	6,000	
Gain on sale of equipment	(4,000)	
Increase in accounts receivable	(5,000)	
Decrease in inventory	1,000	
Increase in prepaid insurance	(1,000)	
Increase in accounts payable	2,000	
Increase in wages payable	1,000	
Cash from operating activities		$24,000
Cash from investing activities		
Sale of equipment	$ 3,000	
Purchase of land	(10,000)	
Purchase of building	(25,000)	
Cash from investing activities		(32,000)
Cash from financing activities		
Issuance of common stock	$26,000	
Dividends	(5,000)	
Cash from financing activities		21,000
Net increase in cash		$13,000

Required: Prepare the cash flow statement for Carol Reitz Enterprises with the direct method.

4. Leon Lyday, Inc. merchandises Spanish clothing. The income statement and the cash flow statement (direct method) for 2003 are

Leon Lyday, Inc.
Income Statement
For the year ended December 31, 2003

Sales		$80,000
Cost of goods sold	$37,000	
Wages expense	14,000	
Depreciation expense	3,000	
Interest expense	2,000	
Loss on sale of equipment	5,000	61,000
Income before taxes		$19,000
Income taxes		9,000
Net income		$10,000

Leon Lyday, Inc.
Cash Flow Statement (direct method)
For the year ended December 31, 2003

Cash from operating activities		
Collected from customers	$76,000	
Paid for inventory	(34,000)	
Paid for wages	(15,000)	
Paid for interest	(2,000)	
Paid for taxes	(4,000)	
Cash from operating activities		$21,000
Cash from investing activities		
Sale of equipment	$10,000	
Purchase of land	(8,000)	
Purchase of building	(19,000)	
Cash from investing activities		(17,000)
Cash from financing activities		
Proceeds from mortgage payable	$11,000	
Dividends	(6,000)	
Cash from financing activities		5,000
Net increase in cash		$ 9,000

Other data: Inventory increased by $3,000 from 2002 to 2003.

Required: Prepare the cash flow statement for Leon Lyday, Inc. with the indirect method.

5. Cisco owns her own horse stable. The income statement and the comparative balance sheet for Cisco are as follows.

Cisco Horse Stables
Income Statement
For the year ended June 30, 2001

Boarding and teaching revenues		$165,000
Wages expense	$60,000	
Supplies expense	40,000	
Insurance expense	10,000	
Depreciation	10,000	
Taxes	15,000	135,000
Net income		$ 30,000

Cisco Horse Stables
Balance Sheets
June 30, 2000 and 2001

	2000	*2001*
Cash	$20,000	$ 25,000
Accounts receivable	10,000	5,000
Supplies	5,000	10,000
Prepaid insurance	1,000	2,000
Barn	50,000	50,000
Accumulated depreciation	(30,000)	(40,000)
Horses	40,000	60,000
Total assets	$96,000	$112,000
Wages payable	$ 1,000	$ 2,000
Taxes payable	1,000	3,000
Cisco, capital	94,000	107,000
Total equities	$96,000	$112,000

Required:

(a) Prepare a cash flow statement using the indirect method.

(b) Prepare a cash flow statement using the direct method.

6. Jean Prior, Inc. buys coal mining supplies and equipment from manufacturers and sells them to coal mining companies. The income statement and the comparative balance sheets for Jean Prior, Inc. are as follows.

Jean Prior, Inc.
Income Statement
For the year ended December 31, 2005

Sales		$200,000
Cost of goods sold		75,000
Gross margin		$125,000
Operating expenses:		
Wages	$20,000	
Utilities	6,000	
Depreciation	5,000	
Advertising	3,000	
Freight out	2,000	36,000
Operating income		$ 89,000
Interest expense		7,000
Income before taxes		$ 82,000
Taxes		34,000
Net income		$ 48,000

Jean Prior, Inc.
Balance Sheets
December 31, 2004 and 2005

	2004	2005
Cash	$ 5,000	$ 7,000
Accounts receivable	10,000	12,000
Inventory	20,000	26,000
Prepaid advertising	2,000	1,000
Current assets	$ 37,000	$ 46,000
Land	$100,000	$120,000
Building	150,000	200,000
Accumulated depreciation	(60,000)	(65,000)
Property plant equipment	$190,000	$255,000
Total assets	$227,000	$301,000
Accounts payable	$ 8,000	$ 13,000
Wages payable	2,000	4,000
Current liabilities	$ 10,000	$ 17,000
Long-term notes payable	$ 40,000	$ 59,000
Mortgage payable	95,000	103,000
Long-term liabilities	$135,000	$162,000
Total liabilities	$145,000	$179,000
Common stock (no par)	$ 51,000	$ 51,000
Retained earnings	31,000	71,000
Stockholders' equity	$ 82,000	$122,000
Total equities	$227,000	$301,000

Required:

(a) Prepare a cash flow statement using the indirect method.

(b) Prepare a cash flow statement using the direct method.

7. Hot-to-Trot paid dividends of $4,000 in 2002. Its comparative balance sheets on December 31, 2001 and 2002 are:

Hot-to-Trot
Comparative Balance Sheets
December 31, 2001 and 2002

Assets

	2001	*2002*
Cash	50,000	30,000
Accounts receivable	15,000	13,000
Inventory	22,000	16,000
Prepaid expenses	2,000	2,500
Equipment	80,000	85,000
Accumulated depreciation	(10,000)	(12,500)
Total assets	159,000	134,000

Liabilities and Stockholders' Equity

Accounts payable	24,000	27,000
Income taxes payable	2,500	4,000
Mortgage payable	10,000	15,000
Common stock	80,000	80,000
Retained earnings	42,500	8,000
Total liabilities and stockholders' equity	159,000	134,000

Required:

(a) No equipment is sold in 2002. Prepare a cash flow statement for 2002.

(b) Suppose that the years 2001 and 2002 are reversed. Dividends of $4,000 are paid in 2002, and the firm sells equipment with a cost of $10,000 and accumulated depreciation of $4,000 for a gain of $2,500. Given these new assumptions, prepare the cash flow statement in 2002.

8. After much thought, Randy Riesterer and Valerie Spooner pool their resources and start a company they call Bodies-R-Us. Its main business is to sell parts and supplies and paints to those in the tattooing industry. The income statement and comparative balance sheets of Bodies-R-Us are as follows.

Bodies-R-Us
Income Statement
For the year ended December 31, 2008

Sales		$219,000
Cost of goods sold		78,000
Gross profit		$141,000
Operating expenses:		
Wages	$57,000	
Rent	18,000	
Depreciation	10,000	
Patent amortization	9,000	94,000
Operating income		$ 47,000
Nonoperating items:		
Gain on sale of trading securities	$13,000	
Loss on sale of available-for-sale securities	(1,000)	
Gain on sale of building	20,000	
Interest expense	(11,000)	21,000
Income before taxes		$ 68,000
Taxes		15,000
Net income		$ 53,000

Bodies-R-Us
Balance Sheets
December 31, 2007 and 2008

Assets

	2007	*2008*
Cash	$ 20,000	$ 37,000
Trading securities	10,000	25,000
Accounts receivable	23,000	21,000
Inventory	42,000	51,000
Prepaid rent	31,000	42,000
Current assets	$126,000	$176,000
Land	$100,000	$167,000
Building	310,000	415,000
Accumulated depreciation	(75,000)	(80,000)
Property plant equipment	$335,000	$502,000
Patents	$ 28,000	$ 19,000
Intangible assets	$ 28,000	$ 19,000
Securities available for sale	$ 22,000	$ 29,000
Long-term investments	$ 22,000	$ 29,000
Total assets	$511,000	$726,000

Liabilities and Stockholders' Equity

	2007	2008
Accounts payable	$ 22,000	$ 41,000
Wages payable	5,000	14,000
Interest payable	8,000	9,000
Taxes payable	12,000	8,000
Unearned revenue	9,000	26,000
Current liabilities	$ 56,000	$ 98,000
Bonds payable	$102,000	$131,000
Mortgage payable	129,000	142,000
Long-term liabilities	$231,000	$273,000
Total liabilities	$287,000	$371,000
Common stock	$ 50,000	$ 65,000
Additional paid-in capital	129,000	206,000
Retained earnings	45,000	84,000
Stockholders' equity	$224,000	$355,000
Total equities	$511,000	$726,000

Additional information:

(1) Trading securities with a cost of $5,000 are sold for $18,000. The market value of remaining trading securities is equal to their cost.

(2) Securities available for sale with a cost of $4,000, which were bought on May 8, 2008, are sold for $3,000 on September 28, 2008. The market value of remaining securities available for sale is equal to their cost.

(3) A building, which costs $80,000 and has an accumulated depreciation of $5,000, is sold for a gain of $20,000.

Required:

(a) Prepare a cash flow statement using the indirect method.
(b) Prepare a cash flow statement using the direct method.

CHAPTER 6

FUNDAMENTALS OF ACCOUNTING INFORMATION SYSTEMS

Up to this point we have focused on financial statements and on bookkeeping issues. Chapters 2 and 5 looked at the components of the accounting reports sent to investors and creditors and other users, while Chapters 3 and 4 examined the nuts and bolts of bookkeeping. We have assumed that the accounting staff obtains the necessary data to record journal entries for its events and transactions. It is now time to consider how they gather the data from which they enter the transactions into journals and ledgers and to think about outputs they create in addition to the financial report.

The accounting information system must capture the relevant data about the firm's transactions, categorize them, and store them in such a way that one can retrieve the information and prepare the financial statements of the entity. One obtains these relevant data through source documents. Accountants store the data in files, usually computerized files, and retrieve them from these files. In addition, managers want some reassurances that these data are correct, and so they introduce control mechanisms to increase the reliability of the data. This chapter focuses primarily on obtaining and storing the data; the next chapter considers internal control issues.

Accumulating data takes time and effort. To make this process as efficient as possible, transactions are typically categorized by activities or cycles. We think of the firm as a system, and we divide it into various subsystems and focus on these subsystems. Each of these cycles shares a number of common features, and these characteristics are described in this and the next chapter. Later chapters concentrate on the details of the accounting cycles. After defining these cycles, we discuss their inputs—the input documents—and we examine their outputs—output documents, management reports, and queries.

After reading and studying this chapter, you should be able to:

- Define a system and the components of a system;
- Conceptualize a firm as a system;
- Define an accounting information system;
- Describe an accounting cycle and tell why accountants categorize transactions into accounting cycles;
- Name the major accounting cycles and indicate which transactions they deal with;
- Define source document, input document, output document, management report, and query;
- Explain the nature of transactions processing;
- Give examples of input documents and output documents and management reports;
- Distinguish characters, fields, records, files, and databases;
- Name and discuss the six types of accounting files; and
- Describe how to process a file.

THE FIRM AS A SYSTEM

Accounting information systems deal with the flow of information within a corporation. To gain a basic understanding requires recognition of what accounting, information, and systems are. Since we have already looked at what is accounting and what is information, let's begin with systems and later tie them together.

Systems Terminology

A *system* is a set of interacting or interdependent items that form a whole. The human body is a system, for it has various parts that work together, and they form a unit that we call a person. The general schema of a system is shown in Exhibit 6.1. Some other examples of systems are flowers, televisions, computers, and universities. Shortly, we will conceptualize the firm in terms of a system. A *subsystem* is some part of a system that is itself a system. Some subsystems of the human body are the circulatory system and the respiratory system.

The *environment* is everything outside of a system, though discussion frequently is limited to that part of the environment that affects and is affected by the system. The environment of the human body includes other humans, food, houses, cars, pets, light, bacteria, and viruses. It also embraces the planet Pluto, but since Pluto has very little impact on any human body (at least until interplanetary travel is a reality), we typically exclude it from any description of the human body and its environment.

The *boundary* is what divides a system from its environment. Skin and hair separate a body from its environment, and so they form the boundary of the human body.

A system has exchanges with its environment. Two important classes of exchanges are inputs and outputs. An *input* is what a system receives from its environment, whereas an *output* is what is sent from a system to its environment. Inputs of the human body include food, water, light, bacteria, and viruses. Outputs of the human body include sweat and speech. A special type of output is called *feedback* because it, in whole or in part, is directed back to the system as input. Speech is an example of feedback since a person can hear what he or she has uttered.

EXHIBIT *6.1*

SCHEMA OF A SYSTEM

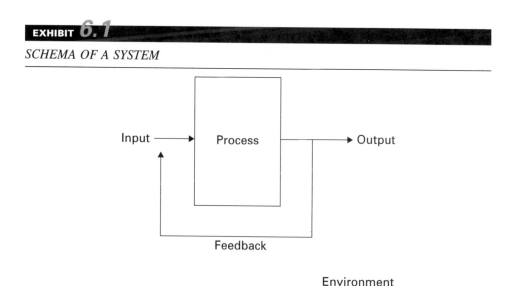

If a person jogs, his or her body will convert water in the body into sweat. We refer to this conversion as a process. In other words, a *process* (or *transformation*) is the changing of a set of inputs into a set of outputs. Another process occurs when a person catches a cold. As the cold virus enters a human, the body responds by creating antibodies to fight the virus, and the body sneezes and coughs and spits out phlegm. As shown in Exhibit 6.1, inputs from the environment enter the system and are processed by it, and then the system exports outputs into the environment.

This discussion, though fairly abstract, helps us because it gives us a vocabulary when talking about systems. We employ this vocabulary as we picture a firm as a system.

Firms Are Systems

Businesses may be conceived as systems, as depicted in Exhibit 6.2, because they have various parts such as marketing and purchasing departments, and these elements work together to form a whole.

The boundary is where the firm engages in exchanges with its environment. Inputs include capital or money from investors and creditors, labor (those who produce the firm's product), management (those who administer or manage the operations of the firm), materials and supplies (inventory), producer goods (buildings, computers, and furniture), and services (painting and legal services). Some outputs are consumer goods and services (what is sold to the customers of the corporation), dividends, interest, salaries, taxes, and wages.

EXHIBIT 6.2

THE FIRM AS A SYSTEM

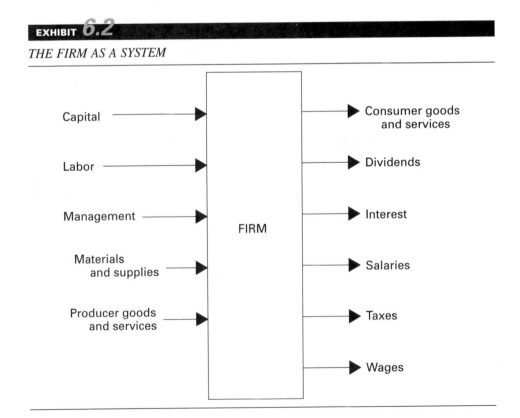

The environment also includes some other parties with which the corporation might interact in the future. Potential customers exist, and the firm would like to sell them goods or services. Other vendors or suppliers exist from whom the company might buy their goods or services. Competitors with whom the firm competes are in the environment, and it is usually good for managers to observe what they are doing. From an accounting viewpoint, we will not concern ourselves much with these other parties, though good managers must maintain a panoramic view as they steer the firm toward its goals. (As accountants expand their services to include assisting managers, they, too, will adopt a broader vision.)

Often, it is more convenient to think of the actors (or players or members) of the environment who interact with the corporation. These actors include customers, vendors or suppliers, investors, creditors, workers, and government agencies. A pictorial for this arrangement is given in Exhibit 6.3. The difference between Exhibit 6.2 and Exhibit 6.3 is that Exhibit 6.2 focuses on the inputs and outputs (thus, it is called an *input-process-output* or *IPO model*) and ignores who is generating the inputs or receiving the outputs, while Exhibit 6.3 does precisely the opposite. The type of diagram in Exhibit 6.3 will be termed the *actors model*.

These actors in the environment both generate inputs and receive outputs. Customers buy goods and services from the firm and pay cash to the company. Vendors ship goods and services to the firm for cash. Workers provide labor services to the corporation in exchange for money. Creditors and investors provide capital to the firm in an effort to earn interest and dividends. Governments provide stability and domestic tranquility and charge for these services via taxes.

Unless the firm is very small, it will partition itself into departments that will focus on one set of these members of the environment. In other words, the system divides into several subsystems. For example, marketing departments are created to deal with customers and attempt to maximize the firm's sales; purchasing departments are organized to interact with vendors; and payroll departments are established to handle wages and salaries. These departments form subsystems of the firm.

Sometimes the processes of the system as well as the other items are exhibited in the diagram. One might include the departments and show the customers interacting with the marketing department and the workers interacting with human resources.

EXHIBIT 6.3

INTERACTIONS OF THE FIRM WITH SIGNIFICANT OTHERS

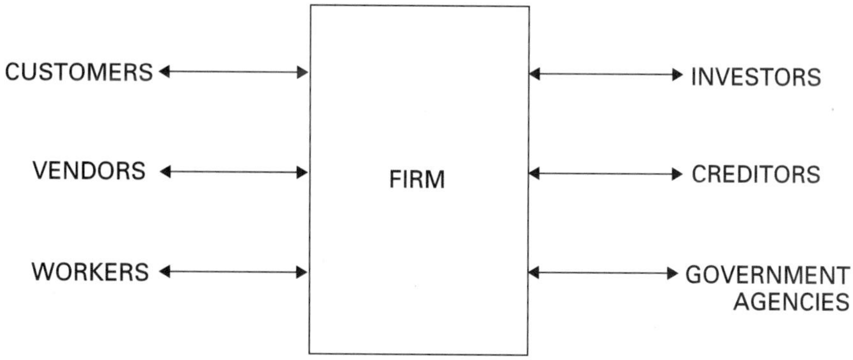

Accounting Information Systems

Accounting departments oversee and direct informational items. In particular, accounting observes the exchanges of the corporation—transactions with customers, vendors, workers, creditors, investors, government agencies, and others—and records the financial effects of the exchanges. Except to provide information to investors, creditors, and governments, accountants typically do not interact with those conducting business with the firm, at least not in their capacity as accountants.

An *accounting information system (AIS)* is a subsystem of a firm that captures financial and other data to process them into financial statements and other reports. The AIS does not have to limit itself to transactions, although this textbook will focus on transactions and transactions processing. In other words, accountants examine the exchanges between the corporate system and its environment, and they record these exchanges in financial terms. Since these data frequently do not convey information because they are too detailed and too limited, the AIS processes the data in order to produce reports informative to management and to investors and creditors.

As discussed later, the data gathering is accomplished with source documents. Data processing is along the lines discussed in Chapters 3 and 4. Then the AIS creates financial statements, output documents, management reports, and queries.

ACCOUNTING CYCLES

The most effective and efficient way of running an accounting information system is by organizing its components or subsystems around certain types of repetitive transactions. These groups of related transactions are called *accounting cycles* or *transaction cycles*. (Unfortunately, this is a second application of the phrase "accounting cycle," the first one discussed in Chapters 3 and 4 and referring to the bookkeeping steps in transactions processing. The context usually indicates which usage is meant.)

Although different companies have different transactions, one common set of cycles is shown in Exhibit 6.4. There are eight accounting cycles:

1. The expenditure cycle
2. The facilities cycle
3. The financing cycle
4. The general ledger cycle
5. The investments cycle
6. The payroll cycle
7. The production cycle
8. The revenue cycle

The general ledger and production cycles generally manage data for internal transactions (e.g., closing entries and transferring costs from resources to work-in-process inventory to finished goods inventory). All of the other cycles concentrate on external transactions engaged in by the corporation. The firm itself is usually organized into departments, and these departments often (though by no means always) will interact with certain groups in the environment. As we define these cycles, be sure to understand which transactions each cycle focuses on, who in the corporate environment interacts with the firm (except for the

EXHIBIT 6.4

ACCOUNTING CYCLES

Cycle	Transactions	Contacts in Environment	Departments
Expenditure cycle	Buy inventory Pay bills	Vendors	Purchasing Accounts payable Cash payments
Facilities cycle	Purchase equipment Purchase buildings	Producers of capital goods	Facilities
Financing cycle	Borrow funds Issue stock	Lenders Investors	Treasury
General ledger cycle	Miscellaneous	—	Accounting (general ledger)
Investments cycle	Buy stocks and bonds	Brokers	Treasury
Payroll cycle	Pay wages	Employees	Payroll
Production cycle	Make finished goods inventory	—	Production
Revenue cycle	Sell goods Collect money	Customers	Marketing Accounts receivable Cash receipts

general ledger and production cycles), and which department of the company is usually responsible for these activities. We present them in the order that they will be covered in this text.

The *general ledger cycle* is the accounting cycle dealing with miscellaneous transactions and the preparation of financial reports. As such, it handles all recording activities that are not the responsibility of any of the other transaction cycles. Such miscellaneous items include adjusting and closing entries. Some companies do not have very many transactions in some cycle, such as the facilities cycle. Consequently, they dispense with the cycle, and any such transactions come under the purview of the general ledger cycle. In addition, this cycle maintains the general ledger, so the other cycles must feed accounting data into this cycle, such as the updated balance of the accounts. This cycle also prepares and distributes the financial accounting statements. Most of the work in this cycle is internal, and so this cycle doesn't interact with players in the environment. Obviously, this work is primarily bookkeeping, so it falls to the accounting department.

The *revenue cycle* is the accounting cycle dealing with selling goods and services to customers and collecting the money. Sometimes this cycle is divided into two cycles: the *sales cycle*, which focuses on the selling activity, and the *cash receipts cycle*, which centers on the collection of the accounts receivable. Attention is placed on customers who buy the goods and services of the firm. The marketing department deals with sales, the accounts receivable department addresses whether to extend credit to the customer and keeps track of what is owed to the firm, and the cash receipts department handles the collection activities.

The *expenditure cycle* is the transaction cycle dealing with the purchase of goods and services and paying for them. Like the revenue cycle, this cycle is sometimes sorted into two cycles. The *purchases cycle* concentrates on the purchase of goods and services, whereas the *cash payments cycle* (or cash disbursements cycle) manages the disbursement of cash to the suppliers. In this cycle, the firm interacts with the vendors of the corporation. The purchasing department is responsible for ordering the goods and services from the vendors, the accounts payable department monitors how much is owed to each vendor, and the cash payments department oversees the actual cash disbursements to the vendors.

The *payroll cycle* is the transaction cycle dealing with the payment of wages and salaries to employees of the firm. In addition to wages and salaries, this cycle also monitors employee benefits such as health and retirement plans. In this cycle the payroll department of the firm interacts with the employees.

The *facilities cycle* is the accounting cycle dealing with the acquisition of property, plant, and equipment. Long-term rentals, or leases, are included in this cycle. The facilities department of the firm interacts with the owners of the property or the producers of the buildings and equipment.

Sometimes the company has excess cash that can be invested to earn more profits. The *investments cycle* is the accounting cycle dealing with buying stocks and bonds of other organizations. The treasury department handles the money of the firm, so it is the primary department involved in the investments cycle. The company buys and sells these securities from brokers and, sometimes, directly from the current owners of the stocks and bonds.

From time to time, the corporation is in short supply of cash and needs to obtain funds. These transactions fall under the financing cycle. The *financing cycle* is the accounting cycle dealing with obtaining money by borrowing funds or issuing stock. The treasury department is responsible for these activities, and it interacts with lenders and investors and their agents.

Manufacturing concerns have an additional cycle, referred to as the production cycle. The *production cycle* is the accounting cycle dealing with the production of finished goods inventory. The production department gathers the raw materials and labor and incurs overhead to produce the products of the firm. These costs are summarized as work-in-process inventory. When the production process is completed, the costs are transferred into finished goods inventory. When the goods are sold, then the costs are transferred into cost of goods sold. (This activity belongs to the revenue cycle.) The work in this cycle is mostly internal, and so this cycle doesn't interact directly with players in the environment. Indirectly, the department interacts with customers, since the finished goods are made for them.

Later chapters describe each of these accounting cycles in detail. The rest of this chapter, as well as the next chapter, discusses features common to all accounting cycles.

TRANSACTIONS PROCESSING: CONVERTING DATA INTO INFORMATION

As explained in Chapters 1 and 3, bookkeepers look at transactions—exchanges, nonreciprocal transfers, events, and allocations—and gather data about these transactions, often measuring the effects in financial terms. We have taken great pains to point out that these data are not valued in their own right, for managers are not helped by such minutia. Accountants utilize transactions processing so that the financial data can be converted into information that managers need to make rational decisions. That part of an AIS that is based primarily on transactions processing is referred to as a *transactions processing system* (TPS). (AISs that are not based on transactions include decision support systems and expert systems; these topics are beyond the scope of this book.)

Transactions Processing System

Exhibit 6.5 details the basics of transactions processing. Earlier versions of this graphic are contained in Chapters 1 and 3. We amend this exhibit (for the last time!) to make two important points. First, accountants obtain the data about the transactions from source documents. A *source document* is a document that captures transaction data. There are two types of source documents: input documents and output documents. *Input documents* trigger transactions processing, whereas *output documents* are produced after transactions processing. In manual systems, source documents are papers; in computerized systems, source documents are often in electronic form. Source documents provide evidence of a transaction and give details about the transaction. The distinction between input documents and output documents is sometimes fuzzy because some output documents later become input documents. It isn't so critical to distinguish between input and output documents. The key point is that source documents are created to prove that the transactions are legitimate and to capture the data necessary to record the transactions.

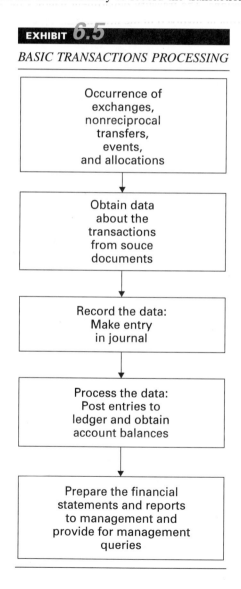

EXHIBIT *6.5*

BASIC TRANSACTIONS PROCESSING

Occurrence of
exchanges,
nonreciprocal
transfers,
events,
and allocations

Obtain data
about the
transactions
from souce
documents

Record the data:
Make entry
in journal

Process the data:
Post entries to
ledger and obtain
account balances

Prepare the financial
statements and reports
to management and
provide for management
queries

Second, managers desire some information about various details not given in the financial statements, and so the AIS is designed to provide this information as well. For example, a manager might like to compare the sales of different products to see which products are generating profits and which are duds or to see how the different sales representatives are performing. The income statement that goes to the public reveals only the aggregate data, but these data are too broad to help answer these issues. The AIS can be designed in such a way that reports are produced that will tell how much profit each product is bringing in and how well each sales representative is doing. These reports are statements or schedules produced by an accounting information system to convey information to management, referred to as *management reports*, and they can be produced weekly, monthly, or as often as is desired.

Related to this point, computerized information systems are being created that give managers the ability to ask ad hoc questions whenever they wish. These questions asked by a manager and addressed to an accounting information system are termed *queries*. The ability to query the system is a powerful tool that helps managers make better decisions.

Thus, the transactions processing system begins with some transaction, the details of which are captured by a source document. Accountants employ the data from these source documents to record the transaction. The TPS processes the data, for example, by posting the entries to the various accounts. The TPS then generates the financial statements and whatever management reports are needed, and it allows managers the ability to query the system.

The TPS also creates output documents that are sent to actors in the environment. Output documents, generated after transactions processing, do such things as authorize the actor to perform some action, or request payment from the actor, or serve as evidence of some transaction.

Input documents trigger transactions processing by some cycle. The processing consists of posting to subsidiary ledgers and the general ledger and other activities to generate the outputs. It also incorporates storage and maintenance of the data. Outputs include financial statements, output documents, management reports, and queries.

Input and Output Documents

To make this discussion more concrete, let's examine some documents. Examples of source documents are tabulated in Exhibit 6.6; more specifically, panel A enumerates some input documents and panel B catalogs some output documents. This listing is certainly not complete and does not include all accounting cycles, but enough examples are given to illustrate the points mentioned above.

From the sales cycle, three examples of input and output documents are customer orders, invoices, and bills of lading. Customer orders (often customer purchase orders) authorize a firm's sale, and they contain the details about what goods are requested by the customer and the quantities of each good. After the company decides to make this sale, it generates an invoice and a bill of lading. An invoice is a bill. This bill lists the price per unit, the quantity, the price per good (price per unit times the quantity sold), the price of all goods (summing up the prices per good), taxes, and shipping and handling charges. The bill of lading gives the shipping instructions, such as the address where to deliver the goods and how to send the goods to the customer (truck, airplane, or whatever).

Two examples of input documents from the cash receipts cycle are the customer check and the remittance advice. When a customer pays its bill, it sends the check to the firm along with the remittance advice. The remittance advice tells who is sending the money so that the customer's accounts receivable account will be properly reduced. An

EXHIBIT *6.6*

EXAMPLES OF SOURCE DOCUMENTS

Panel A: Input Documents

Cycle	Input Document	Purpose
Sales	Customer order	Authorizes a sale to the customer
Cash receipts	Customer check	Provides payment
	Remittance advice	Indicates who is paying the bill
Purchases	Purchase requisition	Requests a purchase from a vendor
Cash payments	Vendor invoice	Requests payment from vendor
Payroll	Time card	Gives proof of work
Production	Production order	Authorizes a work department to make some good

Panel B: Output Documents

Cycle	Output Document	Purpose
Sales	Invoice	Requests payment from the customer
	Bill of lading	Gives shipping instructions
Cash receipts	Deposit slip	Proves that the funds are deposited in the bank
Purchases	Purchase order	Authorizes a purchase from a vendor
Cash payments	Check	Gives proof of payment
Payroll	Payroll check	Gives proof of payment

output document in this cycle is the deposit slip. It provides evidence that the money received from the customers was placed in a company account at the bank.

The purchases cycle is in many ways the mirror image of the sales cycle. An input document in this cycle is the purchase requisition. This document asks the purchasing department to acquire some good or service. If the request is approved, then the purchasing department creates an output document called a purchase order. The purchase order authorizes the purchase of some goods from a supplier. It tells which goods the firm desires to purchase and the quantities purchased.

An input document in the cash disbursements cycle is the vendor invoice. The vendor invoice is a bill from the supplier that requests payment from the firm. Assuming that the vendor invoice is correct, the firm will pay the supplier with a check. The check not only pays the bill, but also acts as proof of payment. Obviously, it indicates to whom the money is paid and how much the payment is. Sometimes a memorandum gives other data, such as which invoice is being paid.

The reader should observe the following naming convention. If the document is initiated by our firm, call it simply what it is, such as invoice or purchase order. If the document originates with somebody in the environment, name them as well as the document, such as vendor invoice or customer purchase order. Thus, an invoice is prepared by our company and sent to one of our customers, whereas a vendor invoice is created by a supplier and it requests payment from us to them.

The payroll cycle has several documents, one of which is the time card. The time card gives the hours worked by a particular employee, and it is signed by a supervisor to vouch that the employee actually worked those hours. The time card thus acts as evidence that the worker performed service for the corporation, and it provides data for figuring how much his or her wages are. Once approved and processed, the firm pays the worker with a check. These payroll checks not only pay the employees for their work, but also serve as evidence that the payments were made.

Our last example comes from the production cycle. One input document is the production order, and it serves primarily as authorization to commence production. For example, the production order might indicate that a certain department is to produce 1,000 microwave ovens. Once the shop floor supervisor receives a production order, he or she obtains the raw materials and initiates the production process.

As stated earlier, these and other documents provide evidence of a transaction and they give details about the transaction. Often they authorize a person in the company to take certain actions, such as sending goods to a customer, or to make a payment to a vendor. Moreover, the details should be sufficient so that the proper journal entry can be made.

Management Reports

In addition to output documents, financial statements, management reports, and queries constitute the outputs of a transactions processing system. We have adequately traveled the road of financial statements in earlier chapters of this text, so nothing needs to be added to those comments. We will provide an example of a query after presenting several accounting files and discussing file processing.

It would be helpful, however, to consider management reports in more depth, so let's consider some examples of management reports. A listing is supplied in Exhibit 6.7. As with the input and output documents, this set is not complete and does not include all accounting cycles, but enough examples are given to illustrate the main points.

Three examples are shown for the sales cycle, namely, a sales analysis report, a back order report, and a sales returns and allowances report. A sales analysis report breaks down sales activity by whatever factor management deems important to influence sales. These variables might include product line, region, and salesperson. The report should therefore help managers to see which products are selling well and which are not, where the products are selling well and where they are not, and who is selling the products and who isn't.

EXHIBIT 6.7

EXAMPLES OF MANAGEMENT REPORTS

Cycle	*Management Report*	*Purpose*
Sales	Sales analysis	Analysis of sales made by product, region, and salesperson
	Back orders	List of orders not fulfilled by the firm
	Sales returns and allowances	List of how much the firm incurred in returns and allowances and why
Cash receipts	Aging of accounts receivable	Determination of which accounts are getting overdue
Purchases	Inventory status	Listing of inventory and the quantity held
	Overdue deliveries	Indication of orders made but not received
Cash payments	Purchase discounts lost	Evidence of late payments
Payroll	Labor costs by department	Determination of labor costs and where incurred
Production	Cost analysis	Measurement of product costs

When a customer desires a product that the firm does not have in inventory, then the company back orders the sale. In other words, the product will be shipped to the customer as soon as the firm can send it. The problem is that the customer may not be very patient and will cancel the order and buy the product from a competitor. To stay on top of the issue, managers look at a back order report to see which products are back ordered and for how long. This information also may lead managers to investigate why there are so many back orders or why it takes a long time to fulfill the order.

Sales returns and allowances are a necessary part of the business world, but firms like to keep them to a minimum. It costs money and takes time and effort to deal with sales returns and allowances. Managers can receive a report that shows the levels of sales returns and allowances. This informs management about whether these levels are within bounds or whether management needs to take action in dealing with a problem.

Aging of accounts receivable is one report generated in the cash receipts cycle. The idea is to segregate the accounts receivable by age, for example, by organizing them into groups according to how many months they are overdue. The idea is to warn management about problems with the collectibility of accounts receivable and to indicate when credit lines to customers might be stopped.

The purchases cycle has several management reports, including an inventory status report and an overdue deliveries report. The inventory status report registers the various items in inventory and states how many of these items are held in inventory. Obviously, it helps managers assess whether the levels are too high or too low, and it assists in deciding when to buy more inventory.

The overdue deliveries report provides a catalog of items which have been purchased by the entity but which have not yet been received. The report not only lists the items purchased but also includes the vendor's name and the date of purchase. This helps managers to follow up with purchases they have made and to evaluate vendors in terms of their performance and reliability. A vendor who is often late with deliveries might be replaced by a supplier that provides better service.

In the cash payments cycle, one report that might interest management is the purchase discounts lost report. In practice, many organizations provide a cash discount, such as 2%, if the bill is paid within a certain time period, such as 10 days. If the bill is not paid within this discount period, then the total amount is due within 30 days. Such an arrangement has an implicit interest rate of about 36%. (How to compute this number is left for Chapter 9.) Since most companies can borrow money at rates significantly below 36%, it is foolish not to take advantage of these cash discount offers. The purchase discounts lost report lists those times when the firm forfeits this cash discount, thereby allowing managers to investigate why the discounts were not taken.

One management report that can be generated within the payroll department is a labor cost report. The costs of wages and salaries can be divided by department (or some other important dimension). This report allows managers to have a better feel about how the labor costs are generated within the company.

The last example is a cost analysis report prepared within the production cycle. The report enumerates each product produced by the firm and shows its cost. The cost can be divided into direct materials, direct labor, and factory overhead components. The report might also give their costs in previous time periods to allow comparisons to be drawn. Such a report assists managers in keeping an eye on production costs.

Some of these reports might contain budgeted numbers. A *budget* is simply a forecast or an estimate of some future outcome. The report might include the actual numbers so that the manager can contrast the budgeted and actual numbers. The difference between the budgeted and actual number is termed the *variance*. This variance is considered favorable if it is good for the company, such as higher actual revenues than predicted or less expenses than forecasted. The cost analysis report, for example, could include budgeted costs, actual costs, and cost variances. The variances could help managers to evaluate the efficiency of the production process.

Note that all of these management reports are statements or schedules produced by an AIS to communicate information to management. Of course, companies tailor the reports to their individual needs. The key factor is to get the AIS to massage data into information that is responsive to the concerns of managers.

ACCOUNTING FILES

Up to this point, we have essentially ignored how accounting data are stored and retrieved. We will continue to omit any discussion of hardware and software (the so-called physical viewpoint), leaving those topics for more advanced accounting and information systems books, but in the rest of this chapter we consider issues of storage and retrieval from a conceptual or logical viewpoint.

The description of journals and ledgers and trial balances and worksheets in Chapters 3 and 4 adopted a manual processing perspective. Not surprisingly, data processing in the real world frequently utilizes computers. A computerized system can be set up either with files or a database, and we will limit our discussion to files. The reader should also acknowledge that learning a manual data processing system is useful because some parts of some firms' data processing is still manual and, more importantly, because manual systems and computerized systems rely on the same accounting terminology and concepts. For example, a balance sheet outputted from a manual system will be the same balance sheet if distributed by a computerized system.

Files and Components of Files

Let's begin with some definitions. A *character* is a unit of data, such as a letter or a numeral. So the name "John Smith" is composed of ten characters—nine letters and one blank space. A *field* is a collection of related characters. The name "John Smith" might be a field denoting a customer of the firm. A *record* is a collection of related fields. Customer name might constitute one record within some file. Other records might join this record to form a file on the customers of the corporation. A *file* is a collection of related records. Finally, a *database* is a collection of related files.

In designing a file, it is common to prepare what is called a record layout. The layout for a given file shows what fields make up any particular record of a file. Exhibit 6.8 presents two examples of record layouts. The first example focuses on the customer master file, a file that lists each customer of the business. Each record yields data about a particular customer. In our example, the fields comprising the record are the customer name, customer number, address, phone number, and credit limit. In the second example, the file is the sales invoice file in which each record gives data pertaining to a particular invoice of the firm. The fields that make up the record are the invoice number, customer number, product number, quantity, price per unit, and total price. (For now we will keep things simple by assuming that the customer buys only one product per invoice.)

Files usually have a field that is designated the key. This *key* uniquely identifies a record within a file. From Exhibit 6.8 one observes that customer number is the key to the customer master file. Customer name would not be used as a key because there may very well be two customers with the name "John Smith." Each individual customer is

EXHIBIT 6.8

EXAMPLES OF A RECORD LAYOUT

Panel A: Customer master file

Customer Name	Customer Number (Key)	Address	Phone Number	Credit Limit
Ed Ketz	101	220 Dorcas Ave. Beckley WV 25801	340-555-4302	$ 2,000
Paul Miller	102	3590 Moonbeam Dr. Colorado Springs CO 80919	079-555-3494	$ 5,000
Rick Telberg	103	2085 Lake Shore Dr. New York NY 10021	212-555-1234	$10,000

Panel B: Sales invoice file

Invoice Number (Key)	Customer Number	Product Number	Quantity	Price Per Unit	Total Price
A601	103	CZ909	10	$ 109.00	$1,090.00
A602	101	GH321	5	$ 44.00	$ 220.00
A603	103	EK604	1	$5,230.00	$5,230.00

therefore given a customer number that differentiates him or her from all other customers. In the second example in Exhibit 6.8, notice that invoice number is the key of the sales invoice file. Also recognize that the customer who is sent the bill is identified by the customer number. To see who the customer is or to find out the address or phone number of the customer, one has to go back to the customer master file.

Types of Files

Accounting information systems can have lots of files. To help understand them, we classify accounting files into six types. These types are defined in Exhibit 6.9, along with examples for each type of file. The six types of accounting files are master, transaction, open, report, history, and reference files.

A *master file* is a file pertaining to subjects within the environment or account balances. Customer master files, vendor master files, and employee master files contain important data about customers, vendors, and employees, respectively. The accounts receivable file, the finished goods inventory file, and the property, plant, and equipment file list the individual accounts receivable, each inventory item, and each piece of property, plant, and equipment, respectively. By summing across the records, the account balances are easily obtained.

A *transaction file* is a file of related transactions, usually within a certain time period such as the current fiscal year. A sales order file lists all the sales orders obtained by the organization. A sales invoice file contains all the invoices sent to the customers of

EXHIBIT 6.9

TYPES OF ACCOUNTING FILES

Type of File	Definition of File	Examples of File
Master	A file pertaining to subjects within the environment or account balances	Customer master file Vendor master file Accounts receivable master file Inventory master file
Transaction	A file of related transactions	Sales order file Cash receipts file Purchase order file Cash disbursements file
Open	A type of transaction file that contains data of incomplete transactions	Open sales invoice file Open purchase order file
Report	A file that creates a financial statement or a management report	Sales analysis report file Labor cost report file
History	A file pertaining to transactions over a period of time	Sales history file Vendor history file
Reference	A file of data that helps update other files or produce financial statements or management reports	Price data file Shipping data file Payroll taxes file

the firm. A cash receipts file gives the cash receipts; the purchase order file registers the purchases by the company; and the cash disbursements file reveals the cash payments by the firm.

An open file is a special type of transaction file; specifically, an *open file* is a type of transaction file that contains data of incomplete transactions. Consider, for example, the situation in which the company has issued invoices to customers, yet has not received their money. The firm certainly wants to monitor this circumstance and be sure that the customer pays off the bill. One way of handling this situation is to use an open sales invoice file, and this file includes only those invoices that have not yet been paid by the customers. An open purchase order file includes only purchase orders for which the firm has not yet received the goods. An open vendor invoice file includes vendor invoices for which the goods have been received but the firm has not paid the bill.

Another type of accounting file is the *report file*, a file that creates a financial statement or a management report. In essence, this file accepts data from other files and manipulates the data in order to print out a financial statement or a management report. Some report files create computer screens so that a user can observe the reports on a computer monitor. Such report files can be made for any of the financial statements and for any of the management reports mentioned earlier in the chapter.

A *history file* is a file pertaining to transactions over a period of time. A sales history file, for example, contains data on all sales activities over the last (say) five years. By analyzing these data, managers might obtain a better sense of what has been accomplished by product line, by sales representatives, by customer, and by region. Another illustration of a history file is the vendor history file. This file could be useful in assessing the time it takes vendors to deliver the ordered goods and whether they shipped the correct goods and the extent to which the corporation has had to send the goods back to the supplier.

The last type of file is called a *reference file*, a file that helps update other files or produce financial statements or management reports. A price data file is like a catalog, for it lists the products offered by the company and their prices. A sales invoice file might access the price data file in order to obtain the price of an item bought by a customer. A shipping data file lists the various means of transporting goods to customers or from vendors and their prices. A payroll taxes file would contain the IRS tables for determining withholding amounts or social security taxes.

As we consider the accounting cycles in detail, we will enumerate the files involved. There will be lots of accounting files, so we will classify them by these six types. Hopefully, this classification scheme can help the reader remember the files and their purposes.

File Processing

Given the pace of the business world, the accounting files will change. Some files, such as the reference files, will change slowly, but transaction files and open files will fluctuate rapidly. The three types of changes to the contents of a file are additions, deletions, and updates. Consider a customer master file. As the company sells to new customers, they will be added to the list of customers. When the firm loses customers, for example, by their declaring bankruptcy, they will be removed from the file. Customers might move from one location to another, or they might change telephone numbers. As these modifications occur, the firm will update the customer master file.

There are two other types of processing, though they do not change the contents of the file. One is sorting, in which the records are put in a particular order, for example, arranged in ascending order of the customer account number. This is done primarily to facilitate other file processing or queries. The last type of processing creates a new file by merging two or more other files. For example, the accountant might possess the accounts receivable master file as of June 21. That file can be merged with the sales invoice file for June 22 and the cash receipts file for June 22 to create an accounts receivable master file as of June 22. In this manner, current values for accounts receivable can be maintained.

Queries

Earlier, we defined queries as questions asked of an AIS. As managers think about the business, various issues will come to mind, and they will want the data to answer these concerns. As an example, see Exhibit 6.10.

Panel A of Exhibit 6.10 gives the records in the sales invoice file. (A real-world file likely would include a number of other fields, but the illustration shows only those fields needed to answer the queries.) For the time period under consideration, only those sales associated with invoice numbers between 2028 and 2036 belong to the period.

Panel B of the exhibit shows two possible queries and the responses from the AIS. A manager might regard the customer with customer number 101 as special for some reason. The manager wanting to know how much this customer bought from the firm can type such a request into the computer, and the AIS will look at the file and respond $12,700.

Another possibility is that the manager would like to find out who is the most successful sales rep during the period. The manager asks who sold the most, and the AIS replies Goldner with sales of $16,700.

This completes the narration of accounting information systems, including an examination of the accounting cycles, of how data are captured from source documents, of the many management reports in addition to the four main financial statements, and of accounting files. These concepts are used extensively later as we explore the accounting cycles in depth.

EXHIBIT **6.10**

EXAMPLE OF QUERIES

Panel A: Sales invoice file

Invoice Number	Customer Number	Sales	Sales Representative
2028	101	$10,000	Smith
2029	104	1,500	Black
2030	102	700	Hope
2031	101	2,000	Weber
2032	109	4,900	Goldner
2033	121	11,100	Goldner
2034	104	500	Smith
2035	131	6,000	Weber
2036	101	700	Goldner

Panel B: Example of Queries

1. What are the dollar sales to customer #101?
   ANS: $12,700

2. Which sales rep had the highest sales?
   ANS: Goldner, who sold $16,700

SIGHTS ALONG THE INTERNET

Two interesting sites to examine are:

World Lecture Hall/ Accounting	www.utexas.edu/world/lecture/acc
XBRL	www.xbrl.org

The first site lists a number of courses on accounting information systems and discusses some basic concepts of AIS. The second describes a site jointly worked on by the AICPA and several other organizations. The purpose of the association is to build a "language" that customizes electronic reports and increases efficiency by reducing data redundancies. Some day it could be the language that firms employ to put their financial reports on the web.

CHAPTER SUMMARY IN TERMS OF LEARNING OBJECTIVES

Define a System and the Components of a System. A system is a set of interacting or interdependent items that form a whole. The environment is everything outside of a system, though the discussion frequently is limited to that part of the environment that affects and is affected by the system. The boundary is what divides a system from its environment. A system has exchanges with its environment: inputs are what are received by a system from its environment, and outputs are what are sent from a system to its environment. A process is the changing of a set of inputs into a set of outputs.

Conceptualize a Firm as a System. Firms can be viewed as systems because they have several interdependent parts, such as marketing and purchasing and production departments, and these elements work as a team. The boundary is where the firm engages in exchanges with its environment. Inputs include capital from investors and creditors, labor, management, materials and supplies, and producer goods and services. Outputs include consumer goods and services, dividends, interest, salaries, taxes, and wages.

Define an Accounting Information System. An accounting information system (AIS) is a subsystem of a firm that captures financial and other data to process them into financial statements and other reports.

Describe an Accounting Cycle and Tell Why Accountants Categorize Transactions into Accounting Cycles. Accounting information systems are typically organized around certain types of repetitive transactions, which are termed accounting cycles. Such an organization leads to effective and efficient accounting information systems.

Name the Major Accounting Cycles and Indicate Which Transactions They Deal With. There are eight major accounting cycles. (1) The general ledger cycle deals with miscellaneous transactions and the preparation of financial reports. (2) The revenue cycle is the accounting cycle that gathers data about selling goods and services to customers and collecting the money. Sometimes this cycle is divided into two cycles: the sales cycle, which focuses on the selling activity; and the cash receipts cycle, which centers on the collection of the accounts receivable. (3) The expenditure cycle converges on the purchase of goods and services and paying for them. It is sometimes divided into two cycles: the purchases cycle, which concentrates on the purchase of goods and services, and the cash payments cycle, which handles the disbursement of cash to the suppliers. (4) The payroll cycle converges on the payment of wages and salaries to employees of the firm. (5) The facilities cycle deals with the acquisition of property, plant, and equipment. (6) The investments cycle is the accounting cycle emphasizing the buying of stocks and bonds of other organizations. (7) The financing cycle is the accounting cycle dealing with obtaining money by borrowing funds or issuing stock. (8) The production cycle accents the production of finished goods inventory.

Define Source Document, Input Document, Output Document, Management Report, and Query. A source document is a document that captures transaction data. There are two types of source documents: input and output documents. Input documents trigger transactions processing. An output document is a document generated after transactions processing. Input documents and output documents provide evidence of a transaction and give details about the transaction.

Statements or schedules produced by an accounting information system to convey information to management are called management reports. The reports are designed to give managers information about certain aspects of the firm on a periodic basis.

Queries are questions asked by a manager and addressed to an accounting information system. The ability to query the system is a powerful and flexible tool that helps managers make better decisions.

Explain the Nature of Transactions Processing. The transactions processing system begins with some transaction, the details of which are captured by a source document, and is then used to record the transaction. The TPS processes the data. The TPS then generates output documents, the financial statements, and whatever management reports are needed, and it allows managers the ability to query the system.

The inputs of a TPS are the input documents. The outputs are output documents, financial statements, management reports, and queries.

Give Examples of Input Documents and Output Documents and Management Reports. Some input documents are customer orders, customer checks, remittance advices, purchase requisitions, vendor invoices, time cards, and production orders. Illustrations of output documents include invoices, bills of lading, deposit slips, purchase orders, and checks. Some management reports are the sales analysis report, the back order report, the sales return and allowances report, the aging of accounts receivable report, the inventory status report, the overdue deliveries report, the purchase discounts lost report, the labor cost report, and the cost analysis report.

Distinguish Characters, Fields, Records, Files, and Databases.   A character is a unit of data, such as a letter or a numeral; a field is a collection of related characters; a record is a collection of related fields; a file is a collection of related records; and a database is a collection of related files.

Name and Discuss the Six Types of Accounting Files.   The six types of accounting files are master files, transaction files, open files, report files, history files, and reference files. (1) A master file is a file pertaining to subjects within the environment or account balances. (2) A transaction file is a file of related transactions, usually within a certain time period. (3) An open file is a type of transaction file that contains data of incomplete transactions. (4) The report file is a file that creates a financial statement or a management report. (5) A history file is a file pertaining to transactions over a period of time. (6) A reference file helps update other files or produce financial statements or management reports.

Describe How to Process a File.   The contents of a file can be modified in three ways: through additions, deletions, and updates. Additions append new records to the file, while deletions reduce the number of records. Updates do not change the number of records; instead, updates change the values of some of the fields of some records within the file.

There are two other types of file processing, and neither changes the contents of the file. Sorting a file places the records into some particular order according to the values of some record. Merging two or more files creates a new file, such as an updated listing.

GLOSSARY

Accounting cycle—a group of related transactions.

Accounting information system (AIS)—a subsystem of a firm that captures financial and other data to process them into financial statements and other reports.

Actors model—a diagram of a system that shows the system and the major players in the environment with which the system interacts.

Boundary—that which divides a system from its environment.

Budget—a forecast of some future outcome.

Cash payments cycle—that portion of the expenditure cycle dealing with the payment of money to vendors.

Cash receipts cycle—that portion of the revenue cycle dealing with collecting money from customers.

Character—a unit of data, such as a letter or a numeral.

Database—a collection of related files.

Environment—everything outside of a system.

Expenditure cycle—the accounting cycle dealing with the purchase of goods and services and paying for them.

Facilities cycle—the accounting cycle dealing with the acquisition of property, plant, and equipment.

Feedback—an output of a system that becomes an input to the same system.

Field—a collection of related characters.

File—a collection of related records.

Financing cycle—the accounting cycle dealing with obtaining money by borrowing funds or issuing stock.

General ledger cycle—the accounting cycle dealing with miscellaneous transactions and the preparation of financial reports.

History file—a file pertaining to transactions over a period of time.

Input—what is received by a system from its environment.

Input document—a document that triggers transactions processing.

Input-process-output (IPO) model—a diagram of a system that shows the system and its major inputs and outputs.

Investments cycle—the accounting cycle dealing with buying stocks and bonds of other organizations.

Key—a field that uniquely identifies a certain record within a file.

Management report—a statement or schedule produced by an accounting information system to convey information to management.

Master file—a file pertaining to subjects within the environment or account balances.

Open file—a type of transaction file that contains data of incomplete transactions.

Output—what is sent from the system to its environment.

Output document—a document produced after transactions processing.

Payroll cycle—the accounting cycle dealing with the payment of wages and salaries to employees of the firm.

Process; also called transformation—the changing of a set of inputs into a set of outputs.

Production cycle—the accounting cycle dealing with the production of finished goods inventory.

Purchases cycle—that portion of the expenditure cycle dealing with the purchase of goods and services.

Query—a question asked by a manager and addressed to an accounting information system.

Record—a collection of related fields.

Reference file—a file that helps update other files or produce financial statements or management reports.

Report file—a file that creates a financial statement or a management report.

Revenue cycle—the accounting cycle dealing with selling goods and services to customers and collecting the money.

Sales cycle—that portion of the revenue cycle dealing with selling goods and services to customers.

Source document—a document that captures transaction data. There are two types of source documents: input and output documents.

Subsystem—a part of a system that is itself a system.

System—a set of interacting or interdependent items that form a whole.

Transaction cycle—accounting cycle.

Transaction file—a file of related transactions.

Transactions processing system (TPS)—the part of an accounting information system that is based primarily on transactions processing.

Transformation—process.

Variance—the difference between a budgeted number and an actual number.

REVIEW QUESTIONS

1. What is a system? What is a subsystem?
2. What is the environment? Why is it important?
3. Define boundary, input, output, feedback, and process.
4. In what sense is a firm a system?
5. What is an accounting information system? How is an AIS a system?
6. When designing an accounting information system, why do accountants focus on accounting cycles?
7. Name the eight major accounting cycles and explain what each of them focuses on.
8. What is a transactions processing system? How is a TPS a system?

9. What is a source document? Why are source documents important?

10. What is an input document? Give some examples of input documents.

11. What is an output document? Why are output documents important?

12. Give some examples of output documents.

13. What is a query?

14. What is a management report? Why are they important?

15. Give some examples of management reports.

16. Define budget and variance.

17. What is a file, and what is its significance?

18. Distinguish character, field, record, file, and database.

19. What is a key, and what is its function?

20. Name and define the six types of accounting files.

21. For each type of accounting file, give an example.

22. Accounting files may be processed in five ways. What are they?

DISCUSSION QUESTIONS

1. How is a university a system? Keep things simple by considering only the teaching mission of the university. Graph the university as a system using (a) the IPO model and (b) the actors model.

2. Flip'n Flop is a greasy hamburger joint that handles cash sales only. List the accounting cycles for Flip'n Flop.

3. Some input documents and some output documents also serve as legal documents. Which documents are the most likely to serve as legal documents? Why?

4. At year-end the accountant prepares the balance sheet and the income statement. One item on the balance sheet is accounts receivable, and one item on the income statement is sales. The accountant places the ending balance of accounts receivable on the balance sheet, while placing the year's total for sales on the income statement.

   The above data come from two files: the sales invoice file and the accounts receivable master file. What difference exists between the files in order to choose the ending balance from one and the year's total for the other?

5. The accounting cycle is the set of steps in transactions processing, and those steps are shown in Exhibit 4.1 in Chapter 4. If the accounting information system is computerized, what steps in the accounting cycle can be automated or eliminated?

EXERCISES

1. Graph a transactions processing system in terms of the IPO model. Utilize the inputs and outputs discussed in this chapter.

2. Kendel's Kennels had the following transactions during the month of January. Determine which accounting cycle processes each of the transactions.

   January 2. Obtained $5,000 from a bank by signing a note.
   January 5. Paid electric bill for $300.
   January 7. Obtained $3,000 worth of dog food on account.
   January 10. Charged customers $20,000 for kenneling services.
   January 14. Paid employees $1,000.
   January 16. Customers paid $16,000 on their accounts.
   January 20. Paid rent of $2,000.
   January 24. Obtained paper supplies on account for $1,000.

January 26. Paid insurance bill of $3,000.
January 28. Paid employees $1,000.
January 30. Kendel withdraws $2,500 for personal use.
January 31. Paid the January 7 bill.

3. February's transactions for Nester's Nostrums are given below. For each of them indicate which accounting cycle is activated.

February 1. Purchased goods for $60,000 on account. A 2% discount is allowed if the bill is paid within 10 days.
February 2. Nester pays the transportation charges of $500.
February 4. Nester sent back $5,000 worth of the goods purchased because they were damaged.
February 5. Nester has cash sales of $6,500.
February 7. The February 1 bill is paid in full.
February 10. Nester has credit sales of $40,000. A 2% discount is allowed if the bill is paid within 10 days.
February 15. Nester purchases $1,000 of trading securities.
February 16. Customers return $3,500 of goods because they have the wrong color.
February 17. Nester has credit sales of $30,000. A 2% discount is allowed if the bill is paid within 10 days.
February 20. Customers pay off their bills from the February 10 sales.
February 25. The securities acquired on the fifteenth are sold for $1,700.
February 28. Operating expenses of $10,000 are paid.

4. Consider the accounting cycles: the general ledger, sales, cash receipts, purchases, cash disbursements, payroll, facilities, investments, financing, and production cycles. List the most common transactions that are contained within each of these accounting cycles.

5. There are three large companies—a service firm, a merchandiser, and a manufacturer. What are the similarities and differences about the accounting cycles that they employ?

6. When a corporation receives a customer order, or when it issues a purchase order, it does not prepare a journal entry.

(a) What is the purpose of the customer order or the purchase order?
(b) What document triggers the recording of the transaction?
(c) Why is the transaction recorded at that point rather than when the customer order is issued or when the firm distributes a purchase order?
(d) What data are contained on a customer order or a purchase order?

7. Consider the following six documents: invoice, bill of lading, remittance advice, vendor invoice, check (written), and time card. Each of them is associated with a transaction that needs recording. For each document, answer the following questions.

(a) What transaction is recorded when the document is generated or received?
(b) What data are required to be contained on the document in order to make the journal entry?
(c) Are other data required when recording the journal entry?

8. A manager could raise the following questions. For each question, name the report that the manager could examine to help answer the question.

(a) Is our firm paying off its short-term debts on a timely basis?
(b) Do we have an excess amount of returns from customers?
(c) How high is factory overhead?
(d) Are sales growing fast enough?
(e) Are vendors sending us our purchases quickly?
(f) How much is the firm paying for overtime?
(g) How many back orders does the company have?
(h) Can I verify that we don't have the inventory to send the customers?
(i) Do we need to adjust the amount of bad debts expense?

9. Stephen Jablonsky is president of Jabo's Gazebos, Inc. He observes that the payroll costs for 2003 are: $80,000 for the art department, $120,000 for the marketing department, and $200,000 for the production department. Mr. Jablonsky wonders whether these numbers are good news or bad news. The budgeted payroll costs are $90,000 for the art department, $145,000 for the marketing department, and $165,000 for the production department. Prepare a report that will help the president to assess the payroll costs for 2003. Does the report completely answer the president's question?

10. Several of the accounting files are essentially computerized versions of some of the special journals or the subsidiary ledgers of a manual system. For each item from a manual system that is listed here, name the accounting file that is its counterpart in a computerized system.

(a) Accounts payable subsidiary ledger   (d) Cash receipts journal

(b) Accounts receivable subsidiary ledger   (e) Purchases journal

(c) Cash disbursements journal   (f) Sales journal

11. For each of the following files, indicate which accounting cycle is involved. Some files are associated with more than one cycle.

(a) Accounts receivable master file   (j) Price data file

(b) Cash disbursements file   (k) Purchase order file

(c) Cash receipts file   (l) Sales analysis file

(d) Customer master file   (m) Sales history file

(e) Inventory master file   (n) Sales order file

(f) Labor cost report file   (o) Shipping data file

(g) Open purchase order file   (p) Vendor history file

(h) Open sales invoice file   (q) Vendor master file

(i) Payroll taxes file

PROBLEMS

1. Sometimes systems that are graphed in terms of the IPO model show components of the processing as well as the inputs and outputs. Prepare a graph of the transactions processing model as an IPO model and include the processing elements—labeled as various accounting cycles. Consider only those inputs and outputs for five cycles: the sales, cash receipts, purchases, cash payments, and general ledger cycles. Include only the following management reports: sales analysis report, aging of accounts receivable, inventory status report, and purchase discounts lost report.

2. For each of these generic transactions, indicate which accounting cycle processes the transaction.

(a) Pay rent   (g) Cash sales

(b) Adjusting entries   (h) Closing entries

(c) Credit sales   (i) Purchase inventory for cash

(d) Purchase land on account   (j) Reversing entries

(e) Issue stock for cash   (k) Purchase inventory on account

(f) Pay employees their wages

3. For each of these generic transactions, indicate which accounting cycle processes the transaction.

(a) Cash sales   (i) Depreciation of equipment

(b) Credit sales   (j) Sale of used equipment

(c) Cash receipts from accounts receivable   (k) Issuance of common stock

(d) Cash purchases of inventory   (l) Declaration of dividends

(e) Credit purchases of inventory   (m) Payment of cash dividends

(f) Cash payments of accounts payable   (n) Obtain cash from a mortgage

(g) Purchases of equipment for cash   (o) Make a payment on a mortgage loan (the payment includes a portion of principal and interest)

(h) Purchases of equipment on credit

4. Banks offer checking and savings accounts to customers, and typically refer to them as noninterest-bearing and interest-bearing deposits. Of course, the money belongs to the customers, and the bank must repay them.

Banks earn profits by taking these deposits and creating loans such as mortgages. To the bank, these loans are receivables since the debtor is obligated to repay the bank the amount of the loan plus interest. Banks also buy securities to earn dividends and interest, and they try to earn trading profits.

What accounting cycles would a bank have?

5. An insurance company charges customers for the insurance policy, which is termed insurance premiums. Besides premiums, insurance companies make money by investing the proceeds and earning dividends or interest or capital gains.

When the customer or the beneficiary is éntitled to receive cash from the insurance company because of the insurance policy, then a payment is made. These are referred to as insurance claims.

What accounting cycles would an insurance company have?

6. There are five transactions with the following journal entries. When is the entry made? What are the minimum data needed to record this entry, and where are the data obtained?

(a) Credit sales

Accounts receivable	$X	
Sales		$X

(b) Payment from customer

Cash	$X	
Accounts receivable		$X

(c) Credit purchase

Purchases	$X	
Accounts payable		$X

(d) Payment to vendor

Accounts payable	$X	
Cash		$X

(e) Pay transportation charges

Transportation in (or out)	$X	
Cash		$X

7. You need to prepare the following three reports. Where would you obtain the data to compose these reports?

(a) Back order report   (c) Overdue deliveries report
(b) Aging of accounts receivable report

8. For the following list of files, determine the records of the file. Also consider whether the file has a key, and if it does, what the key is likely to be. If it probably does not have a key, indicate that situation.

(a) Accounts receivable master file   (g) Open sales invoice file
(b) Cash disbursements file   (h) Price data file
(c) Cash receipts file   (i) Purchase order file
(d) Customer master file   (j) Sales analysis report file
(e) Merchandise inventory master file   (k) Sales order file
(f) Open purchase order file   (l) Vendor master file

9. Give a record layout for (a) the vendor master file and (b) the merchandise inventory master file. Include some sample records within the file.

CHAPTER 7

FUNDAMENTALS OF INTERNAL CONTROL SYSTEMS

Chapters 6 and 7 provide the fundamentals for viewing accounting information systems (AIS) as a whole. The previous chapter examines the framework of the transactions processing system (TPS) which captures the data about the business's transactions needed to issue financial statements, prepare management reports, and allow queries by managers. In the present chapter we focus on the internal control aspects of AIS.

Readers of an organization's financial reports need some assurance that the information the reports contain is factual. This need for confirmation of the truthfulness and accuracy of the information gives rise to auditing and the publication of audit reports. In addition, managers realize that the information that they obtain from management reports and from queries to the AIS needs to be as reliable as possible; otherwise, the information managers obtain will prove useless to them. Therefore, managers also like the comforting assurance that the data are not contaminated or unrepresentative of what they are purportedly measuring. To address the concerns of both investors and managers, accountants create internal control systems.

The fundamental aim of internal contraol systems is to produce relevant and reliable data. The attribute of relevance calls our attention to the desirability of collecting information pertinent to the user's decision needs. Relevance of information to the investment community is monitored and regulated by the SEC and the FASB; hence, corporations must comply with SEC and FASB rules. Managers obviously can design the AIS to capture and store the data they want, so we will assume that managers receive relevant data. The characteristic of reliability informs us that the information represents what it is supposed to represent and is free from bias and measurement error, at least as much as is possible. Much of the chapter will emphasize the assurance of data reliability.

During the 1980s, the Treadway Commission investigated fraudulent financial reporting and accentuated the importance of internal control in reducing the problem of fraudulent financial reporting. After the Treadway Commission issued its report in 1987, five organizations formed a committee to study issues surrounding internal control. Those five organizations were the American Institute of Certified Public Accountants, the American Accounting Association, the Institute of Internal Auditors, the Institute of Management Accountants, and the Financial Executives Institute. This group, called the Committee of Sponsoring Organizations of the Treadway Commission (COSO), issued its report in 1992 entitled *Internal Control—Integrated Framework*. This publication became the standard for internal control, so our discussion will rely heavily on its contents.

In this chapter we construct a framework for discussing internal control systems. Examples primarily will investigate the cash account. Later chapters will apply these concepts to specific situations within the various accounting cycles.

After reading and studying this chapter, you should be able to:

- Explain the five types of management assertions;
- Define an internal control system;

- Describe the five components of an internal control system;
- Discuss the role of control objectives;
- Enumerate and explain major control policies and procedures;
- Demonstrate the importance of controlling cash;
- List common audit procedures of the cash account;
- Discuss usage of cash registers;
- Describe electronic funds transfers;
- Perform a bank reconciliation; and
- Summarize the purpose of petty cash funds and how they operate.

MANAGEMENT ASSERTIONS

Consider investors in a corporation's stocks or bonds. These investors gather information from a variety of sources, including the company's financial statements. As they read the financial statements and the accompanying schedules and footnotes, they come across several assertions made by the firm's management team. To assess the reliability of the financial statements as a whole, these investors can break down the statements into a series of assertions and then investigate the trustworthiness of these assertions.

When managers prepare a financial report—and always keep in mind that the corporate managers assemble the financial statements and have responsibility for them—they basically are making a series of assertions. These assertions fall into five categories: assertions about existence or occurrence; assertions about completeness; assertions about valuation or allowance; assertions about rights and obligations; and assertions about presentation and disclosure. Exhibit 7.1 summarizes this list of assertions. The exhibit also provides four examples for each assertion. The examples include an asset, a liability, a revenue, and an expense.

Assertions about existence or occurrence are statements that items on the balance sheet really existed on the balance sheet date and that transactions reported in the income statement in fact took place during the year (assuming the income statement is for one year). In other words, the assertions claim that all recorded assets (e.g., inventory) and all recorded liabilities (e.g., accounts payable) really existed on the balance sheet date. On the income statement the assertions state that all recorded revenues (e.g., sales) and all recorded expenses (e.g., cost of goods sold) actually occurred during the year. Financial statement users are particularly concerned about the existence of assets (e.g., inventory) and the occurrence of revenues (e.g., sales) because managers might have a bias to overstate assets and revenues.

Assertions about completeness deal with the issue of whether all accounts and all transactions have been properly accounted for. The question is whether the balance sheet displays all of the entity's assets and liabilities. It also addresses the problem of whether the income statement reveals all of the firm's revenues and expenses. Investors are particularly concerned about the completeness of liabilities (e.g., accounts payable) and expenses (e.g., cost of goods sold), for managers might have a bias to understate liabilities and expenses.

Assertions about valuation or allowance pertain to the measurement of the financial statement elements. At the lowest level, the assertion is that each transaction demonstrates the correct quantity and the correct price or cost of the items. At the aggregate level, the assertion is that the accountant has properly included all items and has summed them

EXHIBIT 7.1

MANAGEMENT ASSERTIONS

Management Assertions	As Applied to Inventory	As Applied to Accounts Payable	As Applied to Sales	As Applied to Cost of Goods Sold
Existence or occurrence	All recorded inventory at the balance sheet date exist.	All recorded accounts payable at the balance sheet date exist.	All recorded sales during the period occurred during the period.	All recorded COGS during the period occurred during the period.
Completeness	All existing inventory are included in the inventory account.	All existing accounts payable are included in the accounts payable.	All sales occurring during the period are included in the sales account.	All COGS occurring during the period are included in the COGS account.
Valuation or allowance	Recorded quantities and costs of inventory are correct; totals are correct; any inventory needing write-down has been written down.	Recorded quantities and costs of items bought on credit are correct; and totals are correct.	Recorded quantities and prices of goods sold are correct; totals are correct; and recognition criteria for sales have been met.	Recorded quantities and costs of items sold are correct; and totals are correct.
Rights and obligations	The firm has legal title to the inventory.	The firm has an obligation to pay the accounts payable.	n/a	n/a
Presentation and disclosure	Measurement basis of inventory is disclosed.	Measurement basis is disclosed (if not short-term cash basis).	Recognition and measurement bases are disclosed.	Measurement basis of COGS is disclosed.

correctly. Sometimes assets are required to be reduced in value, that is, written down, because their value has somehow been impaired. Amounts of liabilities increase as the corporation's obligations grow. Assertions about valuation include these potential decreases in an asset's value and potential increases in a liability's measurement. Firms can recognize a revenue only when certain conditions are met (as discussed in Chapter 12). When applied to revenues, this assertion also claims that these recognition criteria have been met.

Assertions about rights and obligations deal with the issue of whether the assets are really the rights of the company and whether the debts are really its obligations. As to assets, the assertion is that the company has property rights to the asset, either by legal title to the asset or through a long-term lease. When applied to liabilities, the assertion is that the firm indeed has an obligation to another entity. Because this assertion is restricted to assets and liabilities, it is not applicable to revenues and expenses.

Assertions about presentation and disclosure essentially are assertions that everything that needs to be disclosed and explained to the investment community has been disclosed and explained in the report. Such an assertion implies that the measurement basis and the recognition criteria have been clarified, especially when the corporation has a choice about how to measure and when to recognize the item. In addition, this assertion states that any additional information necessary to make the financial report not misleading has been communicated to the readers. Note that this assertion is closely connected with the disclosure principle presented in Chapter 1.

These, then, are the five financial statement assertions that managers make when they produce a financial report. To test the reliability of these assertions, external auditors conduct various tests, and, very importantly, they rely on the firm's internal control system.

INTERNAL CONTROL SYSTEMS

So far, we have observed that the study of internal control systems is motivated by the desire of investors and creditors to have reliable financial statements, which in turn possess reliable assertions. An internal control system that is working well can provide additional confidence that the financial statements contain reliable assertions.

Managers also need capable internal control systems to help them with their work. Managers have the responsibility of running the company effectively and efficiently, they want to publish reliable financial reports, and they need to ensure company compliance with the federal, state, and local statutes that apply to the organization. An internal control system that is working well can provide a foundation to help managers operate the firm effectively and efficiently, to issue reliable financial reports, and to meet the corporation's legal obligations. Thus, managers also benefit from internal control systems.

Of these management activities, the most important is effectiveness and efficiency of operations because it produces profits for the corporation. This goal includes the safeguarding of assets, the protection of accounting records, and the production of information that helps managers make rational decisions.

During the congressional investigations of Watergate, congressional staff members discovered that several large corporations were paying bribes to foreign officials and were covering them up by including them with other operating expenses. The firm's internal control mechanisms did not catch these transgressions. As a result of the hearings, in 1977 Congress passed the Foreign Corrupt Practices Act. Among other things, this act prohibits bribes to foreign officials for the purpose of obtaining or retaining business, and it requires companies to maintain good financial reporting practices, including a good internal control system. So another advantage of having an effective internal control system is to comply with the Foreign Corrupt Practices Act.

Internal Control Systems

Internal control is the process of reasonably assuring the realization of corporate goals. According to COSO, these goals include effective and efficient operations, production of reliable financial reports, and compliance with laws and regulations. An *internal control system* (sometimes referred to as an internal control structure) is a set of policies and procedures that collectively provide reasonable assurance that the entity accomplishes its goals of effective and efficient operations, reliable financial reports, and compliance with laws and regulations.

Components of an Internal Control System

As enumerated in Exhibit 7.2, internal control systems can be viewed as having five components: control environment, risk assessment, control activities, information and communication, and monitoring.

The *control environment* comprises the actions and behaviors that indicate how managers and directors feel about control issues. It shapes the internal control system, for it helps to establish whether the firm is serious about internal controls or is merely putting on a show. In other words, the control environment demonstrates the overall attitude toward ethics. A moral tone throughout the organization not only assists people to understand their responsibilities within the firm, but also encourages them to act diligently and courageously. In addition, it establishes the concepts that each person is accountable for his or her actions and that one must act in accordance with management's authority.

To promote an active and healthy control environment, the organization ought to demonstrate integrity and ethical values, display a commitment to competence, provide an organizational structure that supplies the necessary checks and balances—including the operation of an effective board of directors—employ a management style that encourages high ethical principles, delegate authority and assign responsibility clearly so that individuals understand what they can and cannot do, and possess human resource policies and practices that encourage good behavior and discourage unethical actions.

Three structural elements that promote a good control environment are the existence of a board of directors, an audit committee, and internal auditors. A *board of directors* is a group of persons who govern the activities of the corporation. The board's major function is to provide a check on the affairs of managers; in other words, managers become accountable to the board. When managers are not doing their job or are making decisions that are not in the best interests of the corporation, then the directors must intervene and discipline the managers. An *audit committee* is a committee under the board of directors, consisting of members who are independent of management. Often directors themselves,

EXHIBIT 7.2

COMPONENTS OF AN INTERNAL CONTROL SYSTEM

Component	*Explanation of Component*
Control environment	Ethical setting of firm
Risk assessment	Understand risks to corporate goals
Control activities	Specific methods to carry out management goals
Information and communication	Produce reports to notify managers and directors of pertinent information
Monitoring	Assurance that the control system is working

the members of this committee, help control and supervise managers by assisting the external auditors. The idea is to ensure that the external audit uncovers any material internal control problems that exist. Internal auditors work for the firm itself, and part of their job is to evaluate the internal control system and determine its effectiveness. Having a strong and independent board of directors, audit committee, and internal audit staff promotes a dynamic and effective control environment.

The second component of an internal control system is risk assessment. *Risk assessment* deals with the identification and analysis and, where applicable, the quantification of the risks that managers face in their attempts to achieve corporate goals. The idea is simple: everybody faces risks in whatever they do. To minimize losses, one has to manage these risks, and to manage these risks, one has to obtain information relating to the risks that the company actually faces. This analysis includes the identification of risk and an understanding of what the probabilities of loss are and what the potential losses could be. Quantification of risk may be difficult, but managers need to assess risk as well as they can. Areas to analyze include a changed operating environment, new competition, rapid growth, changing technology, product innovation, and foreign operations.

Control activities, the third component of internal control systems, are policies and procedures implemented by managers to assure that specific goals are met. A *policy* is a statement of what ought to be done when certain conditions are met, whereas a *procedure* is a particular course of action. The following example clarifies the distinction. Managers might say that potential customers with income greater than $50,000 should have a credit limit of $5,000 and those with less income should have a credit limit of only $2,000. This policy covers how much credit the firm ought to grant to its customers. The actual review of a customer's application for credit is a procedure. Thus, procedures carry out policies.

These control activities—these policies and procedures—are enacted to reduce the risks and to help meet the corporation's control objectives. This category is an umbrella for many activities, such as authorizations, independent verifications, and segregation of duties. (These policies and procedures are discussed further in a later section of this chapter.)

The fourth aspect of internal control systems is information and communication. Information ought to be sent to managers and directors to help them evaluate the firm's current position and determine what needs to be done to meet the corporate goals. The firm has stated its goals, and it has assessed the risks to achieving those goals, and it has instituted policies and procedures to remedy or control the risks. Communication of information about these goals and risks and control activities helps coordinate the actions of the entity's managers and directors.

Designing an internal control system does not mean that the system will work, nor does it mean that once it is operating, it will always do so. Thus, the fifth component of an internal control system is the monitoring of the system. By *monitoring* we mean a continual assessment of the system's performance. The internal control system is evaluated, perhaps by internal auditors, to assure that it is working the way it was designed to work.

Summary Comments

The five components given in Exhibit 7.2 reflect different aspects of an internal control system. Together they provide a reasonable assurance that the firm accomplishes its goals of effective and efficient operations, reliable financial reports, and compliance with laws and regulations.

The assurance that is given does not guarantee 100% reliability, but it does yield a high degree of confidence that these goals are met. No system in practice can be completely effective. In other words, certain practical considerations limit the effectiveness of internal control systems. Besides, enacting control mechanisms costs money, and firms want to pay for internal controls only as long as they are receiving sufficient benefits.

The fundamental concepts behind internal control systems do not depend on the information processing system. The components of internal control systems are the same regardless of whether the AIS is manual or file-based or uses database technology. These goals and concepts remain the same no matter how the AIS is implemented.

Before leaving this topic, we should also observe that the COSO model is quite broad and may be applied to areas besides accounting. Accountants, managers, and others can utilize this COSO model in any context where goals and risks to those goals exist.

CONTROL OBJECTIVES

Given the COSO framework, we are now in a position to implement and develop an internal control system. Eventually we will link these controls with the various accounting cycles. Before we do so, however, let's consider how to tie these control tools to the accounting cycles.

As the accounting cycles are explored in depth in the remainder of the book, the aspect of control is broached by asking what managers are trying to accomplish in the cycle. In other words, we begin by specifying the control objectives for the cycle. In general terms, each cycle has four goals: (1) to safeguard the assets of the entity; (2) to engage only in those transactions authorized by management; (3) to record all transactions completely and accurately; and (4) to safeguard the accounting records. Exhibit 7.3 tabulates

EXHIBIT 7.3

CONTROL OBJECTIVES FOR SOME ACCOUNTING CYCLES

Common Goals	General Ledger Cycle	Sales Cycle	Facilities Cycle
1. Safeguard the assets of the entity.	N/A	Inventories are safeguarded while in stock and when shipped.	Property, plant, and equipment are safeguarded.
2. Engage only in those transactions authorized by management.	All general ledger cycle transactions are authorized by management.	All sales cycle transactions are authorized by management.	All facilities cycle transactions are authorized by management.
3. Record all transactions completely and accurately.	All valid general ledger cycle transactions are accurately recorded.	All valid sales cycle transactions are accurately recorded.	All valid facilities cycle transactions are accurately recorded.
4. Safeguard the accounting records.	All documents and reports generated in the general ledger cycle are safeguarded.	All documents and reports generated in the sales cycle are safeguarded.	All documents and reports generated in the facilities cycle are safeguarded.

these four objectives. They are applied to three accounting cycles as illustrations, and later chapters give greater details.

Safeguarding assets simply means that the company wants to protect its resources from theft and from damage. Managers want to protect the asset's value to the extent that they can.

The firm wants employees to participate only in transactions that are authorized by management. The corporation does not want to enter into bogus transactions, nor does it desire to engage in transactions that privately benefit someone, whether employed by the firm or an outsider. For example, companies do not want to buy supplies from a fictitious vendor; such a scenario invites the firm to pay cash and not receive anything in return. In addition, corporations do not want employees to make wild and extravagant transactions, even if in the name of the firm. They try to prevent an employee from buying (say) a million dollars' worth of lottery tickets.

All accounting cycles have the control objective of accurately recording all transactions. Obviously, the management team desires reliable information, and this reliability can be achieved only when all transactions are recorded by the AIS.

Safeguarding accounting records should be an evident control objective. These records serve as evidence about the transactions of the firm, and loss of this evidence could prove harmful to the corporation. Consider when a firm is trying to collect an accounts receivable and the customer replies that no sale was made and no goods were received. If the company has no record of the transaction, then it likely will be unable to collect the receivable. If, on the other hand, it has a purchase order from the customer and it possesses a copy of the bill of lading that proves the goods were shipped to the customer, then the company will have a much easier time collecting its money.

After the control objectives are established, the managers set up various control activities that help fulfill the control objectives.

CONTROL POLICIES AND PROCEDURES

When implementing and developing an internal control system, accountants and managers choose control objectives for the firm and its accounting cycles. After determining these goals, accountants and managers set several policies and procedures to achieve the control objectives. These control activities fall into six categories: (1) assignment of authority and responsibility; (2) authorization of transactions; (3) maintenance of adequate accounting records; (4) limited access to assets; (5) independent verifications; and (6) segregation of duties. Exhibit 7.4 provides a reference on control policies and procedures, tying these control activities with the control objectives. Authorization of transactions and limited access to assets support the first two control objectives. The rest of the control activities buttress all four control objectives. As we discuss the various control policies and procedures, the reader should verify that they do help to achieve the company's control objectives.

Assignment of Authority and Responsibility

A starting point is to provide managers and employees with a clear understanding of their authority and responsibility. By *authority* we mean the legitimate power to determine certain issues and command others to do certain things. *Responsibility* refers to having accountability for one's actions.

EXHIBIT 7.4

ACHIEVING CONTROL OBJECTIVES THROUGH CONTROL POLICIES AND PROCEDURES

Which Control Activities Support Which Control Objectives	*Safeguard the Assets of the Entity*	*Engage Only in Those Transactions That Are Authorized by Management*	*Record All Transactions Completely and Accurately*	*Safeguard the Accounting Records*
Assignment of authority and responsibility	Yes	Yes	Yes	Yes
Authorization of transactions	Yes	Yes	No	No
Maintenance of adequate accounting records	Yes	Yes	Yes	Yes
Limited access to assets	Yes	Yes	No	No
Independent verifications	Yes	Yes	Yes	Yes
Segregation of duties	Yes	Yes	Yes	Yes

CAR

custody authorization Record

Consider the corporation's purchasing activities. Managers will invest authority in some individuals, usually limited to some of the employees working in the purchasing department, to buy inventory on behalf of the firm. Other managers and employees will not possess such authority and cannot legitimately engage in such transactions. By reducing this ability to purchase inventory on behalf of the corporation to only a few individuals, the firm reduces the problem of people buying items for their own personal gain.

At the same time, corporate managers hold the purchasing agents responsible for their activities. Managers require them to buy quality inventory at the best possible prices as the goods are needed. This policy holds purchasing agents responsible for not purchasing items necessary in the course of business on a timely basis, for buying inferior goods, for spending too much money on inventory, and for buying unwanted items.

It is desirable to match authority and responsibility. To grant authority to somebody without holding the person responsible for his or her actions invites an abuse of power. Conversely, to require responsibility without giving the person authority often leads to frustration and demoralization.

Providing supervision is one way of holding people accountable for their actions. The supervisor checks the employee's work and verifies that he or she is performing as expected and is not engaging in undesirable activities.

Authorization of Transactions

The first control activity focuses on the workers and managers hired by the company and invests them with authority and responsibility. The second control activity is related to the first, but it concentrates on the transactions of the organization. Simply put, the firm should engage in no transaction unless it has been authorized by management.

Authorizations are policies set up by management with respect to certain types of transactions. Continuing with the purchasing illustration, a company might establish the policy that purchasing agents can buy inventory only when the current level of the inventory goes below a certain level and they can buy only from certain vendors. Purchasing employees act within proper and legitimate limits if they restrict themselves to acting within management's authorizations. In this case they are allowed to buy inventory when their levels fall below some set limit—something that the purchasing agents need to verify. They also may proceed with the purchase, providing that they stick with the list of acceptable suppliers.

A related concept is an *approval,* an implementation of some authorization, which is often evidenced by the signature of a person with the authority to engage in the transaction. For example, before a purchasing agent buys (say) 100 television sets, he or she reviews the requisition from those with the appropriate authority to request the purchase. Among other things, a manager needs to approve the requisition. If everything looks acceptable and if some manager has approved the purchase, then the purchasing agent may proceed with the transaction. The purchasing department prepares the purchase order, and the purchasing department manager approves it by signing the purchase order. Note also that when an employee signs the document, the worker is accepting responsibility for the transaction.

In a computerized information system, the computer can initiate transactions. For example, when an inventory level dips below some preset number, the computer could automatically create a purchase order to buy more of the item. Even then it is important that these transactions be undertaken only upon management authorization.

Maintenance of Adequate Accounting Records

The term *accounting records* signifies the input documents, output documents, journals, and ledgers of a firm. To publish reliable financial statements and management reports, the entity needs trustworthy data as captured by documents, recorded in journals, and summarized in ledgers. The company must have enough documents and records of the right kind to gather the appropriate data. In addition, these data need to be maintained as evidence that only legitimate and properly authorized transactions occurred.

Maintenance of the accounting records forms an *audit trail,* references that link various documents and accounting data. Recall the posting process in a manual system in which the posting reference column of the ledger contains the page number of the journal where the transaction is recorded and the posting reference column of the journal gives the account number to which it has been posted. The idea behind these cross-references is that an auditor (or other appropriate employee of the firm) can trace the various records that form the basis for recording a transaction. In other words, the audit trail helps justify the legitimacy for recording a transaction.

Documents should be prenumbered. Prenumbered documents deter their misuse since gaps in the numbers raise questions in the minds of those working in the department. Prenumbering also makes it easier to trace a specific document to a specific transaction. Sometimes documents are voided because of errors. Firms retain voided documents in order to account for all of the prenumbered documents.

Responsible individuals should fill out the documents at the time of the transactions or as near to that time as practicable. Preparation of the documents at that time helps to maintain accountability for the exchange, and it helps the person gather the data in an efficient manner.

Suppose that a business enterprise purchases an item and the supplier sends the firm the vendor invoice. The company pays the bill. Later, however, an employee observes the purchase order and the vendor invoice and might think it should be paid. What prevents a firm from paying a bill twice? The usual technique is to *cancel* the document—writing something on the document or marking it in some way that prevents people from using the document twice. In this example, when the bill is paid the first time, an employee should stamp the invoice "paid." This notation tells others not to pay the bill again.

Limited Access to Assets

Limited access implies that the entity allows access to certain assets only to those individuals who have the authority to obtain access. The idea is simple: if everybody can get their hands on the assets of the firm, then the chance of theft or misuse increases. Besides, if many people are allowed access to the resources of the company and something happens, it may be difficult to determine whose fault it is. If few are permitted such access, then it is much easier to decide who deserves the blame for the problem.

Authorizing just a few people to deal directly with the assets helps establish limited access. Some physical ways of limiting access are to install locks, to have storage areas for the assets, and to monitor the area with electronic devices.

Companies sometimes create special cash funds called *imprest funds*. For example, imprest funds can be set up for payroll needs (payroll imprest fund) or for small, miscellaneous purchases (petty cash fund). These funds usually have one person designated as the fund officer or fund manager, and only this person can dispense these funds. This individual keeps tabs on the funds and supports any cash disbursements with vouchers and receipts that explain the nature of the transactions. This organizational setup thus provides limited access to the imprest fund.

Independent Verifications

When unchecked, people sometimes act in unethical, and perhaps even illegal, ways. Individuals who know that they are monitored from time to time probably are less likely to steal assets or engage in activities against the wishes of management. *Independent verification*—procedures that check up on individuals and the TPS or parts of the TPS—provide such a restraint.

Notice that the definition of independent verification applies to the TPS as well as to individuals. The reason for this inclusion is that managers and auditors do not want to assume that the internal control system is working as designed. They want proof. Independent verification of the performance of the system provides evidence on whether it is operating as it should.

One type of independent verification is a reconciliation. A *reconciliation* is a computation that supports some specific amount with other evidence. For example, an auditor might review the accounting records which indicate that the inventory includes 50 refrigerators. The auditor then observes that the physical inventory contains only 47 refrigerators. Before claiming a discrepancy, the auditor also considers whether any refrigerators have been purchased and whether any have been sold. It is possible that any refrigerators in transition from the vendor or to the customer have not yet been accounted for. In this case, if three refrigerators have been sent to customers but the transactions have not yet been recorded, then the discrepancy can be explained. The recorded inventory is reconciled with the physical count.

Segregation of Duties

Suppose the next time you watch *Jeopardy,* Alex Trebek is a player as well as the host. Most people will think that is unfair because he can see the answers (or should we say the questions?) ahead of time and because he judges whether the contestant's response is correct. In an analogous fashion, firms do not want employees to engage in overlapping functions that challenge the integrity of the process. Furthermore, when a person carries out two or more overlapping jobs, then he or she is more likely to be tempted to do something against the policies of the corporation.

To mitigate these potential problems, firms segregate functions that, if combined, might cause difficulties with achieving the objectives of the internal control system. *Segregation of duties* ensures that no one performs duties that are incompatible from an internal control perspective. Among other functions, organizations want to keep the custody of assets separate from authorization of transactions and from accounting.

Let's continue working with the purchasing area as an illustration. If one person can authorize a purchase and has access to it once the firm receives the goods, then the person can more easily order something wanted for the home and, upon arrival, put it in the trunk of the car. If one person can authorize a purchase and has recordkeeping responsibilities, then he or she can make an unauthorized purchase and cover it up by expensing some account. By not putting the inventory on the books, this individual avoids direct accountability for it. Finally, if one person has custody of the assets and recordkeeping responsibilities, then the individual can take something out of the storage area and put it in the trunk of the car. He or she then erases accountability for the inventory, for example, by claiming that it was returned to the vendor. None of these schemes is a perfect way to steal and not get caught, but they certainly make it easier, just what the firm wants. Not!

Summary

Exhibit 7.4 lists the control objectives of an organization, as well as its control policies and procedures. We show which control activities support which control objectives. As a whole, the six control policies and procedures help the company meet all of its control objectives.

CONTROL OF CASH

To add some specificity to this narrative on internal control systems, we will explore the control of cash. Perhaps the most vulnerable of assets, cash requires protection from unauthorized uses. Thus, the company needs to provide several control activities to protect this asset. In this section we consider some audit procedures, usage of cash registers, electronic funds transfers, bank reconciliations, and petty cash.

Not only does cash include the green stuff and the coins in the cash registers, but it also consists of what the firm has in its bank accounts. Large companies can have several checking accounts and one or more savings accounts. Often they will have an imprest payroll account, which simply means that one checking account is devoted solely to payroll transactions. Firms do this for control purposes, and we discuss it further in Chapter 11. They also might have an imprest petty cash fund, a small fund to handle certain routine transactions. Petty cash funds are described later in this chapter.

Near cash items, such as certificates of deposit and money market funds, often are combined with the cash account when the balance sheet is prepared. Accountants do this as long as the certificates of deposit (CDs) and the money market funds mature in a short time period (say, under three months) and they have no restrictions on how they may be used (such as to pay off some debt). For our purposes, however, transactions involving CDs and money market funds belong to the investments cycle, so we will exclude them from further discussion in this chapter.

Cash Audit Procedures

The ultimate control objective, as far as cash is concerned, is its safeguarding. To bring about this goal, the firm requires management's authorization of cash transactions and evidence of proper transactions, perhaps by documents with signatures from managers who have the authority to approve the transactions. Adequate documents and records are maintained to demonstrate that each transaction is legitimate. The firm also restricts who in the company can handle cash to as few people as possible. Independent verifications take place, for example, by having internal auditors make surprise visits to those who work with cash. The internal auditor counts the cash to make sure that the amount of cash actually there is what ought to be there. Finally, the corporation segregates the various functions involving cash. The finance department of a firm is often split into the treasury (or treasurer's department) and the controller's department. Among other duties, the treasury handles the money while the controller's department has responsibility for accounting. Within these two departments the firm can segregate duties even further.

Of course, the entity will audit the cash account and the cash transactions to verify that the internal control system is working effectively. In one procedure, the auditor compares canceled checks with the cash disbursements journal (or cash disbursements transactions file) for the date, payee, and amount. The auditor does this to verify that the recording in the cash disbursements journal is correct and that the payee is a legitimate vendor of the firm. A related audit procedure involves examination of the canceled checks for signature, endorsement, and cancellation by the bank.

As to cash inflows, the auditor compares deposits in the bank with the cash receipts journal (or the cash receipts transactions file). The idea is to compare the date, customer, and amount to verify that the transactions are proper and that they have been recorded correctly.

Another audit procedure has the auditor perform a bank reconciliation, which we will explain shortly. Bank reconciliations contrast the firm's cash balance with the bank's cash balance reported in the monthly bank statement. The only differences between the two balances are timing differences and errors. The auditor reconciles all timing differences between the company and the bank, and so is left with errors. These errors should be small in number, and they should occur randomly and be the result of mistakes, not robbery or coverups of any misappropriations.

One of the reconciling items in a bank reconciliation is outstanding checks. Some outstanding checks, however, could be a coverup for cash shortages. The auditor, therefore, needs to follow up on the outstanding checks and make sure that they clear the banking system in the near future and that they represent legitimate transactions.

An auditor can employ many more procedures to audit the cash account. The techniques given here indicate how one might begin to audit cash and verify that the internal control system is working. Other procedures are detailed in auditing textbooks.

Cash Registers

When firms have cash sales, they typically employ cash registers. Cash registers record transactions twice, once for the customer and once internally. The printed receipt for the customer and the visibility of the numbers on the register itself allow a customer to view them and complain when there are inaccuracies. The internal copy provides a basis for recording the day's transactions and indicates how much cash should be in the drawer.

At the end of the day or the work period, the cashier counts the amount of cash in the register. Another employee examines the internal record to see how much cash should be in the cash register and contrasts this number with how much cash is actually there. Any discrepancies should be small and random. The day's cash sales would be recorded as a debit to cash for the amount of cash in the cash register and a credit to sales as indicated by the internal record. The difference is treated as cash short and over, which is an income statement account. When the account has a debit balance, it represents a miscellaneous expense; when it has a credit balance, it indicates a miscellaneous revenue. (Compare this treatment with that for petty cash described later in the chapter.) The individual who prepares this entry should not be the cashier.

Cash generated from these cash sales should be deposited in the bank daily. The person who deposits the cash should not be the same person who operates the cash register or who records the transactions.

In today's world, cash registers may themselves be microcomputers that can do many more things than just record cash sales. For example, if linked with bar code scanners, these cash registers could keep tabs on the company's inventories. This possibility is discussed more fully in Chapters 9 and 10 when we present point-of-sale systems. For now, the reader should concentrate on the control issues of using cash registers.

Electronic Funds Transfers (EFT)

Before the advent of computers, money transfers from one party to another resulted from the buyer's giving bills, coins, or checks to the seller. Computers, however, provide an electronic means of moving money from one entity to another. Banks can do this because the checking accounts are maintained electronically, and banks can easily take money out of one account and convey it to another by giving a computer certain commands. We refer to cash flows effected by computerized instructions rather than bills, coins, or checks as *electronic funds transfers (EFTs)*.

Accounting for cash does not change when electronic funds transfers are utilized. Cash is cash no matter what form it takes. If the firm agrees with an electric utility to have the electric bills paid via EFTs, then it still records the payments as a debit to utility expense and a credit to cash.

EFTs do, however, affect the control system. The firm needs to use passwords and employ encryption techniques that encode and decode messages to keep computer hackers from stealing money from the corporation by simulating an EFT. Corporations might also employ digital signatures, which allow senders to have unique identifiers and makes forgery virtually impossible. Routine transactions, as the above-mentioned deal with an electric company, can be authorized by some general statement from management. Notices of the EFT, sometimes called EFT advices or EFT transaction advices, should be mailed to somebody other than those who have the authority to engage in EFT transactions, thus maintaining a segregation of duties. As we explore the other cycles, we will encounter EFTs again.

Bank Reconciliations

One way of obtaining independent verification of the cash account is through a statement issued by the bank. In practice, the bank's statement about the cash balance usually differs from the firm's balance because of various timing differences. But if the balances are adjusted for the timing differences, then any remaining discrepancies are errors. This audit procedure is called a *bank reconciliation.*

Let's suppose the company has an account called cash in bank. This account, as the name suggests, represents money in the bank. The account increases as the firm deposits money into the account, and the account decreases as checks are written against it. Periodically—usually every month—the bank will send a statement to its customers. The statement summarizes the activity within the account during the month and presents an ending balance. Except for timing differences and for errors, the checkbook balance of the firm will agree with the bank's ending balance.

Checks written by the firm take time to arrive at its destination, get cashed by them, clear their bank, and clear the corporation's bank. Similarly, deposits by the company require some time before the bank adds them to the firm's account. At the end of the month, the bank may not have administered the check clearing or the cash deposits, even though the firm has recorded the cash flows on its books. These inconsistencies represent timing differences, items recorded by the firm but not yet dealt with by the bank.

Sometimes the bank performs some service for the firm, such as collecting a note receivable. When the bank receives the cash, it adds the amount to the firm's account, even if the company has not yet recorded the transaction. Another possibility exists when the bank completes an EFT on behalf of the firm, such as a payment to the electric company. The firm may have signed an agreement to allow the electric utility to obtain its money via an EFT, and so the bank proceeds to honor the request for money from the electric company, even if the firm has not recorded the transaction. These discrepancies represent timing differences. In this case they are transactions engaged in by the bank on behalf of the company, but the firm has not recorded the items.

In addition to these timing differences, both parties might make errors. Any errors have to be corrected.

Reconciling the bank's ending balance with the firm's ending balance is a simple two-step procedure. Adjust the bank balance for items accounted for by the firm but not by the bank, such as outstanding checks and outstanding deposits. This includes any adjustments for bank errors. Next, adjust the book balance for items accounted for by the bank but not by the firm, such as service charges and EFTs. Adjust also for any errors by the company. The two adjusted balances should equal, and the balance is referred to as the true cash balance. This process is summarized as follows:

Bank balance	$ X	Book balance	$ X
Items considered		Items considered	
by the firm but		by the bank but	
not by the bank	±X	not by the firm	±X
Bank errors	±X	Firm errors	±X
True cash balance	$ X	True cash balance	$ X

Once the true cash balance is determined, the accountant prepares journal entries for the items considered by the bank but not by the firm. The accountant also makes correcting entries to correct the errors entered into the books of the firm. No entries are made for the items considered by the firm but not by the bank. The bank makes its own journal entries.

If the bank reconciliation is going to have maximum effectiveness, then it should not be prepared by anybody who handles cash or who makes journal entries involving cash. The reason for this restriction is simple: it would be so easy to steal cash and cover it up by fudging the bank reconciliation. We will assume that the internal auditing department prepares the bank reconciliation.

As an example of a bank reconciliation, consider the affairs of Sam Hartman and Associates. The company receives its bank statement, and it notices that:

(a) The balance per the cash account is $9,870.
(b) The balance per the bank statement is $11,200.
(c) Outstanding checks total $2,350.
(d) The bank imposes a service charge of $35.
(e) The bank has disbursed $313 to the electric company, pursuant to the firm's agreement about EFTs.
(f) Outstanding deposits equal $730.
(g) Sam Hartman discovers that check number 2345 for $212 is unrecorded. It was for rent expense.
(h) Check number 2543 was written for $140, but it is recorded incorrectly as $410. The check had paid off the firm's accounts payable to Zola, Inc.

The internal auditor prepares the bank reconciliation from these data, and Exhibit 7.5 presents this bank reconciliation. The internal auditor adjusts the bank balance for outstanding checks and for outstanding deposits. Next the internal auditor adjusts the book balance for the service charge and for the EFT to the electric utility and corrects the two errors. After converting both balances, the internal auditor obtains the true cash balance of the corporation.

Finally, the bookkeeper prepares the four journal entries for the adjustments to the book balance. These journal entries are as follows:

Bank fees		$ 35	
	Cash		$ 35
Electricity expense		$313	
	Cash		$313
Rent expense		$212	
	Cash		$212
Cash		$270	
	Accounts payable (Zola, Inc.)		$270

EXHIBIT 7.5

EXAMPLE OF A BANK RECONCILIATION

Sam Hartman and Associates
Bank Reconciliation
For the month of July

Bank balance	$11,200	Book balance	$9,870
Outstanding checks	2,350	Service charge	35
	$ 8,850		$9,835
Outstanding deposits	730	EFT:	
		electric bill	(313)
		Error-omitted check #2345	(212)
		Error in check #2543	270
	$ 9,580		$9,580

Petty Cash

Many corporations encounter some small expenditures of cash for items that need imme-diate payment. The postal officer, for example, might deliver the mail and state that the firm owes so much money because somebody didn't include enough postage. Typically, the postal worker will not wait for the company to get lots of paperwork printed and signed by all of the right people. The solution to this situation is to create a *petty cash fund*, a special cash fund set up to make relatively small cash payments.

The petty cash fund is established by giving the money to one person who is in charge of the fund; this person is called the petty cash officer (or custodian). When something comes up for which the petty cash fund appropriately can disburse money, the custodian pays out the cash and prepares a *petty cash voucher* stating what the transaction is and what the cash was disbursed for. Exhibit 7.6 displays an example of a petty cash voucher. To verify the legitimacy of the transaction, the petty cash officer also obtains other docu-ments, such as receipts. From time to time the fund is replenished; that is, the petty cash fund receives additional money such that the fund is restored to its original balance. Of course, the firm could increase or decrease the fund balance. The sum of the expenditures, as evidenced by the petty cash vouchers, should equal the amount of replenished cash.

Accounting for a petty cash fund is straightforward. When the firm sets up the fund, it creates a separate cash account called petty cash. To do this, debit petty cash and credit cash. No entries are made while transactions occur. When the fund is replenished, how-ever, the accountant analyzes the petty cash vouchers and records the transactions in the usual way. The fund is replenished not only when funds become small, but also at fiscal year-end. In this way, the entries are placed in the correct accounting period. When a bal-ance sheet is prepared, the accountant usually combines petty cash into the cash account.

One new wrinkle occurs when the amount of cash added to the fund does not equal the sum of the expenditures as documented by the vouchers. An account called cash short and over is used as a plug for this difference. The account cash short and over is an in-come statement account. If it has a debit balance, it represents a miscellaneous expense; if it possesses a credit balance, it portrays a miscellaneous revenue.

To explain this, consider the following problem. Hall Enterprises authorizes a $200 petty cash fund and places Elma Wilkins in charge of it. At the end of the month the fund has cash of $70 and petty cash vouchers that indicate payments of $20 for flowers, $60 for freight in, and $45 for postage. Not only is the fund replenished, but it is increased to $300. Prepare the necessary journal entries.

Before answering the problem, recognize that the expenditures add up to $125, but it takes $130 to restore the fund to its original balance. In other words, there is a short-age of $5 and this amount needs to be expensed.

EXHIBIT 7.6

EXAMPLE OF A PETTY CASH VOUCHER

CRUMMER'S BIKES
Petty Cash Voucher

Number   3041   Date   May 31, 2002

Paid to: U.S. Post Office

Amount paid: $4.20

Explanation: To pay postage because of insufficient stamps

Account to charge: Postage expense

Signature of petty cash officer: *Jenny Lynde*

The entry to create the fund is:

Petty cash	$200	
Cash		$200

The journal entry that records the month's transactions and replenishes the fund to its original balance is:

Miscellaneous expense	$20	
Freight in	$60	
Postage expense	$45	
Cash short and over	$ 5	
Cash		$130

Notice that cash is credited, not petty cash. The balance in petty cash is $200, just as you want. Besides, the $130 came from the general cash funds, not the petty cash fund.

To recognize the change in the amount of the petty cash fund, make the following entry:

Petty cash	$100	
Cash		$100

After this entry, petty cash has a balance of $300.

Having spelled out how to account for the petty cash fund, we now need to examine internal control issues with respect to the fund. Several simple principles cover its operation. Only one person is placed in charge of the petty cash fund. That way, if there is a cash shortage, you know who is responsible. This person is vested with the power to engage in certain transactions, but management needs to list which transactions are appropriate for the petty cash fund.

The petty cash officer should prepare a petty cash voucher, such as the one shown in Exhibit 7.6, for each transaction and should obtain evidence from the other party to support the transaction, such as a receipt for cash. These documents provide evidence that the officer is engaging only in authorized transactions and is not spending the money on personal things.

Once used, the petty cash vouchers and the supporting documents should be canceled. Bills can be marked "paid" to keep the custodian from using the same invoice as evidence for bogus transactions.

From time to time, the firm should have surprise counts of the petty cash fund. These inspections serve as independent verifications that help to curb any temptation by the petty cash officer to spend the money improperly.

The journal entries prepared to record the petty cash fund transactions ought to be made by somebody other than the petty cash officer. If the duties were not segregated, then it would be trivial to steal cash and cover it up.

Finally, the amount of money in the petty cash fund should be small. Large amounts might offer too great a temptation to the petty cash officer.

As you review this setup, notice how all of the control activities discussed above and enumerated in Exhibit 7.4 are implemented here.

SIGHTS ALONG THE INTERNET

Since the foundation for this chapter rests on the COSO report, the student might want to find out more information about COSO and its implications. Two sites worth looking at are:

COSO	www.coso.org
A COSO audit-process outline	members.aol.com/mrsciacfe/cosoaudt.htm

Electronic funds transfers is an important topic in business today. Additional information can be gleaned from:

EFT security issues	www.asicomm.com/prod06.htm
EFT and payments by the federal government	www.fms.treas.gov/eft/general.html
NPS Global, a vendor of EFT services	npsglobal.com

Finally, some accounting sites look at the audit process (or, more broadly, assurance services) and provide resources. See:

AICPA (click on "Assurance Services")	www.aicpa.org
AuditNet	www.auditnet.org
CPA Net (click on "Assurance")	www.cpanet.com/index.asp

The AICPA site also contains some material on electronic commerce. After getting to the site, click on "CPA Webtrust: The Future of E-Commerce."

CHAPTER SUMMARY IN TERMS OF LEARNING OBJECTIVES

Explain the Five Types of Management Assertions.   There are five categories of management assertions: assertions about existence or occurrence; assertions about completeness; assertions about valuation or allowance; assertions about rights and obligations; and assertions about presentation and disclosure. Assertions about existence or occurrence are statements that items on the balance sheet really existed on the balance sheet date and that transactions reported in the income statement really took place during the year. Assertions about completeness deal with the issue of whether all accounts and all transactions have been properly accounted for. Assertions about valuation or allowance pertain to the measurement of the elements. Assertions about rights and obligations deal with the issue of whether the assets are really the rights of the company and whether the debts are really its obligations. Assertions about presentation and disclosure are assertions that everything that needs to be disclosed and explained has been.

Define an Internal Control System.   An internal control system is a set of policies and procedures that collectively provide a reasonable assurance that the entity accomplishes its goals of effective and efficient operations, reliable financial reports, and compliance with laws and regulations.

Describe the Five Components of an Internal Control System.   Internal control systems can be viewed as having five components: control environment, risk assessment, control activities, information and communication, and monitoring. Internal control systems begin with a control environment that is concerned with the overall attitude toward ethics. A moral tone throughout the organization can assist people in understanding their responsibilities within the firm. Second, one should have a clear understanding of the risks that are faced in trying to achieve the corporate goals. With this comprehension of the risks, the firm can develop plans to reduce the risks to acceptable levels. Third, managers develop control activities to supply specific policies and procedures to implement the firm's control objectives. Fourth, information ought to be communicated to managers and directors to help them in evaluating the firm's current position and in determining what needs to be done to meet the corporate goals. Reports are prepared with the pertinent information and distributed to the appropriate managers and directors. Finally, designing an internal control system does not mean that it will work, nor does it mean that once it is operating, it will always do so. The internal control system needs to be monitored to see that it is working the way it was designed to work.

Discuss the Role of Control Objectives. When implementing an internal control system, one begins by stating the control objectives for the AIS or for the accounting cycle within the AIS. For the most part, each accounting cycle has four goals: (1) to safeguard the assets of the entity; (2) to engage only in those transactions authorized by management; (3) to record all transactions completely and accurately; and (4) to safeguard the accounting records.

Enumerate and Explain Major Control Policies and Procedures. There are six categories of control activities: (1) assignment of authority and responsibility; (2) authorization of transactions; (3) maintenance of adequate accounting records; (4) limited access to assets; (5) independent verifications; and (6) segregation of duties.

Assigning authority and responsibility allows managers and employees to understand clearly what they can and cannot do.

Authorizations are policies set up by management with respect to certain types of transactions, while approvals are implementations of some authorization, often evidenced by the signature of a person with the authority to engage in the transaction. Requiring transactions to have authorizations helps maintain control by insisting that employees execute only those transactions that meet management's approval.

To maintain adequate accounting records provides the evidence that legitimate transactions have taken place. Maintenance of the accounting records also provides an audit trail, references that link various documents and accounting data, yielding evidence of what took place.

By limiting access to the firm's assets, management can decrease the chances of theft or misuse. It also makes it relatively easy to ascertain who is responsible if problems develop.

Independent verifications are procedures that check up on individuals and the TPS or parts of the TPS. These independent and random checks help to assure that individuals are acting within their proper scope of authority and that the TPS is working as designed.

Segregation of duties ensures that no one performs duties that are incompatible from an internal control perspective. Firms want to keep the custody of assets separate from authorization of transactions and from accounting.

Demonstrate the Importance of Controlling Cash. Cash is the most vulnerable of assets since it is desired by everybody and, without proper controls, it is easily misappropriated.

List Common Audit Procedures of the Cash Account. In one procedure the auditor compares canceled checks with the cash disbursements journal for the date, payee, and amount. Another audit procedure involves examination of the canceled checks for signature, endorsement, and cancellation by the bank. In yet another audit procedure, the auditor compares deposits in the bank with the cash receipts journal as to the date, customer, and amount. A fourth audit procedure has the auditor perform a bank reconciliation. The last audit procedure covered in the text is a followup of the outstanding checks from a bank reconciliation.

Discuss Usage of Cash Registers. Cash registers record transactions internally to indicate how much cash should be in the cash register. They also record transactions externally to induce the customer to check for errors in the processing of the transaction. One individual operates the cash register, a second person compares the cash in the drawer with the internal records, and a third deposits the cash in the bank.

Describe Electronic Funds Transfers. Computers provide an electronic means of moving money from one entity to another. Banks can do this because the checking accounts are maintained electronically, and banks can easily take money out of one account and convey it to another by giving a computer certain commands. These cash flows effected by computerized instructions rather than bills, coins, or checks are termed electronic funds transfers (EFTs). Accounting for cash does not change when electronic funds transfers are utilized, though new control policies and procedures are needed to protect the cash account when electronic funds transfers are utilized.

Perform a Bank Reconciliation. A bank reconciliation is an audit procedure of the cash account in which the cash balance per the firm's books is compared with the cash balance per the bank statement. To conduct a bank reconciliation, carry out the following two-step procedure. Adjust the bank balance for items accounted for by the firm but not by the bank, such as outstanding checks and outstanding deposits. Also adjust for bank errors, if any. Second, adjust the book balance for items accounted for by the bank but not by the firm, such as service charges and EFT. Adjust also for any errors by the company. The two adjusted balances should be equal, and the balance is referred to as the true cash balance.

Summarize the Purpose of Petty Cash Funds and How They Operate. A petty cash fund is a special cash fund set up to make relatively small cash payments. The petty cash fund is established by giving the money to one person who is in charge of the fund, called the petty cash officer. When a need arises for the petty cash fund, the custodian pays out the cash and prepares a petty cash voucher stating what the transaction is and what the cash was disbursed for. The petty cash officer also obtains other documents to verify the legitimacy of the transaction. From time to time the fund is replenished. That is, the petty cash fund receives additional money such that the fund is restored to its original balance. The sum of the expenditures, as evidenced by the petty cash vouchers, should equal the amount of replenished cash.

GLOSSARY

Accounting records—input documents, output documents, journals, and ledgers of a firm.

Approval—an implementation of some authorization, often evidenced by the signature of a person with the authority to engage in the transaction.

Audit committee—a committee under the board of directors, consisting of members who are independent of management, which interacts with external auditors.

Audit trail—references that link various documents and accounting data.

Authority—legitimate power to determine certain issues and command others to do certain things.

Authorization—a policy set up by management with respect to certain types of transactions.

Bank reconciliation—an audit procedure of the cash account in which the cash balance per the firm's books is compared with the cash balance per the bank statement.

Board of directors—a group of persons who govern the activities of the corporation.

Cancel—identifying documents in such a way that they cannot be used as evidence for more than one transaction.

Control activities—policies and procedures implemented by managers to assure that specific goals are met.

Control environment—actions and behaviors that indicate how managers and directors feel about control issues.

Electronic funds transfer—a cash flow effected by computerized instructions rather than bills, coins, or checks.

Imprest fund—a cash fund, usually fixed in amount, that is set aside for a special purpose.

Independent verification—procedures that check up on individuals and the TPS or parts of the TPS.

Internal control—the process of reasonably assuring the realization of corporate goals.

Internal control system—a set of policies and procedures that collectively provide a reasonable assurance that the entity accomplishes its goals of effective and efficient operations, reliable financial reports, and compliance with laws and regulations.

Limited access—allowing access to certain assets only to those individuals who have the authority to do so.

Monitoring—an assessment of the system's performance.

Petty cash fund—a special cash fund set up to make relatively small cash payments.

Petty cash voucher—a document filled out by the petty cash officer that states what the transaction is and what the cash was disbursed for.

Policy—a statement of what ought to be done when certain conditions are met.

Procedure—a particular course of action.

Reconciliation—a computation that supports some specific amount with other evidence.

Responsibility—accountability for one's actions.

Risk assessment—the identification and analysis and, where applicable, the quantification of the risks that managers face in their attempts to achieve corporate goals.

Segregation of duties—ensuring that no one performs duties that are incompatible from an internal control perspective.

REVIEW QUESTIONS

1. What was the subject of the Treadway Commission's inquiry?
2. Who is COSO, and what is its significance?
3. Of what importance are management assertions?
4. What financial-statement assertions do managers make when they publish financial reports? Explain each of them.
5. What three groups desire good internal control systems? Why are they yearning for good internal control systems?
6. How did the Foreign Corrupt Practices Act of 1977 affect the accounting profession?
7. Define internal control and internal control systems.
8. Name the components of an internal control system.
9. Define control environment and indicate its importance.
10. Managers control those employees under them, but who controls the managers of the corporation?
11. What is meant by risk assessment?
12. What are control activities?
13. In terms of an internal control system, what is meant by information and communication?
14. What is monitoring, and why is it necessary?
15. Most organizations have four general control objectives. Name them.
16. There are six main control policies and procedures. What are they?

17. Explain the significance of the assignment of authority and responsibility.

18. Authorization of transactions is one of the control activities of the firm. Discuss what this activity entails.

19. Why should a corporation maintain adequate accounting records?

20. When a person cancels a document, what is done to the document? What is the purpose of canceling documents?

21. Why is it important to limit access to the firm's resources?

22. What are imprest funds?

23. What is meant by independent verifications, and what role do they play in an internal control system?

24. What are reconciliations? In what sense is a bank reconciliation a reconciliation?

25. When a firm segregates duties, what does it accomplish?

26. List some audit procedures for the cash account.

27. Discuss control aspects of cash registers.

28. What are electronic funds transfers? How do they affect financial accounting? How do they affect internal control systems?

29. What is a bank reconciliation? How does one conduct a bank reconciliation?

30. Explain why a firm might have a petty cash fund and how it operates.

31. Discuss briefly how to account for a petty cash fund.

32. What internal control issues exist with respect to a petty cash fund?

DISCUSSION QUESTIONS

1. Firms set up internal control systems to safeguard assets and to generate reliable reports. What do internal control systems imply about human nature?

2. From a coldly analytical point of view, dating has benefits and costs and risks (okay, that's just reality). Lynn Brighton has just received a proposal of marriage from Mark Pringle. Desiring objectivity, Lynn solicits your help in making a rational decision with regard to this offer. Help Lynn to perform this analysis by viewing the issue from an internal control perspective (though you don't have to tell Lynn that!).

3. To protect the privacy of students, many universities release grades only to students and their faculty advisors and to deans who deal with students. Using the framework of internal control, as developed by COSO, discuss how universities ought to establish a strategy to minimize the probability and the problems of releasing grades to unauthorized individuals.

4. Kryfelt Chemical manufactures highly explosive materials. Using the framework of internal control, as developed by COSO, discuss how Kryfelt's management should establish a strategy to minimize the probability and costs of an explosion.

5. You receive a fax that contains an interesting business proposition. Are there any control issues with respect to this fax?

6. Would it ever make sense for a firm to audit the addresses of customers and suppliers?

7. In electronic commerce (sometimes referred to as e-commerce), the parties transact their business electronically, for example, over the Internet. What are the control objectives of the buyer? the seller?

Many Americans still do not buy anything via the Internet. When asked why not, most claim that they are afraid of getting gypped by the seller or that they are afraid of revealing their credit card number to some computer hacker. Firms have begun hiring accountants to provide assurance services to these potential customers.

How is this situation analogous to independent, external CPAs auditing the financial statements of a company? What would you expect these accountants to assure?

EXERCISES

1. The text presents five types of management assertions:

(a) existence or occurrence,   (d) rights and obligations, and

(b) completeness,   (e) presentation and disclosure. *—footnotes*

(c) valuation or allowance,

For each of the following items, indicate which assertion is being made. In some cases, more than one assertion is being made.

(1) The balance sheet says that inventory is $2,300,000. *a,b,c e*

(2) The footnotes indicate that the firm uses the LIFO method for valuing the inventory.

(3) The income statement gives operating expenses of $560,000.

(4) The balance sheet claims that total liabilities are $3,000,000.

(5) The footnotes describe the major lawsuits facing the corporation.

(6) The allowance for doubtful accounts is $200,000.

(7) Sales are $4,200,000.

(8) Sales are recognized upon shipment of the goods.

(9) The entity has paid $300,000 for trading securities, which now have a market value of $290,000.

(10) The footnotes explain the contingent liabilities of the firm (items that may become liabilities in the future).

2. As explained in the text, internal control systems have five components:

(a) control environment,   (d) information and communication, and

(b) risk assessment,   (e) monitoring. *—feedback*

(c) control activities,

For each of the following items, indicate which component is being applied. In some cases, more than one component is exercised.

(1) The firm prints and distributes to all employees a copy of the firm's policies and procedures.

(2) An internal audit committee is formed.

(3) Internal auditors perform a bank reconciliation.

(4) The firm creates a code of ethics.

(5) Internal auditors test whether a computer hacker can break into the firm's computers.

(6) The company determines the consequences if a warehouse is destroyed (e.g., by fire).

(7) An employee is fired for embezzling funds. This fact is announced in a company newsletter.

(8) The corporation doesn't allow bookkeepers to have a key to the warehouse.

(9) The firm considers the consequences of the firm's computers being destroyed physically or by viruses.

(10) Keys to the computer office are limited to only certain personnel.

3. Control objectives in part establish goals to substantiate management assertions. Show how the control objectives for the sales cycle, given in Exhibit 7.3, corroborate management assertions as applied to sales, which are listed in Exhibit 7.1.

4. As explained in the text, there are six control activities. They are:

(a) assignment of authority and responsibility,

(b) authorization of transactions,

(c) maintenance of adequate accounting records,

(d) limited access to assets,

(e) independent verifications, and

(f) segregation of duties.

For each of the following items, indicate which control activity is being applied. In some cases, more than one control activity is utilized.

(1) The firm keeps stock and bond investments in a safe that can be opened only by certain personnel.

(2) The personnel who can open the safe cannot record transactions involving investments.

(3) The company does not allow investments in derivatives. —policy no high risk

(4) The vice-president of investments decides what stocks and bonds the firm invests in.

(5) Internal auditors inspect the stock and bond securities on a random, surprise basis.

(6) The vice-president of investments can decide the investment strategy of the firm but does not account for investments.

(7) Before a buy or sale of stock is carried out, the treasurer of the firm must give her approval.

(8) The board of directors examines the investment strategy of the firm.

(9) When purchases or sales of investments are made by the company, the broker reports are obtained and saved.

(10) Market prices of the stock and bond investments are obtained.

5. Organization charts depict the various segments of the organization in terms of superior–subordinate relationships. A very simple example of an organization chart is shown on the next page.

Organization charts are useful both as a component of the control environment and as a control activity. Explain.

6. Give at least one example of an authorization/approval for every cycle except for the general ledger cycle. (Break the expenditure and revenue cycles into two cycles each.)

7. Image processing is a technology that allows organizations to copy documents into electronic form. This is done by scanning the paper version and storing the image in a computerized form. When somebody wants to see the document, he or she retrieves the electronic image and views it on a computer screen. As desired, the user can print hard copies from the computerized file.

(a) The technology permits firms to destroy the paper documents by saving the electronic images of those documents. Is this technology an acceptable means of maintaining adequate accounting records?

(b) Suppose that this is an acceptable form of maintaining accounting records. Are there any other control issues that need to be addressed?

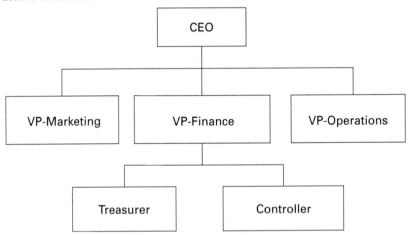

8. The sales journal included a column for the invoice number. The purchases journal had a column for the purchase order number. What is the purpose of these columns?

9. Cash includes cash on hand, cash in the bank, payroll cash, and petty cash. The accountant can have these items as four different accounts in the general ledger and informally aggregate these items when a balance sheet is prepared. Alternatively, the bookkeeper can have one cash account and have the various items as subsidiary accounts. What are the advantages and disadvantages of these two methods of handling the various cash accounts?

10. Purchasing departments buy supplies and inventories from vendors; they do so by writing a purchase order. A purchase order is a document sent by the entity to purchase goods from a vendor. Receiving departments receive goods that have been purchased by the firm; when they receive supplies and inventories, they create a receiving report. A receiving report is a document generated by the receiving department to show what goods they have received and what condition they are in. Why would an auditor reconcile purchase orders with receiving reports? (*Hint:* What potential problems exist if goods that are purchased have not been received? if goods have been received for which there are no purchase orders?)

11. On the next two pages are the cash receipts journal and the cash disbursements journal of the Bold Nold Express for the first week of November.

Required:

(a) Given the cash receipts journal, what do you expect the daily deposits to be?

(b) Given the cash disbursements journal, what checks do you expect to find in the corporate checkbook?

12. Bob McLaughin owns his own retail business. He feels that the business is doing very well but wonders why he doesn't have more cash. He hires you to investigate his firm and help him out.

In your examination, you discover that the business enterprise has two cash registers, and they are operated by several part-time workers. The last cashiers for the day count the cash in the cash register they were using. They also compare the cash total with the amount indicated by the internal tape. The assistant manager then takes the cash and deposits it at the bank. The next day the assistant manager prepares a journal entry for the amount of cash deposited in the bank.

You also discover that during rush times, since there are only two cash registers, Bob allows those customers who have the exact amount of the sale to simply give the cash to one of the cashiers and leave. The cashier will then ring up the sale later when it is less busy.

Finally, you find out that the return policy for McLaughlin's business is to return the item to a cashier. The cashier receives the returned goods and gives them cash out of the cash register.

Required: Write a report to Bob McLaughlin and make suggestions on how he can improve his business.

13. Mackey Company just received its bank statement in the mail, and you have been assigned the bank reconciliation. The ending balance per the bank statement is $4,810; per Mackey's books it is $4,545. Outstanding checks total $1,725, and there is a deposit in transit of $1,200. The bank charges Mackey a service charge of $25. You also discover two errors. Check number 2315 for $145 was omitted from the check register. Check number 2401 was for $545 but the bookkeeper recorded the check as $455. Prepare the bank reconciliation.

14. On April 1, the Tomfoolery Company created a petty cash fund of $500. On April 32 the petty cash officer presented vouchers for the following disbursements:

Freight paid on purchases	$110
Office supplies purchased	50
Withdrawal by Thomas Dunce, proprietor	150

Cash in the fund totaled $200 on April 32; the fund was replenished on that date.
Required: Prepare the journal entries on April 1 and April 32.

PROBLEMS

1. What assertions do managers make with respect to the cash flow statement?

2. Recall the management responsibility report and the unqualified audit report, both deliberated in Chapter 1. What assertions do managers make in the management responsibility report? What assertions do auditors make in the unqualified audit report?

3. State the control objectives for the following accounting cycles: cash disbursements cycle, cash receipts cycle, financing cycle, investments cycle, payroll cycle, production cycle, and purchases cycle.

4. Firms use a receiving department to admit items into the entity's possession. The receiving department receives goods that have been purchased by the firm, and it receives goods that are being returned by customers.

(a) Why do companies employ receiving departments? Why not let the purchasing department receive items from vendors? Why not let the sales department receive goods returned from customers?

(b) Receiving departments typically fill out a receiving report. What data are written down on this report?

(c) What control objectives are supported by a receiving department? How is this accomplished?

BOLD NOLD EXPRESS

Cash Receipts Journal

Date	Cash (DR)	Sales Discount (DR)	Accounts receivable Customer	F	(CR)	Sales (CR)	Other Account	F	(DR)	(CR)
11-1	$ 800					$800				
11-2	$ 980	$ 20	Dan Dorsey	*	$ 1,000					
11-2	$ 2,000		Steve Heinz	*	$ 2,000					
11-5	$ 5,000						Common Stock	320		$5,000
11-5	$ 400		Stacy Sublett	*	$ 400					
11-6	$ 500		Liz Hainey	*	$ 500					
11-7	$ 3,000		Joan Andrews	*	$ 3,000					
11-7	$ 4,900	$100	Dan Miller	*	$ 5,000					
TOTAL	$17,580	$120			$11,900	$800				*
	(100)	(620)			(120)	(600)				

BOLD NOLD EXPRESS

Cash Payments Journal

Date	Cash (CR)	Purchase Discount (CR)	Accounts payable Vendor	F	(DR)	Purchases (DR)	Other Account	F	(DR)	(CR)
11-1	$ 150					$150				
11-2	$ 98	$ 2	Meriam Smith	*	$ 100					
11-6	$ 9,000						Auto (Kleinart's Kars)	161	$9,000	
11-7	$ 1,000		Pat Barbash	*	$1,000					
TOTAL	$10,248	$ 2			$1,100	$150				
	(100)	(510)			(200)	(500)				

223

5. Joy Saftner, the controller of Aerie International, looked at the CEO Tom Sneed and said, "We are hurting this year. Earnings are down, and there is no way that we will meet the forecasts by financial analysts."

> "That's not good," replied Tom. He swiveled his chair back and forth as he meditated this bad news. Then he asked, "What would happen if sales increased?"
> "Oh, things would improve a lot. If revenues were up another 10% or so, we could come close to budget. Real close." She sighed. "Assuming that there are no other expenses." She paused again. "But how can we do that when the fiscal year ends tomorrow."
> Tom Sneed smiled fiendishly. "Don't worry about it. I'll talk things over with Mike." He was referring to Michael Barzloff, the chief operating officer.

Joy wondered what her boss was thinking. Not willing to probe any further, she left his office.

Two weeks later Saftner was looking at the financial statements, and she noticed that revenues somehow had increased 11% over her original number and that the corporation had hit the analysts' forecasts. At the same time, Joy noticed that sales in the new year so far were zero. Suspecting that Tom and Mike moved current sales into the previous year, she confronted the CEO.

Unabashed, Tom Sneed laughed at her questions. "Yes, of course, we moved the sales from these two weeks into last December. They're legitimate sales, so we aren't hurting anybody."

> "But how about the auditors? Won't they find out what happened?"
> "No, of course not," replied Tom. "But just to make sure, we covered it up by changing the date function in the computers. The dates were moved back to December 14. Tonight Mike will move them to January 15. Nobody will know."

As Joy comprehended that the invoices would be dated December of last year and not January of this year, she realized that the documents were tainted by the erroneous data.

Required: Answer the following questions about this case.

(a) Did Tom and Mike do anything wrong?

(b) What should Joy do?

(c) Would any internal control procedure have prevented Tom and Mike from changing the date function in the firm's computers?

6. Hope Valley Scents went belly up. After entering corporate bankruptcy, the investment community learned that corporate officers from Hope Valley Scents had falsified the corporate financial statements by overstating sales and by understating cost of goods sold, thereby increasing income. They understated cost of goods sold by overstating ending inventory.

Required: Answer the following questions about this case.

(a) If the fictitious sales are booked as cash sales, how would an auditor likely discover the fraud? What does this imply about the journal entries for these sham transactions?

(b) Explain fully how overstating ending inventory leads to lower cost of goods sold.

(c) To detect this fraudulent scheme, the auditors could have counted which two assets?

(d) How does counting assets help one to discover whether somebody is overstating income?

7. Ashish & Jolly, Limited is preparing its bank reconciliation. Its October 31 balance in the cash in bank account is $24,311, while the bank statement shows a balance of $26,579. After looking at the bank statement, the canceled checks, and other records, the clerk performing the reconciliation discerns the following:

(a) Checks outstanding total $3,151.

(b) Outstanding deposits total $1,100.

(c) The bank charges a service charge of $30.

(d) The bank has collected a note receivable for Ashish & Jolly, principal of $1,000 and interest of $70. The firm has not yet recorded the transaction.

(e) The firm erroneously omitted writing check number 3392 in the check register. Written to a vendor for merchandise received, the check equals $787.

(f) The firm's check number 3189, written for $59, was erroneously charged by the bank for $95.

Required

(1) Prepare the October bank reconciliation for Ashish & Jolly, Limited.

(2) Prepare the necessary journal entries for Ashish & Jolly, Limited.

8. Elliott & Sons has just received its September bank statement. Mark Elliott, who is responsible for the bank reconciliation, has asked for your help. He shows you the following documents.

September Bank Statement

The overview of the statement shows:

Balance, August 31	$22,333
Deposits and other credits	2,093
Checks and other debits	(5,124)
Balance, September 30	$19,302

Deposits, per the bank statement:

Date of deposit	Amount
September 7	$ 410
September 14	785
September 21	898
	$2,093

Checks, per the bank statement:

Check Number	Amount	Check Number	Amount
191	$680	265	$ 64
254	92	268	115
257	991	269	51
259	100	270	248
260	32	271	198
261	249	273	45
262	358	275	560
263	47	276	850
264	151		

Other debits, per the bank statement:

Service charge	$ 35
EFT: phone company	258

Ledger Account: Cash in Bank

The overview of the account shows:

Balance, August 31	$19,542
Deposits	2,516
Checks	(4,181)
Balance, September 30	$17,877

Deposits made in September:

Date of Deposit	Amount
September 5	$ 410
September 11	785
September 19	898
September 29	423
	$2,516

Checks written during September:

Check Number	Amount	Check Number	Amount
259	$100	268	$115
260	32	269	51
261	249	270	248
262	358	271	198
263	47	272	45
264	151	273	45
265	64	274	945
266	123	275	560
267	void	276	850

Bank Reconciliation—August

Bank balance	$22,333	Book balance	$19,572
Outstanding checks	2,791	Service charge	30
	$19,542		$19,542

where the outstanding checks are:

Check Number	Amount
191	$ 680
252	1,100
254	92
257	919

Required
(a) Help Mark Elliott to prepare the bank reconciliation for September. Assume that any errors are made by Elliott & Sons and are due to an incorrect debit or credit to accounts payable.
(b) Tell Mark which journal entries ought to be prepared as a result of the bank reconciliation.

9. Karen Ruddy, clerk for Smiley & Daughters, needed a little cash to hold her over until the next payday. So she "borrowed" $100 from the cash receipts. Unfortunately, another employee keeps the books, so the receipt of the $100 was recorded. While Karen was trying to think of how to cover up her "temporary loan," she looked at the mail and noticed the monthly bank statement. Her bank reconciliation, without the "loan," would have been:

Bank balance	$600	Book balance	$550
Outstanding checks	300	Service charge	50
	$300		
Deposits in transit	200		
	$500		$500

where the outstanding checks are:

Check Number	Amount
3177	$ 75
3281	150
3293	25
3297	50

Given the "loan," however, the actual bank balance is $500.

Required
(a) How can Karen cover up her "borrowing" through the bank reconciliation?
(b) How can Karen get away with this "loan"?

(c) How can this "borrowing" be discovered?

(d) What can the firm do to discourage this scheme in the future?

10. Mork Barnes and Mindy Kondracke are the petty cash officers for Hamre, Inc. One Tuesday morning Eddie Bissell and Sheila Adams, both from the internal audit department, paid a surprise visit to Mork and Mindy. It lasted a brief time, and then they left.

Suspicious, Eddie and Sheila returned only two weeks later. Eddie looked at the following voucher:

HAMRE, INC.
Petty Cash Voucher

Date   March 17, 2002

Paid to: Sam Stone

Amount paid: $250.00

Explanation: To give a customer money for a sales return

Account to charge: Sales returns and allowances

Signature of petty cash officer: *Mork Barnes*

Eddie Bissell said, "I swear this same voucher was here last time."

"No," protested Mork. "Probably it was just a different customer. I'm forever giving money to a customer for a return."

Sheila looked at the cash receipt signed by Sam Stone and noted that it wasn't dated. "What's going on, Mork?"

Eddie added, "What did Sam Stone return?"

Mork Barnes continued to complain, but Eddie and Sheila continued looking into the matter. So Mork changed his tune, "If there's a problem, you should be talking with Mindy, not with me."

Required: Evaluate the petty cash fund from an internal control perspective.

CHAPTER *8*

THE GENERAL LEDGER CYCLE

The general ledger cycle is the accounting cycle that handles miscellaneous transactions, adjusting entries, closing entries, correcting entries, reversing entries (if used), and the preparation of financial reports. This cycle is unlike any of the other cycles because it does not involve any interaction with other entities, such as customers and suppliers, and it does not undertake any economic activity, such as producing goods. Essentially, the general ledger function maintains the general journal and the general ledger, and then outputs financial reports to investors and creditors as well as other management reports, and allows managers to query the accounting database.

To carry out its task, the general ledger department interacts with all of the other cycles, principally obtaining accounting data from them, so that the accounting department can update the accounts and produce up-to-date financial reports. In a manual system, this transfer of data is often accomplished by transmittal of a journal voucher, a document that contains the appropriate accounting data. In a computerized system, much of this work is performed electronically and automatically.

Before discussing the general ledger cycle, we need to provide some additional details about accounting information systems. These issues pertain to the initial establishment of the accounting system and the methods for documenting how the accounting system operates. We also sketch a template for describing the accounting cycles.

After reading and studying this chapter, you should be able to:

- Define accounting manual, standard accounting entries, chart of accounts, and coding schemes;
- Explain the importance of documenting an accounting system;
- Describe flowcharting symbols and the principles of flowcharting an accounting cycle;
- State the various aspects in the template for examining the accounting cycles;
- Define the general ledger cycle, explain its functions, and tell who is responsible for the cycle;
- List the control objectives of the general ledger cycle;
- Describe a journal voucher and its use;
- State the files employed in the general ledger cycle;
- Indicate how the general ledger master file is kept up to date;
- Explain the flowchart for maintenance of the general ledger; and
- Explain the flowchart for the general ledger end-of-period procedures.

SOME GENERAL ISSUES

Consider a new firm that is in the process of getting organized. (Similar issues exist when companies install new accounting systems.) Although much of the managerial effort will be directed toward getting customers, establishing relationships with suppliers, and hiring talented workers, some effort will be aimed at setting up a corporate infrastructure that can successfully compete with other businesses. Part of that endeavor will focus on creating an AIS that can provide relevant and reliable information on a timely basis.

When establishing a new accounting system, managers often will create an accounting manual, determine the standard accounting entries, produce a chart of accounts, and invent appropriate coding schemes. These steps provide a means for deciding various accounting issues, such as which accounting method to adopt (when the firm has a choice) and who is responsible for collecting and transmitting the data. It also provides a foundation for the internal auditors and external auditors to understand the corporate AIS.

The Accounting Manual

An *accounting manual* is a book that indicates how the accounting system is set up and provides the basic instructions on how it operates. It lists the positions within the accounting department and provides a job description for each position. More importantly, the accounting manual states the company's policies with respect to financial reporting issues. It also describes the particular accounting cycles for the firm and states the responsibilities within each cycle. The manual supplies the firm's standard accounting entries, chart of accounts, and its coding scheme.

Standard Accounting Entries

When designing the AIS, the accountant needs to consider the likely transactions in which the corporation will engage. For these transactions, the management team chooses how to account for them in what are termed standard accounting entries or standard journal entries.

Standard accounting entries are an enumeration of the suggested journal entries for transactions in which the firm might engage. In practice, the accountant considers the standard accounting entries after organizing the firm's transactions into accounting cycles. Accountants classify repetitive transactions into these cycles because it provides an effective and efficient way of operating an AIS. As described in Chapter 6, many entities have eight transaction cycles: the expenditure, facilities, financing, general ledger, investments, payroll, production, and revenue cycles. Business enterprises add to, delete from, or modify this list as is appropriate for their corporate needs.

For each cycle, the accountant considers the specific transactions that might occur. A standard accounting entry is selected for each possible transaction. This choice is especially important in those cases in which the firm has several different ways of booking the transaction.

For example, consider the purchase of supplies for $1,000 with the terms that a 2% discount can be taken if the bill is paid in 10 days; otherwise, the full amount must be paid in 30 days. In Chapter 3 we gave only one journal entry for the initial purchase. In fact, the company can record this transaction in four possible ways, depending on whether the firm wants to charge (i.e., debit) supplies or supplies expense and whether the company desires to employ the gross method or the net method. (Remember that it doesn't matter which account is initially debited as long as the accountant makes the correct adjusting entry to update the accounts. Also, it doesn't matter whether the firm measures the purchases at gross or net amounts, although the choice will affect how the corporation accounts for later transactions.) The four choices are:

1. Supplies; gross method

Supplies	$1,000	
Accounts payable		$1,000

2. Supplies; net method

Supplies	$ 980	
Accounts payable		$ 980

3. Supplies expense; gross method

Supplies expense	$1,000	
Accounts payable		$1,000

4. Supplies expense; net method

Supplies expense	$ 980	
Accounts payable		$ 980

This example is discussed further in Chapter 10.

The key point is that the firm needs to choose which method it will apply for various possible transactions. These standard accounting entries are placed in the accounting manual to assist accountants, managers, and auditors in understanding the corporate AIS.

The Chart of Accounts

Once the standard entries are determined, one can draw up a chart of accounts. We briefly discussed the chart of accounts in Chapter 3. You will recall that the *chart of accounts* is a list of all accounts used by an entity and the numbers used to code the accounts. Exhibit 8.1 contains an example of a chart of accounts. The idea is for the accountant to conceive of all possible transactions of the firm and then have an account established that can be employed for this set of possible transactions.

The numbers assigned to the accounts are, of course, arbitrary. Some meaning can be infused into the numbers by assigning like accounts with similar numbers. For example, Exhibit 8.1 depicts current assets as ranging between 100 and 199, property, plant, and equipment as 200–299, current liabilities as 300–399, long-term liabilities as 400–499, stockholders' equity as 500–599, revenues as 600–699, expenses as 700–799, and miscellaneous accounts as 900–999.

In past chapters we booked transactions by using the account titles. For example, to record a credit sale of $1,000, the accountant makes the following journal entry:

Accounts receivable	$1,000	
Sales		$1,000

With assigned account numbers, the accountant could just as easily make the entry with the account numbers instead of the account titles. Thus, employing the chart of accounts in Exhibit 8.1, we could record the above transaction as:

120	$1,000	
601		$1,000

Accountants usually apply the account titles because humans can more easily make sense of the titles instead of the account numbers. When computers record and store the transactions, it will be more efficient to use the account numbers.

Coding Schemes

Computers gain efficiency by using the account numbers because accountants employ coding schemes that help to classify the data into useful categories. This concept can be extended by adding details to the numbers such as indicating which store or salesperson made the sales.

EXHIBIT 8.1

CHART OF ACCOUNTS

Current Assets (100–199)
- 101 Cash in bank
- 102 Petty cash
- 110 Trading securities
- 120 Accounts receivable
- 121 Allowance for doubtful accounts
- 130 Merchandise inventory
- 140 Office supplies
- 150 Prepaid insurance
- 160 Prepaid rent

Property, Plant, and Equipment (200–299)
- 210 Land
- 220 Buildings
- 221 Accumulated depreciation—buildings
- 230 Machinery
- 231 Accumulated depreciation—machinery
- 240 Equipment
- 241 Accumulated depreciation—equipment

Current Liabilities (300–399)
- 310 Accounts payable
- 320 Notes payable (short-term)
- 330 Wages and salaries payable
- 340 Interest payable
- 341 Taxes payable
- 350 Bonds payable—current portion
- 360 Mortgage payable—current portion

Long-term Liabilities (400–499)
- 420 Notes payable (long-term)
- 470 Bonds payable
- 471 Discount on bonds payable
- 472 Premium on bonds payable
- 480 Mortgage payable

Stockholders' Equity (500–599)
- 510 Preferred stock
- 515 Additional paid-in capital—preferred stock
- 520 Common stock

Stockholders' Equity (500–599) (*continued*)
- 525 Additional paid-in capital—common stock
- 540 Retained earnings
- 560 Treasury stock
- 565 Additional paid-in capital—treasury stock

Revenues (601–699)
- 601 Sales
- 620 Investment income (trading securities)
- 630 Gain on sale of land
- 631 Gain on sale of buildings
- 632 Gain on sale of machinery
- 633 Gain on sale of equipment
- 690 Miscellaneous income

Expenses (700–799)
- 700 Cost of goods sold
- 705 Wages and salaries expense
- 710 Supplies expense
- 715 Telephone expense
- 720 Electricity expense
- 725 Insurance expense
- 730 Rent expense
- 740 Depreciation expense—buildings
- 741 Depreciation expense—machinery
- 742 Depreciation expense—equipment
- 750 Loss on sale of land
- 751 Loss on sale of buildings
- 752 Loss on sale of machinery
- 753 Loss on sale of equipment
- 755 Investment losses (trading securities)
- 760 Interest expense
- 770 Bad debts expense
- 790 Miscellaneous expense

Miscellaneous (900–999)
- 900 Dividends—preferred stock
- 910 Dividends—common stock
- 950 Cash short and over
- 999 Income summary

A *coding scheme* is a system of representing economic phenomena by a set of numbers or letters or other symbols. In the coding scheme involved in Exhibit 8.1 every number has three digits. The first digit reveals the type of account it is:

1—current assets

2—property, plant, and equipment

3—current liabilities

4—long-term liabilities

5—stockholders' equity

6—revenues

7—expenses

9—miscellaneous

The next two digits identify the specific account within the category. Thus, account 631, which is a revenue, corresponds to gain on the sale of land.

The AIS can garner additional data if managers believe them to be worthwhile. For example, the management team of an automobile dealer might want to keep track of the type of car sold and who makes the sale. This goal can be implemented by creating a sales number that is a five-digit code, as illustrated in Exhibit 8.2.

Panel A of Exhibit 8.2 registers the coding scheme. The first three digits are "601" for sales. The fourth digit represents the type of automobile sold:

1 = Chrysler

2 = Mazda

3 = Hyundai

The fifth digit denotes the sales representative:

1 = Mohamed Hussein

2 = David Jensen

3 = Rajib Doogar

4 = Yong Kim

5 = Dick Kochanek

Thus, "60111" means that Mohamed Hussein has sold a Chrysler to some customer.

Panel B of Exhibit 8.2 provides hypothetical data for a given month. Panel C massages the data so that managers can see which type of car was sold and how much sales were generated by the sales staff. In practice, the AIS can publish management reports that show this information, or it can allow managers to query the database and discover the answers to specific questions.

The process that is followed to ascertain the specific results is fairly straightforward. For example, to find out the dollar sales of Hyundai's, select all the transactions in which the fourth digit is "3." There are three such transactions:

Code	Amount($)
60134	8,000
60132	8,000
60134	9,500

By adding up the second column, one determines that the dollar sales of Hyundai's amounted to $25,500. This process is repeated for all of the other attributes, and the reader should verify the results in panel C of Exhibit 8.2.

We discussed management queries in Chapter 6. Coding schemes are very useful in providing a means whereby the computer system can answer queries. An example is given in panel D of Exhibit 8.2. The query asks how much sales of a particular type of car did one particular sales representative produce. The AIS can answer this question by utilizing the code for the particular auto and the code for the particular individual; with these codes the computer searches the file and sums the data.

EXHIBIT *8.2*

EXAMPLE OF A CODING SCHEME

Panel A: Sales code (5 digits)

First three digits, 601, designate sales revenue.
Fourth digit indicates the type of automobile sold:

$$1 = \text{Chrysler}$$
$$2 = \text{Mazda}$$
$$3 = \text{Hyundai}$$

Fifth digit denotes the sales representative:

$$1 = \text{Mohamed Hussein}$$
$$2 = \text{David Jensen}$$
$$3 = \text{Rajib Doogar}$$
$$4 = \text{Yong Kim}$$
$$5 = \text{Dick Kochanek}$$

Panel B: Sales data for one month

Account Code	Amount of Sales
60134	$ 8,000
60111	32,000
60125	7,500
60124	9,000
60132	8,000
60121	10,000
60113	25,000
60125	12,000
60124	12,000
60134	9,500
60121	10,500
60114	29,000
TOTAL	$172,500

Panel C: Analysis of sales data

Sales by type of automobile

Chrysler	$ 86,000
Mazda	61,000
Hyundai	25,500
Total	$172,500

Sales by sales representative

Mohamed Hussein	$ 52,500
David Jensen	8,000
Rajib Doogar	25,000
Yong Kim	67,500
Dick Kochanek	19,500
Total	$172,500

Panel D: Example of a query

Query: "How many Mazda's did Yong Kim sell?"
Process: Look at all records that have "2" as the fourth digit and
"4" as the last digit.
Answer: There are two sales that total $21,000.

These processes are mechanical, and the computer excels at this type of computation. Account numbers add to this efficiency.

DOCUMENTATION OF AN ACCOUNTING SYSTEM

As stated earlier, the accounting manual shows the accounting cycles that the managers will utilize and describes each of them in detail. These representations include not only a description of the standard accounting entries and the accounts and their coding, but also a narration of the input documents that trigger the cycles, the output documents generated in the cycles, who is responsible for preparing the source documents, and how they are distributed. The usual format of these portrayals is via flowcharts. (Although most cycle activities are initiated by some input document, an exception should be noted. A few cycles begin with the passage of time; for example, firms typically make adjusting entries at the fiscal year-end.)

A *flowchart* is a graphical representation of some phenomena of interest. Of course, our concern is with accounting systems. Flowcharts come in many different flavors; we will restrict our focus to document flowcharts. *Document flowcharts* are flowcharts that depict input and output documents and indicate who creates the documents and who receives them. Other popular types of flowcharts include systems flowcharts (which are concerned with the hardware involved), entity relationship diagrams (which show the relationships among resources, events, and actors), and data flow diagrams (which portray processes, data sources, and data flows). These and other types of flowcharts are discussed in more advanced courses.

Flowcharting is important because it paints a picture of how the accounting system operates. At a minimum, accountants must know how to read flowcharts so that they can understand how an AIS is organized. Some accountants and information specialists also need the ability to prepare flowcharts so that others can read them. Auditors also use flowcharts to evaluate the internal controls of the AIS and their effectiveness.

Document Flowcharts

As stated, document flowcharts sketch an accounting cycle's documents and tell how they are processed. To draw the picture, accountants use standardized symbols. Exhibit 8.3 offers a list of the symbols that will be utilized in this text. More symbols exist, but we leave them to other courses. The six symbols we employ are the document, operation, file, records, connector, and document flowline symbols.

The *document symbol* will represent either an input or output document. It also signifies financial statements and management reports. Frequently, more than one copy of a document is prepared; for example, the firm would keep a sales order document for itself and also send a copy to the customer. Multiple copies are indicated in the flowchart by nesting the document symbols together and overlaying them onto one another. The multiple copies are also numbered. The flowchart will denote the path of each copy of each document.

An example is provided in Exhibit 8.4; it is actually a subset of a flowchart in the sales cycle and will be seen again in Chapter 9. Note that there is only one document, the sales order, and there are two copies of this document. One copy (copy #1) is sent to the customer, while the other (copy #2) is retained by the sales department.

The *operation symbol* (sometimes called a process symbol) depicts the processing

EXHIBIT 8.3

SYMBOLS FOR DOCUMENT FLOWCHARTS

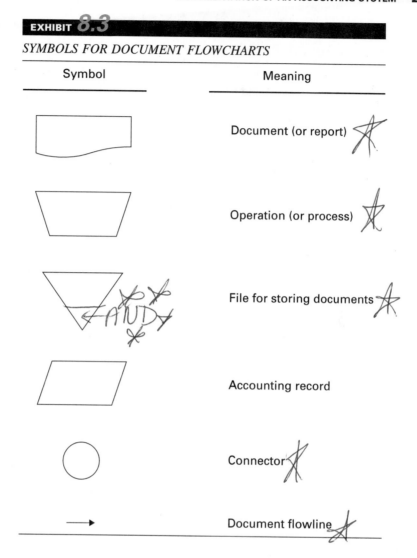

Symbol	Meaning
	Document (or report)
	Operation (or process)
	File for storing documents
	Accounting record
	Connector
	Document flowline

of documents or accounting data. This processing might include authorizing a credit sale or approving a purchase requisition. More advanced flowcharts distinguish among different types of processes, such as manual or computerized processes. We will keep things simple by using only one operation or processing symbol. In Exhibit 8.4 there is only one process: the sales department prepares the sales order.

The *file symbol* indicates that documents (or reports) are stored and how they are stored. For example, when money is deposited into the bank, the bank typically verifies the transaction with a bank deposit slip. The firm will store these deposit slips to prove that the transactions occurred. The file symbol in a flowchart indicates that the documents are stored. The letter A, D, or N, placed inside the file symbol, shows how they are stored. "A" signifies that the documents are stored alphabetically, "D" by date, and "N" by the document number.

Exhibit 8.4 reveals that the sales department files copy #2 of the sales order by the sales order number. The firm does not show what outsiders, such as customers, do with the sales order. That is their business.

EXHIBIT **8.4**

EXAMPLE OF A DOCUMENT FLOWCHART

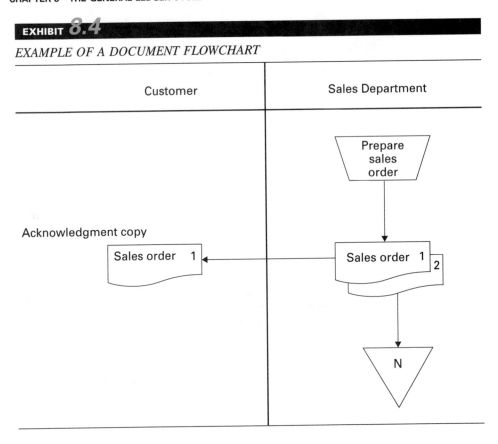

The *records symbol* is a flowchart symbol that represents accounting records, such as journals and ledgers. It shows who is responsible for the accounting records and maintains them. Although Exhibit 8.4 does not include a records symbol, one can be seen later in the chapter, specifically in Exhibits 8.9 and 8.10.

The *connector symbol* represents where one process interfaces another process that is shown elsewhere in the flowchart. Connector symbols are utilized when the graph is too big to be placed on one page or to reduce the clutter of placing lots of lines on the flowchart. In practice, two symbols are used, one to show an on-page connection and another to show an off-page connection. Since our document flowcharts will not be too large, we use the symbol in Exhibit 8.3 for both purposes. Exhibit 8.4 does not show a connector symbol, but we will see an example in Exhibit 8.10.

Finally, a *document flowline symbol* represents the direction in which data and documents flow during processing. Arrowheads show the direction of the flow. The flowlines in Exhibit 8.4 disclose that the process begins with the preparation of the sales order. Afterward, the sales department sends one copy to the customer to acknowledge the sale and retains one copy for its own records. This second copy is filed by sales order number. Thus, these flowlines show the order in which the various steps are carried out.

Good Flowcharting Techniques

Although this text concentrates on your ability to read document flowcharts, some exercises and problems will require their construction. Good techniques need to be employed

EXHIBIT 8.5

FIVE RULES OF GOOD FLOWCHARTING

1. Show the different departments and entities involved in the process.
2. Show the source of each document.
3. With an operation (process) symbol denote the preparation of each document.
4. Indicate the disposition of each document. *where do they go*
5. Provide written comments when they can clarify the process.

documentation

to allow others to read the flowchart and understand what is meant. For example, auditing relies in part on the documentation of the corporation's internal control system. Auditors do this by flowcharting the system.

Document flowcharts depend on a few proper techniques. First, show the different departments and entities involved in the process. Typically, a column is provided for each of them, and the documents it prepares or receives and the processing it does are sketched in the column. For example, Exhibit 8.4 shows the sales department and the customer. The customer column indicates that the customer receives a copy of the sales order, while the sales department column says that the department processes the sales order, sends a copy to the customer, and retains one copy for itself.

The next three techniques of good flowcharting deal with the creation, processing, and disposition of each document. These rules are: show the source of each document; with an operation (process) symbol denote the preparation of each document; and indicate the disposition of each document. Exhibit 8.4 communicates that the sales department prepares the sales order and that both the customer and the sales department receive a copy of the sales order.

Flowcharts can also be enhanced with some clarifying comments. Exhibit 8.4 does this by showing why the customer receives a copy of the sales order: it acts as an acknowledgment that the firm received the customer's order and is processing it. These comments help the reader to understand the purpose of various steps.

These five flowcharting rules are summarized in Exhibit 8.5. They will help keep the flowchart as simple as possible, which aids readability, and yet be thorough in capturing the details of what the company is doing.

TEMPLATE FOR EXAMINING ACCOUNTING CYCLES

Except for the last chapter, the remainder of the book examines the eight accounting cycles. We finish this chapter by looking at the general ledger cycle. Chapter 9 discusses the revenue cycle, and Chapter 10 examines the expenditure cycle in detail. Chapter 11 focuses on the payroll cycle and outlines the facilities cycle, the investments cycle, the financing cycle, and the production cycle.

We follow a similar pattern in describing these transaction cycles. To understand each cycle, let's begin by looking at the functions of the cycle. Knowing the functions of a particular cycle will help us understand what is expected in each accounting cycle. Next, we glance at the departments involved, so as to determine who is responsible for undertaking certain actions within the cycle. Each chapter also mentions the basic journal en-

---
EXHIBIT 8.6

TEMPLATE FOR EXAMINING ACCOUNTING CYCLES

---

1. Functions of the cycle
2. Departments involved in the cycle
3. Basic journal entries
4. Control objectives
5. Documents
6. Management reports and queries
7. Files
8. Document flowcharts

---

tries in the cycles, sometimes extending the bookkeeping knowledge gained in earlier chapters. We also present the control objectives within each cycle, utilizing the principles stated in Chapter 7.

To gather the data and process them into understandable form, and to provide the evidentiary matter that the transactions have management's authorization and they are properly accounted for, accountants employ documents. In each accounting cycle we enumerate the appropriate source documents. We also list some important management reports that can be prepared and management queries that the system ought to be able to handle. Using the concepts presented in Chapter 6, we also catalog the major files involved in each cycle, assuming a file-based computerized AIS. This will prepare the student for advanced courses that focus on computerized accounting systems. Finally, we either furnish the document flowcharts and explain them thoroughly, or we ask the student to prepare them in the chapter exercises and problems.

These steps for examining the accounting cycles are summarized in Exhibit 8.6. The reader need not study this list; rather, it is presented merely to help anticipate what will be covered as we dissect all of the accounting cycles.

THE GENERAL LEDGER CYCLE

The first cycle to place under a microscope is the general ledger cycle. The *general ledger cycle* is the accounting cycle that deals with miscellaneous transactions and the preparation of financial reports. Its ultimate objective is to publish the balance sheet, the income statement, the statement of changes in stockholders' equity, and the cash flow statement.

Functions of the Cycle

The general ledger cycle has three functions. First, this cycle handles all recording activities that are not the responsibility of any of the other accounting cycles. These recording activities include adjusting entries, closing entries, correcting entries, and, if they are utilized, reversing entries. The cycle employs the general journal (or journal vouchers, described later) for recording these particular transactions. Second, this cycle maintains the general ledger, so the other cycles must feed accounting data into the general ledger cycle, usually, a summary of the other cycle's transaction activities. Third, this cycle also prepares and distributes the financial accounting statements.

In practice, some companies do not have very many transactions in a paticular cycle, such as the investments cycle, so the firms eliminate the cycle, thereby requiring the general ledger cycle to journalize any transactions that normally are part of the investments cycle. We will ignore this possibility in the rest of the book.

Departments Involved in the Cycle

The department responsible for this cycle is termed the general ledger department. Rather than immediately moving on, we should consider this department's relationship with other departments, particularly those dealing with accounting issues.

The *finance department* handles all accounting and finance issues for the corporation. Although there are many variations in practice, one way of organizing the finance department is pictured in Exhibit 8.7. The *vice-president of finance* heads this department, which is subdivided into two parts, the treasury and the controller's department.

The *treasury department* is the group within the finance department that receives, maintains, and disburses cash. The *treasurer* is the chief executive of the treasury department. This department is responsible for cash inflows (called cash receipts) and cash outflows (labeled cash disbursements). The credit department reviews applications from customers for credit. It also approves or rejects credit sales to customers, depending on their credit history. In addition, the treasury manages financing issues whenever the enterprise needs to obtain additional funds (financing). On the other hand, when the business has excess cash and would like to invest it, this department also manages these

EXHIBIT 8.7

ORGANIZATION OF THE FINANCE DEPARTMENT

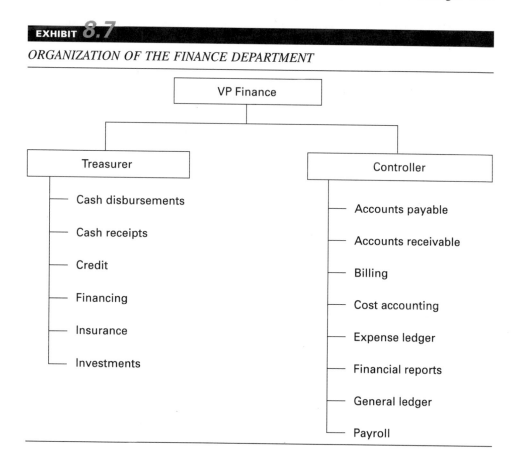

activities (in the investments department). Finally, the treasury is responsible for the insurance needs of the business enterprise.

The *controller's department* zeroes in on accounting concerns. This department is within the finance department, and it conducts the various accounting responsibilities, such as recording transactions and preparing financial statements. The *controller* (sometimes called the comptroller) is the chief executive of the controller's department. There exists several groups within the controller's department. As the names indicate, the accounts payable and the accounts receivable departments supervise credit purchases and credit sales. Billing supervises the billing of customers when sales are made. Cost accounting determines the cost of products and services. Expense ledger handles the accounting for operating expenses. Financial reports prepares the financial statements, both those issued to investors and creditors and those designed for corporate managers. The *general ledger department*, the focus of this half of the chapter, summarizes all the accounting data and updates the general ledger. Payroll deals with the accounting for wages and salaries.

Before leaving this organizational detail, the reader should notice the separation of the treasury department (those who handle the money) and the controller's department (those who account for the money) and the partitioning of each of these departments into various groups. Besides enhancing organizational efficiency, this organizational structure achieves segregation of duties. This setup keeps people from performing duties that are incompatible from an internal control perspective, as described in the previous chapter.

Basic Journal Entries

Bookkeeping aspects in this cycle comprehend adjusting entries and closing entries, which were explained in Chapter 3, and correcting entries and reversing entries, which were introduced in Chapter 4. These topics have already been thoroughly spelled out, and so there is no need to discuss them further.

Control Objectives

We are not going to discuss all, or even many, of the internal control issues in these accounting cycles, for they are adequately covered in auditing textbooks. However, we will note the control objectives in each accounting cycle to reinforce the importance of internal controls. When building real-world AIS, the accountant constructs internal control policies and procedures to meet these objectives.

The general ledger cycle is fairly simple, relative to the other cycles, and so has three straightforward internal control objectives:

> All general ledger cycle transactions are authorized by management.
> All valid general ledger cycle transactions are accurately recorded.
> All documents and reports generated in the general ledger cycle are safeguarded.

If these objectives are met, then the firm is reasonably assured that the financial statements reflect the transactions in this cycle (i.e., adjusting, closing, correcting, and reversing entries) and that the company retains evidentiary matter to prove them.

Documents

Documents in the general ledger cycle are the worksheet, the various trial balances, the financial statements, and the journal voucher. Since the worksheet, trial balances, and financial statements have been examined in detail already, we concentrate on the one new document. The *journal voucher* is a document in which a department records a summary entry for its transactions. Its purpose is to transmit this accounting information to the general ledger department so that it can update the general ledger for the effects of these transactions.

An example of a journal voucher is presented in Exhibit 8.8. The document is uncomplicated. It contains a space for a journal voucher number, which permits easier tracing of documents should an auditor want to follow a trail of documents. The number also minimizes the problem of double counting some set of transactions. The document also holds a place for the date and the name of the department submitting the document to the general ledger department. It then reflects the summary journal entry or entries. Finally, it has a place for an appropriate individual to sign off and accept responsibility for the document.

Notice that we claimed that the originator of the journal voucher would provide a summary entry. This simply means that there is no need to report each and every transaction to the general ledger department. For example, the sales department could make lots of credit sales in one day. At the end of the day, it could tally up the total credit sales for the day and send as the summary entry a debit to accounts receivable and a credit to sales for the total amount. (Of course, there is the issue of how much each particular customer owes, but that is not within the province of the general ledger cycle. This issue is explained in the next chapter.)

This arrangement also gives the entity the option of getting rid of the general journal. In other words, if the firm records all transactions on journal vouchers, then it could save the journal vouchers and this file of journal vouchers would take the place of the general journal.

Management Reports and Queries

The output from this cycle is the financial reports. These reports include not only those sent to external readers, but also those for management purposes only, such as monthly statements.

EXHIBIT 8.8

THE JOURNAL VOUCHER

JOURNAL VOUCHER		
Number: Date: Department:		
Accounts	Debits	Credits
		Authorized by: _____

Outputs could also include any specialized reports for managers, such as financial statements for subsets of the entity, such as various departments or divisions. Computers could also allow managers to raise ad hoc questions, such as "How much sales did we make last week?" Although these outputs are made available in practice, we restrict our discourse to the financial reports to investors and creditors; we have already discussed these statements at great length in Chapters 2 and 5.

Files in an EDP Environment

In a computerized system (sometimes referred to as electronic data processing, or EDP), this cycle would have several files. The *general ledger master file* contains all of the firm's accounts and the account balances. When we say all of the accounts, we mean all of the ledger accounts—we do not mean the subsidiary accounts. Subsidiary account balances are contained in other files. (Why is the general ledger file a master file?)

The *journal voucher file* contains a listing of all the journal vouchers received by the general ledger department. In effect, it acts like a general journal. (What type of file is the journal voucher file?)

In a manual system, the entries in the general and special journals are posted to the general and subsidiary ledgers. Posting of the entries updates the balances in the various journals by adding or subtracting the effects of the transactions to the beginning balances to obtain the new balances. In this manner, account balances in the ledgers stay current.

Updating accounts in a computerized file system requires the balances from the old general ledger master file and a summary of the transactions from the journal voucher file. Effects of the transactions are added to or subtracted from the old account balances to attain the new balances. These new balances are recorded in the new general ledger master file. Notice that this process of updating the general ledger master file replaces (and is equivalent to) posting.

(A database system updates the accounts automatically and directly when the transaction is first recorded, much as spreadsheets update certain cells automatically.)

A *financial reporting file* takes the account balances in the general ledger master file and prints out (or spools to a computer monitor screen) the financial statements. While taking care of the mechanical details of preparing the financial statements, these documents must be supplemented with appropriate footnotes so that all necessary disclosures are made to the external readers. In addition, multiple years of data can be published with a *financial reporting history file*.

Document Flowcharts

There are two flowcharts for the general ledger cycle: one to depict the maintenance of the general ledger and another to show the preparation of the financial statements. Exhibit 8.9 gives the document flowchart for the maintenance of the general ledger, and Exhibit 8.10 furnishes the document flowchart for the end-of-period procedures.

Maintenance of the General Ledger.   In Exhibit 8.9, activities are initiated whenever an accounting cycle summarizes transactions on a journal voucher and submits the journal voucher to the general ledger department. As one might expect, the sales cycle summarizes various sales transactions, the facilities cycle summarizes various transactions pertaining to property, plant, and equipment, the payroll cycle summarizes transactions dealing with wages and salaries, and so on. Each cycle summarizes its transactions, typically for one day, and conveys these summary journal entries on the journal voucher. (The general ledger department itself will initiate activity by preparing a journal voucher for adjusting and closing entries; see Exhibit 8.10.)

EXHIBIT 8.9

MAINTENANCE OF GENERAL LEDGER

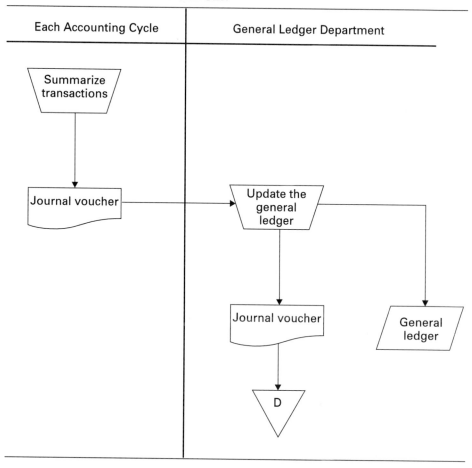

Once a journal voucher is received, the general ledger department posts the transactions to the general ledger and obtains the new ledger balances. In the flowchart, this process is referred to as updating the general ledger. Upon updating, the accountant files the journal vouchers in the journal voucher file by date. One could file them instead by journal voucher number, but filing by date maintains them in chronological order, and so the set of journal vouchers looks a lot like a general journal.

Some firms will show the general ledger twice in this flowchart. The old general ledger, with its old account balances, is placed as an input to the updating process. With the new account balances, the output from this process is called the new general ledger. We will reduce the clutter in a flowchart like that in Exhibit 8.9 by only showing the updated general ledger.

End-of-Period Procedures. The document flowchart in Exhibit 8.10 depicts the preparation of the financial statements and the various steps involved at the end of the accounting period. Essentially, this flowchart graphically represents the accounting cycle summarized in Exhibit 4.1 in Chapter 4.

The flowchart indicates that time sets up this data processing. Most other flowcharts

EXHIBIT 8.10

GENERAL LEDGER END-OF-PERIOD PROCEDURES

General Ledger Department	Readers of Financial Report

At the end of the fiscal period

```
 _____
/Prepare /
\worksheet/
 --------
     |
     v
 _____
| Worksheet |
 --------
     |
     v
 _____
/Prepare /
/trial   /
/balance /
 --------
     |
     v
 _____
| Trial    |
| balance  |
 --------
     |
     v
 _____          _____          _____
/Prepare adjusting/    | Journal  |      /Update  /
/entries and the / --> | voucher  | -->  /general /
/adjusted TB     /      --------        /ledger  /
 ------------             |              --------
     |                    v                 |
     v                    \/                v
   ( A )                 ( D )          /General /
                                       /ledger  /
```

(continued)

reveal a process initiated by some document either coming from an outsider (such as a customer's purchase order or a vendor's invoice) or from another department (such as a journal voucher). Rather than being triggered by some input document, this process is activated by the calendar. When the end of the accounting period is reached, then the general ledger end-of-period procedures are run. The worksheet encapsulates much of the work in this process.

As explained in Chapter 4, the end-of-period process is to make a trial balance, prepare the preliminary adjusting entries in the worksheet, construct an adjusted trial balance, prepare the financial statements, and enter and post the adjusting and closing entries. The adjusting and closing entries are actually placed in journal vouchers, both of which are filed by date (though filing by journal voucher number is possible), and the AIS updates the general ledger.

EXHIBIT *8.10*

GENERAL LEDGER END-OF-PERIOD PROCEDURES (continued)

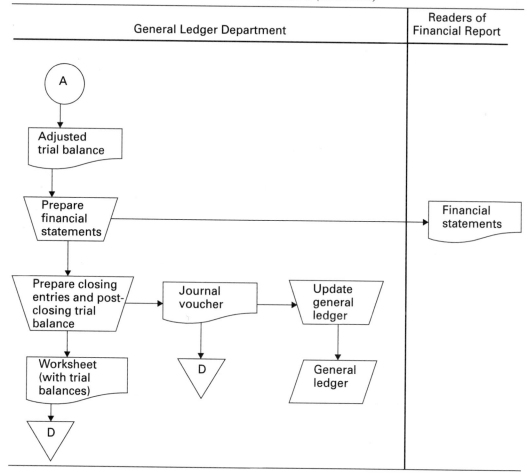

When the process is completed, the firm has published its financial statements for investors and creditors and other interested readers. It has updated the general ledger and prepared the way for the next accounting cycle. Finally, the general ledger department saves the journal vouchers with the adjusting and closing entries, and it saves the worksheet with the various trial balances.

SIGHTS ALONG THE INTERNET

A number of sites discuss general ledger software packages. For a few examples, see (in each case go to the site and click on "software" or "accounting software"):

Accountants World	www.accountantsworld.com
Accounting Web	www.accountingweb.co.uk
Electronic Accountant	www.electronicaccountant.com
Rutgers Accounting Web	www.rutgers.edu/Accounting

CHAPTER SUMMARY IN TERMS
OF LEARNING OBJECTIVES

Define Accounting Manual, Standard Accounting Entries, Chart of Accounts, and Coding Schemes. An accounting manual is a book that indicates how the accounting system is set up and provides the basic instructions of how it operates. It indicates who is responsible for what, and it states the company's policies with respect to financial reporting issues.

Standard accounting entries are an enumeration of the suggested journal entries for transactions in which the firm might engage. In practice, the accountant usually determines the standard accounting entries after organizing the firm's transactions into accounting cycles.

The chart of accounts is a list of all accounts used by an entity and the numbers used to code the accounts. A coding scheme is a system of representing economic phenomena by a set of numbers or letters or other symbols. Managers and accountants choose codes (such as account numbers) in such a way that the AIS can generate additional information.

Explain the Importance of Documenting an Accounting System. Documenting an accounting system describes the accounting cycles of the firm, standard accounting entries, the accounts, and their coding. This description includes a narration of the documents generated in the cycles, who is responsible for preparing them, and how they are distributed. This documentation helps accountants, information specialists, and auditors to understand how the accounting system operates.

Describe Flowcharting Symbols and the Principles of Flowcharting an Accounting Cycle. The document symbol represents either an input document or an output document. The operation symbol depicts the processing of documents or accounting data. The file symbol indicates that documents (or reports) are stored and how they are stored. "A" signifies that the documents are stored alphabetically, "D" by date, and "N" by the document number. The records symbol represents the accounting records, such as journals and ledgers, and it shows who is responsible for them. The connector symbol represents where one process interfaces another process that is shown elsewhere in the flowchart. A document flowline symbol represents the direction in which data and documents flow during processing. Arrowheads show the direction of the flow.

There are five rules to follow when creating document flowcharts. They are: (1) show the different departments and entities involved in the process; (2) show the source of each document; (3) with an operation (process) symbol, denote the preparation of each document; (4) indicate the disposition of each document; and (5) provide written comments when they can clarify the process.

State the Various Aspects in the Template for Examining the Accounting Cycles. The investigation of the eight accounting cycles will require an examination of various components of the cycles. These include the functions of the cycle, the departments involved in the cycle, the basic journal entries for the cycle, the control objectives, the input and output documents, the management reports and queries, the files, and, most importantly, the document flowcharts.

Define the General Ledger Cycle, Explain Its Functions, and Tell Who Is Responsible for the Cycle. The general ledger cycle is the accounting cycle that deals with miscellaneous transactions and the preparation of financial reports. The general ledger cycle has three functions: it handles all recording activities that are not the responsibility of any of the other accounting cycles (such as adjusting entries, closing entries, correcting entries, and reversing entries); it maintains the general ledger; and it prepares and distributes the financial accounting statements.

The department responsible for this cycle is the general ledger department. The general ledger department is part of the controller's department, which is a subset of the finance department.

List the Control Objectives of the General Ledger Cycle. There are three control objectives: all general ledger cycle transactions are authorized by management; all valid general ledger cycle transactions are accurately recorded; and all documents and reports generated in the general ledger cycle are safeguarded.

Describe a Journal Voucher and Its Use. The journal voucher is a document in which a department records a summary entry for its transactions. Its purpose is to transmit this accounting information to the general ledger department so that it can update the general ledger for the effects of these transactions.

State the Files Employed in the General Ledger Cycle. The general ledger master file contains all of the firm's ledger accounts and the account balances. The journal voucher file contains a listing of all the journal vouchers received by the general ledger department, and so it looks like a general journal. The financial reporting file takes the account balances in the general ledger master file and prints out the financial statements. The financial reporting history file analyzes several years of accounting data.

Indicate How the General Ledger Master File Is Kept Up to Date. To keep accounts up to date in the general ledger master file, the firm takes the account balances in the old general ledger master file and adds to or subtracts from the balances the activities listed in the journal voucher file. The new account balances are then placed in a new general ledger master file.

Explain the Flowchart for the Maintenance of the General Ledger. Each accounting cycle summarizes its transactions and conveys these summary journal entries on the journal voucher. Once a journal voucher is received, the general ledger department posts the transactions to the general ledger and obtains the new ledger balances. Upon updating, the accountant files the journal vouchers in the journal voucher file by date.

Explain the Flowchart for the General Ledger End-of-Period Procedures. The flowchart graphically represents the accounting cycle when a worksheet is used. The end-of-period process entails making a trial balance, preparing the preliminary adjusting entries in the worksheet, building an adjusted trial balance, preparing the financial statements, and making and posting the adjusting and closing entries. The general ledger department makes journal vouchers for the adjusting and closing entries and files them by journal voucher number. When the process is completed, the firm has published its financial statements for investors and creditors and other interested readers, and it has updated the general ledger and prepared the way for the next accounting cycle.

GLOSSARY

Accounting manual—a book that indicates how the accounting system is set up and provides the basic instructions of how it operates.

Chart of accounts—a list of all accounts used by an entity and the numbers used to code the accounts.

Coding scheme—a system of representing economic phenomena by a set of numbers or letters or other symbols.

Connector symbol—a flowchart symbol that represents where one process interfaces another process that is shown elsewhere in the flowchart.

Controller—the chief executive of the controller's department.

Controller's department—the group within the finance department that carries out accounting responsibilities.

Document flowchart—a flowchart that depicts input documents and output documents and indicates who creates the documents and who receives them.

Document flowline symbol—a flowchart symbol that represents the direction in which data and documents flow during processing.

Document symbol—a flowchart symbol that represents a source document.

File symbol—a flowchart symbol that indicates that documents (or reports) are stored and how they are stored.

Finance department—the department within a corporation that manages all accounting and finance issues.

Financial reporting file—a report file that takes the account balances in the general ledger master file and prints out (or spools to a computer monitor screen) the financial statements.

Financial reporting history file—a history file that reveals the financial statements of the corporation for several years.

Flowchart—a graphical representation of some phenomena of interest.

General ledger cycle—the accounting cycle dealing with miscellaneous transactions and the preparation of financial reports.

General ledger department—the group in the controller's department that summarizes all the accounting data and updates the general ledger.

General ledger master file—a master file that contains all of the firm's accounts and the account balances.

Journal voucher—a document in which a department records a summary entry for its transactions.

Journal voucher file—a transaction file that lists all the journal vouchers received by the general ledger department.

Operation symbol—a flowchart symbol that represents the processing of documents or accounting data.

Records symbol—a flowchart symbol that represents accounting records, such as journals and ledgers.

Standard accounting entries—an enumeration of the suggested journal entries for transactions in which the firm might engage.

Treasurer—the chief executive of the treasury department.

Treasury department—the group within the finance department that receives, maintains, and disburses cash.

Vice-president of finance—the chief executive of the finance department.

REVIEW QUESTIONS

1. What is an accounting manual?
2. What are standard accounting entries?
3. How can entries be recorded without using account titles?
4. What is a coding scheme?
5. Why is it important to document the accounting information system?
6. What is a flowchart? What is a document flowchart?
7. Enumerate the list of symbols employed in the construction of document flowcharts.
8. How are input and output documents differentiated in a document flowchart?
9. What symbol is used to represent financial statements?
10. How does one sketch a processing step in a document flowchart?
11. What is the file symbol, and how does it show the manner in which the documents are filed?
12. What symbol reflects the general journal, the general ledger, the special journals, and the subsidiary ledgers?

13. If a document flowchart occupies several pages, how does the flowchart indicate the manner in which one goes from one page to the other?

14. How is the direction of processing shown in a document flowchart?

15. State the five principles of good flowcharting. *essay*

16. What is the general ledger cycle?

17. What are the functions of the general ledger function?

18. Briefly explain the structure of the finance department in a typical corporation.

19. Why is the treasury department separated from the controller's department?

20. What are the basic journal entries in the general ledger cycle?

21. State the internal control objectives within the general ledger cycle.

22. What is the journal voucher? What information is contained on the journal voucher?

23. What are the outputs from the general ledger cycle?

24. Name the files utilized in the general ledger cycle, and briefly define each file.

25. How are the account balances kept up to date in the general ledger master file?

26. Who initiates activity within the general ledger cycle?

27. How are journal vouchers filed?

DISCUSSION QUESTIONS

1. Flip'n Flop is a greasy hamburger joint. As the enterprise sets up business, the managers have hired you to help set up the accounting information system. Flip'n Flop is a sole proprietorship, operates at only one location, rents rather than owns the property, accepts no credit for sales, and has no security investments. Outline an accounting manual for the company.

2. Prepare a chart of accounts for Flip'n Flop, as described in the previous question.

3. A financial reporting file consists of the line items in the various financial statements.

(a) The financial reporting file gets most of its data from the general ledger master file. At what point in the accounting cycle does the financial reporting file obtain these data?

(b) If the firm is a merchandiser that does not have a cost of goods sold account, does the general ledger master file have all of the data it needs to make an income statement and balance sheet?

(c) How does the financial reporting file get the data to prepare a statement of changes in shareholders' equity?

(d) What data does the financial reporting file need to construct a cash flow statement? Where does the file get the inputs so that it can make the statement?

4. Investors and creditors and managers employ financial ratios to help them analyze corporations. For example, the current ratio (current assets divided by current liabilities) and the return on investment (let's compute it as net income divided total assets; variations exist in how to measure the ratio) may be of interest to financial statement readers. Another popular ratio is the price-earnings (p-e) ratio, which is the common stock price per share divided by the earnings per share. Assume that managers want the financial statements to include a ratio analysis.

(a) Which file would contain these ratios?

(b) Where would the file obtain the input data to construct the ratios?

5. Does the general ledger department really have to prepare a journal voucher for closing entries in a computerized accounting system?

EXERCISES

1. A company with a computerized AIS likely would want the chart of accounts placed in a file.

(a) What type of file would this be?

(b) What records would make up this file?

(c) Give a record layout for the chart of accounts file.

2. Helen Huff, president of Huff's Appliances, is curious about the idea of using accounts numbers to make journal entries. For the transactions below, use the chart of accounts in Exhibit 8.1 and prepare the journal entries.

(a) Huff's Appliances purchases a building for $100,000, paying 20% down payment and mortgaging the rest.

(b) The corporation issues 1,000 shares of preferred stock with a market value of $103 per share and a par value of $100 per share.

(c) Huff's sells trading securities that have a value of $45,000 for $41,000.

(d) Huff's sells some old machinery for $10,000. The machinery has a cost of $97,000 and accumulated depreciation of $79,000.

(e) Huff's depreciates the building acquired in (a) using the straight-line method. The building has a salvage value of $20,000 and an estimated life of 40 years.

3. Sundar's Shoes has two branches, the North Store and the South Store. The company employs the chart of accounts given in Exhibit 8.1. To keep track of how each of the stores is performing, Sundar's Shoes sets up a coding scheme that adds a "1" to the account number for transactions affecting the North Store and a "2" for those involving the South Store. Thus, "6011" refers to sales made by the North Store.

Following is a set of transactions for July; for the sake of brevity, only the portion dealing with income statement accounts is given. Based on the data, prepare an income statement for each store.

Account Code	Dollar Amount
6012	20,000
6011	15,000
7052	5,000
7251	2,000
6012	10,000
7201	2,000
6011	7,000
7302	6,000
7051	2,000
7301	5,000
7202	1,000
6011	14,000
7002	16,000
7001	18,000

4. Compare and contrast a service corporation, a merchandiser, and a manufacturer in terms of their general ledger cycles. Assume that all three are large firms and that they utilize a file system as described in this chapter.

5. The general ledger cycle has three control objectives. What control policies might be implemented to achieve these objectives? (*Hint:* See Exhibit 7.4 in Chapter 7.)

6. Consider the following three practices that often occur within the general ledger cycle. What is their purpose?
(a) The controller approves the adjusting entries prepared by her assistant.
(b) Journal vouchers should be prenumbered.
(c) Access to the general ledger master file is controlled via password protection.

7. Grant Borbridge, Inc. has the following transactions for the second week in August.

Cash		$1,000	
	Sales		$1,000
Cash		$ 500	
	Sales		$ 500
Cash		$1,200	
	Sales		$1,200
Cash		$ 400	
	Sales		$ 400
Cash		$1,900	
	Sales		$1,900

Aggregate ("batch") these transactions into one summary entry and record it on a journal voucher for Grant Borbridge, Inc. Date it August 13, 2001, and let's say it is voucher number 6221. Dana Goldstein signs off on the journal voucher.

Who makes up the journal voucher? Who receives it?

8. What type of file is the (a) general ledger master file, (b) journal voucher file, (c) financial reporting file, and (d) financial reporting history file?

9. What is the key of the (a) general ledger master file, (b) journal voucher file, (c) financial reporting file, and (d) financial reporting history file?

10. Name the records that comprise the (a) general ledger master file, (b) journal voucher file, (c) financial reporting file, and (d) financial reporting history file.

11. How can the journal voucher file replace the general journal? Can it replace the special journals? What replaces the general ledger? Can it replace subsidiary ledgers?

12. The following is a list of queries that a manager might raise. Which file is accessed to answer the query?

(a) What is the net income of the period?

(b) What is the balance of the firm's accounts receivable?

(c) What is the balance in a particular customer's account?

(d) How does this year's sales compare with last year's?

13. A manager likely would pose no query for which file in the general ledger cycle? Auditors, on the other hand, might be interested in this file. Why?

PROBLEMS

1. Keith Miska, president of Miska Scientific Associates, and his staff must choose the standard entries that the enterprise will use when making journal entries. He has hired you to assist the firm in doing this. At your first meeting, Barb Baldner, the VP of Operations, asks you to list the typical transactions of a business. Do this, framing your answer in terms of the eight business cycles.

2. Jon and Jennifer Goodson are owners and managers of Danks Department Store. Because they have many different types of inventory and there is a need to control the activities involving the inventory, the Goodsons have asked you to create a coding scheme for their inventory.

The corporation has stores in Park Forest, Ferguson, and Halfmoon. Each store has the following sales departments: automotive supplies, books and CD's, boy's clothing, garden needs, girl's clothing, household items, men's clothing, sporting goods, toys, and women's clothing.

Required: Create a coding scheme for the merchandise inventory of Danks.

3. Creating computer coding schemes for some account, such as sales, accomplishes similar goals as making a subsidiary ledger for a manual system.

(a) If the coding scheme encodes exactly one attribute, then the coding scheme and the subsidiary ledger produce exactly the same effects. Explain how, using the example in Exhibit 8.2 and ignoring the fifth digit (which indicates the sales representative).

(b) If the coding scheme encodes more than one attribute, then the coding scheme and the subsidiary ledger produce similar but not exactly the same results. Explain, using the example in Exhibit 8.2. (*Hint:* What type of query can the subsidiary ledger not answer?)

(c) How can the traditional subsidiary ledger be amended to handle the problem noted in (b)?

(d) When there is more than one attribute, why would a manager be more likely to use a coding scheme rather than a subsidiary ledger (besides the efficiency of a computer)?

4. (a) Draw an input-output model of the general ledger cycle.

(b) Draw an actors model of the general ledger cycle.

5. On the next several pages are the four special journals of the Centraband Corporation for the month of December 2002. Prepare a journal voucher for each of them.

(a)

Sales Journal
Page S7

Date	Invoice Number	Customer	F	Amount
12-1	1302	Solloway	*	$1,000
12-3	1303	Hamman	*	850
12-4	1304	Wei	*	3,450
12-4	1305	Goldman	*	200
	TOTAL			$5,500

(b)

Purchases Journal
Page P13

Date	Purchase Order Number	Vendor	F	Amount
12-2	2516	Cohen	*	$ 800
12-7	2517	Bergen	*	1,200
12-9	2518	Granovetter	*	240
12-14	2519	Mahmood	*	300
	TOTAL			$2,540

6. Consider a firm whose chart of accounts is given in Exhibit 8.1. For each account, indicate which cycle (or cycles) sends a journal voucher to the general ledger department of a summary transaction that affects the balance of the account. For those cases in which more than one entry is possible (e.g., one can record the purchase of insurance with a debit to prepaid insurance or a debit to insurance expense), assume that the income statement account is used.

7. Assume that the entity has a chart of accounts file. Also assume that all transactions have exactly one debit and exactly one credit. Prepare a record layout for (a) the general ledger master file, (b) the journal voucher file, (c) the financial reporting file, and (d) the financial reporting history file.

8. On October 8, 2001 the general ledger master file for Kantar Bridge Club would reveal the following balances:

Accounts	Debits	Credits
Cash	10	
Land	100	
Common stock		50
Retained earnings		50
Sales		40
Electricity expense	25	
Dividends	5	
Totals	140	140

Cash Receipts Journal
Page CR5

(c)

Date	Cash (DR)	Sales Discount (DR)	Accounts Receivable			Sales (CR)	Other		
			Customer	F	(CR)		Account	(DR)	(CR)
12-1	$ 800					$800			
12-2	$ 980	$20	Goren	*	$1,000				
12-5	$5,000						Common Stock		$5,000
12-8	$ 500		Blackwood	*	$ 500				
TOTAL	$7,280	$20			$1,500	$800			*

Cash Payments Journal
Page CP30

(d)

Date	Cash (CR)	Purchase Discount (CR)	Accounts Payable			Purchases (DR)	Other		
			Vendor	F	(DR)		Account	(DR)	(CR)
12-1	$ 150					$150			
12-4	$ 90	$10	Stayman	*	$ 100				
12-6	$ 9,000						Auto	$9,000	
12-14	$ 1,000		Sobel	*	$1,000				
TOTAL	$10,240	$10			$1,100	$150		*	

There are four transactions on October 9, 2001 for Kantar Bridge Club:

Issued at par common stock for $100 (voucher number 1101).
Purchase land for $75 (voucher number 2192).
Cash sales of $10 (voucher number 6302).
Pay electricity bill of $5 (voucher number 4887).

Required:

(a) From the October 8 trial balance, prepare a record layout for the general ledger master file. Use the chart of accounts in Exhibit 8.1.

(b) From the transaction data, prepare a record layout for the journal voucher file. Use the chart of accounts in Exhibit 8.1.

(c) Update the general ledger master file by giving the record layout on October 9, 2001 for Kantar Bridge Club.

9. To query a system about various aspects of the sales requires setting up the data in some manner that allows these questions to be answered easily. One way of doing this is via the chart of accounts. Suppose that sales has 600 as the account number. Then we can append additional numerals to this number so that it provides additional information.

Consider Frankie's Furniture Store that sells furniture. Frankie wants to keep track of the type of furniture sold and who is selling the furniture. So the sales number becomes a five-digit code. The first three digits are "600" for sales. The fourth digit represents the type of furniture sold:

$$1 = \text{living room}$$
$$2 = \text{dining room}$$
$$3 = \text{bedroom}$$

The fifth digit denotes the sales representative:

1 = Sally Thompson	4 = Jim Hicks
2 = Wayne Leininger	5 = Polly Corn
3 = Floyd Beams	

Thus, "60011" means that Sally Thompson has sold some living room furniture.
    Given the data below, answer the following queries:

(a) How much dining room furniture was sold?
(b) How much did Polly Corn sell?
(c) How much living room furniture was sold by Wayne Leininger?
(d) Which sales rep sold the most?

August sales for Frankie's Furniture Store are as follows (specific dates are omitted):

Account Code	Amount of Sales
60015	$3,200
60024	4,900
60013	9,700
60022	7,500
60031	5,400
60034	9,100
60023	8,800
60011	4,600
60012	8,100
60035	9,000
60023	8,400
60021	7,500
60032	6,900
60014	9,900
60025	6,600

CHAPTER 9

THE REVENUE CYCLE

Managers probably focus on the revenue cycle more than any other, for sales are needed to create profits and cash receipts are necessary to produce positive cash flows from operations. Because of this importance, the AIS must generate the information managers need to stay abreast of these activities, and it must have an internal control system that allows managers to operate the firm effectively and efficiently and to meet the entity's legal obligations. External auditors must be concerned with this cycle as well because many of the financial statements discovered to be fraudulent began with inflated revenues.

This chapter begins with an overview of the revenue cycle—the cycle dealing with the selling of goods and services to customers and the collection of the money owed the firm. It discusses the cycle's functions and the accounting information to develop, the business departments involved in the cycle, the basic steps and journal entries, and the control objectives. In this chapter, we also briefly mention point-of-sales systems, electronic data interchange, and the effect of the Internet on this cycle.

The rest of the chapter considers four activities in this cycle: the creation of a credit sale, a sales return, a receipt of cash, and a write-off of an uncollectible account. For each of these activities, we explore the documents, the management reports and queries, the document flowcharts, and the files necessary to computerize the cycle.

After reading and studying this chapter, you should be able to:

- Define revenue cycle, sales cycle, and cash receipts cycle;
- Discuss the functions of the revenue cycle;
- Name the departments involved in the revenue cycle;
- List the basic steps in the cycle;
- Describe the basic journal entries in the revenue cycle;
- State the control objectives of this cycle;
- Define the customer order, sales order, bill of lading, invoice, and customer statement;
- Summarize the credit sales flowchart;
- State what files are necessary to support the accounting of credit sales;
- Identify the sales return memo and the credit memo;
- Describe the sales return flowchart;
- Name the files necessary to support the accounting of sales returns;
- Define check, remittance advice, deposit slip, and cash receipts prelist;
- Explain the cash receipts flowchart;
- Discuss the files that support the accounting of cash receipts;
- Identify the write-off memo and the aged accounts receivable report; and
- Clarify the write-off of accounts receivable flowchart.

OVERVIEW OF THE REVENUE CYCLE

The *revenue cycle* is the accounting cycle dealing with selling goods and services to customers and collecting the money. Some accountants split this cycle into two cycles: the *sales cycle*, which focuses on the selling activity, and the *cash receipts cycle*, which centers on the collection of the accounts receivable. Attention is placed on customers who buy the goods and services of the firm.

Functions of the Cycle

The functions of the revenue cycle are to sell products or services to customers and to collect the money from them. With respect to the revenue cycle, managers need to ask such questions as the following:

(a) Which product or service should we provide customers?
(b) What price should we charge for these products and services?
(c) How should the products be advertised? In other words, how do we obtain customers for our products and services?
(d) How should we distribute the products and services?
(e) What should the credit policy be?

The revenue and expenditure cycles help to answer (a) and (b) by pointing out the profits earned per product and service. If the profit is deemed small, then managers need to consider raising the price, trying to lower the cost, or discarding the product or service. Accounting provides little help in answering (c) or (d), though the expenditure cycle will provide a cost for these activities. Data from the revenue cycle might indirectly help to answer (e) by showing how much sales increase when the credit policy is loosened.

In the rest of the chapter, we assume that management has decided on the array of goods and services to offer, their price, and the credit terms. We will ignore the advertising strategy and the issue of how to distribute the products to the customers since the accounting aspects of the revenue cycle do not touch on these concerns. Once management has selected the strategic issues, it can concentrate on selling the goods and services and on collecting cash from the customers.

Business Departments

Several departments are engaged in the revenue cycle. Besides the controller's department, the marketing, logistics, and treasurer's departments also play a role in this cycle.

Bookkeeping activities are carried out by the general ledger, billing, and accounts receivable departments. From the previous chapter, you know that the general ledger department receives data via a journal voucher and thus keeps the general ledger up to date. The *billing department* handles the bills—it prepares the invoice when a sale is made, adjusts the bill upon a sales return or a sales allowance, and has responsibility for the sales journal. The *accounts receivable department* supervises the accounts receivable subsidiary ledger, adjusting the customer's account as sales are made and cash receipts are collected.

Although the *marketing department* deals with all five questions mentioned above, we will focus only on their activities of selling a specific set of products to some customer. This part of marketing is referred to as the *sales order department*. In particular, the sales staff will make a sale to a customer and will jot down the data about the sale. The accountant uses these data when journalizing the transaction, whether to the sales journal for a credit sale or to the cash receipts journal for a cash sale. In the remainder of this chapter, we restrict discussion to credit sales, although some of the exercises and problems will have cash sales.

In general, the *logistics department* deals with the procurement and movement of equipment, facilities, and personnel. As we discuss the accounting cycles, we focus on that part of logistics that concerns inventory. In this cycle, accountants emphasize the movement of inventory from the business enterprise to the consumer. In the purchases cycle, the spotlight is on the procurement of the inventory. Logistics has three departments that affect the revenue cycle: the warehouse, the shipping department, and the receiving department. The *warehouse* holds the goods in storage and releases them upon proper authorization. The *shipping department* sends the products from the firm to the customers. When a customer returns the good, for whatever reason, the *receiving department* receives them.

Within the treasurer's office, the credit department and the cash receipts department work within the revenue cycle. The *credit department* grants customers a line of credit and approves credit sales to them. It also tracks whether the customers are paying on time and, when necessary, determines that some accounts receivable cannot be collected. The *cash receipts department* collects the cash from the customers and deposits the cash into the firm's bank.

Two other departments play a role in the revenue cycle. The mailroom opens the mail and notes those pieces of mail in which the customer makes a payment. The internal auditor enters the cycle, for that department obtains and stores the deposit slips once the cash receipts department takes the money to the bank.

Thus, the accountants record the transactions as they occur, the marketing department makes sales to customers, logistics has custody over the inventory, and the treasurer's department processes the cash. This division of labor also brings about a segregation of duties and so enhances internal control.

Basic Steps

Credit memo

The revenue cycle proceeds in eight basic steps. They are:

1. Obtain the customer order.
2. Check the customer's credit.
3. Enter the sales order.
4. Ship the goods to the customer (if out of stock, back order).
5. Bill the customer.
6. If the customer is dissatisfied, then provide for a sales return or a sales allowance.
7. Collect the cash from the customer.
8. Periodically write off bad accounts receivable.

The credit sale flowchart, shown later, covers steps (1)–(5), the sales returns flowchart step (6), the cash receipts flowchart step (7), and the write-off of accounts receivable flowchart step (8).

One comment is in order. *Back orders* are customer orders for goods that are temporarily not in the warehouse. Although the company does not have the item in stock, it plans either to buy them (if a merchandiser) or construct them (if a manufacturer). Once this stage is carried out, the business enterprise can fill the customer's order. The company needs to act quickly, for the customer might decide to cancel the order and place a similar order with one of the company's competitors.

Basic Journal Entries

Previous chapters have already presented the basic journal entries, although we need to discuss two new wrinkles. These concern the amount to record when the corporation offers a cash discount to the customers and how to record the cost of sales when the perpetual method is utilized.

Corporations sometimes offer a cash discount to provide incentives to customers to send in the cash promptly. A common offer allows customers to take a 2% discount if the customer pays the cash within 10 days; otherwise, the full amount must be paid within 30 days. This offer is typically written as "2/10, n/30" and reads as "two-ten, net thirty." Since not paying this discount is roughly equivalent to paying 36% interest, customers have a strong motivation to pay the bill within the discount period. (How to calculate the 36% is left as a discussion question; the solution depends on the interest formula— interest equals principal times the interest rate times time. Solve for the interest rate.)

When cash discounts are presented, corporations may account for the sales and cash collections with either the gross method or the net method. Under the *gross method*, sales are recorded at the full amount, including the cash discount. If the customer does pay within the discount period, then this fact is recorded with the sales discount account. Recall from Chapter 3 that the sales discount is a contra-revenue account. With the *net method*, however, sales are recorded at the full amount less the cash discount. If the customer pays the bill outside the discount period, then the extra amount paid is recorded as finance revenue or interest revenue.

With this distinction, let's proceed to list the basic journal entries for the revenue cycle. They are: (1) recording the credit sale; (2) recording the cash collection; (3) recording a sales return or allowance; and (4) recording a write-off of accounts receivable.

Exhibit 9.1 provides an example of the first three basic transactions and records them under both the gross and net methods. First, let's assume that Toni Irvin Fashions sells on credit $10,000 worth of goods. The entity gives customers credit terms of 2/10,

EXHIBIT 9.1

GROSS AND NET METHODS TO RECORD SALES

Toni Irvin Fashions sells $10,000 worth of goods and offers customers a 2% discount if paid within 10 days. Show the accounting under the gross and net methods.

Gross Method			Net Method		
When sold:					
Accounts receivable	$10,000		Accounts receivable	$ 9,800	
Sales		$10,000	Sales		$9,800
If paid within the discount period:					
Cash	$ 9,800		Cash	$ 9,800	
Sales discounts	$ 200		Accounts receivable		$9,800
Accounts receivable		$10,000			
If paid after the discount period:					
Cash	$10,000		Cash	$10,000	
Accounts receivable		$10,000	Accounts receivable		$9,800
			Interest revenue		$ 200
If goods are returned:					
Sales returns and allowance	$10,000		Sales returns and allowance	$ 9,800	
Accounts receivable		$10,000	Accounts receivable		$9,800

n/30. It is recorded as a debit to accounts receivable and a credit to sales. Under the gross method, the amount entered is the full $10,000, but under the net method it is $9,800, since the discount is 2% of $10,000 or $200.

The second basic entry is for the collection of cash. Here we have to consider two cases. First, assume that the customers pay their bills within the 10-day discount period. Toni Irvin Fashions will then receive $9,800 and will, of course, debit cash for that amount. The gross method measures the accounts receivable at the full amount, so the bookkeeper credits accounts receivable for $10,000. The difference is shown as a debit to sales discounts. If the net method is employed, then debit cash $9,800 and credit accounts receivable for $9,800. Note that both methods show net sales of $9,800.

Second, assume that the customers pay after the 10-day discount period. This implies that they pay Toni Irvin Fashions $10,000. Under the gross method, the entry is a debit to cash and a credit to accounts receivable for $10,000. The net method also debits cash for $10,000 but credits accounts receivable for the net amount $9,800 and places the $200 difference as a credit to interest revenue (sometimes called sales discounts not taken). Note that total revenues are $10,000 for both methods.

The third basic journal entry in the revenue cycle occurs when the customer returns the goods for a refund or obtains an allowance because of some problem with the product. As shown in Exhibit 8.1, the entry is a debit to sales returns and allowances, a contra-revenue account, and a credit to accounts receivable. The gross method puts it for the full amount, while the net method subtracts the amount of the cash discount.

The last basic entry in this cycle takes place when the accounts receivable department decides that a customer is not going to pay the bill. The journal entry is:

Allowance for doubtful accounts	$X	
Accounts receivable		$X

Recall from Chapter 3 that in the adjusting entry process the corporation makes an estimate of its bad debts expense and records it as a debit to bad debts expense and a credit to allowance for doubtful accounts. Later, we will observe a new method that estimates the final balance in the allowance account. Allowance for doubtful accounts increases when the adjusting entry is made but decreases when the customer account is written off.

One last accounting issue remains to be discussed, and this involves inventory. There are two general ways to account for a firm's inventory: the periodic and the perpetual methods. The *periodic method* counts the inventory only at the end of accounting periods. This implies that the amount in the inventory account is the amount of beginning inventory, except at the end of the accounting period, when it is the amount of the ending inventory. This method is rather easy to use. Its chief disadvantage is that managers have little control over the inventory account and thus little control over the inventory itself. The *perpetual method* keeps a record of inventory after each and every sale and purchase. It can be tedious and costly to use, but this method allows managers to have a good idea of what is in (or should be in) inventory at all times. Computers and other technological innovations have significantly reduced these bookkeeping costs in recent years.

Chapters 2–4 used the periodic method without saying so. There is nothing further to do in the accounting for the revenue cycle if the business enterprise uses the periodic method. If the company applies the perpetual method, then when a sale is made to a customer, the firm has to record the sale and it must account for the cost of the sale. The latter entry is:

Cost of sales	$X	
Inventory		$X

In addition, if the customer returns the goods, the inventory would have to be added back and the cost of sales reduced. The perpetual method will be described further in the next chapter.

Control Objectives

The control objectives in the revenue cycle are fairly straightforward. Following the discussion in Chapter 7, these objectives deal with protecting the firm's assets and accounting records, participating only in authorized transactions, and keeping proper records. These control objectives are as follows:

- Inventories are safeguarded while in stock and when shipped.
- Cash is safeguarded when received from customers and is deposited in the bank as soon as possible.
- Credit is extended only to those customers who probably will repay the accounts receivable.
- Once credit is extended, management tries to collect the accounts receivable.
- All revenue-cycle transactions are authorized by management.
- All valid revenue-cycle transactions are recorded accurately.
- All documents and reports generated in the revenue cycle are safeguarded.

Selling in Today's Technological World

Computers have had an important effect on how firms sell products. Three ways that we will look at briefly are point-of sales systems, electronic data interchanges, and Internet sales.

Retailers often make use of *point-of-sale (POS) systems*. A POS system combines various aspects of the revenue cycle together and gets its name because the transaction data are collected where the sale takes place. The customer brings some goods to the sales staff and presents his or her charge card. The goods have a bar code on them, and this bar code is scanned by the sales clerk. The bar code indicates to the computer what goods the customer is purchasing, their price, and their cost. In effect, the bar code enables the company to maintain a perpetual inventory system.

After scanning the credit card number on the customer's credit card, the POS evaluates the customer's credit status. If it is acceptable, the sale proceeds; if the customer is over the limit or hasn't paid the bill in a long time, then the sale is halted.

POS systems provide an efficient and effective means of handling the credit checking and sales recording activities, as well as providing a feasible means to keep track of the inventory under a perpetual system. The only disadvantage is the increased costs of the scanners, the computer hardware, and software necessary to have a POS system. The accounting does not change when using a POS system, though the control activities will.

Whereas POS systems enhance sales to consumers, electronic data interchange systems enrich sales to corporations. An *electronic data interchange (EDI)* is a computer-to-computer exchange of business documents. For example, a maker of auto engines could have a deal to sell engines to some automobile manufacturer. As the automobile manufacturer needs engines, it could send its requests to the engine maker via EDI. Upon receipt of the virtual or electronic purchase order, the engine maker can send the engines (and, if necessary, start making more so the order can be fulfilled on a timely basis). When it ships out the engines, the firm can then send an invoice electronically to the automobile manufacturer.

As with POS systems, the accounting does not change when using EDI but the control activities will. The benefits from EDI include the increased speed of communication between customer and seller, increased accuracy of the transmissions, and the elimination of some business documents. The disadvantages are the costs and the threats of theft by computer hackers.

With the invention of the web, firms have started advertising and selling electronically to customers. This setup has many advantages, including convenience and speed and better customization to customer wants. The accounting for sales made via the Internet is no different from a manual system. The technology simply offers another, often better, way of making the sale.

Later courses in accounting information systems will build on these exciting dimensions. We will continue this chapter by taking a closer look at four activities within the revenue cycle: credit sales, sales returns, collection of cash from customers, and the write-off of an account receivable.

CREDIT SALES

The major activity in the revenue cycle is making credit sales. This section explains the documents for this activity, as well as management reports and queries, and discusses the document flowchart for credit sales at length. We conclude with a brief look at what files the AIS must have to account for these transactions and maintain good internal controls.

Documents

The AIS receives or generates five documents for credit sales: the customer order, sales order, bill of lading, invoice, and customer statement.

The receipt of the customer order initiates credit sales activities. By *customer order* we mean the document by which a customer offers to buy goods from the corporation. In practice, the customer order typically is the customer's purchase order. We will illustrate the purchase order in the next chapter.

When the business enterprise accepts the customer order, it prepares a sales order. To accept an order not only requires that the firm have the goods (or get them quickly) to sell them, but also that the company grant further credit to the customer. The *sales order* itself is the document by which a corporation records details about a sale to a customer. Several copies of the sales order are made so that the customer can be informed that the sale is being processed, the warehouse knows what goods to pick for the customer, and the billing department knows what to charge the customer.

An example of a sales order is shown in Exhibit 9.2. It incorporates the corporation's name and address, the customer's name and address, the date, the customer number, the sales order number, and the customer's purchase order number. The last-named is included to help answer questions about the order. The sales order shows the quantity ordered, the item number, a description of the product ordered, the quantity shipped, and the unit price, the total price per product, and the overall total price.

The *bill of lading* is the document that specifies details about the shipment of goods from the seller to the buyer. Exhibit 9.3 contains a bill of lading. The document shows how the goods will be shipped, for example, by truck or by rail. It displays the customer's name and shipping address, which may be different from the address for billing purposes, and it provides details about the shipper. The bill of lading designates what goods are being shipped, how many there are, and their weight (assuming the shipping fees are determined by weight), and the shipping fees. It tells whether the goods are being shipped COD, in which case the shipper must collect the money before delivering the goods, and

EXHIBIT 9.2

SALES ORDER

Sales Order
Krumrine Productions
100 Old Main Street
Clarksburg PA 16899-1950

Customer: _____

Address: _____

_____

_____

_____

Date: _____

Sales Order Number: _____

Customer Number: _____

Customer Purchase Order

Number: _____

Quantity Ordered	Item Number	Product Description	Quantity Shipped	Unit Price	Total
			TOTAL	PRICE	

it shows how the freight charges are going to be paid. "Shipper, per" and "Carrier, per" are where the appropriate employee of the shipper and the carrier sign the document, thus authorizing the transaction.

Either the seller or the buyer is responsible for the transportation charges. The acronym FOB stands for "free on board" and designates who is not paying for the transportation of the goods. Specifically, "FOB shipping point" denotes that the seller is not paying the shipping charges, whereas "FOB destination" says that the buyer is not paying them. Thus, the buyer owes the carrier the funds when the goods are shipped FOB shipping point, and the seller must pay the carrier when the goods are shipped FOB destination. Incidentally, whoever pays the transportation charges has legal title to the goods during transit.

A fourth document that enters the picture when a credit sale is made is the invoice. The *invoice* is the document sent to a customer indicating the price for goods or services provided by the seller and the terms for settlement. Exhibit 9.4 illustrates an invoice. The reader should compare Exhibit 9.2 and Exhibit 9.4 and note that the invoice is very much like the sales order, differing only in the inclusion of sales taxes (if any) and shipping costs. Because of this overlap, some firms combine the sales order and invoice.

EXHIBIT 9.3

BILL OF LADING

STRAIGHT BILL OF LADING
FROM:

Krumrine Productions
100 Old Main Street
Clarksburg PA 16899-1950

Bill of lading No. _____

Shipper No.   _____
Carrier No.   _____
Date   _____

TO:
Name   _____
Address _____
        _____
        _____

Shipper, per   _____

Carrier, per   _____

No. of packages	Kind of package, description of articles, special marks, and exceptions	Weight	Rate	Charges
	TOTAL CHARGES			

The agreed or declared value of the property is hereby specifically stated by the shipper to be not exceeding:

$ _____ per _____

FREIGHT CHARGES
  [ ] Freight prepaid
  [ ] Collect
  [ ] Bill to shipper

IF WITHOUT RECOURSE:
The carrier shall not make delivery of this shipment without payment of freight

_____
(Signature of Consignor)

Signature below signifies that the goods described above are in apparent good order, except as noted. Shipper hereby certifies that he is familiar with all the bill of lading terms and agrees with them.

_____

EXHIBIT **9.4**

INVOICE

Invoice
Krumrine Productions
100 Old Main Street
Clarksburg PA 16899-1950

Invoice Number: _____

Sold to: _____
Address: _____
_____
_____
_____

Date: _____
Sales Order Number: _____
Customer Number: _____
Customer Purchase Order
　　Number: _____

Shipped to: _____
_____
_____

Terms: _____
Shipped: _____

Quantity Ordered	Item Number	Product Description	Quantity Shipped	Unit Price	Total
			TOTAL	PRICE	
			TAXES		
			SHIPPING	COSTS	
				TOTAL	

The last document is the customer statement. Periodically—in practice, often monthly—the company prepares a *customer statement*, a document that informs the customer how much is owed on the account. This statement usually presents the beginning balance, the additional credit sales, and the cash remittances, and it computes the ending balance owed the corporation. Usually, the customer statement is accompanied by a remittance advice, which we discuss later.

Management Reports and Queries

Before a sale is made, the credit department needs to assess the creditworthiness of the customer; it must therefore be able to query the system on this matter. Sales analyses reports are quite common in practice, and these are described in Chapters 6 and 8. Managers also want to know about back orders, so that they can speed up the process and hopefully not lose any business to competitors.

Credit Sales Flowchart

The flowchart for a credit sale is tabulated in Exhibit 9.5. Because of its complexity, we will walk through it step by step. Notice that the "cast of characters" consists of the customer, the sales order department, the credit department, the warehouse, the shipping department, the billing department, the accounts receivable department, and the general ledger department. As you study this exhibit, pay attention to who receives the documents and who prepares them and try to understand the purpose for these actions.

It all gets started when a customer submits a customer order to the company. The sales order department receives this customer order and then prepares the sales order. Five copies are made of the sales order. Before proceeding, the sales order department must get permission from the credit department. So it sends one copy (specifically, copy #5) to the credit department which examines the customer's creditworthiness. Once the credit is approved, the credit department sends the sales order back to the sales order department. If the credit is rejected, then the sales department must reject the customer's order and halt the process. This case is not shown in the flowchart.

When the sales order department receives the approved sales order from the credit department, then it sends one copy to the customer. The customer's copy acts as an *acknowledgment copy*. In other words, the seller sends this document to the buyer to indicate receipt of the customer order and agreement to the sale. Such acknowledgment might be omitted if the sale is fulfilled immediately, but it becomes important if the process takes time so that the customer is kept informed of what is taking place.

The sales order department also sends two copies of the sales order to the warehouse and one copy to the billing department. The last copy is filed by sales order number. (For control purposes, it is important to maintain unique numbers for the sales order, and this is often accomplished by prenumbering the documents.)

When the warehouse receives two copies of the sales order, it files one copy by the sales order number. The other copy is used as a *picking list*, a document that informs the warehouse which goods to move to the shipping department because of a sale. The warehouse then sends the goods along with the sales order to the shipping department. The warehouse also updates the inventory records by recording the decreases in the *inventory subsidiary ledger*. This ledger works similar to the accounts receivable or accounts payable subsidiary ledger, and it would detail the specific goods that comprise the inventory account; it is further discussed in the next chapter. If the warehouse does not have the products desired by the customer, then it either fills out a back order document (not shown in this diagram) or it simply indicates that the quantity shipped is less than the quantity ordered.

The shipping department has responsibility for distributing the goods to the customer. When it receives authorization for such a shipment, via the sales order and the goods from the warehouse, then the shipping department prepares the bill of lading. One copy of the bill of lading is given to the shipper, and one copy is sent to the billing department. When the goods are shipped to the customer, a packing list is often included. The *packing list* is a document sent by the seller to the customer when the goods are

EXHIBIT *9.5*

CREDIT SALES FLOWCHART

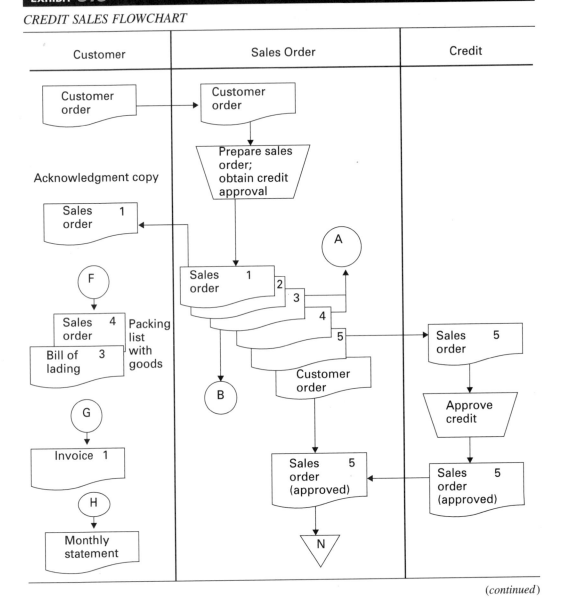

(*continued*)

shipped displaying the sale and the shipping terms. In practice, and as presented in Exhibit 9.5, the packing list is just a copy of the sales order and a copy of the bill of lading.

The billing department joins the party when it receives a copy of the sales order and a copy of the bill of lading. The department compares the two documents and makes sure that there is no discrepancy between them. If there is, the billing department must resolve the problem. It waits for the bill of lading so that it knows that the goods have actually been sent to the customer. Shipment of goods is the usual indicator that the revenue can be recognized under generally accepted accounting principles. Thus, the billing department will create the invoice, and it will record the sale in the sales journal.

EXHIBIT *9.5*

CREDIT SALES FLOWCHART (continued)

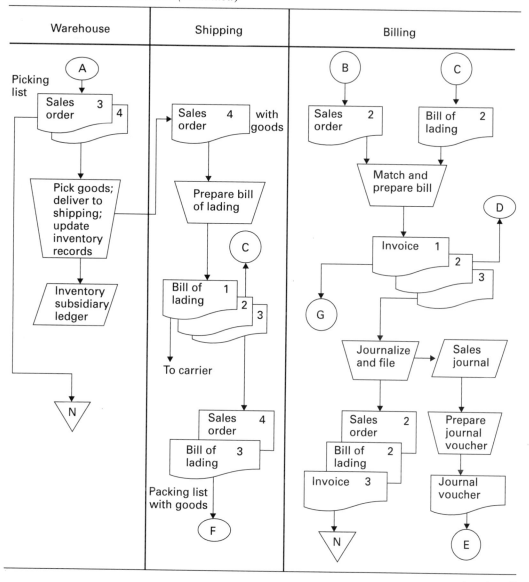

(continued)

After the billing department creates the invoice, it sends one copy to the customer and another copy to the accounts receivable department. The last copy is employed by the billing department to record the transaction in the sales journal. It will then file its copy of the sales order, the bill of lading, and the invoice by the invoice number. Periodically, the billing department will summarize the entries in the sales journal on a journal voucher, which is then sent to the general ledger department.

The accounts receivable department obtains a copy of the invoice. When it does, the accounts receivable department posts the credit sale to the accounts receivable subsidiary ledger. This keeps the customers' accounts up to date. It will file the invoice by invoice

EXHIBIT *9.5*

CREDIT SALES FLOWCHART (continued)

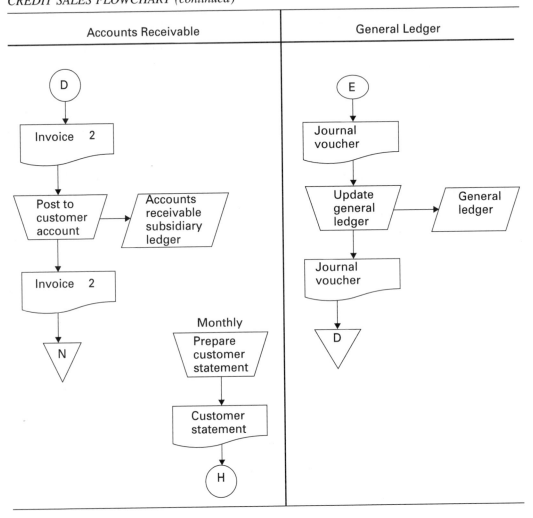

number. Monthly, the department will prepare the customer statement and send it to the customer.

The general ledger department accepts a journal voucher from the billing department for the credit sale. The general ledger department will then make a journal entry of a debit to accounts receivable and a credit to sales for this batch of sales. The reader may notice that the activity for the general ledger department is exactly the same as that depicted in Exhibit 8.9 from Chapter 8. (Of course, the journal entry varies from activity to activity.)

This completes the process of handling a credit sale. Although the progression is a bit involved, the many steps are necessary to process the sale and maintain good internal controls. The reader is encouraged to read and study this material until he or she thoroughly understands the process. One should have a clear comprehension of what departments participate in the process, which documents are employed, who creates the documents, and who receives them.

Files in an EDP Environment

To move toward a computerized accounting system, several files are needed to handle the accounting for credit sales. There should be three master files: the customer master file, the accounts receivable master file, and the inventory master file. More specifically, the last-named consists of the merchandise inventory master file for a merchandiser and the finished goods inventory master file for a manufacturer. Both can have a supplies inventory master file, and the manufacturer may also utilize a raw materials inventory master file and have a work-in-process inventory master file. We needn't bother with these additions since they don't affect the revenue cycle.

The *customer master file* is the file that enumerates each customer of the firm and various details about each of them. The record layout consists of the customer account number (the key), the customer name, the customer address (billing and shipping if they are different), the customer phone number, and the credit status.

The *accounts receivable master file* is a file that shows what each customer owes the firm. It is a computerized version of the accounts receivable subsidiary ledger. We leave the record layout as an exercise.

The *inventory master file* is a file showing the specific goods that comprise the inventory accounts. It is the analog of the inventory subsidiary ledger. A possible record layout includes the product number (which is the key), the product name, a brief description, the warehouse location, the unit of measure code, the quantity on hand, and the reorder point (that is, the point at which the firm would restock the inventory).

Two more files that are introduced into an EDP system are the *sales order file* and the *sales invoice file,* and they contain the entity's sales orders and invoices, respectively. (Sometime they are combined into one file.) One way of implementing the AIS is to have them both as open transactions files. In other words, the open sales order file would contain those sales orders that have not yet been filled; once they are filled, an invoice is prepared and the sales order is transferred to the open sales invoice file. The open sales invoice file would contain those orders that have been filled and for which an invoice has been sent, but the bills have not yet been paid. Once paid, the amounts are removed from the open sales invoice file.

Possible reference files are a shipping data reference file that gives the possible carriers and their cost structures and a price data reference file that lists prices for all products sold by the firm.

This concludes the activities surrounding credit sales. We still need to discuss sales returns, cash collections from customers, and write-offs of uncollectible accounts. The good news is that they are less detailed than the processing of credit sales.

SALES RETURNS

We now turn our attention to sales returns.

Documents

We need to consider only two documents here: the sales return memo and the credit memo. The *sales return memo* (sometimes combined with allowances and called the sales returns and allowance memo) is a document that indicates a return of goods previously sold to a customer. The memo contains the customer name and customer number, the quantity and description of the returned products, and a reason for the return. It also should be prenumbered. For control reasons, some manager must approve the return, and many companies have the credit manager perform this role.

The *credit memo* is a document that indicates that a customer's account should be reduced because of a sales return or a sales allowance. The credit memo is prepared by the billing department upon receipt of a sales return memo signed by the credit manager. The credit memo itself has the customer name, the customer number, and the amount to credit to the customer's account, and it is signed by somebody in the billing department. It, too, is prenumbered.

Management Reports and Queries

Managers sometimes desire a report on the sales returns and allowances, and this report states the amount of the sales returns and allowances. Managers hope to keep the sales returns and allowances small because it is expensive to process these returns and allowances and because it might indicate problems with the firm's products. The report might break down the sales returns and allowances by product, customer, and sales staff. Categorizing the data in these ways might reveal a defective product, a grumpy customer, or careless sales clerks.

Sales Returns Flowchart

Exhibit 9.6 displays the document flowchart for processing sales returns. Two documents are employed, namely, the sales return memo and the credit memo. The departments that are involved are receiving, credit, warehouse, billing, accounts receivable, and general ledger.

The customer kicks off the activities by returning the goods to the corporation. The receiving department takes delivery of the goods. Before accepting them, the receiving department verifies that the firm sold the goods to this particular customer, and it inspects the goods. It determines either that the goods have been returned within a reasonable time period or that they are under warranty.

Once the receiving department accepts the goods from the customer, it fills out the sales return memo. Both copies go to the credit manager for his or her approval. When the credit manager signs the sales return memo, the receiving department sends one copy to the warehouse, along with the returned goods, and one copy to billing. (An additional copy might be given to the customer.)

In some firms, the receiving department makes a *receiving report* that shows what goods they have received and what condition they are in. In this case, however, there is no need to prepare this document since those data are already contained in the sales return memo.

When the warehouse receives the goods and the sales return memo, it replaces the goods in the warehouse and it updates the inventory records. It files the sales return memo by its number.

After the billing department obtains its copy of the sales return memo, it composes the credit memo and the journal voucher. One copy of the credit memo goes to the accounts receivable department, and the journal voucher goes to the general ledger department. The billing department files the sales return memo and the credit memo by the credit memo number.

SALES RETURN FLOWCHART

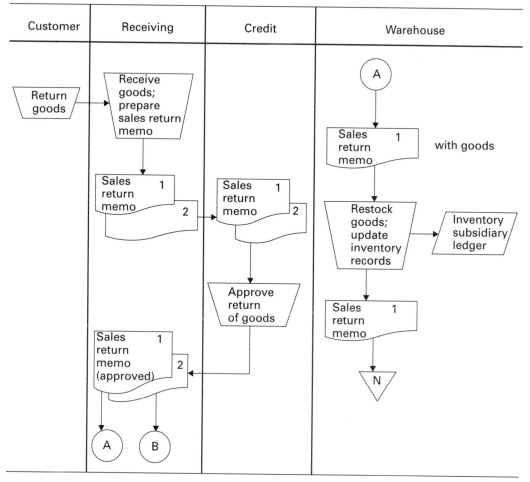

(continued)

The accounts receivable department gets a copy of the credit memo and uses the data in the document to adjust the customer's account. Then it files the memo by the credit memo number.

Finally, the general ledger department receives the journal voucher, and it does its usual spiel. This covers all the activities necessary to handle a sales return.

Files in an EDP Environment

In a computerized accounting system, one would continue to utilize the accounts receivable master file and the inventory master file. The only change is to add a *sales returns and allowances file* that lists the sales returns and allowances. Essentially, this file enumerates all of the sales return memos created by the entity.

EXHIBIT **9.6**

SALES RETURN FLOWCHART (continued)

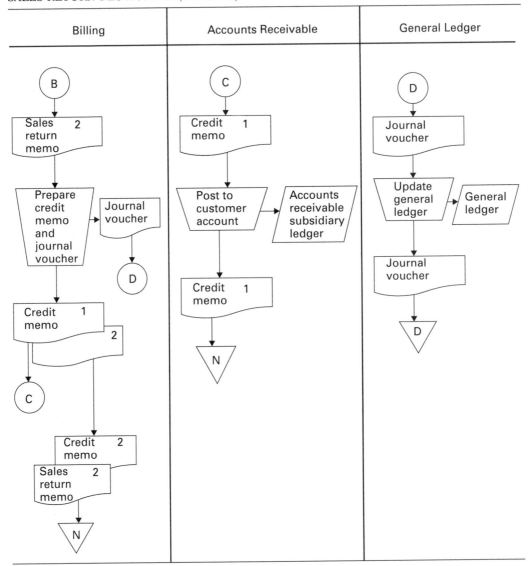

CASH RECEIPTS

The third activity in the revenue cycle examined here is the collection of cash from customers. This activity has four documents: the remittance advice, the cash receipts prelist, checks, and deposit slips. The departments engaged in this process are the mailroom, cash receipts, accounts receivable, internal audit, and general ledger. Besides interfacing with the customer, the firm also transacts business with its bank.

Documents

Administering this process requires remittance advices, the cash receipts prelist, checks, and deposit slips. A *remittance advice* is a document sent by a customer when making a

EXHIBIT *9.7*

REMITTANCE ADVICE

Krumrine Productions
100 Old Main Street
Clarksburg PA 16899-1950

Remittance Advice

Customer Name   _____
Customer No.   _____
Amount Paid   _____
Date Paid   _____

Total Amount Due: _____

Make checks payable to Krumrine Productions.

payment to ensure that the correct account is reduced. Customers obviously don't want to pay a bill and have somebody else take the credit. The corporation sends the customer the remittance advice at the same time that it sends the customer statement, and then the customer returns the remittance advice when it pays the bill.

An example of a remittance advice is shown in Exhibit 9.7. At a minimum it needs to state the customer name, the customer number, and the amount paid. It often shows the amount owed and gives a place to record the date paid. It should also say to whom to make the check payable.

A cash receipts prelist is used for control purposes. The *cash receipts prelist* is a document that shows the customers who have mailed cash to the corporation and how much. Exhibit 9.8 demonstrates how a cash receipts prelist might look. Each day a clerk in the mailroom fills out this form. For each receipt of cash (hopefully by check), the clerk writes down the customer's name, the check number, the invoice number, the amount of the invoice, and the amount received. This form of the document assumes that the firm bills by the invoice. If the corporation adds together multiple invoices to find the total owed by the customer, it can omit the columns in the prelist that pertain to invoices. This document will go to the cash receipts department, which in turn will use it as a safeguard on how much cash was received.

Checks, of course, are documents requesting a bank to pay money to the payee, that is, the person or corporation listed on the check that is entitled to the money. *Deposit slips* are documents signifying cash deposited in a bank account.

Management Reports and Queries

Cash managers generally want to know the cash receipts on a timely basis, and a report can be produced for them, or the system can allow them to query the system.

Cash Receipts Flowchart

Exhibit 9.9 depicts the document flow when cash is received from customers. We will assume that customers pay their bills by sending the money through the postal system. They may also use an EFT.

EXHIBIT **9.8**

CASH RECEIPTS PRELIST

Krumrine Productions
Cash Receipts Prelist

Date: _____

Source of cash receipts	Check No.	Invoice No.	Amount of invoice	Amount received

Clerks in the mailroom open the mail from customers. They separate the remittance advices from the checks. A cash receipts prelist is then made from the list of remittance advices, and all checks are immediately endorsed. The mailroom sends one copy of the cash receipts prelist and the endorsed checks to the cash receipts department. It also sends a copy of the cash receipts prelist and the remittance advices to accounts receivable. It then files a copy of the cash receipts prelist by date.

The cash receipts department receives the endorsed checks and a copy of the cash receipts prelist from the mailroom. It prepares two copies of a deposit slip and takes the endorsed checks and deposit slips to the bank. From the cash receipts prelist, the cash receipts department updates the cash receipts journal and files the cash receipts prelist by date. Periodically, the cash receipts department summarizes the data in the cash receipts journal on a journal voucher and sends it to the general ledger department.

The accounts receivable department takes action when it acquires the cash receipts prelist and the batch of remittance advices. It files the cash receipts prelist by date. It alphabetically sorts the remittance advices and uses the data to update the customer accounts in the accounts receivable subsidiary ledger. It then files the remittance advices alphabetically.

EXHIBIT *9.9*

CASH RECEIPTS FLOWCHART

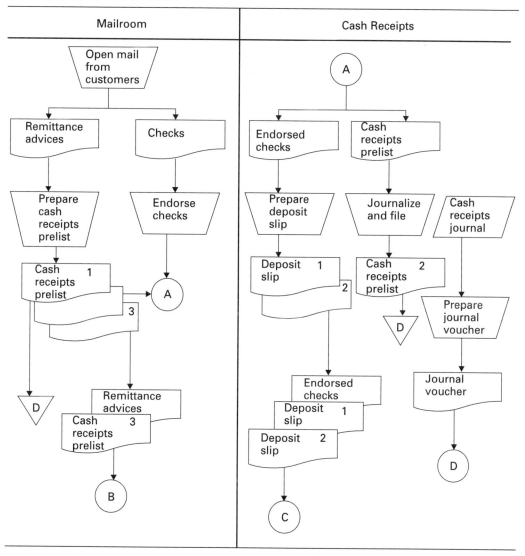

(continued)

When a person from the cash receipts department takes the cash to the bank, the bank accepts the cash and validates the deposit. One copy of the deposit is given back to this individual. This deposit slip, validated by the bank, is handed over to the internal audit department, which files them by date.

The general ledger does its usual work when it obtains a journal voucher.

Files in an EDP Environment

These activities employ the customer master file and the accounts receivable master file. A new file is needed, however, namely, a *cash receipts file*, which replaces the cash receipts journal.

EXHIBIT **9.9**

CASH RECEIPTS FLOWCHART (continued)

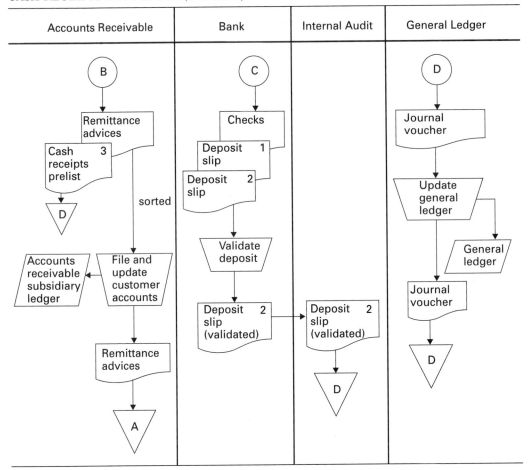

WRITE-OFFS OF ACCOUNTS RECEIVABLE

Write-offs complete this discussion of the revenue cycle. Keep in mind that we are concentrating on the writing off of specific accounts that are deemed uncollectible. We are less concerned with determining how much to record as bad debts expense, although we demonstrate the aging method for making this adjusting entry. The flowchart does not include this activity, but it could easily be amended to provide this information.

Documents

The only document in this sector of the revenue cycle is the *write-off memo,* a document specifying which accounts to write off as uncollectible. The memo lists the accounts to write off, including the customer names, customer numbers, amounts to write off, and age of the accounts or other reasons that justify the write-off.

Management Reports and Queries

The *aged accounts receivable report* describes the existing customer accounts in terms of how long they have been unpaid. The logic is simple: the older the account, the more likely the customer will never pay the bill.

The report itself segregates the accounts receivables into several groups. For example, Krumrine Productions might have $100,000 of accounts receivable. We make categories of how many 30-day periods old the account is, and we place the accounts into the proper age group. Suppose Krumrine Productions does this and finds the following information:

Current accounts (1–30 days)	$ 60,000
31–60 days old	25,000
61–90 days old	10,000
over 90 days old	5,000
	$100,000

Krumrine Productions can apply this information in two ways. First, at the end of an accounting period, Krumrine can estimate how many worthless accounts are included in the accounts receivable. Let's assume from past experiences that Krumrine Productions has had 1% of the accounts which are 1–30 days old go bad, 2% of those 31–60 days old go rotten, 10% of those 61–90 days old become uncollectible, and 50% of the accounts unpaid for over 90 days never paid. Then the accounts receivable department of Krumrine Productions can assess that the uncollectible accounts total $4,600, determined in the following manner.

Current accounts (1–30 days)	1% of $60,000 = $ 600
31–60 days old	2% of 25,000 = 500
61–90 days old	10% of 10,000 = 1,000
over 90 days old	50% of 5,000 = 2,500
Uncollectible accounts	$4,600

This computation shows what the final balance in the allowance for doubtful accounts ought to be. So, if the account already has a credit balance of $600, then the adjusting entry is:

Bad debts expense	$4,000	
Allowance for doubtful accounts		$4,000

On the other hand, if the allowance account has a debit balance of $600, then the amount in the adjusting entry is $5,200. The key to understanding this is to realize that the aging of receivables method is estimating the amount that is uncollectible at the end of the accounting period.

The second way that the aged accounts receivable report can be used is to assess the viability of individual accounts. For example, it could be company policy to write off all accounts that become 120 days old. Journalizing this write-off, as discussed earlier in the chapter, requires a debit to the allowance account and a credit to accounts receivable.

Write-off of Accounts Receivable Flowchart

Exhibit 9.10 presents the document flowchart for writing off accounts receivable. One document used is the write-off memo, and one report is the aged accounts receivable report. The departments that play a part in this process are accounts receivable, the credit department, the treasurer, and general ledger.

EXHIBIT 9.10

WRITE-OFF OF ACCOUNTS RECEIVABLE FLOWCHART

(*continued*)

Generally, this activity is conducted periodically, such as monthly. At the end of the month, the accounts receivable department takes the data in the accounts receivable subsidiary ledger and ages the accounts, thereby coming up with the aged accounts receivable report. They send this report to the credit department.

The credit department peruses the aged accounts receivable report, and it decides which customer accounts to write off. It then prepares the write-off memo and ships it off for the treasurer's signature. Once the treasurer approves the write-off, the credit department sends one copy back to accounts receivable and files the other copy by date.

When the accounts receivable department gets the write-off memo, it updates the accounts receivable subsidiary ledger and it prepares the journal voucher that summarizes

EXHIBIT *9.10*

WRITE-OFF OF ACCOUNTS RECEIVABLE FLOWCHART (continued)

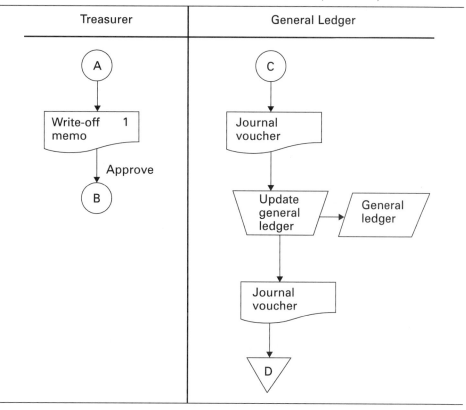

this internal transaction. The journal voucher is sent to the general ledger department. The write-off memo is filed by date.

The general ledger receives the journal voucher and updates the general ledger.

Files in an EDP Environment

The firm does not have to have any additional files to support these write-offs. If it wants a file, it can create an accounts receivable write-off file that essentially is a collection of the write-off memos.

This completes the revenue cycle. In the next chapter we look at the expenditures cycle, which, for the most part, is the flip side of what we have discussed in this chapter.

SIGHTS ALONG THE INTERNET

Several sites explore electronic data interchange (EDI) in greater depth. They are:

EC/EDI Insider	www.wpc-edi.com/insider
Executive overview of EDI	fox.nstn.ca/~cottier/overview/EDI/edi.html
Medicare EDI	www.hcfa.gov/medicare/edi/edi.htm
Software vendors of EDI	www.excite.com/business/internet_services/organizations/ edi_associations/software/?search=EDI

Another exciting topic is point of sale (POS). Some sites to explore are:

POS hardware	www.pointofsale-barcode.com/barcode/toc.html
Software vendors of POS	www.excite.com/business/a_z_industries/retailing/software/ ?search=POS

Finally, the Accounting Web references some generalized revenue software.

Accounting Web	www.accounting.web.co.uk/software

Once at the site, click on "Sales & marketing."

CHAPTER SUMMARY IN TERMS OF LEARNING OBJECTIVES

Define Revenue Cycle, Sales Cycle, and Cash Receipts Cycle. The revenue cycle is the accounting cycle dealing with selling goods and services to customers and collecting the money. The sales cycle focuses on the selling activity, while the cash receipts cycle concentrates on the collection of the accounts receivable.

Discuss the Functions of the Revenue Cycle. The functions of the revenue cycle are to sell products or services to customers and to collect the money from them. To carry out these functions, managers need to decide which products or services to offer, what price to charge for them, how to advertise and distribute them, and what credit terms to offer customers.

Name the Departments Involved in the Revenue Cycle. Billing prepares the invoice when a sale is made, adjusts the bill when necessary, and has responsibility for the sales journal. The accounts receivable department supervises the accounts receivable subsidiary ledger, adjusting the customer's account as sales are made and cash receipts are collected. The sales order department makes the sales to the customers of the firm. The warehouse holds the goods in storage and releases them upon proper authorization. The shipping department sends the products from the firm to the customers. The receiving department receives goods sent to the company. The credit department grants customers a line of credit and approves specific credit sales to them. The cash receipts department collects the cash from the customers and deposits the cash into the firm's bank.

List the Basic Steps in the Cycle. The revenue cycle proceeds in eight basic steps: (1) obtain the customer order; (2) check the customer's credit; (3) enter the sales order; (4) ship the goods to the customer; (5) bill the customer; (6) if the customer is dissatisfied, then provide for a sales return or a sales allowance; (7) collect the cash from the customer; and (8) periodically write off any bad accounts receivable.

Describe the Basic Journal Entries in the Revenue Cycle. When cash discounts are presented, corporations may account for the sales and cash collections with either the gross method or the net method. Under the gross method, sales are recorded at the full amount, including the cash discount. If the customer does pay within the discount period, then this fact is recorded with the sales discount account. With the net method, sales are recorded at the full amount less the cash discount. If the customer pays the bill outside the discount period, then the extra amount paid is recorded as interest revenue.

There are four basic journal entries in the revenue cycle. When a credit sale is made, debit accounts receivable and credit sales, either at gross or at net. When cash is received, debit cash for the amount remitted and credit accounts receivable. The amounts and other accounts depend on whether the cash is remitted within the discount period and whether the entity applies the gross or net method. When a customer returns goods or obtains an allowance, debit sales returns and allowances and credit accounts receivable, either at gross or at net. Periodically, the company needs to assess the collectibility of the accounts receivable. Bad accounts are written off with a debit to allowance for doubtful accounts and a credit to accounts receivable.

State the Control Objectives of This Cycle. Inventories are safeguarded while in stock and when shipped. Cash is safeguarded when received from customers and is deposited in the bank as soon as possible. Credit is extended only to those customers who probably will repay the accounts receivable. Once credit is extended, management tries to collect the accounts receivable. All revenue-cycle transactions are authorized by management. All valid revenue-cycle transactions are accurately recorded. All documents and reports generated in the revenue cycle are safeguarded.

Define the Customer Order, Sales Order, Bill of Lading, Invoice, and Customer Statement. The customer order is the document by which a customer offers to buy goods from the corporation. The sales order is the document by which a corporation records details about a sale to a customer. The bill of lading is the document that specifies details about the shipment of goods from the seller to the buyer. The invoice is the document sent to a customer indicating the price for goods or services provided by the seller and the terms for settlement. The customer statement is a document that informs the customer how much is owed on the account.

Summarize the Credit Sales Flowchart. The customer sends the customer order to the corporation. The sales order receives the customer order and prepares the sales order. The credit department approves the sale if the customer is in good standing with respect to its credit. The warehouse receives the sales order and picks the goods and sends them along with the sales order to the shipping department. The shipping department prepares the bill of lading and ships the goods to the customer along with the packing list, which is usually a copy of the sales order and a copy of the bill of lading. When it receives the sales order and the bill of lading, the billing department prepares the invoice, makes the entry in the sales journal, and summarizes the entries in a journal voucher. The accounts receivable takes its copy of the invoice and updates the customers' accounts. It also produces the monthly customer statement. The general ledger department uses the journal voucher to update the general ledger.

State What Files Are Necessary to Support the Accounting of Credit Sales. The customer master file is the file that enumerates each customer of the firm and various details about them. The accounts receivable master file is a file that shows what each customer owes the firm. The inventory master file is a file showing the specific goods that comprise the inventory accounts. The sales order file and the sales invoice file contain the entity's sales orders and invoices, respectively.

Identify the Sales Return Memo and the Credit Memo. The sales return memo is a document that indicates a return of goods previously sold to the customer. The credit memo is a document that indicates that a customer's account should be reduced because of a sales return or a sales allowance.

Describe the Sales Return Flowchart.   The customer returns the goods. The receiving department accepts the goods and prepares the sales return memo, which is okayed by the credit department. The warehouse restocks the inventory and updates the inventory records. Billing prepares the credit memo and a journal voucher. Accounts receivable updates the customer's account, while the general ledger department updates the general ledger.

Name the Files Necessary to Support the Accounting of Sales Returns.   The only additional file needed to support these activities is a sales returns and allowances file, which basically is a collection of the sales return memos.

Define Check, Remittance Advice, Deposit Slip, and Cash Receipts Prelist.   A check requests a bank to pay money to the payee. A remittance advice shows which customer is paying its bill. A deposit slip shows that cash is deposited in a bank account. And a cash receipts prelist spells out the customers who have mailed cash to the corporation and how much.

Explain the Cash Receipts Flowchart.   The mailroom receives the customer's check and remittance advice. Checks are endorsed and sent to cash receipts. The mailroom prepares the cash receipts prelist and distributes copies to cash receipts and to accounts receivable. The cash receipts department takes the money, prepares a deposit slip, and deposits the checks into its bank, and turns the deposit slips over to the internal audit department. It also updates the cash receipts journal. When accounts receivable obtains a copy of the cash receipts prelist and the remittance advices, it updates the customers' accounts. The general ledger department updates the general ledger.

Discuss the Files That Support the Accounting of Cash Receipts.   The new file needed to computerize recording these activities is a cash receipts file, which would replace the cash receipts journal.

Identify the Write-Off Memo and the Aged Accounts Receivable Report.   The write-off memo is a document specifying which accounts to write off as uncollectible. The aged accounts receivable report is a report segregating accounts receivable by the length of time they have been unpaid.

Clarify the Write-Off of Accounts Receivable Flowchart.   Monthly, the accounts receivable department prepares an aged accounts receivable report and sends it to the credit department. Based on the information in this report, the credit department decides to write off some customer accounts and lists them in a write-off memo. Once this is approved, it goes back to accounts receivable which updates the accounts receivable subsidiary ledger.

GLOSSARY

Accounts receivable department—that branch of the controller's department that supervises the accounts receivable subsidiary ledger.

Accounts receivable master file—a file that shows what each customer owes the firm.

Acknowledgment copy—a document sent by the seller to the buyer indicating receipt of the customer order and agreeing to the sale.

Aged accounts receivable report—a report segregating accounts receivable by the length of time they have been unpaid.

Back order—a customer order for goods that are temporarily not in the warehouse.

Billing department—that branch of the controller's department that prepares the invoice when a sale is made and adjusts the bill when necessary.

Bill of lading—a document that specifies details about the shipment of goods from the seller to the buyer.

Cash receipts cycle—that portion of the revenue cycle dealing with collecting money from the customers.

Cash receipts department—that branch of the treasurer's department which collects the cash from customers and deposits the cash into the firm's bank.

Cash receipts file—a file that records the cash receipts of the firm.

Cash receipts prelist—a document that shows the customers who have mailed cash to the corporation and how much. *Should agree w/ deposit slip.*

Check—a document requesting a bank to pay money to the payee.

Credit department—that branch of the treasurer's department that grants customers a line of credit and approves credit sales to them.

Credit memo—a document that indicates that a customer's account should be reduced because of a sales return or a sales allowance.

Customer master file—a file that enumerates each customer of the firm and various details about each of them.

Customer order—a document by which a customer offers to buy goods from the corporation.

Customer statement—a document that informs the customer how much is owed on the account.

Deposit slip—a document signifying cash deposited in a bank account.

Electronic data interchange (EDI)—a computer-to-computer exchange of business documents.

Gross method—the accounting method that records sales and purchases at the full amount, including any cash discount that is offered.

Inventory master file—a file showing the specific goods that comprise the inventory account.

Inventory subsidiary ledger—a subsidiary ledger that details the specific goods that comprise the inventory account.

Invoice—a document sent to a customer indicating the price for goods or services provided by the seller and the terms for settlement.

Logistics department—the department that deals with the procurement and movement of equipment, facilities, and personnel.

Marketing department—the department that deals with selling goods and services to customers, including advertising and distribution.

Net method—the accounting method that records sales and purchases at the full amount less any cash discount that is offered.

Packing list—a document sent by the seller to the customer when the goods are shipped displaying the sale and the shipping terms.

Periodic method—the accounting method that counts inventory only at the end of accounting periods.

Perpetual method—the accounting method that keeps a record of inventory after every sale and purchase.

Picking list—a document that informs the warehouse which goods to move to the shipping department because of a sale.

Point-of-sales (POS) system—an electronic system by which many steps of a retail sale are performed by a computer.

Receiving department—that branch of the logistics department which receives goods that come to the firm.

Receiving report—a document generated by the receiving department to show what goods they have received and what condition they are in.

Remittance advice—a document sent by a customer when making a payment to ensure that the correct account is reduced.

Revenue cycle—the accounting cycle dealing with selling goods and services to customers and collecting the money.

Sales cycle—that portion of the revenue cycle dealing with selling goods and services to customers.

Sales invoice file—a file listing the firm's invoices during some accounting period.

Sales order—a document by which a corporation records details about a sale to a customer.

Sales order department—that branch of the marketing department which makes sales to the customers of the firm.

Sales order file—a file listing the firm's sales orders during some accounting period.

Sales return memo—a document that indicates a return of goods previously sold to a customer.

Sales returns and allowances file—a file listing the firm's sales returns and sales allowances during some accounting period.

Shipping department—that branch of the logistics department which ships goods from the firm to others.

Warehouse—that branch of the logistics department that holds the goods in storage and releases them upon proper authorization.

Write-off memo—a document specifying which accounts to write off as uncollectible.

REVIEW QUESTIONS

1. What is the revenue cycle, and how might it be further subdivided?
2. What are the functions of the revenue cycle?
3. What are the responsibilities of the controller's department in the revenue cycle?
4. What does the marketing department do in the revenue cycle?
5. What is logistics, and what is its role in the revenue cycle?
6. What are the duties of the treasurer's department in the revenue cycle?
7. What are the basic steps in the revenue cycle?
8. What does 2/10, n/30 mean? What does 1/20, n/60 mean?
9. Distinguish between the gross method and net method for recording credit sales.
10. Summarize the basic journal entries in the revenue cycle.
11. Distinguish the periodic method and the perpetual method for accounting for inventory. How do the methods impact the revenue cycle?
12. What are the control objectives in the revenue cycle?
13. Explain POS systems and EDI.
14. Define customer order, sales order, bill of lading, invoice, and customer statement.
15. Summarize the credit sales flowchart.
16. Define acknowledgment copy, picking list, and packing list.
17. What are the customer master file, the accounts receivable master file, the inventory master file, the sales order file, and the sales invoice file?
18. What are the sales returns memo and the credit memo?
19. Summarize the sales returns flowchart.
20. What is a receiving report?
21. What is the sales returns and allowances file?
22. Define remittance advice, cash receipts prelist, check, and deposit slip.
23. Briefly explain the activities in the cash receipts flowchart.
24. What is a cash receipts file?
25. Define write-off memo.
26. What is an aged accounts receivable report?
27. Explain the aging method of estimating uncollectible accounts. Does this method estimate bad debts expense?
28. Summarize the write-off of accounts receivable flowchart.

DISCUSSION QUESTIONS

1. We covered the sales journal in Chapter 4 and illustrated it in Exhibit 4.3. At that time we implicitly assumed the gross method.

Required: Reconfigure the sales journal shown in Exhibit 4.3 of Chapter 4 if the company employs the net method and offers terms of 2/10, n/30.

2. We covered the cash receipts journal in Chapter 4 and illustrated it in Exhibit 4.5 of that chapter. At that time we implicitly assumed the gross method.

Required: Reconfigure the cash receipts journal shown in Exhibit 4.5 of Chapter 4 if the company employs the net method and offers terms of 2/10, n/30.

3. When a customer is offered terms of 2/10, n/30 but does not remit the cash within the 10-day discount period, the customer incurs an interest rate of about 36%. Use the interest formula (I=PRT) and verify this rate. Assume a 360-day year.

4. What are some principles for creating good documents?

5. Suppose a business enterprise does not have the goods a customer orders and so must make a back order.
(a) The firm might prepare a back order memo. Design this document, and tell who would prepare it and who would receive a copy of it.
(b) Instead of preparing a new document, the sales order could indicate the existence of a back order by showing that the quantity shipped is less than the quantity ordered. Some companies place "BO" in the column to indicate that the product is back-ordered. Who prepares this information, and who receives it?
(c) However the company indicates back orders, management will want to monitor the situation so that the firm does not lose the business. How can managers monitor the back order?
(d) When the goods are received, how does the sales process continue?

6. Compare and contrast the sales order with the invoice and the sales return memo with the credit memo. Data in the sales order greatly overlaps that in the invoice, and similarly for the sales returns and allowance memo and the credit memo.
(a) Why are there both a sales order and an invoice?
(b) Why are there both a sales return memo and a credit memo?
(c) Suppose management wants to cut down on the paperwork. If the firm combines these pairs of documents, what must it do to ensure good internal controls?

EXERCISES

1. Chocolate Dot Com has the following transactions in June. All credit sales are made with terms of 2/10, n/30.

June 3. Penny Stewart buys on credit 1,000 boxes of chocolate at $3 each.
June 5. Anthony Watts buys on credit 500 cartons of chocolate bars at $5 each.
June 6. Penny Stewart returns 100 boxes of chocolate because they were crushed during transit.
June 14. Anthony Watts pays his bill.
June 30. Penny Stewart pays her bill.

Required: Journalize the transactions if Chocolate Dot Com employs (a) the gross method and (b) the net method.

2. On December 31 Blakely, Inc. applies the aging method and decides that the allowance for doubtful accounts should have a balance of $1,000. It currently has a debit balance of $100. Then on January 31 of the next year, Blakely, Inc. decides that the $600 receivable from JC Mann is uncollectible.
Prepare the two journal entries for Blakely, Inc.

3. Agrawal Engineering has $50,000 of accounts receivable. When these receivables are analyzed, Agrawal Engineering determines that 40% are 1–30 days old, 30% are 31–60 days old, 20% are 61–90 days old, and the rest are over 90 days old. The corporation has further decided, based on past experience, that 1% of the accounts 1–30 days old, 2% of the accounts 31–60 days old, 4% of the accounts 61–90 days old, and 10% of the accounts older than 90 days will eventually turn bad.
Required:
(a) Prepare an aged accounts receivable report.
(b) Assuming that the allowance account presently has a credit balance of $100, prepare the adjusting entry.
(c) Assuming that the allowance account presently has a debit balance of $200, prepare the adjusting entry.

4. On July 31 the Adikes Company writes off the $13,000 receivable from Josh Steinberg. But on September 23, Josh Steinberg remits $8,000 and promises to pay the rest in one month. Prepare the journal entries on July 31 and September 23.

5. Vernis Welmon Company retails kitchen appliances. Inventory costs $200 per unit and is sold at $400 per unit. Beginning inventory consists of 50 units. During November the firm buys 420 units from the manufacturer and sells 400 units to consumers. Prepare the journal entries for Vernis Welmon Company if it uses (a) the periodic method and (b) the perpetual method.

6. Ronda Williams is on the sales staff for Krumrine Productions. On March 4, 2002 she makes a sale to Yaa Asante, Inc. for 100 shirts at $9 each (product number SH-120) and 40 belts at $5 each (product number BL-920). The sales order number is SO-1234, and the customer's purchase order is PO-6789. Krumrine Productions has assigned Yaa Asante the customer number 1081. The address for the customer is Yaa Asante, Inc., 1001 Cliff View Dr., Columbus, Ohio 43210. The shipping address is the same.

The sales tax is 3%, and shipping and handling charges come to $45. Krumrine's invoice number for this transaction is IN-3579. Terms of the sale are 1/10, n/30. The goods are shipped via Yippie Trucks on March 6, 2002.

Required: (a) Prepare the sales order for this transaction, and (b) prepare the invoice once the goods are sent to the customer.

7. Exercise 6 discusses the sale to Yaa Asante, Inc. by Krumrine Productions. Krumrine ships the goods via Yippie Trucks, shipper number 9020, which uses carrier number 333 to ship these particular goods. The shirts and belts are placed in three packages, each weighing about 7.5 pounds. The rate charged by Yippie is $2 per pound. The freight is prepaid by Krumrine Productions. Bob Smith signs for the shipper, and Liz Miles signs for the carrier. Prepare the bill of lading.

8. Dave Hersh from Probe, Inc. is interviewing you for a job as an accountant with his firm. He gives four scenarios and asks you to answer who pays for the transportation charges in each case.
(a) Probe is the buyer; terms are FOB shipping point.   **(c)** Probe is the buyer; terms are FOB destination.
(b) Probe is the seller; terms are FOB shipping point.   **(d)** Probe is the seller; terms are FOB destination.

9. Mae Avenilla had bought $421 worth of goods from Krumrine Productions. She is now remitting the full amount on October 16, 2002. As she mails a check for $421, she also includes the remittance advice. Her address is 934 Order Boulevard, Barney, Utah 84300, and her customer number is 1421. Prepare the remittance advice.

10. On February 13, 2002, the mailroom of Krumrine Productions receives four checks. The first concerns Ingrid Robinson, invoice IN-2013 for $930. She remits all $930 in check number 2346. The second remittance is from Cary Ritter, invoice IN-2011 for $510. He remits $200 in check number 989. The third cash receipt comes from Tamara Stewart, who is making a payment on the note receivable held by Krumrine. The check is for $350, and the check number is 1506. The fourth check, number 4555, is written by Keith Orni for invoice IN-2132. The invoice is for $700, but Orni takes the 1% discount he is entitled to. Prepare the cash receipts prelist for Krumrine Productions.

11. Following is a sales journal for the Richard Jones Company (with the folio column omitted). Prepare the journal voucher for the billing department to send to the general ledger department. Jill Kanoff signs the voucher, number B-210, on January 31, 2002.

Date	Invoice No.	Customer	Amount
1-3	2501	Mulkey	$ 400
1-7	2502	Demers	1,200
1-11	2503	Ndubueze	300
1-29	2504	Petrov	700
	TOTAL		$2,600

Assume the periodic method is used to account for inventory.

12. David Alderson returns several crates of wine to Good Tasting, claiming that the wine in fact tastes terrible. The billing department for Good Tasting prepares a credit memo that credits Alderson's account for $2,200. Prepare the journal voucher for this return if the billing department assigns it voucher number SRA-567 and if Anson Chow signs the voucher on May 29, 2003. Assume that Good Tasting accounts for its accounts receivable with the gross method and its inventory with the periodic method.

13. Jacob Ponemon manufactures auto parts. Following is page 338 of the firm's cash receipts journal for May 8, 2001 (date and folio columns omitted). Prepare the journal voucher for the cash receipts department to send to the general ledger department. Julia Nelson signs the voucher, number CR-9801, the evening of May 8.

Cash (DR)	Sales Discount (DR)	Accounts Receivable		Sales (CR)	Other		
		Customer	(CR)		Account	(DR)	(CR)
$ 500				$500			
$2,000		Bush	$2,000				
$5,000					Land		$3,500
					Gain		$1,500
$ 900		Gore	$ 900				
$ 980	$ 20	Ventura	$1,000				
$9,380	$ 20		$3,900	$500			
(100)	(620)		(120)	(600)			

14. The credit department of Jump Up! is reviewing its accounts receivable and decides to write off two accounts. Lance Killmeyer owes the company $3,350, and Chris Curran owes the firm $2,800. Ebru Cankaya, who works in the accounts receivable department, prepares the journal voucher on June 7, 2001. The number of the voucher is WO-666.

15. When reviewing the four flowcharts for the revenue cycle, you should notice that journal vouchers are prepared from the sales journal and the cash receipts journal, and this process, in effect, posts the transactions to the general ledger. Journal vouchers, however, are not prepared from the accounts receivable subsidiary ledger or from the inventory subsidiary ledger. Why not?

16. In a computerized AIS, what is the counterpart to the sales journal, cash receipts journal, accounts receivable subsidiary ledger, and inventory subsidiary ledger?

17. What are the keys to the accounts receivable master file, cash receipts file, customer master file, inventory master file, sales invoice file, sales order file, and sales returns and allowances file?

18. Using the examples in Chapter 6, Exhibit 6.8, develop a record layout for (a) the accounts receivable master file and (b) the sales order file.

PROBLEMS

1. (a) Draw an input-output model of the sales cycle and the cash receipts cycle.

(b) Draw an actors model of the revenue cycle.

2. (a) List all of the documents in the revenue cycle. For each document, indicate who prepares it and who receives a copy. If the copy has a name, state it (e.g., the copy of the sales order that goes to the customer is referred to as the acknowledgment copy).

(b) List all of the accounting journals and ledgers in the revenue cycle. For each journal and ledger, state who has responsibility for it.

3. Krumrine Productions has hired you to assist them in developing their AIS. Specifically, your job is to design a

(a) customer statement

(b) sales return memo

(c) credit memo and

(d) write-off memo

4. We can classify management assertions into five categories: existence or occurrence, completeness, valuation or allowance, rights and obligations, and presentation and disclosure. State management's assertions with respect to sales, cash receipts, accounts receivable, and inventory. Assume all transactions are in U.S. dollars.

5. The control objectives for the revenue cycle are: (1) inventories are safeguarded while in stock and when shipped; (2) cash is safeguarded when received from customers and is deposited in the bank as soon as possible; (3) credit is extended only to those customers who probably will repay the accounts receivable; (4) once credit is extended, management tries to collect the accounts receivable; (5) all revenue-cycle transactions are authorized by management; (6) all valid revenue-cycle transactions are accurately recorded; and (7) all documents and reports generated in the revenue cycle are safeguarded. For the following list of activities, indicate by number the control objectives that the activity is fulfilling.

Activity Within the Revenue Cycle	*Control #*
1. Credit sales need approval from the credit department.	
2. The warehouse doesn't pick inventory without an approved sales order.	
3. The warehouse takes responsibility for the inventory subsidiary ledger.	
4. Shipping doesn't ship goods without an approved sales order.	
5. Billing compares the sales order and the bill of lading.	
6. Billing has responsibility for the sales journal.	
7. Billing files the sales order, bill of lading, and invoice.	
8. Accounts receivable sends the invoice to the customer.	
9. Accounts receivable takes cares of the accounts receivable subsidiary ledger.	
10. General ledger receives and files journal vouchers.	
11. Receiving inspects sales returns.	
12. Customers are offered terms of 2/10, n/30.	
13. The credit department approves sales returns.	
14. The mailroom prepares a cash receipts prelist.	
15. The mailroom endorses checks immediately.	
16. Cash receipts has responsibility for the cash receipts journal.	
17. Accounts receivable files the remittance advices.	
18. Validated deposit slips go to internal audit.	
19. The credit department analyzes the age of the accounts receivable.	
20. The treasurer approves write-off memos.	

6. Documents fulfill the control objectives of the business enterprise. Following is a list of the documents in the revenue cycle. Each document serves to meet one of the following control objectives: (1) safeguard inventories; (2) safeguard cash; (3) safeguard accounts receivables; (4) all revenue-cycle transactions are authorized by management; and (5) all valid revenue-cycle transactions are accurately recorded. For the following list of documents, indicate by number the control objectives that the activity is fulfilling.

Documents Within the Revenue Cycle	Control #
1. Bill of lading	
2. Cash receipts prelist	
3. Check	
4. Credit memo	
5. Customer order	
6. Customer statement	
7. Deposit slip	
8. Invoice	
9. Journal voucher	
10. Remittance advice	
11. Sales order	
12. Sales return memo	
13. Write-off memo	

7. **(a)** How would the following three errors likely be discovered?

(i) The billing clerk enters the wrong amount for sales.

(ii) The cash receipts clerk credits Redd for the payment when it actually was Tullock who made the payment.

(iii) An invoice was put into the wrong envelope and thus sent to the wrong party.

(b) How would the AIS prevent the following irregularities from occurring?

(i) The shipping clerk sends goods to a friend.

(ii) A billing clerk prepares a credit memo for a friend.

(iii) A customer takes a cash discount but pays after the discount period.

8. Sara Seidensticker opens a furniture store and has asked you to help design the AIS. Specifically, you are asked to design the flowchart for the cash sales.

The sales clerk will take the customer's order, draft a sales order, and ring it up on the cash register. Checks are immediately endorsed. The customer receives one copy of the sales order and the cash register receipt. Two copies go to the warehouse, and the last is filed. At the end of the day, there is a reconciliation between the cash register tape and the cash in the drawer. Assuming no discrepancies, two deposit slips are prepared and the checks are deposited in the bank.

The warehouse uses the sales order to pick the appropriate furniture and sends the goods and one copy of the sales order to shipping. The shipping department prepares a shipping document and sends the goods to the customer via a company truck. (No bill of lading needs to be prepared since Seidensticker uses its own trucks.)

Required: Draw the cash sales flowchart for Seidensticker Furniture.

9. Florida Electric Power Company sends out its meter readers each month to read the customers' meters. They record these measurements on a "monthly meter readings" document, which is turned over to the billing department. The billing department records these measurements in a ledger it calls "customer meter readings." It then subtracts the beginning meter reading from the ending amount to determine the monthly usage of electricity, and it multiplies this amount by the appropriate rate to obtain the charge for the month.

Required:

(a) Prepare a flowchart for these credit sales. *Hint:* Use Exhibit 9.5 as a guide, but note that you may omit the credit department, warehouse, and shipping.

(b) What does the customer meter readings ledger look like?

(c) The electric company rotates who takes the meter readings, and it rotates where it takes the readings. Why?

10. Assume that the cash receipts for Weigle, Inc. are made via EFT. Specifically, customers authorize their banks to remit cash to Weigle, Inc.'s bank through EFT. Weigle has arranged that its bank prepares three copies of an EFT voucher for the cash remittances as the bank deposits the money into Weigle's account. The three copies are sent to cash receipts, accounts receivable, and internal audit.

Required: Prepare the flowchart for cash receipts at Weigle, Inc.

11. The Cole Van Hooser Company employs a sales order file and a sales invoice file in its accounting information system. The files are presented below and on the next page.

The sales order file enumerates all of the sales made during the month of October 2003. Assume that each sales order is for only one product. When the sale is made, all of the data are entered by the sales clerk except for the bill of lading. When the goods are actually shipped, the shipping clerk enters the bill of lading number. Thus, a blank in the bill-of-lading-number column indicates that the goods have not yet been shipped to the customer.

The sales invoice file lists all unpaid invoices plus all invoices sent out during October 2003. Each sales invoice corresponds to one sales order. The billing clerk enters all of the data into the file except for the date of the cash receipt. When the customer remits the cash, the cash receipts clerk enters the date into the file. Thus, a blank in the date-of-cash-receipt column implies that the customer has not yet paid the invoice.

Required:

(a) What data are contained in the open sales order file?

(b) What is sales for October 2003?

(c) What data are contained in the open invoice file?

(d) How much cash is received from customers in October 2003?

(e) Using the formula from Chapter 5, show the relationship between monthly sales and monthly cash receipts from customers.

Sales Order Number	Date	Customer Number	Product Number	Quantity Ordered	Price per Unit	Bill of Lading Number
SO-3646	9-17	102	NL-110	1	5,000	BL-808
SO-3679	10-2	121	ZN-322	10	1,000	BL-801
SO-3680	10-6	110	IJ-658	50	50	BL-802
SO-3681	10-8	101	AW-319	10	200	BL-803
SO-3682	10-9	115	ZN-322	5	1,000	BL-805
SO-3683	10-13	121	BL-462	100	100	BL-804
SO-3684	10-15	108	HI-111	50	60	
SO-3685	10-16	126	IJ-658	70	50	BL-806
SO-3686	10-21	114	SW-098	100	40	BL-811
SO-3687	10-21	108	QW-468	50	300	BL-809
SO-3688	10-24	119	AW-319	50	200	BL-807
SO-3689	10-27	110	FL-300	10	400	BL-810
SO-3690	10-29	103	NL-110	1	5,000	
SO-3691	10-31	111	ZN-322	20	1,000	BL-812

Sales Invoice Number	Sales Order Number	Date of Invoice	Customer Number	Amount Billed	Date of Cash Receipt
IN-3195	SO-3499	8-17	120	16,000	
IN-3239	SO-3668	9-22	104	8,000	10-21
IN-3245	SO-3679	10-2	121	10,000	10-29
IN-3246	SO-3680	10-7	110	2,500	10-14
IN-3247	S0-3681	10-8	101	2,000	10-3
IN-3248	SO-3683	10-13	121	10,000	
IN-3249	SO-3682	10-14	115	5,000	10-21
IN-3250	S0-3685	10-16	126	3,500	10-21
IN-3251	SO-3688	10-24	119	10,000	10-28
IN-3252	SO-3646	10-24	102	5,000	
IN-3253	S0-3687	10-24	108	15,000	10-27
IN-3254	SO-3689	10-28	110	4,000	10-31
IN-3255	SO-3686	10-28	114	4,000	
IN-3256	SO-3691	10-31	111	20,000	

CHAPTER 10

THE EXPENDITURE CYCLE

As the name suggests, the expenditure cycle deals with the firm's outlays. Managers concentrate on this cycle so that they can utilize the company's resources in an effective and efficient manner. By controlling costs, managers can increase profits for a given revenue level, since, of course, income equals revenues minus expenses. In addition, managers want to control the outflow of cash so that they can use this scarce resource as advantageously as possible. The AIS must deliver the information managers need to do these things. The firm also must have an internal control system that allows managers to operate the firm effectively and efficiently, meet the entity's legal obligations, and protect the company's resources. External auditors are also concerned with this cycle so that they can attest that expenses and cash outflows are properly reported.

This chapter begins with an overview of the expenditure cycle—the cycle dealing with the purchase of goods and services from the suppliers of these goods and services and the payment of the money owed them. As found in practice, we omit wages and salaries from this discussion, even though they comprise services to the corporation and require cash outlays because they have some special features that lead accountants to utilize a separate payroll cycle. This chapter discusses the cycle's functions and the accounting information to be developed, the business departments involved in the cycle, the basic steps and journal entries (including a discussion of the inventory subsidiary ledger), and the control objectives. We also touch on electronic data interchange, Internet purchases, and just-in-time inventory systems.

The rest of the chapter considers three activities in this cycle: a credit purchase of some good, a purchase return, and a disbursement of cash to a vendor. For each of these activities, we explore the documents, management reports and queries, document flowcharts, and files necessary to computerize the cycle.

As we explore the expenditure cycle, our work is made relatively easy with the realization that this cycle is the mirror image of the revenue cycle, which was featured in the previous chapter. Instead of customers sending us purchase orders, we send purchase orders to our suppliers. Rather than recording a credit sale, we record a credit purchase. And we pay out cash instead of receiving cash. There are some differences in the two cycles, however. For example, the expenditure cycle has a purchase requisition document for which there is no counterpart in the revenue cycle. For the most part, however, the two cycles are very much alike—the firm simply switches roles.

After reading and studying this chapter, you should be able to:

- Define expenditure cycle, purchases cycle, and cash payments cycle;
- Discuss the functions of the expenditure cycle;
- Name the departments involved in the expenditure cycle;
- List the basic steps in the cycle;
- Describe the basic journal entries in the expenditure cycle;
- Distinguish between periodic and perpetual inventory systems;
- Explain the inventory subsidiary ledger;

- State the control objectives of this cycle;
- Define purchase requisition, purchase order, vendor invoice, vendor packing list, and purchase voucher;
- Summarize the credit purchases flowchart;
- State what files are necessary to support the accounting of credit purchases;
- Identify the debit memo (the purchase returns memo);
- Explain the cash disbursements flowchart; and
- Discuss the files that support the accounting of cash payments.

OVERVIEW OF THE EXPENDITURE CYCLE

The *expenditure cycle* is the accounting cycle dealing with the purchase of goods and services and paying for them. Like the revenue cycle, this cycle is sometimes divided into two cycles: the *purchases cycle*, which concentrates on the purchase of goods and services, and the *cash payments cycle* (or cash disbursements cycle), which manages the disbursement of cash to the suppliers. In the expenditure cycle, the firm interacts with the vendors of the corporation. The purchasing department is responsible for ordering the goods and services from the vendors, the accounts payable department monitors how much is owed to each vendor, and the cash disbursements department oversees the actual cash disbursements to the vendors.

To keep things manageable, we focus on only one type of expenditure—the purchase of merchandise inventory. Fortunately, much of what is discussed here extends to other types of expenditures.

Functions of the Cycle

The expenditure cycle focuses on obtaining resources at a reasonable cost and paying the money owed to the vendors but no other money. If the entity is a merchandiser, it will obtain the merchandise inventory that it desires to sell to the public. If the business enterprise is a manufacturer, it must acquire its raw materials from vendors. Manufacturers utilize this cycle in almost the same way as merchandisers. All firms, whether service organizations, merchandisers, or manufacturers, obtain various goods and services needed to keep the business going, such as utilities, insurance, rentals, and office supplies.

Having said this, we assume, after some general observations, that the firm is a merchandiser just to give some specificity to the remaining exposition. Furthermore, we assume that the managers have already decided which goods to buy from vendors and then resell. The expenditure cycle takes that decision as a given.

With these observations in mind, managers needs to ask questions such as the following:

1. Which products or services do we need to obtain from suppliers?
2. How much do we stock, and what quantity do we purchase? (Together, the answers to these two questions will indicate at what level the firm should restock its inventory.)
3. What quality level should the products have?
4. Given the quality level desired, how do we find the cheapest products?
5. How do we store the goods to protect them as long as the firm holds them?

6. How do we ensure that we pay only for the goods and services provided the corporation?

7. How do we make sure that we take advantage of all cash discounts?

Accounting does not provide information that will help answer the first four questions. Decisions made for the revenue cycle will help managers to answer the first question here. For example, a merchandiser will obtain the merchandise inventory that managers have already decided to sell. A manufacturer will procure the raw materials that are needed in the manufacturing process. The quantity to purchase and the amount to stock are often functions of ordering costs, carrying costs, stock-out costs, and the like. The area of operations management has developed formulas to assist managers in making these decisions. Quality level is dictated by the quality desired by the firm's customers. To obtain reasonable costs on inventory, the firm scans its environment to find the best prices. It also sometimes agrees to long-term contracts to obtain favorable terms. Accounting will, of course, keep track of the costs; it can also develop metrics to help measure quality.

The logistics department has responsibility for the inventory, so it must decide how to store and safeguard the inventory. This is critical to the control aspects of the AIS.

Accounting does, however, help to answer the last two questions. Internal control procedures help to ensure that the firm pays only the legitimate bills. The AIS will also notify managers about the existence of cash discounts.

In the rest of the chapter we assume that management has decided on the array of goods and services to purchase and from which vendors, the quality level desired, and the quantity of goods to purchase and keep in stock. Once these issues are decided, then accounting can assist managers in controlling costs and protecting the assets of the corporation.

Business Departments

The controller's department, the logistics department, and the treasurer's department participate in this cycle. Let's discuss their roles in the expenditure cycle.

Bookkeeping activities are carried out by the general ledger department, the accounts payable department, and inventory control. As is the usual case, the general ledger department receives data via a journal voucher and keeps the general ledger up to date. The *accounts payable department* supervises the accounts payable subsidiary ledger. It adjusts the suppliers' accounts as purchases, purchase returns and allowances, and cash payments are made. *Cost accounting* determines the cost of a product or of a service. Manufacturing firms are the most likely to have an inventory control department, which then calculates the direct material costs, the direct labor costs, and the overhead costs for each product produced by the company.

As noted in the previous chapter, the *logistics department* deals with the procurement and movement of equipment, facilities, and personnel. We continue to focus on that part of logistics that concerns inventory. In the expenditure cycle, accountants emphasize the movement of inventory from the vendor to the business enterprise. Logistics has four departments that affect this cycle: purchasing, receiving, shipping, and warehouse. The *purchasing department* is that branch of the logistics department that procures supplies and inventory. Individuals in the purchasing department who approve a purchase by signing the purchase order are called *purchasing agents*. The *receiving department* takes delivery of the good after the vendor ships it to the firm. If the company decides to reject the goods and send them back, then the *shipping department* processes them. The *warehouse* holds the goods in storage and releases them upon proper authorization.

The only department in the treasurer's office that assists in the expenditure cycle is the cash disbursements department. The *cash disbursements department* is that part of the treasurer's department which pays out cash to the suppliers.

Thus, the accountants record the transactions as they occur, logistics receives the inventory and has custody over it, and the treasurer's department processes the cash payments.

Basic Steps

The expenditure cycle proceeds in six basic steps. They are:

1. Determine when a product is needed.
2. Acquire the product.
3. Receive the goods and inspect them.
4. If the goods are unacceptable, return or obtain a purchase allowance.
5. Validate the order
6. Pay the cash to the vendor.

The credit purchase flowchart, shown later, covers steps 1–3; the purchase returns flowchart, which is left as a problem, covers step 4; and the cash disbursements flowchart covers steps 5 and 6.

If the entity makes a purchase and the vendor indicates that the goods are on back order, then the managers can decide either to wait for the goods or cancel the order. Neither possibility affects or changes the accounting for purchases. Of course, the accountants want to make sure that a canceled order is not paid. This can be accomplished by appropriately marking up the original business documents.

Basic Journal Entries

Earlier chapters have already described the basic journal entries employed in this cycle. As with Chapter 9, however, we have several additional items to explain. Fortunately, two of them are the flip side of what we did in the preceding chapter, so we can build on those foundations. Specifically, we need to address three areas: the accounting for cash discounts offered by suppliers to the corporation; the employment of either a periodic inventory system or a perpetual inventory system; and the inventory subsidiary ledger.

Gross and Net Methods for Recording Cash Discounts.   Sellers sometimes offer a cash discount to provide incentives for customers to send in the cash promptly, and these discounts are offered to businesses as well as people. As a company buys inventory from its suppliers, it, too, may be offered such a cash discount. If a supplier gives terms of 2/10, n/30 (an explanation of this notation can be found in the previous chapter), the transaction implicitly carries an interest rate roughly equal to 36%. Thus, given the usual interest rates in the United States, the entity should take advantage of these proposals.

When cash discounts are presented, corporations may account for the purchases and cash payments with either the gross method or the net method. Under the *gross method,* purchases are recorded at the full amount. If our firm pays within the discount period, then this fact is recorded with the contra-expense account called purchases discount. (Let's assume that the periodic inventory method is applied; shortly, we will explore the perpetual inventory method and explain what changes are involved.) With the *net method,* however, purchases are recorded at the full amount less the cash discount. If the corporation pays the bill outside the discount period, then the extra amount paid is recorded as finance expense or purchase discounts lost.

With this distinction, let's proceed to list the basic journal entries for the expenditure cycle. The basic journal entries pertain to recording (1) the credit purchase; (2) the cash payment; and (3) a purchase return or purchase allowance.

Exhibit 10.1 illustrates these three basic transactions and records them under both the gross and net methods. Charu Varshney and Associates buys on credit $10,000 worth of goods. The supplier gives Charu Varshney credit terms of 2/10, n/30. The credit purchase is recorded as a debit to purchases and a credit to accounts payable. Under the gross method, the accountant enters the full amount $10,000, but under the net method the discount (2% of $10,000 or $200) is deducted and so the accountant records the credit purchase at $9,800.

The second basic entry records the disbursement of cash. Let's consider two cases. The first case assumes that the company pays the liability within the 10-day discount period. Charu Varshney and Associates distributes $9,800 to the vendor and records the transaction with a credit to the cash account for $9,800. The gross method measures the accounts payable at the full amount, so the bookkeeper credits accounts payable for $10,000. The difference is shown as a credit to purchase discounts. If the entity uses the net method, then it debits accounts payable for $9,800 and credits cash for $9,800. Both methods disclose net purchases of $9,800.

The second case covers the situation when the firm pays the vendor after the 10-day discount period; thus, Charu Varshney and Associates must pay the supplier $10,000. Under the gross method, the entry is a debit to accounts payable and a credit to cash for

EXHIBIT 10.1

GROSS AND NET METHODS TO RECORD PURCHASES

Charu Varshney and Associates buys $10,000 worth of goods from a supplier who offers a 2% discount if paid within 10 days. Show the accounting under the gross and net methods. Assume the periodic inventory system. (If the perpetual system is employed, then CVA would replace the purchases, purchase discounts, and purchase returns and allowances accounts with the inventory account.)

Gross Method			*Net Method*		
When purchased:					
Purchases	$10,000		Purchases	$9,800	
Accounts payable		$10,000	Accounts payable		$ 9,800
If paid within the discount period:					
Accounts payable	$10,000		Accounts payable	$9,800	
Cash		$ 9,800	Cash		$ 9,800
Purchase discounts		$ 200			
If paid after the discount period:					
Accounts payable	$10,000		Accounts payable	$9,800	
Cash		$10,000	Purchase discounts lost	$ 200	
			Cash		$10,000
If goods are returned:					
Accounts payable	$10,000		Accounts payable	$9,800	
Purchase returns and allowances		$10,000	Purchase returns and allowances		$ 9,800

$10,000. The net method also credits cash for $10,000 but debits accounts payable for the net amount $9,800 and places the $200 difference as a debit to purchase discounts lost or to finance expense. Note that once the goods are sold and the inventory costs are passed into cost of goods sold, total expenses are $10,000 for both methods.

The third basic journal entry in this cycle occurs when the firm returns the goods for a refund or obtains an allowance because of some problem with the product. As shown in Exhibit 10.1, the entry is a debit to accounts payable and a credit to purchase returns and allowances, a contra-expense account. The gross method records the transaction for the full amount, while the net method subtracts the amount of the cash discount.

The reader should compare this explanation and example with that given in Chapter 9. Notice that there is great similarity between the two expositions. The only difference arises from the fact that in one case the firm is the seller, while in the other it is the buyer.

Periodic Versus Perpetual Inventory System. There are two general ways to account for a firm's inventory: the periodic and the perpetual methods. The *periodic method* counts the inventory only at the end of accounting periods. This implies that the amount in the inventory account is the amount of beginning inventory, except at the end of the accounting period, when it is the amount of the ending inventory. The major advantage of the periodic method is its ease of use; its chief disadvantage is that managers have little idea of what belongs in the inventory account, except at year-end, and thus they can exert little control over the inventory. The *perpetual method* keeps a record of inventory after each and every sale and purchase. Its chief advantage is that it gives managers a good idea of what is in (or should be in) inventory at all times; its only disadvantages are that it can be tedious to implement and costly to use. However, computers and product scanners, as seen in grocery stores, have significantly reduced these problems.

Conventionally, accountants use the term "purchases" when they apply the periodic method but use the term "inventory" when they employ the perpetual method. In addition, accountants typically debit or credit the inventory account when there is a purchase discount or when there is a purchase return or allowance. This naming convention, however, is a minor point. The more substantive point is that the perpetual method requires the firm to make two journal entries when it has a sale. When the company sells a product to a customer, it first records the sale, and then it must account for the cost of goods sold. The second entry is obvious:

Cost of sales	$X	
Inventory		$X

In addition, if the customer returns the goods, the inventory will have to be added back and the cost of sales reduced. (How is cost of goods sold recognized under the periodic method? *Hint:* See Chapter 3.)

Both methods can record the inventory at the gross or net amount. This implies that the perpetual method could be employed in Exhibit 10.1. If it is, then the purchases, purchase returns, and purchase returns and allowances accounts are replaced with the inventory account. Since there are no sales in that exhibit, the naming change is the only modification one needs to make.

Inventory Subsidiary Ledger. To assist managers in controlling inventory, the AIS must have an inventory subsidiary ledger, especially if the firm has a perpetual inventory system. Just as an accounts receivable subsidiary ledger helps the manager find out what each customer owes the firm or an accounts payable subsidiary ledger helps the manager assess how much is owed to each supplier, the inventory subsidiary ledger provides information about each product that makes up the inventory of the firm. The inventory ledger account reveals the company's total inventory. To get the amount of a particular product, one must look in the inventory subsidiary ledger.

Recall from Chapter 4 that a *subsidiary ledger* simply lists the components of some general ledger account. Thus, the *inventory subsidiary ledger* is a subsidiary ledger that details the specific goods that comprise the inventory account. The *controlling account* in this context is the general ledger inventory account. A particular product in the inventory is listed in its own *subsidiary account*.

As an example, assume the business enterprise has three products in inventory, a widget, a gadget, and a gidget. The firm has paid $400 for widgets, $700 for its gadgets, and $900 for the gidgets. The inventory account will have a balance of $2,000. The general ledger account inventory is the controlling account, and the sum of the cost of the individual products must equal $2,000. The inventory subsidiary ledger will have three accounts: inventory—widgets; inventory—gadgets; and inventory—gidgets. These latter accounts are termed subsidiary accounts. As with the other subsidiary ledgers, these subsidiary accounts do not go on the balance sheet because that would double count them. The existence of these subsidiary accounts allows managers to find out the balance of any product.

Recall that accountants can prepare an accounts receivable subsidiary schedule or an accounts payable subsidiary schedule, which would show the balances in the subsidiary accounts. In like manner, accountants can produce a *subsidiary schedule* for the inventory account. This schedule lists all the products that comprise the inventory account, and it gives the total for all inventory.

Consider the following example, which is also reported in Exhibit 10.2. Fran's Furniture keeps an inventory subsidiary ledger so that the managers can see the levels of the different products it sells. The store maintains the inventory on the perpetual system. Assume that Fran's Furniture has five products. The products and their balances at the beginning of February are:

Chair: CH-300	$ 30,000
Chair: CH-410	22,000
Chair: CH-502	59,000
Coffee Table: CT-190	37,000
Sofa: SO-335	21,000
Total	$169,000

The controlling account will also have a balance of $169,000. Let's assume that the beginning balance is $42,610 in accounts receivable and $63,000 in accounts payable. We will also assume that Fran's closes its nominal accounts monthly, so sales and cost of goods sold have beginning balances of zero. Other accounts are ignored.

Fran's buys furniture from its suppliers and retails them to consumers. The vendor's terms are n/30 so we can concentrate specifically on the inventory subsidiary ledger. Fran's Furniture (FF) engages in the following transactions during February:

February 13: FF buys $2,000 of chairs (product number CH-502).
February 14: FF buys $5,000 of sofas (product number SO-335).
February 15: FF returns $500 of the chairs purchased on the 13th because of a defect.
February 25: FF sells chairs (product number CH-502) to its customers. The goods cost $5,000 and sell for $9,000.
February 28: FF buys $3,000 of coffee tables (product number CT-190).

EXHIBIT 10.2

EXAMPLE OF AN INVENTORY SUBSIDIARY LEDGER

Panel A: Journal entries in the general journal

GENERAL JOURNAL

PAGE 89

Date	Description	F	Debit	Credit
2-13	Inventory	130	$2,000	
	Accounts payable	210		$2,000
	Chairs: CH-502	*		
2-14	Inventory	130	$5,000	
	Accounts payable	210		$5,000
	Sofas: SO-335	*		

GENERAL JOURNAL

PAGE 90

Date	Description	F	Debit	Credit
2-15	Accounts payable	210	$ 500	
	Inventory	130		$ 500
	Chairs: CH-502	*		
2-25	Accounts receivable	120	$9,000	
	Sales	400		$9,000
2-25	Cost of goods sold	610	$5,000	
	Inventory	130		$5,000
	Chairs: CH-502	*		
2-28	Inventory	130	$3,000	
	Accounts payable	210		$3,000
	Coffee table: CT-190	*		

Panel B: General ledger (partial)

GENERAL LEDGER
ACCOUNTS RECEIVABLE

Account No. 120

Date	Description	F	Debits	Credits	Balance
	Opening Bal				$42,610
2-25	Credit sale	90	$9,000		$51,610

(continued)

EXHIBIT *10.2*

EXAMPLE OF AN INVENTORY SUBSIDIARY LEDGER (continued)

INVENTORY

Account No. 130

Date	Description	F	Debits	Credits	Balance
	Opening Bal				$169,000
2-13	Purchase	89	$2,000		$171,000
2-14	Purchase	89	$5,000		$176,000
2-15	Return	90		$ 500	$175,500
2-25	Sale	90		$5,000	$170,500
2-28	Purchase	90	$3,000		$173,500

ACCOUNTS PAYABLE

Account No. 210

Date	Description	F	Debits	Credits	Balance
	Opening Bal				$63,000
2-13	Purchase	89		$2,000	$65,000
2-14	Purchase	89		$5,000	$70,000
2-15	Return	90	$ 500		$69,500
2-28	Purchase	90		$3,000	$72,500

SALES

Account No. 400

Date	Description	F	Debits	Credits	Balance
2-25	Credit sale	90		$9,000	$9,000

COST OF GOODS SOLD

Account No. 610

Date	Description	F	Debits	Credits	Balance
2-25	Sale	90	$5,000		$5,000

(continued)

EXHIBIT *10.2*

EXAMPLE OF AN INVENTORY SUBSIDIARY LEDGER (continued)

Panel C: Subsidiary ledger

INVENTORY SUBSIDIARY LEDGER
Chair: CH-300

Date	Description	F	Debits	Credits	Balance
	Opening Bal				$30,000

Chair: CH-410

Date	Description	F	Debits	Credits	Balance
	Opening Bal				$22,000

Chair: CH-502

Date	Description	F	Debits	Credits	Balance
	Opening Bal				$59,000
2-13	Purchase	89	$2,000		$61,000
2-15	PRA	90		$ 500	$60,500
2-25	Sale	90		$5,000	$55,500

Coffee Table: CT-190

Date	Description	F	Debits	Credits	Balance
	Opening Bal				$37,000
2-28	Purchase	90	$3,000		$40,000

Sofa: SO-335

Date	Description	F	Debits	Credits	Balance
	Opening Bal				$21,000
2-14	Purchase	89	$5,000		$26,000

Panel D: Schedule of inventory

Fran's Furniture
Inventory Schedule
February 28, 2001

Product	Amount
CH-300	$ 30,000
CH-410	22,000
CH-502	55,500
CT-190	40,000
SO-335	26,000
Total	$173,500

Your mission is to make the appropriate journal entries in the general journal, post them to the general ledger and to the inventory subsidiary ledger, and publish an inventory subsidiary schedule at the end of the month. Exhibit 10.2 displays the solution to this problem. Panel A gives the journal entries in the general journal, panel B indicates the affected accounts in the general ledger, panel C shows the inventory subsidiary ledger and all of the subsidiary accounts, and panel D displays the schedule of inventory at February 28.

The journal entries in panel A of Exhibit 10.2 are straightforward. Keep in mind that the perpetual inventory method is in place. Acquisition of new inventory is shown as a debit to inventory and a credit to accounts payable. The purchase return is accounted for as a debit to accounts payable and a credit to inventory. Notice that the sale has two entries. One entry shows the credit sale in the usual fashion, with a debit to accounts receivable and a credit to sales. The other entry reflects the cost of this particular sale. There is a debit to cost of goods sold and a credit to inventory. Of course, the sale is measured at the selling price to the consumer, whereas the cost of goods sold is measured at the firm's cost to its suppliers.

Posting to accounts receivable, the inventory controlling account, accounts payable, sales, and cost of goods sold is carried out as explained in Chapter 3. The amount is carried from the general journal to the general ledger and placed in the debit or credit column as is appropriate. The account number is placed in the folio column of the general journal.

We also record which product is involved in the transaction. After the journal entry, the accountant writes the name and product number of the inventory item. Once he or she posts the item to the inventory subsidiary ledger, the accountant places an asterisk ("*") or a similar notation in the folio column to indicate that the posting has been made.

Panel B presents the partial general ledger. All postings have been performed, which means that the page number of the general ledger where the journal entry occurs is listed in the folio column of the general ledger. If the reader has difficulty following panel B, he or she should review general ledgers as they are constructed and discussed in Chapter 3.

The inventory subsidiary ledger is given in panel C of Exhibit 10.2. As defined, each subsidiary account has a separate position within the subsidiary ledger. An accountant can look up the details for any product, examine the beginning balance for that product, see the changes that have been made during the period, and observe the ending balance. The inventory subsidiary ledger operates like the other subsidiary ledgers. The date column states the date of the transaction. The description column optionally provides a short statement of what took place. The folio column is used for posting purposes and gives the page in the general or special journal in which the original transaction is recorded. The debits and credits columns show whether the inventory increased or decreased, and the balance column gives the product's total balance after the particular transaction.

In practice, the inventory subsidiary ledger could hold other data, such as the quantity of the product and where stored. Whatever information managers consider important can be placed there.

As is always the case, the amount of the controlling account equals the sum of the balances of the subsidiary accounts. For example, look at Fran's accounts at the end of February. If the ending balances for all five products in the inventory subsidiary ledger are added up, one will obtain $173,500, the same number that is the ending balance in the controlling account. This fact is placed in a more readable format in panel D and is referred to as the inventory schedule.

This example placed the entries in the general journal. In practice, the bookkeepers put purchases in the purchases journal, sales in the sales journal, and purchase returns in the general journal. They would also employ an accounts receivable subsidiary ledger and an accounts payable subsidiary ledger. We ignored these items in this example to concentrate on the inventory subsidiary ledger.

Control Objectives

The control objectives in the expenditure cycle are similar to those in the revenue cycle to the extent that both deal with cash and inventory. They differ a bit, since the revenue cycle concerns itself with cash inflows, whereas the expenditure cycle looks at cash outflows. Since both cycles involve credit purchases/sales, both deal with accounts awaiting settlement. The revenue cycle manages accounts receivable, and the expenditure cycle handles accounts payable. Following the discussion in Chapter 7, these objectives continue to focus on protecting the firm's assets and accounting records, participating only in authorized transactions, and keeping proper records. These control objectives are as follows.

Purchases of inventory are made only when needed by the firm and only from legitimate suppliers.

Inventories are safeguarded when received and while in stock.

Cash is safeguarded by disbursing cash only for valid accounts payable of the corporation.

All expenditure-cycle transactions are authorized by management.

All valid expenditure-cycle transactions are recorded accurately.

All documents and reports generated in the expenditure cycle are safeguarded.

Buying in Today's Technological World

Just as science and technology have affected selling activities, they have also had a major impact on buying. We discussed point-of-sale (POS) systems, EDI, and web-based transactions in the revenue cycle. As POS systems are aimed primarily at retail customers, corporate buyers do not often use them. In the expenditure cycle, we briefly touch on EDI, web-based transactions, and just-in-time (JIT) systems.

An *electronic data interchange (EDI)* is a computer-to-computer exchange of business documents. For example, a restaurant may have a contract with a food wholesaler that covers inventory purchases. As the restaurant manager notices that the food supplies are getting low, he or she could send electronic requests to the wholesaler through the computer. With a well-programmed perpetual inventory system, managers could even permit the computer to automatically trigger the request when the inventory becomes low. These exchanges of business documents between the restaurant and the food wholesaler provide an example of EDI. The restaurant sends an electronic version of the purchase order, and the wholesaler sends the food along with an electronic invoice.

Some retailers connect their POS system to their EDI system. This connection allows the firm's vendors to access information as the sales are being made to the firm's customers.

Accounting does not change when using EDI, but the control activities will. As stated in the previous chapter, the benefits from EDI include increased speed of communication between customer and seller, increased accuracy of transmission, and elimination of some business documents. The disadvantages are the costs, though they are decreasing, and the threats of theft by computer hackers.

The Internet has affected society greatly, and one effect is that it provides a mechanism for trading between buyers and sellers. Doing business over the Internet has many advantages, including convenience and speed and better customization to customer wants.

News features about web-based sales are frequently misleading because they focus on re-tail sales. In fact, business-to-business (sometimes written as B2B) sales on the Internet far exceed corporate-to-consumer sales. The Internet provides a marvelous, exciting way for companies to obtain their inventory.

Accounting for purchases made via the Internet is exactly the same as accounting for purchases made through a manual system. The technology simply offers a different way of purchasing the goods.

In the past, firms managed their inventories by determining the needs, considering the time it took to process an order and receive the goods, and figuring out the cost of running out of stock. They held enough inventories to avoid stock-outs. This process had lots of costs, from interest on the accounts payable for holding lots of inventory to pil-ferage and breakage, and to the requirement of having lots of warehouse space to house the goods. Firms have looked for ways to reduce these costs.

One way to decrease inventory costs is to implement a just-in-time system. *Just-in-time (JIT) systems* basically refer to systems in which inventory is not obtained until nec-essary. To implement JIT, managers frequently negotiate long-term contracts with their suppliers for limited and speedy deliveries. The contract helps ensure that the company need not keep a buffer of goods by agreeing to buy a lot of inventory over a specified amount of time. The primary advantage of JIT is that it allows a company to reduce its levels of inventories, sometimes to very low levels.

JIT is especially beneficial to manufacturers. It permits them to have low raw ma-terials inventory. It also lets them not start production until sales have already been made. Thus, JIT should also reduce work-in-process inventory and finished goods inventory.

Unfortunately, JIT does require some changes in accounting, but these changes are beyond the scope of this course. Clearly, however, businesses have the potential to save lots of money with JIT by holding smaller amounts of inventory.

Later courses in accounting information systems will build on this foundation. We continue this chapter by taking a closer look at the three major activities within the ex-penditure cycle: credit purchases, purchase returns, and cash disbursements to vendors.

CREDIT PURCHASES

The major activity in the expenditure cycle is making credit purchases. In this section we explain the documents for this activity and the management reports and queries, and we direct most of our attention to the document flowchart for credit purchases. The section concludes with a brief look at what files the AIS must have to account for these transac-tions and maintain good internal controls.

Documents

When a credit purchase takes place, the AIS receives or generates six documents: the pur-chase requisition, the purchase order, the vendor invoice, the vendor packing list, the re-ceiving report, and the journal voucher. In addition, the term "purchase voucher" refers to the set of four documents: the purchase requisition, purchase order, vendor invoice, and receiving report.

Generation of the purchase requisition initiates this cycle. A *purchase requisition*, as the name suggests, is a document that asks the purchasing department to obtain cer-tain goods. In our flowchart, we assume that an employee in the warehouse notices that the firm is short in some products and reports this fact via the purchase requisition. (The process can, of course, be automated.)

Exhibit 10.3 contains an illustration of a purchase requisition. The document shows the corporation's name and address, the purchase requisition number, the date, the name of the employee filling out the document, and optionally a suggested vendor. The document enumerates the inventory items, giving the product description, item number (if known), quantity desired, and unit price. It also has a line for a supervisor to approve the request and indicate the date of the approval.

The purchase order is the second document created in the expenditure cycle. The *purchase order* is a document sent by the entity to purchase goods from a vendor. The purchasing department fills it out and sends it to the vendor. Sometimes the supplier provides a formal acceptance of the sale by sending the company a copy of its sales order; this copy is called the acknowledgment copy. This sales order also gives some assurance that the vendor has correctly interpreted the purchase order.

Exhibit 10.4 displays a purchase order. The purchase order is very much like the purchase requisition inasmuch as it contains the corporation name and address, purchase order number, date, product description, item number, quantity desired, and unit price.

EXHIBIT 10.3

PURCHASE REQUISITION

PURCHASE REQUISITION
Krumrine Productions
100 Old Main Street
Clarksburg PA 16899-1950

PRQ No. _____

Date: _____
Prepared by: _____
Suggested Vendor: _____

Quantity Ordered	Item Number	Product Description	Unit Price	Total
			COST	

Approved by: _____
Date approved: _____

EXHIBIT *10.4*

PURCHASE ORDER

PURCHASE ORDER
Krumrine Productions
100 Old Main Street
Clarksburg PA 16899-1950

PO No. _____

Vendor: _____

Address: _____

_____

_____

_____

Date: _____

Vendor Number: _____

Shipping terms: _____

Requisition Number: _____

Shipping date: _____

Ship to:

Address: _____

_____

_____

Quantity Ordered	Item Number	Product Description	Unit Price	Total

Purchasing agent: _____

The document portrays the purchase requisition number to allow an auditor or a supervisor or any other interested party to find the underlying request to purchase the inventory. The purchase order shows the shipping terms and a date by which the firm would like the goods shipped. Sometimes the billing address is different from the address where the products should be sent. If so, the purchase order also lists the shipping address. Finally, a purchasing agent in the purchasing department signs the document.

The third document in this cycle is the vendor invoice. The *invoice* is the document sent to the customer indicating the price for the goods or services provided by the vendor and the terms for settlement. We covered the invoice and included an example in the previous chapter. There is nothing new to offer here, except to say that the corporation is now the customer and so receives the invoice from the seller. The copy of the vendor invoice asks the firm to pay the bill; it also gives additional evidence that a valid transaction has taken place between the firm and a supplier.

The vendor sends a packing list (sometimes called a packing slip) when the goods are shipped to our firm. As discussed previously, a *packing list* is a document sent by the seller to the customer when the goods are shipped, and it displays the sale and shipping terms. Often the packing list is merely a copy of the sales order and a copy of the bill of lading.

Another document found in the expenditure cycle is the receiving report. The *receiving report* is generated by the receiving department to show what products they have received and what condition they are in. In Chapter 9 we talked about the receiving report in terms of sales returns. There the focus was on verifying that the customer actually bought the goods from our company and that there was a legitimate reason for returning the goods. The concern in the expenditure cycle is that the business enterprise has sent a purchase order to the supplier, that the goods received are in fact the goods ordered by the company, and that they are in acceptable condition.

In practice, the receiving report is often a copy of the purchase order except that the quantity column is blank. Also, the price per unit and the total price are not displayed since one could figure the quantity based on those data. If the counters in the receiving department had access to the original purchase order in its entirety, they might be tempted to slack off and just say that the quantity received was the quantity ordered. By blanking out these data, the receiving department is forced to perform a *blind count* of the goods received. Thus, this version of the purchase order is called a *blind copy*.

The last document is the journal voucher, which we have amply described.

Management Reports and Queries

Two reports coming out of this cycle concern the usage of inventory and the inventories on hand (sometimes called the inventory status report). To publish them, the firm needs to have a perpetual inventory system, especially if managers want this information more frequently than once per year. Inventory usage simply shows what inventory has been used during a specific period of time, while the inventories on hand report states what is still in inventory. The reports often list all types of inventory as well as a total amount.

Another report is the overdue deliveries report. As the name suggests, the report states which goods have been ordered from a vendor but have not been received. This declaration calls attention to items that need followup by the managers, and it suggests, if a vendor is repeatedly late, that the firm might consider finding a different supplier.

Credit Purchases Flowchart

Exhibit 10.5 presents the credit purchases flowchart. The actors involved in this activity are the warehouse, purchasing department, vendor, receiving department, accounts payable, and general ledger department. The documents that flow among these actors are the purchase requisition, purchase order, vendor invoice, vendor packing list, receiving report, and journal voucher.

Somebody working within the warehouse notices that some inventory item is low. (As always, variations exist in practice.) He or she then fills out a purchase requisition so that the company will have additional units when the ones presently on hand are depleted. The individual prepares three copies of the purchase requisition. One copy goes to ac-

EXHIBIT **10.5**

CREDIT PURCHASE FLOWCHART

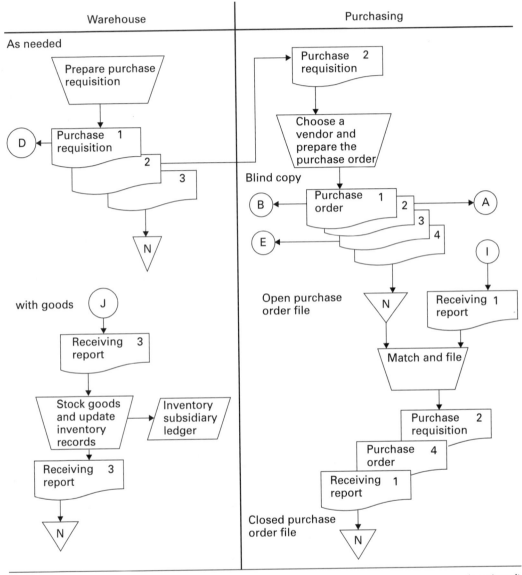

(continued)

counts payable; a second proceeds to the purchasing department—the department that actually buys the products from suppliers; and the third copy stays in the warehouse and is filed by the purchase requisition number.

Once the purchasing department receives its copy of the purchase requisition, it first decides on a vendor. The purchasing department might use the suggested vendor, assuming one is named by the warehouse. It might see who the firm has employed before, examine their past performance, and choose who it thinks is the best. The department could also put the order up for bid and go with the best deal it can make.

EXHIBIT 10.5

CREDIT PURCHASE FLOWCHART (continued)

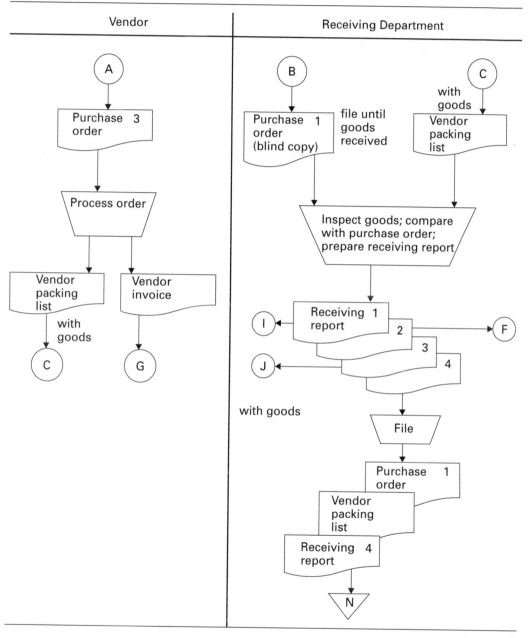

(continued)

After it determines the supplier, the purchasing department prepares four copies of the purchase order. The first copy is sent to the vendor so the order can be processed. The purchasing department gives a second copy to the receiving department, usually with the quantity and price data deleted. As stated before, this copy of the receiving report is termed the blind copy. The purchasing department also sends a copy to accounts payable. The

EXHIBIT 10.5

CREDIT PURCHASE FLOWCHART (continued)

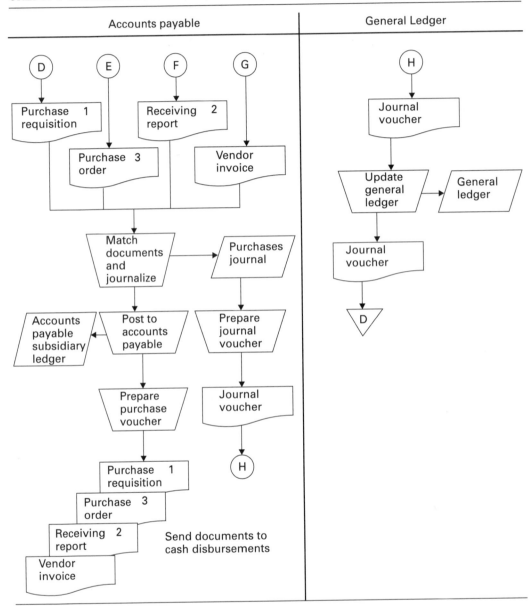

last copy is temporarily filed by purchase order number. At this juncture, the file is named the open purchase order file. An *open purchase order file* includes only those purchase orders for which the firm has not yet received the goods. Having a file with only unfilled purchase orders helps the entity follow up with slow vendors. Purchase orders stay in this file until the purchasing department obtains a copy of the receiving report, indicating that the order is now filled.

Meanwhile, the vendor receives its copy of the purchase order. The supplier processes the order, as explained in the previous chapter. The vendor ships the goods to the firm along with a packing list. It also sends the business enterprise an invoice for the sale, usually with a remittance advice.

The receiving department receives the goods from the vendor. It inspects the goods and compares it with a copy of the purchase order. The latter step is followed so as not to accept an order not made by the corporation. Assuming that everything is okay, the receiving department prepares four copies of the receiving report. The receiving department sends one copy of this document to the warehouse (along with the goods themselves), another copy to the purchasing department, a third copy to accounts payable, and it files one copy. The last-named copy is filed with a copy of the purchase order and the packing list. They are filed by the purchase order number.

Let's now go back to the purchasing department, which is holding the open purchase order file. It obtains a copy of the receiving report. When this is done, the purchasing department compares the receiving report with the purchase order. This comparison is especially important if the receiving department blindly counts the inventory it receives. Assuming that the two documents agree, the purchasing department files its copy of the purchase requisition, purchase order, and receiving report by the purchase order number.

Now we will return to the warehouse, the group that initiated the purchase process. Once it acquires the goods and attains its copy of the receiving report, the warehouse stocks the goods in the warehouse and updates the inventory subsidiary ledger. It also files its copy of the receiving report either by the receiving report number or by the purchase order number (assuming that the number is written on the receiving report). The latter number is better since it would facilitate communication among departments if there are any snafus.

You should notice that the accounts payable department gets a copy of four documents: the purchase requisition, purchase order, receiving report, and vendor invoice. This set of documents is frequently called the *purchase voucher package* or disbursement voucher package, or voucher package for short. Together they provide the evidence that a valid transaction has occurred. The accounts payable department first compares these documents. Assuming that they match, the department next journalizes the transaction in the purchases journal. (If necessary, you should review the mechanics of the purchases journal, as presented in Chapter 4.) After that, it posts the transaction to the accounts payable subsidiary ledger. Accounts payable then sends the purchase voucher package to cash disbursements. Periodically, the accounts payable department will summarize the entries in the purchases journal on a journal voucher. It then sends the journal voucher to the general ledger department.

When the general ledger department acquires the journal voucher, it performs its usual routine of updating the general ledger and filing the journal voucher.

This completes the flowchart for credit purchases. Of particular note is the creation of the purchase voucher package to provide evidence of the transaction with the supplier. The process also builds in checks and balances, which make it very difficult to make unauthorized purchases.

Files in an EDP Environment

As the business enterprise moves from a manual system to a computerized accounting system, the AIS creates several computer files. There will be three master files: the vendor master file, the accounts payable master file, and the inventory master file. The last-named are the merchandise inventory master file for a merchandiser and the finished goods inventory master file for a manufacturer. Both types of business organizations, as well as service organizations, have a supplies inventory master file. Furthermore, the manufacturer also has a raw materials inventory master file and a work-in-process inventory master file. Our comments about the inventory master file apply to a merchandise inventory file but can easily be amended to suit other needs.

The *vendor master file* is the file that enumerates each vendor of the firm and various details about each of them. The record layout consists of the vendor account number (the key), vendor name, vendor address, and vendor phone number. The file might also contain data about the quality of the services provided by the vendor, though that information is more frequently kept in a vendor history file.

The *accounts payable master file* is a file that shows what the corporation owes to each of its suppliers. It is a computerized version of the accounts payable subsidiary ledger. We leave the record layout as an exercise.

The *inventory master file* is a file showing the specific goods that comprise the inventory accounts. It is the analog of the inventory subsidiary ledger, described earlier and illustrated in Exhibit 10.2. A possible record layout includes the product number (which is the key), the product name, a brief description, the warehouse location, the unit of measure code, the quantity on hand, and the reorder point (that is, the point at which the firm would restock the inventory).

An EDP system in the expenditure cycle would create two transaction files: an open purchase order file and an open vendor invoice file. Recall that open files are special transaction files that contain data of incomplete transactions. An *open purchase order file* is a file that includes only those purchase orders for which the firm has not yet received the goods. The file allows managers to easily keep track of which purchases have not been received and might need attention. The *open vendor invoice file* (also called the open voucher file) is a file that includes only those vendor invoices that have not yet been paid. This file permits the firm to hold cash until the last possible moment and then pay the bill and still obtain the cash discount. Such cash management helps the company to earn as much interest off the money as it possibly can.

The corporation might also maintain a shipping data file, a file that has some reference data pertaining to shipping information. It could also keep a vendor history file, a file that tells how well the suppliers fulfilled the orders and how quickly.

Having finished the development of the credit purchases activities within the expenditure cycle, we now move to a consideration of purchase returns and allowances and, later, cash disbursements.

PURCHASE RETURNS

Let's briefly look at purchase returns and allowances. We only sketch this set of activities and leave the details to the exercises and problems at the end of the chapter. As with most items in this chapter, purchase returns and allowances are the flip side of their counterpart in the revenue cycle, viz., sales returns and allowances, where the firm becomes the buyer instead of the seller.

Initially, the vendor sends the products to the firm's receiving department. Workers in that department inspect the goods and the purchase order. If there is a problem—such as the company didn't order the inventory, the wrong product was sent, or the goods are damaged—then the receiving department can refuse to accept the goods from the supplier. Nothing special has to be done by the receiving department, and we do not include those refusals in this section.

Instead, let's assume that the receiving department has accepted the products from the supplier. Somebody has accepted the goods for the company and filled out the receiving report. This receipt of the inventory constitutes the purchase transaction and requires the firm to record the purchase. Later, an employee determines that something is amiss and that the inventory ought to be returned to the vendor (or an allowance made). This activity leads to the purchase return or allowance, including making the necessary journal entries.

Documents

Once the decision to return the goods (or obtain an allowance) is made, a debit memorandum is prepared. A *debit memo* is a document indicating that the firm's account should be reduced because of a purchase return or purchase allowance. The document gets its name from the observation that, when the company reduces its accounts payable, it debits the account. An exercise asks you to construct a debit memo. Just keep in mind that it will be similar to a credit memo.

Management Reports and Queries

Some reports about purchase returns and allowances help to pinpoint problems with the firm's vendors. Relevant statistics, perhaps summarized, can be placed in the vendor history file so that the purchasing department has a better idea of which vendors to use and which to avoid.

Purchase Returns Flowchart

This is left as an exercise. We will assume that somebody finds a defect in the products and notifies the purchasing department, and purchasing then prepares the debit memo. We assume that the goods are in the warehouse, and it sends the goods to the shipping department, along with a blind copy of the debit memo. Who else needs a copy of the debit memo? What else must the warehouse do? Why have a blind copy of the debit memo?

Files in an EDP Environment

A firm might have a *purchase returns and allowances file*, which is the counterpart to the sales returns and allowances file.

CASH DISBURSEMENTS

The third and last activity to examine in the expenditure cycle is the cash payments to vendors. Documents for this activity include the purchase requisition, purchase order, receiving report, vendor invoice, and check. Departments that participate in cash disbursements consist of accounts payable, cash disbursements, and general ledger.

Documents

Although the corporation purchases its inventory on credit, the accounts payable department collects four documents. These documents, as mentioned earlier, are the purchase requisition, purchase order, receiving report, and vendor invoice. Together, they comprise what is known as the purchase voucher package, or simply the voucher package. Exhibit 10.5 showed that accounts payable receives a copy of each of them and then sends them to cash disbursements. Their purpose is to prove that a valid purchase has taken place.

The last document in this activity is the check. The cash disbursements department writes the check, states that the payee is the vendor, signs it, and then mails it to the vendor. Alternatively, the firm could employ EFT and pay the vendor electronically.

Management Reports and Queries

Corporate managers want to know about the coming bills and when they are due so that they can better manage the firm's cash flow. They want to use the cash while they can, so they try to pay the bills at the last possible moment. If nothing else, they can put the cash in the bank and earn interest on the days they hold it before paying the suppliers. At the same time, managers want to pay the bills in time so that the entity can obtain any cash discounts and avoid the implied finance charges. Thus, managers want to query the system about the bills and their due dates.

A report could be made of cash payments to suppliers. Another report could be made to show any disbursements that miss the cash discount; this report is termed the lost discounts report.

Cash Disbursements Flowchart

Exhibit 10.6 displays the cash disbursements flowchart. As already discussed, the exhibit is implicitly linked with Exhibit 10.5, for the accounts payable department holds the voucher package and eventually sends it to cash disbursements. In fact, this is where Exhibit 10.6 begins. The accounts payable department has the voucher package, which may be called the open vendor invoice file or the open voucher file. As the due date approaches, the accounts payable department sends the voucher package to cash disbursements.

The cash disbursements department examines the voucher package. When it is convinced that the purchase is legitimate, it writes the check to the vendor. It also cancels the voucher package by writing or stamping "PAID" on the voucher package. Some firms will also write the check number on the voucher package to provide an audit trail. If the vendor sends a remittance advice with the invoice, then the firm will include the remittance advice with the check. Cash disbursements enters the transactions into the cash disbursements journal. (You may wish to review the discussion of the cash disbursements journal in Chapter 4.) At appropriate intervals, it summarizes the transactions on a journal voucher and sends the journal voucher to the general ledger department.

After writing the check and recording the transaction in the cash disbursements journal, the department returns the voucher package to accounts payable, which files it by the purchase order number. The accounts payable department also updates the vendor accounts in the accounts payable subsidiary ledger.

The vendor receives the check, deposits it, and records the transaction.

The general ledger department receives the journal voucher, records it in the general ledger, and files the journal voucher by the date.

Files in an EDP Environment

To computerize these processes, the firm needs a vendor master file and an accounts payable master file. These files have been described already. The only new file it needs

EXHIBIT *10.6*

CASH DISBURSEMENT FLOWCHART

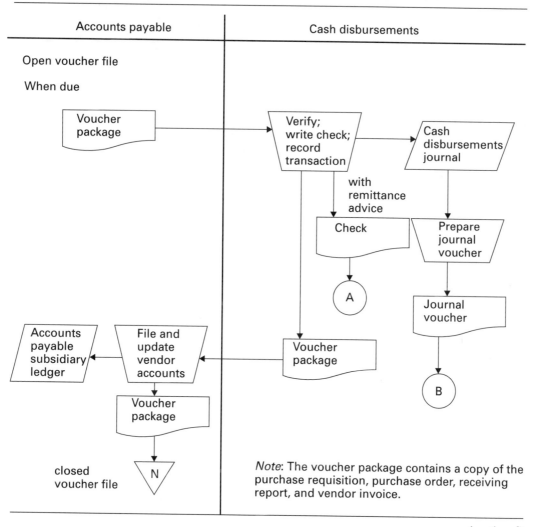

(continued)

is a *cash disbursements file*; this is a transactions file that records the cash disbursements of the firm.

SIGHTS ALONG THE INTERNET

Some sites that explore inventory systems are:

AMPS	www.amps-aai.com/inventory.htm
CIS chemical inventory system	www.chemsw.com/12220.htm
Materials inventory	www.mcsphanet.com/wmsinv.html

EXHIBIT *10.6*

CASH DISBURSEMENT FLOWCHART (continued)

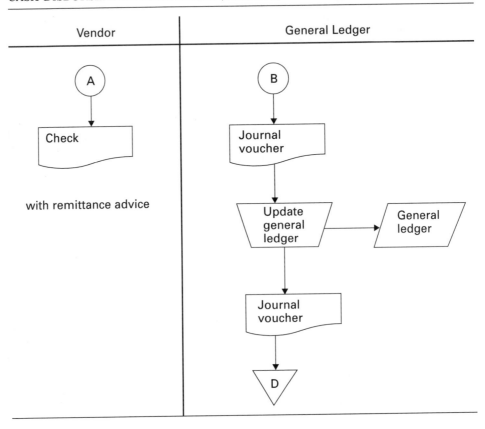

The reader can learn more about JIT by investigating these sites:

JIT Manufacturing Supply	www.jitmfg.com
JIT vendors (Los Alamos National Laboratory)	bus.lanl.gov/bus4/jit/jitcon.htm
JIT-Kaizen (Hitachi Shimizu Tech Technology)	www.tokai.or.jp/hst/kaizen/E-HTM/jit.htm
Kanban—an integrated system	www.geocities.com/TimesSquare/1848/japan21.html

Enterprise resource planning is in vogue today when accounting for and controlling and budgeting inventory. See the following site for more information about ERP:

Inventory software vendors	www.excite.com/business_and_investing/other_business_topics/companies_by_type/computers_and_internet/companies_by_region/latin_america/?search=ERP

CHAPTER SUMMARY IN TERMS OF LEARNING OBJECTIVES

Define Expenditure Cycle, Purchases Cycle, and Cash Payments Cycle. The expenditure cycle is the accounting cycle dealing with the purchase of goods and services and paying for them. The purchases cycle concentrates on the purchase of goods and services, and the cash payments cycle (or cash disbursements cycle) manages the disbursement of cash to the suppliers.

Discuss the Functions of the Expenditure Cycle. The functions of the expenditure cycle are to obtain resources at a reasonable cost and to pay the money owed to the vendors but no other money. Managers need to decide which products and services to obtain, how much to acquire, what quality level the products are to have, and where to find the cheapest prices. They also need to determine how to store the products, assure that payments go only for valid payables, and take advantage of all cash discounts.

Name the Departments Involved in the Expenditure Cycle. The accounts payable department supervises the accounts payable subsidiary ledger. Cost accounting determines the costs of the products. The purchasing department procures supplies and inventory. The receiving department takes delivery of the good after the vendor ships it to the firm. The shipping department returns to the vendor any rejected goods. The warehouse holds the goods in storage and releases them upon proper authorization. The cash disbursements department pays out cash to the suppliers.

List the Basic Steps in the Cycle. The expenditure cycle has six steps: (1) determine when a product is needed; (2) acquire the product; (3) receive the goods and inspect them; (4) if the goods are unacceptable, return them or obtain a purchase allowance; (5) validate the order; and (6) pay the cash to the vendor.

Describe the Basic Journal Entries in the Expenditure Cycle. When cash discounts are offered, business enterprises may account for the purchases and cash disbursements with either the gross method or the net method. Under the gross method, purchases are recorded at the full amount, including the cash discount. If the firm pays the bill within the discount period, then this is recorded with a purchase discount account. With the net method, purchases are recorded at the amount less the cash discount. If the firm pays the bill after the discount period ends, then the extra amount paid is recorded as purchase discounts lost or as interest expense.

There are three basic journal entries in the expenditure cycle. When a purchase is made, debit purchases or inventory and credit accounts payable. When cash is paid out, credit cash for the amount disbursed and debit accounts payable. The amounts and other accounts depend on whether the cash is paid within the discount period and whether the corporation applies the gross or net method. When the company returns goods or obtains an allowance, debit accounts payable and credit purchase returns and allowances, either at gross or at net.

Distinguish Between Periodic and Perpetual Inventory Systems. The periodic method counts the inventory only at the end of the accounting periods, and in between there is no record about what the inventory level should be. The perpetual inventory system keeps a record of inventory after each and every sale and purchase.

Explain the Inventory Subsidiary Ledger. The purpose of inventory subsidiary accounts is to allow a manager to find out the balance in any particular product, which is a component of inventory. The inventory subsidiary ledger lists each of these products in the inventory of the firm. As with all controlling accounts, the inventory controlling account is the sum of the related subsidiary accounts.

State the Control Objectives of this Cycle.   Purchases of inventory are made only when needed by the firm and only from legitimate suppliers. Inventories are safeguarded when received and while in stock. Cash is safeguarded by disbursing cash only for valid accounts payable of the corporation. All expenditure-cycle transactions are authorized by management. All valid expenditure-cycle transactions are accurately recorded. All documents and reports generated in the expenditure cycle are safeguarded.

Define Purchase Requisition, Purchase Order, Vendor Invoice, Vendor Packing List, and Purchase Voucher.   The purchase requisition is a document that asks the purchasing department to obtain certain goods. The purchase order is a document sent by the entity to purchase goods from a vendor. The vendor invoice is the invoice sent by the vendor to the corporation. The vendor packing list accompanies the items purchased, and it displays the sale and the shipping terms. The purchase voucher, or voucher package, is the set of the purchase requisition, purchase order, receiving report, and vendor invoice.

Summarize the Credit Purchases Flowchart.   The warehouse prepares the purchase requisition. The purchasing department prepares the purchase order. Upon receipt of the purchase order, the vendor sends the goods to the firm, along with a packing list. Later it sends its invoice. The receiving department receives the goods from the vendor and inspects them. If acceptable, the receiving department takes the inventory and sends the goods to the warehouse. It also prepares a receiving report. When the warehouse receives the goods, it stocks them and updates the inventory subsidiary ledger. In the meantime, the accounts payable department receives a copy of the purchase requisition, purchase order, receiving report, and vendor invoice. If everything checks out, it sends the voucher package to cash disbursements. It also updates the accounts payable subsidiary ledger.

State What Files Are Necessary to Support the Accounting of Credit Purchases.   Five files are necessary. The vendor master file enumerates each vendor of the firm. The accounts payable master file shows what the corporation owes to each of its suppliers. The inventory master file shows the specific items in inventory. The open purchase order file contains those purchase orders for which the firm has not yet received the goods. The open vendor invoice file (also called the open voucher file) includes only those vendor invoices that have not yet been paid.

Identify the Debit Memo (the Purchase Returns Memo).   The debit memo indicates that the firm's account should be reduced because of a purchase return or a purchase allowance.

Explain the Cash Disbursements Flowchart.   The accounts payable department sends the voucher package to the cash disbursements department. Once it approves payment, it writes the check and sends it to the vendor. It also updates the cash disbursements journal.

Discuss the Files that Support the Accounting of Cash Payments.   In addition to the vendor master file and an accounts payable master file, the firm needs a cash disbursements file.

GLOSSARY

Accounts payable department—that branch of the controller's department that supervises the accounts payable subsidiary ledger.

Accounts payable master file—a file that shows what the corporation owes to each of its suppliers.

Blind copy—a copy of the purchase order without any of the price or quantity data.

Blind count—a count of the inventory received from a vendor by the receiving department without any information about the quantity of goods ordered or their prices.

Cash disbursements department—that branch of the treasurer's department which pays out cash to the suppliers.

Cash disbursements file—a file that records the cash disbursements of the firm.

Cash payments cycle—that portion of the expenditure cycle dealing with the payment of money to the vendors.

Controlling account—an account whose balance is the sum of the related subsidiary accounts.

Cost accounting—that branch of the controller's department that determines the cost of goods and services.

Debit memo—a document which indicates that the firm's account should be reduced because of a purchase return or purchase allowance.

Electronic data interchange (EDI)—a computer-to-computer exchange of business documents.

Expenditure cycle—the accounting cycle dealing with the purchase of goods and services and paying for them.

Gross method—the accounting method that records sales and purchases at the full amount, including any cash discount that is offered.

Inventory master file—a file showing the specific goods that comprise the inventory account.

Inventory subsidiary ledger—a subsidiary ledger that details the specific goods that comprise the inventory account.

Invoice—a document sent to a customer indicating the price for goods or services provided by the seller and the terms for settlement.

Just-in-time (JIT) system—a system in which inventory is not obtained until necessary.

Logistics department—the department that deals with the procurement and movement of equipment, facilities, and personnel.

Net method—the accounting method that records sales and purchases at the full amount less any cash discount that is offered.

Open purchase order file—a file that includes only those purchase orders for which the firm has not yet received the goods.

Open vendor invoice file—a file that includes only those vendor invoices that have not yet been paid.

Packing list—a document sent by the seller to the customer when the goods are shipped displaying the sale and the shipping terms.

Periodic method—the accounting method that counts inventory only at the end of accounting periods.

Perpetual method—the accounting method that keeps a record of inventory after every sale and purchase.

Purchase order—a document sent by the entity to purchase goods from the vendor.

Purchase requisition—a document that asks the purchasing department to obtain certain goods.

Purchase returns and allowances file—a file listing the firm's purchase returns and allowances during some accounting period.

Purchase voucher package—the set of four documents relating to the same set of purchases, viz., the purchase requisition, purchase order, receiving report, and vendor invoice.

Purchases cycle—that portion of the expenditure cycle dealing with the purchase of goods and services.

Purchasing agent—the person in the purchasing department who approves a purchase by signing the purchase order.

Purchasing department—that branch of the logistics department that procures supplies and inventory.

Receiving department—that branch of the logistics department that receives goods that come to the firm.

Receiving report—a document generated by the receiving department to show what goods they have received and what condition they are in.

Shipping department—that branch of the logistics department that ships goods from the firm to others.

Subsidiary account—one of the components of the subsidiary ledger for some controlling account.

Subsidiary ledger—a listing of the components of some account.

Subsidiary schedule—a report that enumerates the details of some account.

Vendor master file—a file that enumerates each vendor of the firm.

Warehouse—that branch of the logistics department that holds the goods in storage and releases them upon proper authorization.

REVIEW QUESTIONS

1. What is the expenditure cycle, and how might it be further subdivided?

2. What are the functions of the expenditure cycle?

3. What are the responsibilities of the controller's department in the expenditure cycle?

4. What are the responsibilities of the logistics department in the expenditure cycle?

5. What is the role of the treasurer's department in the expenditure cycle?

6. What are the basic steps in the expenditure cycle?

7. Explain the difference between the gross and net methods for recording inventory.

8. Summarize the basic journal entries in the expenditure cycle.

9. What are the differences between the periodic and perpetual inventory systems?

10. What is the inventory subsidiary ledger, and how does it operate?

11. What are the control objectives in the expenditure cycle?

12. What does EDI refer to?

13. What is JIT, and why is it important?

14. Define purchase requisition and purchase order.

15. The firm receives the vendor invoice and the packing list from the vendor. What are these documents?

16. What is the receiving report?

17. What is a blind copy of the purchase order? Who receives the blind copy and why?

18. Summarize the credit purchases flowchart.

19. What are the vendor master file, accounts payable master file, and inventory master file?

20. Define open purchase order file and open vendor invoice file.

21. What is a debit memo?

22. Define the purchase voucher.

23. Summarize the cash disbursements flowchart.

24. What is a cash disbursements file?

DISCUSSION QUESTIONS

1. We covered the sales journal in Chapter 4 and illustrated it in Exhibit 4.3 of that chapter. At that time we implicitly assumed a periodic inventory system.

Reconfigure the sales journal shown in Exhibit 4.3 if the company employs a perpetual inventory system with an inventory subsidiary ledger. Assume the products cost 40% of the selling price. Also assume that 150 is the account number for inventory and 520 is the account number for cost of goods sold. Assume that Karpov and Kamsky bought four and one chess clocks (product number CL-210), respectively; Kasparov purchased a chess set (product number CS-875), and Short bought a chess computer (product number (CM-450). You do not have to show the accounts receivable subsidiary ledger or the inventory subsidiary ledger.

2. We discussed the purchases journal in Chapter 4 and provided an example in Exhibit 4.4 of that chapter. At that time, we implicitly assumed a periodic inventory system.

Reconfigure the purchases journal shown in Exhibit 4.4 if the business enterprise applies a perpetual inventory system with an inventory subsidiary ledger and if it accounts for purchases with the net method. Assume that all vendors offer us terms of 2/10, n/30. Inventory has 150 as the account number, and accounts payable has 120 as its account number. Our firm buys chess clocks (product number CL-220) from Morphy; a chess computer from Steinitz (product number CM-299); chess sets (product number CS-300) from Lasker; and chess books from Alekhine ($120 of BK-140, $100 of BK-345, and $180 of BK870). You do not have to show the inventory subsidiary ledger or the accounts payable subsidiary ledger.

3. We described the cash disbursements or cash payments journal in Chapter 4 and gave an example in Exhibit 4.6 of that chapter. At that time we implicitly employed the gross method for recording purchases.

(a) Reconfigure the cash disbursements journal shown in Exhibit 4.6 if the corporation uses the net method for recording purchases. (You should recognize that application of a perpetual inventory system with an inventory subsidiary ledger does not impact the cash disbursements journal as long as there are no cash purchases.) Assume that all vendors, except the auto dealer, offer us terms of 2/10, n/30. Inventory has 150 as the account number, and purchase discounts lost 585 as its account number. Ignore the December 1 transaction in the newly designed cash disbursements journal. You do not have to show the accounts payable subsidiary ledger.

(b) There are two ways to modify the journals to handle cash purchases. What are they?

4. Quality is increasingly recognized as one of the crucial attributes to help firms add value and increase profits. With respect to purchases of inventory, the entity could track at least two aspects of quality: time to deliver and quality of the goods delivered.

(a) How can the accountant measure the time of delivery? Who would capture the data?

(b) Let's make the simplifying assumption that goods delivered by the vendor are either acceptable or not acceptable. In this case, how can the accountant measure the quality of the vendor's performance?

EXERCISES

1. Pumpkin Dot Com has the following transactions in June. All credit purchases are made with terms of 2/10, n/30.

June 2. Buys 10,000 boxes of chocolate from Vinnie's Chocolate at $1 per box.
June 5. Buys 1,000 sacks of flour from Flo's Flour Shop. The cost is $5 per sack.
June 10. Pays the bill from Vinnie's Chocolate.
June 11. Buys 8,000 cartons of powdered milk at $0.50 per carton.
June 12. The powdered milk is bad and returned to the supplier.
June 20. Pays the bill from Flo's Flour Shop.

Required: Journalize the transactions if Pumpkin Dot Com employs (a) the gross method and (b) the net method. Use the periodic method for both (a) and (b).

2. Fischer's Flicks retails videos. Beginning inventory consists of 100 units at a cost of $1.20 each. During December, the corporation buys 1,000 videos, each at a cost of $1.20 each. The firm sells for cash 800 of these videos, at a selling price of $4 each. Prepare the journal entries for Fischer's Flicks if it uses (a) the periodic method and (b) the perpetual method. Use the gross method for both (a) and (b). For part (a), assume that Fischer's recognizes the cost of goods sold during the adjusting entry process. For part (c), indicate at what date cost of goods sold is journalized under periodic and perpetual methods.

3. Yeager's Gators sells accounting books. Following is the inventory subsidiary ledger as of October 14, 2001.

Yeager's Gators
Inventory Subsidiary Ledger
October 14, 2001

Book	Unit Cost	Number of Copies	Cost
Accounting for Dummies	$ 5	100	$ 500
Accounting for Idiots	4	200	800
Accounting for Morons	3	300	900
Accounting Jokes	10	400	4,000

During the week Yeager's Gators sells 20 copies of *Accounting for Dummies*, 40 copies of *Accounting for Morons*, and 100 copies of *Accounting Jokes*. It buys 50 more copies of *Accounting Jokes* at $10 per copy, thinking it a potential big seller. The firm also buys 100 copies of a new and wonderful textbook, *Introduction to Accounting Systems and Controls* at $20 per copy.

Required:

(a) What is the amount in inventory—control at October 14, 2001?

(b) Prepare a subsidiary schedule at October 21, 2001.

(c) What is the amount in inventory—control at October 21, 2001?

4. Alexei Kissel notices that Kissel Equipment is low in Gunk Oil and in Hooey Lubricant. On February 13, 2002, she prepares a purchase requisition and suggests Sneffel's Supplies as the vendor. The purchase requisition number is PRQ-2131.

Alexei requests 200 quarts of Gunk Oil at $0.50 per quart and 100 cartons of Hooey Lubricant at $0.80 per carton. For these two products Sneffel's Supplies has product numbers of GO-100 and HL-666.

The address of the firm is 111 Boxline Road, Paddington, Indiana 46666.

Pat Begala, Alexei's supervisor, approves the request on February 14.

Required: Prepare the purchase requisition.

5. Patty Sirmon is the purchasing agent for Kissel Equipment. Upon receipt of the purchase requisition on February 15, 2002 discussed in the previous exercise, Patty Sirmon orders the goods from Sneffel's Supplies (vendor number 239), located at 220 Beckley Avenue, Georgetown IL 60666. The purchase order number is PO-42578.

The suggested shipping date is February 22, 2002 or before, and the shipping terms are FOB shipping, using Yippie Trucks.

The company wants the goods sent to the warehouse at 200 Circleville Road, Lonely Valley, Indiana 47777.

Required: Prepare the purchase order.

6. Below is a purchases journal for Susan Whitson Company (with the folio column omitted). The business enterprise uses the perpetual method at the gross amount. Prepare the journal voucher for the accounts payable department to send to the general ledger department. Bill Covey approves the voucher, number PV-0929, on January 31, 2002.

Date	Purchase Order No.	Vendor	Amount
1-07-2002	3789	Popeye's	$5,100
1-15-2002	3790	Columbo	975
1-24-2002	3791	Chan's	2,050
1-30-2002	3792	Ironside	1,400
		TOTAL	$9,525

7. On the next page is the cash disbursements journal of Yolinda, Inc. on November 29, 2002 (date and folio columns omitted). Prepare the journal voucher for the cash disbursements journal to send to the general ledger department. Andrea Allison approves the voucher, CD-1191, on the same date. Assume that Yolinda, Inc. accounts for inventory with the periodic method at the gross amount.

Cash (CR)	Purchase Discounts (DR)	Accounts Payable		Purchases (DR)	Other		
		Vendor	(DR)		Account	(DR)	(CR)
$ 1,000				$1,000			
$ 1,960	$ 40	Smitt	$ 2,000				
$ 5,000					LTI[a]		$5,000
$ 4,000		Black	$ 4,000				
$ 5,390	$110	Berol	$ 5,500				
$17,350	$150		$11,500	$1,000			*
(100)	(720)		(310)	(700)			

[a]LTI denotes long-term investments (account number 280).

8. When reviewing the flowcharts for the expenditure cycle, you should notice that journal vouchers are prepared from the purchases journal and the cash disbursements journal, and this process, in effect, posts the transactions to the general ledger. Journal vouchers, however, are not prepared from the accounts payable subsidiary ledger or from the inventory subsidiary ledger. Why not?

9. In a computerized AIS, what is the counterpart to the purchases journal, the cash disbursements journal, the accounts payable subsidiary ledger, and the inventory subsidiary ledger?

10. What are the keys to the accounts payable master file, cash disbursements file, inventory master file, open purchase order file, open vendor invoice file, purchase returns and allowances file, and vendor master file?

11. Using the examples in Exhibit 6.8 in Chapter 6, develop a record layout for (a) the accounts payable master file, (b) the open purchase order file, and (c) the open vendor invoice file.

PROBLEMS

1. (a) Draw an input-output model of the purchases cycle and the cash disbursements cycle.

(b) Draw an actors model of the expenditure cycle.

2. (a) List all of the documents in the expenditure cycle. For each document, indicate who prepares it and who receives a copy.

(b) List all of the accounting journals and ledgers in the expenditure cycle. For each journal and ledger, state who has responsibility for it.

3. Alejandro Diaz Productions has hired you to assist them in developing their AIS. Specifically, your job is to design:

(a) a blind copy of the purchase order,   **(c)** a receiving report.

(b) a debit memorandum, and

4. We can classify management assertions into five categories: existence or occurrence, completeness, valuation or allowance, rights and obligations, and presentation and disclosure. State management's assertions with respect to purchases, cash disbursements, accounts payable, and inventory. Assume all transactions are in U.S. dollars.

5. The control objectives for the revenue cycle are: (1) purchases of inventory are made only when needed by the firm and only from legitimate suppliers; (2) inventories are safeguarded when received and while in stock; (3) cash is safeguarded by disbursing cash only for valid accounts payable of the corporation; (4) all expenditure-cycle transactions are authorized by management; (5) all valid expenditure-cycle transactions are accurately recorded; and (6) all documents and reports generated in the expenditure cycle are safeguarded. For the following list of activities, indicate by number the control objectives that the activity is fulfilling.

Activity within the expenditure cycle	Control #
1. Inventory is not ordered unless a purchase requisition is completed.	
2. The warehouse takes responsibility for the inventory subsidiary ledger.	
3. The purchasing department chooses the vendor from whom to purchase the goods.	
4. Purchasing prepares the purchase order for each purchase.	
5. The purchasing department maintains the open purchase order file.	
6. The receiving department receives a blind copy of the purchase order.	
7. The receiving department counts and inspects the goods received from the vendor.	
8. The receiving department prepares a receiving report.	
9. Accounts payable receives a copy of the purchase requisition, purchase order, receiving report, and vendor invoice.	
10. Accounts payable has responsibility for the purchases journal.	
11. Accounts payable has responsibility for the accounts payable subsidiary ledger.	
12. General ledger receives and files journal vouchers.	
13. Cash disbursements receives a copy of the purchase requisition, purchase order, receiving report, and vendor invoice.	
14. The cash disbursements department has responsibility for the cash disbursements journal.	
15. Cash disbursements writes a check to the vendor and mails it with the remittance advice.	
16. Accounts payable maintains the open voucher file.	

6. Documents fulfill the control objectives of the business enterprise. Following is a list of the documents in the expenditure cycle. Each document serves to meet one of the following control objectives: (1) safeguard inventories; (2) safeguard cash; (3) all expenditure-cycle transactions are authorized by management; and (4) all valid expenditure-cycle transactions are accurately recorded. For the following list of documents, indicate by number the control objectives that the activity is fulfilling.

Documents within the Revenue Cycle	Control #
1. Check	
2. Journal voucher	
3. Purchase order	
4. Purchase requisition	
5. Receiving report	
6. Vendor invoice	
7. Vendor packing list	

7. (a) How would the following three errors likely be discovered?

(i) The accounts payable clerk enters the wrong amount for purchases.

(ii) The cash disbursements clerk debits Frodo for the payment when the corporation actually pays Bilbo for the inventory.

(iii) A clerk placed a check into the wrong envelope and thus the check was sent to the wrong vendor.

(b) How would the AIS prevent the following irregularities from occurring?

(i) The receipt of unordered goods.   **(iv)** A vendor overcharges for the goods provided.

(ii) A purchasing agent orders a stereo for himself.   **(iv)** A vendor overcharges for the goods provided.

(iii) A warehouse clerk orders a stereo for herself.

8. Greg Dill operates a Gadget Company. September's inventory subsidiary schedule reveals the following items in inventory and their amounts:

Gizmo (GZ-10)	$ 10,000
Ho-boy (HB-89)	23,000
Atta-girl (AG-07)	41,000
Wham-bam (WB-81)	38,000
	$112,000

The following transactions occur in October:

October 5 Gadget Company buys $7,000 of Ho-boys.
October 10 It gets an allowance of $1,000 on the Ho-boys bought on October 5.
October 15 It buys $5,000 of Atta-girls.
October 20 It sells $8,000 (cost) of Gizmos at a selling price of $14,000.
October 25 It sells $13,000 (cost) of Atta-girls for sales of $30,000.

Required:

(a) Prepare the inventory general ledger account and the inventory subsidiary ledger as of the beginning of October. Verify that the accounts are in balance.

(b) Make journal entries for the above transactions in the general journal on page 774.

(c) Post the journal entries to the inventory general ledger account and to the inventory subsidiary ledger. You may ignore the remaining accounts. Verify that the accounts in the subsidiary ledger balance the controlling account.

(d) Prepare an inventory subsidiary ledger schedule for October.

9. One of the vendors of Charles H. Smith Publishing, Inc. is McKeown Power and Light Company, and they have agreed to have cash payments remitted through EFT. McKeown Company sends a copy of the invoice to its bank, which obtains payments from Smith's bank. Smith's bank makes the disbursement and informs Smith Publishing when it sends the bank statement to the firm. McKeown Company also sends two copies of the invoice to Smith Publishing.

The operating expense department of Smith Publishing receives the two invoices from McKeown Company. After approving the invoice, the operating expense department sends one copy to cash disbursements and files the other copy. The internal audit department receives the bank statement, determines the EFT cash payment to McKeown Company, and notifies the cash disbursements department via an EFT journal voucher. After receiving and comparing the invoice and the EFT journal voucher, the cash disbursements department records the transaction and files the documents.

Required:

(a) Design the EFT voucher.

(b) Prepare the flowchart for these expenditures of Smith Publishing.

10. You are a member of an accounting firm that is doing some consulting work for Harding and Tubbs, Inc., and you are assigned the task of designing procedures for the corporation's purchase returns. Assume that the goods are presently in the warehouse. When notified, the purchasing department prepares five copies of the debit memo, one of which is a blind copy. Once informed by the purchasing department about the return, the warehouse sends the goods to the shipping department with the blind copy of the debit memo. Shipping counts the number of goods and returns this copy to accounts payable. It also ships the goods back to the vendor.

Required: Prepare the flowchart for the purchase returns.

11. The Chris Freisheim Company utilizes a purchase order file and a vendor invoice file. The files are presented on the next page.

The purchase order file states the purchases made in May plus earlier purchases in which the goods are not received until May. Assume that each purchase order is for only one product. The receiving report column is left blank until the goods are accepted by the receiving department, at which time a clerk in the receiving department writes down the number of the receiving report. Thus, a blank in the receiving report number column indicates that the goods have been ordered but not yet received by the company.

The vendor invoice file enumerates the vendor invoices unpaid as of May 1 plus all vendor invoices received during May. Each vendor invoice corresponds to one purchase order. The check number column and the date of cash payment column are left blank until the entity pays the bill. At that time, a clerk in the cash disbursements department enters the check number as well as the date of payment. A blank in these columns implies that the bill is not yet paid.

Required:

(a) Prepare the open purchase order file.
(b) Construct the closed purchase order file.
(c) Are there any purchase orders for which there is no vendor invoice?
(d) Assuming that purchases are recognized only when the firm receives a legitimate invoice from the vendor, how much are purchases in May?
(e) Prepare the open vendor invoice file.
(f) Build the closed vendor invoice file.
(g) How much cash does the firm pay its vendors in May?
(h) Using the formula from Chapter 5, show the relationship between monthly purchases and monthly cash flow disbursements to suppliers. (*Hint:* Remember that cost of goods sold equals beginning inventory + purchases − ending inventory.)

Purchase Order Number	Date	Vendor Number	Product Number	Quantity Ordered	Cost per Unit	Receiving Report Number
PO-205	4-10	105	JK-100	100	200	RR-547
PO-217	4-25	121	ZN-322	500	10	RR-545
PO-219	4-30	106	BL-462	100	100	RR-550
PO-220	5-1	105	HI-111	50	10	RR-553
PO-221	5-5	119	SW-098	100	25	RR-551
PO-222	5-6	106	BL-513	50	1	RR-552
PO-223	5-10	108	JK-350	300	2	RR-555
PO-224	5-14	101	FL-900	200	3	RR-554
PO-225	5-15	121	ZN-322	500	10	
PO-226	5-15	118	IJ-658	1,000	5	RR-556
PO-227	5-20	105	JK-100	200	200	RR-557
PO-228	5-25	107	NL-110	500	3	
PO-229	5-30	111	GA-234	100	9	

Purchase Order Number	Vendor Number	Vendor Invoice Number	Invoice Date	Amount Billed	Check Number	Date of Cash Payment
PO-205	105	IN-098	5-11	20,000	3917	5-20
PO-213	113	RV-2345	5-2	15,000	3910	5-12
PO-217	121	0199082	5-13	5,000	3938	5-22
PO-219	106	INV-710	5-10	10,000	3914	5-19
PO-220	105	IN-136	5-10	500	3918	5-20
PO-221	119	987A7	5-19	2,500	3961	5-27
PO-222	106	345005	5-10	50	3919	5-20
PO-223	108	Y110970	5-20	600	3969	5-30
PO-226	118	S-197	5-28	5,000		

CHAPTER 11

PAYROLL, FACILITIES, INVESTMENTS, FINANCING, AND PRODUCTION CYCLES

So far we have described the general ledger, sales, cash receipts, purchases, and cash disbursements cycles. We wrap up our examination of accounting cycles in this chapter by discussing and explaining the remaining five cycles: payroll, facilities, investments, financing, and production.

Covering five cycles in one chapter might at first seem an overwhelming task, but it really isn't. Because we have covered the basics of accounting cycles in a meticulous manner in previous chapters, we can skim over related topics. In addition, except for the production cycle, these cycles are generally limited and so can be processed simply. The only cycle that could be extensive is the production cycle, but we restrict the coverage to a traditional job-order cost system and leave process costing and more modern production techniques to other textbooks.

The payroll cycle concentrates on wages and salaries; the facilities cycle considers the purchase and sale of property, plant, and equipment; the investments cycle deals with the purchase and sale of investments; and the financing cycle handles the issuance and reacquisition of the company's own securities. Finally, the production cycle focuses on the production of some good; in other words, the firm obtains raw materials and transforms them into its own product that it then sells to its customers.

After reading and studying this chapter, you should be able to:

- Define and explain the payroll cycle;
- Prepare journal entries in the payroll cycle and use the payroll subsidiary ledger;
- Discuss the payroll cycle flowchart;
- Describe the facilities cycle, including the facilities subsidiary ledger;
- Portray the investments cycle;
- Explain the financing cycle;
- Perform job-order costing, including the work-in-process subsidiary ledger; and
- Describe the production cycle process.

PAYROLL CYCLE

Since most employees like getting paid, the firm must provide a mechanism to determine how much they earn, how much the employees owe in taxes and other deductions, and how much is their net pay. The payroll cycle covers these matters. Specifically, the *payroll cycle* is the accounting cycle dealing with the payment of wages and salaries to employees of the firm.

Functions of the Cycle

Broadly speaking, managers need to address the following human resource issues:

(a) How many employees do we need to carry out the tasks of the firm but not have idle workers?

(b) What skills should the employees possess?

(c) How do we recruit and retain the best employees?

(d) How do we recruit and retain minorities?

(e) How much do we pay the workers?

(f) How do we administer the payroll?

The payroll cycle specifically addresses only the last item.

Business Departments

Firms often have a *human resources department*, a department of the firm that deals with such issues as hiring, retaining, and firing employees as well as training them and paying them wages and salaries and various benefits. This department concerns itself with issues (a)–(e) listed above.

To administer the payroll function, at least six departments become involved. The *payroll department*, as the name implies, processes the payment of wages and salaries to the employees. Some workers are paid by the month regardless of how many hours they work; they receive a salary from the company. Other workers are paid by the hour, so their wages are determined by some wage rate times the number of hours worked, for example, during a two-week period. This arrangement necessitates that somebody observe how many hours the employees work, and this group is referred to as *timekeeping*.

Accounts payable assesses whether the company should pay a bill and then prepares the check to pay the bill. (If the corporation is large enough, it might have a section of accounts payable dedicated only to wages and salaries payable.) Cash disbursements signs the checks and distributes them to the employees. Internal audit receives the validated deposit slips, and the general ledger department updates the general ledger for wages and salaries expenses and the associated liabilities and cash flows.

Basic Steps and Basic Journal Entries

Having already been hired, the employees work for a period of time and the corporation pays the employees periodically. An *employee master file* contains the names of all employees of the firm, their social security numbers, addresses and phone numbers, positions, wage rates, and tax data such as how many exemptions they are claiming. Other data could be included as well, such as each individual's skills, schooling, previous positions, references, and birth date. A simple example of an employee master file is shown in Exhibit 11.1.

Further, let's assume that the charge for their work is to wages and/or salaries expense. (Later, when we discuss the production cycle, this assumption will be dropped.) The whole amount that the worker earns is the *gross pay*. But the person must pay federal income taxes and social security taxes (also known as FICA taxes, where FICA stands for Federal Insurance Corporation of America). There can be many other deductions as well, including state and local income taxes, parking fees, and contributions to a retirement fund or a health plan. For simplicity, we will limit the deductions to federal income taxes and social security taxes only. The accounting and AIS concerns are virtually the same for these other deductions. The *net pay* is what the employee actually receives, and it is equal to the gross pay less the deductions paid by the employee.

EXHIBIT 11.1

EMPLOYEE MASTER FILE

Employee	Social Security Number	Address	Phone	Position	Wage Rate	Number of Exemptions
Paul Adams	111-22-3333	100 Douglas Dr. State College PA	843-555-1234	Clerk	$12/hr.	4
George Corman	123-45-6789	432 Stanford Ave. State College PA	843-555-7762	Clerk	$15/hr.	4
Annie Harvey	000-40-0000	43 Mosch Dr. Lemont PA	843-555-0900	Manager	$5,000/mo.	3
Cheryl Putukian	909-09-0909	Apt. 42B Glen Acres Bellefonte PA	843-555-4575	Clerk	$10/hr.	1

Many companies set up a separate checking account to take care of the payments to the employees. This fund, called a *payroll fund*, is an imprest fund and has some features similar to the petty cash fund discussed in Chapter 7. (You may wish to review that material, including the accounting for the petty cash fund and internal controls for such a fund.)

To set up the payroll fund, make the following entry:

Payroll cash	$X	
Cash		$X

Once the payroll department figures out the gross pay and the deductions, the total net pay is deposited into the payroll fund. The entry has the same accounts as before (though a simpler entry is shown later).

The journal entry for the wages and salaries is:

Wages and salaries expense	$X	
Employee federal income taxes payable		$X
FICA taxes payable		$X
Wages payable		$X

Specifically, the accountant charges the expense for the gross pay and credits the wages payable for the net pay. Notice that he or she credits the deductions to the appropriate current liability. The reason for this is that the firm acts as a conduit by collecting the money from the employee and then later paying the appropriate party the amount owed by the employee. In this case, the company pays the federal government for the employees' income taxes (called withholdings) and their social security taxes. Keep in mind that the employee is actually the one paying these taxes.

It should be noted that the account federal income taxes payable differs from the account employee federal income taxes payable. The former indicates the amount the firm owes for its own federal income taxes, whereas the latter shows the amount the firm owes for the employees' federal income taxes, having deducted the amounts from the employees' paychecks.

When the checks are written and distributed to the workers, the entry is:

Wages payable	$X	
Payroll cash		$X

Today, many firms electronically send the cash to the employees' bank accounts. This does not affect the journal entry, although it raises some control issues similar to the ETF control issues discussed in Chapters 9 and 10.

The employer has some additional expenses to pay; for example, employers have to pay federal unemployment taxes (FUT) and must match the social security taxes paid by the employees. Other expenses are possible, such as state unemployment taxes, pensions, health care, and day care centers, but we will restrict the discussion to the first two items. The journal entry for this transaction is:

Payroll expenses	$X	
Federal unemployment taxes		$X
FICA taxes payable		$X

Later, when the corporation pays the employee's deductions and the employer taxes, it debits the liability and credits cash. Notice that this cash is from the general cash fund, not a special fund.

Control Objectives

We leave these as an exercise for the reader. Keep in mind the fact that the payroll fund is an imprest fund and that the firm should prepare bank reconciliations for the fund.

Documents

The payroll cycle has at least five documents: the timecard, payroll summary, payroll voucher, checks, and deposit slips. The last two have been defined in earlier chapters. The *timecard* is a document that shows when an employee has worked for the firm. The supervisor or someone in the payroll department determines the total number of hours worked during a period of time.

The *payroll summary* is a register that records the gross pay, deductions, and net pay to each employee. In many ways it acts like a special journal. An illustration is given in Exhibit 11.2. From the timecards, the payroll clerk writes down the total number of regular hours (those up to 40 hours in one week) and any overtime hours. From the employee master file, the clerk finds the wage rate and multiplies that by the number of regular hours to get the regular pay. The clerk makes a similar calculation to obtain the overtime pay, except that overtime includes a 50% premium ("time and a half"). Total gross pay is the sum of the regular and overtime pay. The deductions and the net pay are then computed (see a text on taxes to determine how they are calculated). Notice that salaried employees do not show the number of hours but merely report the salary for the time period. Sometimes, as shown in Exhibit 11.2, the check number is included to provide an audit trail. In addition, the reference column contains an asterisk (or some other mark) to indicate that the data has been transferred to the *payroll subsidiary ledger*—a subsidiary ledger that provides details of the wages and salaries earned by each employee.

Exhibit 11.3 shows a typical payroll subsidiary ledger. Records within the subsidiary ledger are the employees themselves. The gross pay and deductions for each pay period are shown in this ledger. In addition, the year-to-date (YTD) totals are figured for the gross pay and the deductions. No cross-reference column is given because the dates implicitly provide the cross-reference to the payroll summary.

The *payroll voucher* is a special type of journal voucher used to record wages and salaries. For the example in Exhibit 11.2, the journal entry placed on the payroll voucher is a debit to wages and salaries expense $7,985, a credit to FICA taxes payable $799, a

EXHIBIT 11.2

PAYROLL SUMMARY

Date: February 28

Employee	Ref	Regular Hours	Regular Pay	Overtime Hours	Overtime Pay	Total Gross Pay	FICA Taxes Payable	Fed. Inc. Taxes Payable	Net Pay	Check Number
Paul Adams	*	80	960			960	96	96	768	2345
George Corman	*	75	1,075			1,075	108	70	897	2346
Annie Harvey	*	Salary				5,000	500	800	3,700	2347
Cheryl Putukian	*	80	800	10	150	950	95	95	760	2348
TOTALS						7,985	799	1,061	6,125	

EXHIBIT 11.3

PAYROLL SUBSIDIARY LEDGER

PAUL ADAMS
(SSN:111-22-3333)

Date	Gross Pay	FICA Payable	Federal Inc. Taxes Payable	Gross Pay YTD	FICA YTD	Federal Inc. Taxes YTD
1-15	960	96	96	960	96	96
1-31	1,200	120	120	2,160	216	216
2-14	960	96	96	3,120	312	312
2-28	960	96	96	4,080	408	408

GEORGE CORMAN
(SSN:123-45-6789)

Date	Gross Pay	FICA Payable	Federal Inc. Taxes Payable	Gross Pay YTD	FICA YTD	Federal Inc. Taxes YTD
1-15	0	0	0	0	0	0
1-31	0	0	0	0	0	0
2-14	0	0	0	0	0	0
2-28	1,075	108	70	1,075	108	70

ANNIE HARVEY
(SSN:000-40-0000)

Date	Gross Pay	FICA Payable	Federal Inc. Taxes Payable	Gross Pay YTD	FICA YTD	Federal Inc. Taxes YTD
1-15	0	0	0	0	0	0
1-31	5,000	500	800	5,000	500	800
2-14	0	0	0	5,000	500	800
2-28	5,000	500	800	10,000	1,000	1,600

CHERYL PUTUKIAN
(SSN:909-09-0909)

Date	Gross Pay	FICA Payable	Federal Inc. Taxes Payable	Gross Pay YTD	FICA YTD	Federal Inc. Taxes YTD
1-15	800	80	80	800	80	80
1-31	600	60	60	1,400	140	140
2-14	800	80	80	2,200	220	220
2-28	950	95	95	3,150	315	315

credit to employee federal income taxes payable $1,061, and a credit to cash $6,125. One could make the entries as given before, but the credit to cash simplifies the bookkeeping. Notice that this one entry is equivalent to making the series of entries:

Payroll cash	$6,125	
Cash		$6,125
Wages and salaries expense	$7,985	
FICA taxes payable		$ 799
Employee fed. income taxes payable		$1,061
Wages payable		$6,125
Wages payable	$6,125	
Payroll cash		$6,125

Although the three entries depict what is really going on, it is more efficient—and equivalent—just to make the one entry.

Flowchart

The payroll flowchart is depicted in Exhibit 11.4. This flowchart covers only the payment to the employees. Payments to the federal government for income taxes and social security taxes and unemployment taxes are left as a problem.

Timekeeping starts the cycle by measuring the hours worked by the employees. The payroll department uses the data to prepare the payroll summary, sending one copy to accounts payable. It also posts the data to the payroll subsidiary ledger. It files one copy of the payroll summary and the timecards.

With the data in the payroll summary, the accounts payable department prepares the checks and payroll voucher. The unsigned checks go to cash disbursements for their approval and signature. One copy of the payroll voucher accompanies the checks to cash disbursements, another goes to general ledger, and a third copy is kept within accounts payable.

Cash disbursements signs the checks and distributes them to the workers. It also writes a check for the total net pay and deposits this check into the payroll fund.

The bank accepts this check, validates the deposit slip, and sends one copy to internal audit.

The general ledger department uses the data on the payroll voucher to update the general ledger.

FACILITIES CYCLE

So far we have discussed the general ledger cycle (Chapter 8), the revenue cycle (Chapter 9), the expenditure cycle (Chapter 10), and the payroll cycle. The next three cycles—the facilities, investments, and financing cycles—differ from these cycles inasmuch as they tend to be episodic. In other words, the previous cycles dealt with transactions that are ongoing and often occur many times every business day. The next three cycles we portray deal with transactions that occur only occasionally (at least for most businesses). These cycles tend to be simpler because many corporations establish a committee or task force to conduct these operations for the company.

The *facilities cycle* is the accounting cycle dealing with the acquisition of property, plant, and equipment. The function of this cycle is quite simple: to be sure that the corporation has the land, buildings, equipment, and other long-term assets needed to conduct the business in an effective manner. Often a facilities committee is set up to handle

EXHIBIT **11.4**

PAYROLL CYCLE FLOWCHART

Timekeeping	Payroll

(continued)

these transactions. It buys property, plant, and equipment when needed by the firm, and it sells them either when it is profitable to do so or when the asset is no longer functioning efficiently.

To ensure that the committee acts in accordance with senior management's directives, businesses establish some control mechanisms. Depending on the size of the firm and of the transaction, higher level managers, perhaps even the president, the chief operating officer, or the chief executive officer, reviews the transaction. At some organizations the board of directors examines these transactions. Internal auditors may also join the investigation. In any case, the review consists of an evaluation of the reasons for the transaction, the vendor, the asset and its specifications, the invoice, and a check that the asset is physically on the premises.

Periodically, the facilities committee meets to assess the capital needs of the firm. The process of gathering data about possible capital projects and deciding which to un-

EXHIBIT *11.4*

PAYROLL CYCLE FLOWCHART *(continued)*

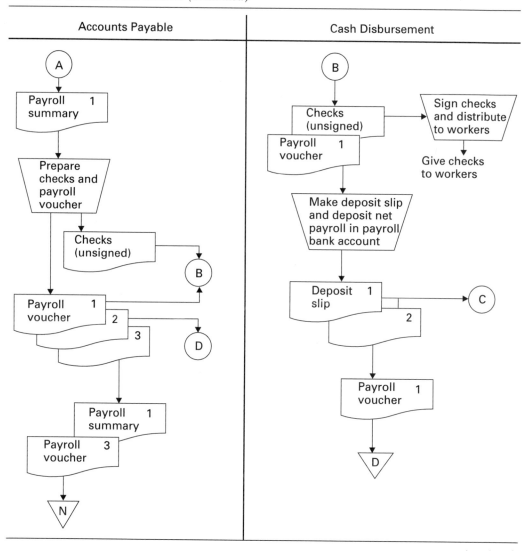

(continued)

dertake is called *capital budgeting* and is a major topic in management accounting. If the members of the committee decide that a purchase should be made, they then investigate vendors and the various deals that can be made. After this fact-finding mission is completed, they decide from whom to purchase the asset. They also may obtain insurance on the asset.

When the fiscal period ends, the committee reviews the depreciation charges on all of the company's depreciable assets. It then prepares a journal voucher and sends it to the general ledger department so that the depreciation charges can be included when making adjusting entries.

We have covered the accounting for the purchase, depreciation, and disposition of these assets. If you need a review, see the material in Chapters 3 and 4. The only new item to consider is the subsidiary ledgers for this cycle.

EXHIBIT *11.4*

PAYROLL CYCLE FLOWCHART (continued)

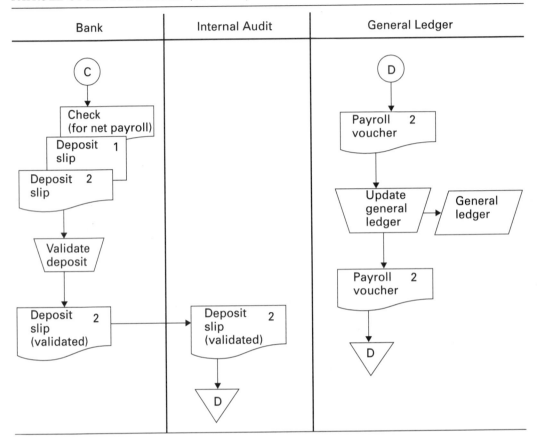

An example of an equipment subsidiary ledger is shown in Exhibit 11.5. Each piece of equipment is named, and its location is stated. In a large firm with many pieces of equipment, each piece is often tagged and given a number. This number is also denoted in the subsidiary ledger. Estimates of the asset's life and salvage value are noted in the subsidiary ledger. The date column tells the date of the transaction. The next three columns show what is in the asset's account, usually the original cost. The next three columns indicate the depreciation on the asset and its balance in accumulated depreciation. The book value is also computed.

A building subsidiary ledger looks the same as the equipment subsidiary ledger. A property subsidiary ledger also looks similar, but it does not contain the accumulated depreciation columns since accountants don't depreciate land.

Documents, at a minimum, include a capital asset proposal. (In practice, it goes by many names.) A *capital asset proposal* suggests the purchase of some property, plant, or equipment and has lines for appropriate managers or directors to approve the transaction. If the item is some equipment, then the process becomes similar to the purchase of inventory. Additional documents include purchase orders, bills of lading, receiving reports, and vendor invoices. Buildings and land also require various legal papers, such as the *title*, which indicates ownership of the described property.

EXHIBIT 11.5

EQUIPMENT SUBSIDIARY LEDGER

Item: Computer
Location: Office
Life: 4 years
Salvage value: $500

| Date | Asset | | | Accumulated Depreciation | | | Book |
	Debit	Credit	Balance	Debit	Credit	Balance	Value
01-02-00	6,300		6,300				6,300
12-31-00					1,450	1,450	4,850
12-31-01					1,450	2,900	3,400
12-31-02					1,450	4,350	1,950

Item: Office furniture
Location: Office
Life: 10 years
Salvage value: $2,000

| Date | Asset | | | Accumulated Depreciation | | | Book |
	Debit	Credit	Balance	Debit	Credit	Balance	Value
01-02-01	23,000		23,000				23,000
12-31-01					2,100	2,100	20,900
12-31-02					2,100	4,200	18,800

Item: Safe
Location: Office
Life: 5 years
Salvage value: $0

| Date | Asset | | | Accumulated Depreciation | | | Book |
	Debit	Credit	Balance	Debit	Credit	Balance	Value
07-01-00	10,000		10,000				10,000
12-31-00					1,000	1,000	9,000
12-31-01					2,000	3,000	7,000
12-31-02					2,000	5,000	5,000

INVESTMENTS AND FINANCING CYCLES

These two cycles are closely related. The *investments cycle* is the accounting cycle dealing with buying stocks and bonds of other organizations, whereas the *financing cycle* is the accounting cycle dealing with obtaining money by borrowing funds or issuing stock.

Often the department overseeing these activities is housed within the treasury department. This makes sense, for the treasury department manages the cash of the enterprise. When the firm has excess cash, it makes temporary investments, which it cashes in when the firm needs the cash. When the firm needs cash, especially on a long-term basis, it considers whether to issue securities to obtain that cash or whether to borrow money from a bank or other lending institution. Its function indeed is to address the financial capital needs of the business. The investments cycle does this by considering profitable uses of excess or idle cash, whereas the financing cycle considers how to raise money for expansion or other corporate needs.

To conduct such transactions, corporations set up an investing committee and a financing committee, similar to the facilities committee. They have the power to engage in both investing and financing activities. Control is provided by requiring approvals for certain transactions either by senior managers or by the board of directors.

Three financial instruments are widespread: preferred stock, common stock, and bonds. Both types of stock legally provide ownership interests in the business enterprise. In addition, both types have *limited liability*, which limits losses on their investments to the investment itself.

Preferred stock has certain preferences or rights when contrasted with common stock. The major preference is that it receives dividends first. If the company pays no dividends to preferred stockholders, then it cannot pay any dividends to common shareholders. Most preferred stock issued in the United States has a cumulative feature. When companies omit a dividend to preferred stock, the cumulative feature requires them to pay both the back and regular dividends before common stockholders receive any dividends. Preferred stock also is preferred during liquidation. If the firm closes, then preferred shareholders recover their investments before common stockholders receive anything back (but creditors stand in line ahead of both preferred and common shareholders). Preferred stock might also have a convertibility feature that allows the owners to turn in preferred stock to receive some other security, usually shares of common stock.

Common stockholders have a residual interest in the firm, which means that, once creditors and preferred shareholders are paid, the assets belong to them. Although dividends to preferred stockholders are limited, dividends to common shareholders may be as large as the board of directors wants to make them. These considerations imply that common stock is the riskiest of these securities but also provides opportunities for the greatest gains.

Bonds are a type of debt. A *bond* is a security in which the issuing corporation usually promises to pay interest periodically and, at the end of a certain time period, promises to pay the principal. The principal amount is often called the *face value* of the bond. In this chapter we assume that the bond is sold to the investors, called bondholders, at the face value. The next chapter drops this assumption. The interest paid on the bonds is determined by a contractual interest rate called the *coupon rate*. Interest is calculated in the usual way with the simple interest formula: interest equals principal times the coupon rate of interest times time. Most bonds in the United States pay interest every six months, so the time is $\frac{1}{2}$ year. Although most bonds pay interest, a few do not, and they are called *zero-coupon bonds*.

When these securities are purchased, the investor records them for the amount paid for them. They are usually placed in an investments account. When the corporation issues stocks, it records the cash received in either common stock or preferred stock at the par value of the stock (assuming it has a par value; see Chapter 2), and places the difference in an additional paid-in capital account. It accounts for dividends received and interest revenue in the usual way.

When the firm issues bonds at their face value, it debits cash for the amount it receives and credits bonds payable for the face amount. It records interest expense in the same way as it would for any creditor. It records the principal repayment as a debit to bonds payable and a credit to cash.

If desired, investment or financing subsidiary ledgers can be constructed. In these contexts, they are often called registers. Some accounting details about these events and transactions are covered in Chapters 2–3, and more details are provided in Chapter 12.

PRODUCTION CYCLE

The *production cycle* is the accounting cycle dealing with the production of finished goods inventory. Recall from Chapter 2 that a manufacturer has four types of inventories: supplies, raw materials inventory, work-in-process (WIP) inventory, and finished goods inventory. Raw materials consists of those goods acquired from vendors that will become part of the production process. WIP measures the amount of goods started in production but not yet complete. Finished goods comprise those goods that are completed and ready for sale to customers.

Production has two prototypes: a job-order system or a process system. A job-order production system tends to be organized around the jobs or the work to do for customers. One job may be to make a certain type of table, and another job might be to make certain kitchen furniture. A process system tends to have flows, such as the conversion of petroleum into oil and gasoline. We restrict our discussion to the job-order system. AIS issues are similar for both methods, but the accounting differs significantly. We will leave the accounting for process systems to courses in management accounting.

In practice, a variety of sophisticated techniques exist, such as just-in-time production. We will omit those considerations here to simplify matters. Future courses in management accounting will address these methods.

Enterprise resource planning (ERP) refers to software packages that integrate the various activities in the production process. These systems capture financial and nonfinancial data to provide relevant information to those working in accounting, human resources, logistics, marketing, and production. The integration of all production data and the assistance to managers in all phases of production decision making make these software packages worthwhile. Further discussion of ERP is beyond the scope of this text; more information about ERP can be found on the Internet.

The production cycle has a simple and straightforward function—to make the finished goods. Inputs into production are the materials, labor, and other resources, generally referred to as factory overhead. The finished goods are the outputs, and they generally are sold to outsiders, although they may be consumed within the firm.

This cycle has a variety of departments, some of which have already been encountered. The *planning department* oversees corporate planning, and this includes the production plans. *Production control* manages the production process, and in particular, it authorizes new production and requisitions materials from the warehouse which will be employed in the manufacturing process. The warehouse, of course, holds the goods in storage and releases them upon proper authorization. In this context, the warehouse releases the materials to production upon receipt of a production order. The *production department(s)* actually carries out the work to produce the goods. *Cost accounting* is assigned the task of accounting for the goods, especially to determine the cost per unit of the product. The acquisition of materials has been described in Chapter 10 under the purchases cycle, and the usage of labor is discussed earlier in this chapter within the payroll cycle.

Accounting Issues

Since we have limited our scope to job-order systems, we need only concern ourselves with job-order costing. A *job* is some work to be done or some specific task. *Job-order costing* attempts to measure the manufacturing cost of a job.

Before filling in the details of job-order costing, let's review some terms from Chapter 2. The three types of manufacturing costs are: direct materials, direct labor, and factory overhead. *Direct materials* are the raw materials that are used in the production of a product and become an integral part of the product. *Indirect materials* are raw materials that are too small or that would require an expensive monitoring system. Because management thinks the benefits of such a monitoring system do not cover the costs, the firm does not track these materials individually. *Direct labor* is labor that is performed during the production process that can be easily traced to the products. *Indirect labor* is other labor expended during the production process that cannot be easily traced to the products. *Factory overhead* refers to any resources employed in the production process except for direct materials and direct labor. Note that factory overhead includes indirect materials and indirect labor.

Overview of Production Accounting.
The production accounts are summarized in Exhibit 11.6. The raw materials inventory account keeps track of the costs of the raw materials maintained by the corporation. As discussed in Chapter 10, the inventory account is debited when materials are acquired, assuming a perpetual inventory system. When materials are placed into production, the account is credited to remove the items from the raw materials inventory account. The offsetting entry depends on whether the materials are considered direct or indirect. The debit portion of the entry is to WIP if the items are direct materials and to factory overhead if they are indirect materials.

Labor requires an adjustment to what was said earlier in the payroll cycle. At that time, we stated that the accountant would debit wages and salaries expense. This is certainly true for service organizations and merchandisers. It is still true for manufacturers when the labor is not related to production, such as the labor of the sales staff or top management. Production-related labor, however, is going to be charged against WIP or factory overhead, depending on whether it is direct or indirect labor. But the payroll department may not know which type of labor is involved. The cost accounting department will know which type of labor is used, and it could adjust the accounts. One solution is as follows. The payroll department will debit payroll control, a temporary account, and make the usual credits (employee federal income taxes payable, FICA taxes payable, and wages payable). Then, when the cost accounting department has the relevant data, it can debit WIP for the amount of direct labor, debit factory overhead for the amount of indirect labor, and debit wages and salaries expense for labor that is not part of the production process. The credit goes to payroll control. After this entry, payroll control ought to have a zero balance.

Accounting for other resources as factory overhead is more problematic. Factory overhead includes such items as factory depreciation, factory insurance, and factory utilities. Some of these items may not be calculated until a later time, so how can the accountant cost a particular job when completed if he or she doesn't have all the cost data? Corporations handle this problem by estimating the amount of factory overhead.

The estimation proceeds as follows. The planning department plans on production for the year (or some other time period). It prepares a budget for the business enterprise,

EXHIBIT 11.6

PRODUCTION ACCOUNTS

Raw Materials Inventory		Payroll Control	
Purchases	Direct materials Indirect materials	Gross pay	Direct labor Indirect labor

Factory Overhead		Work-in-Process	
Indirect materials Indirect labor Other	Applied	Direct materials Direct labor Applied FOH	Transfer to finished goods

Finished Goods		Cost of Goods Sold	
Transferred in from WIP when production completed	Transferred out once goods are sold	Transferred in when finished goods are sold	

and this budget indicates the estimated production for the year and the estimated resources that will be consumed during the production process. Specifically, this budget gives the estimated factory overhead costs for the year, and it reveals the estimated number of direct labor hours for the year. The accountant can then compute the *factory overhead rate* as the estimated factory overhead cost divided by the estimated number of direct labor hours.

This estimation procedure is under attack these days. Improvements for many firms can be attained by finding better estimators than the number of direct labor hours. These estimators are termed cost drivers. In addition, activity-based costing changes the procedure in some fundamental ways. Since the purpose of this text rests primarily on developing basic accounting skills and introducing accounting information systems, we leave these topics to management accounting texts.

Thus, to cost a particular job, the cost accountant measures the direct materials and the direct labor and estimates the amount of factory overhead. This estimated factory overhead number is called *applied overhead*. In terms of journal entries, applied overhead is recognized by making a debit to WIP and a credit to factory overhead.

Actual overhead items are debited to factory overhead. Applied overhead is credited to the account. If the planning department has excellent prognosticators, the actual overhead will equal the applied overhead at the end of the year. This never happens in practice. If the planning department overestimates overhead, then applied overhead exceeds the actual overhead. The factory overhead has more credits than debits. Overhead is said to be overapplied. On the other hand, if planning underestimates overhead, then applied overhead is less than the actual overhead, and the factory overhead account has more debits than credits. Overhead is said to be underapplied. At year-end what do we do with the extra amount? Although several possibilities exist, the simplest way to handle the account is to close out the factory overhead account to cost of goods sold. In the first instance, you would debit factory overhead and credit COGS; in the second case you would reverse the entry. Either way factory overhead has a zero balance at year-end.

When a job is finished, the accountant transfers the costs from WIP to finished goods by debiting finished goods inventory and crediting WIP. When the firm sells the goods, it debits COGS and credits finished goods inventory for their cost.

In practice, firms keep these costs by jobs, for example, by employing a subsidiary ledger. Exhibit 11.7 contains an example. The subsidiary accounts are different jobs in which the firm is engaged. The costs (direct materials, direct labor, and factory overhead) are entered into the subsidiary account for each job. Similarly, the finished goods account and cost of goods sold might also have subsidiary ledgers.

Example. The discussion so far has been very abstract, so let's provide an example of job-order costing. Rathlef Enterprises makes silver-plated gizmos. During the current period, the firm engages in the following transactions:

1. It purchases raw materials on account, $123,000.

2. Factory payroll amounted to $210,000. The workers had to pay federal income taxes of $45,000 and FICA taxes of $30,000.

3. Production control requisitions $75,000 of materials, of which $57,000 is direct materials and $18,000 is indirect materials.

4. Cost accounting determines that the $210,000 labor costs consist of $100,000 of direct labor and $110,000 of indirect labor.

5. Rathlef incurs additional factory overhead of $80,000. Assume these costs are obtained on account.

6. During production there are 10,000 direct labor hours. Factory overhead is applied at a rate of $20 per hour.

7. Completed jobs cost $231,000.

8. Goods that are sold had costs of $172,000.

9. The factory overhead account is closed out to cost of goods sold.

We will now figure out the journal entries for these transactions. Exhibit 11.8 gives the transactions and summarizes the answers.

We encountered transactions like the first one in Chapter 10 so we know how to handle it. Assuming the raw materials inventory involves a perpetual inventory system, the entry is:

(1)	Raw materials inventory	$123,000	
	Accounts payable		$123,000

The second transaction is similar to what we talked about in the early part of the chapter, though we replace wages and salaries expense with payroll control. Later, the cost accounting department will determine to which accounts to charge the labor. Thus, the journal entry is:

(2)	Payroll control	$210,000	
	Employee fed. inc. taxes payable		$ 45,000
	FICA taxes payable		$ 30,000
	Wages payable		$135,000

EXHIBIT 11.7

WORK-IN-PROCESS SUBSIDIARY LEDGER

Job No. 101

Date	Activity	Cost	Balance

Job No. 102

Date	Activity	Cost	Balance

Job No. 103

Date	Activity	Cost	Balance

Job No. 104

Date	Activity	Cost	Balance

Production control requires materials for production during the year. Direct materials total $57,000, while indirect materials sum to $18,000. Recall that direct materials goes into WIP as a separate item; indirect materials is one of many items belonging to factory overhead, and that's where it goes. These facts are reflected as:

(3)	Work-in-process	$57,000	
	Factory overhead	$18,000	
	Raw materials inventory		$75,000

As stated in (2), the production labor equaled $210,000. Cost accounting can divide it into $100,000 of direct labor and $110,000 of indirect labor. Analogous to materials, direct labor goes to WIP, and indirect labor is added to factory overhead. Thus,

EXHIBIT 11.8

EXAMPLE OF JOB-ORDER COSTING

Rathlef Enterprises makes silver-plated gizmos. During the current period, it engaged in the following transactions. For each transaction, prepare the appropriate journal entry.

Transaction	Journal Entry		
1. Purchased materials on account, $123,000	Raw materials inventory	$123,000	
	Accounts payable		$123,000
2. Factory payroll amounted to $210,000, and the workers owe $45,000 federal income taxes and $30,000 FICA taxes	Payroll control	$210,000	
	Employee fed.inc.taxes pay		$ 45,000
	FICA taxes payable		$ 30,000
	Wages payable		$135,000
3. Materials requisition of $75,000, of which $57,000 is direct materials and the rest is indirect	Work-in-process	$ 57,000	
	Factory overhead	$ 18,000	
	Raw materials inventory		$ 75,000
4. Assigned factory payroll to the production jobs, of which $100,000 is direct labor and the rest is indirect	Work-in-process	$100,000	
	Factory overhead	$110,000	
	Payroll control		$210,000
5. Other factory overhead incurred cost $80,000 and was obtained on account	Factory overhead	$ 80,000	
	Accounts payable		$ 80,000
6. There are 10,000 direct labor hours. Factory overhead is applied as $20 per direct labor hour	Work-in-process	$200,000	
	Factory overhead		$200,000
7. Completed production of $231,000	Finished goods	$231,000	
	Work-in-process		$231,000
8. Determined cost of goods sold of $172,000	Cost of goods sold	$172,000	
	Finished goods		$172,000
9. Closed out the overhead account	Cost of goods sold	$ 8,000	
	Factory overhead		$ 8,000

(4) Work-in-process		$100,000	
Factory overhead		$110,000	
Payroll control			$210,000

Please note that payroll control now has a zero balance. It is only a temporary account, allowing the payroll department to account for the various deductions against the workers' gross pay in addition to allowing the cost accounting department to figure out how to charge the labor.

Besides indirect materials and indirect labor, there are other items in factory overhead. Assume that Rathlef Enterprises incurs additional overhead throughout the year that amounts to $80,000. To keep things simple, assume that all of the overhead items were obtained on account. The entry is:

(5) Factory overhead		$80,000	
Accounts payable			$80,000

At the beginning of the year, the planning department estimates that factory overhead will be approximately $20 per direct labor hour. During the year the production department utilizes 10,000 direct labor hour. Thus, during the year the cost accounting department applies $200,000 of overhead to the various jobs. In summary, the entry becomes:

(6)	Work-in-process	$200,000	
	Factory overhead		$200,000

The production department completes a number of jobs; these completed jobs have a cost of $231,000. Essentially the accountant just transfers these costs from WIP to finished goods inventory. The entry:

(7)	Finished goods	$231,000	
	Work-in-process		$231,000

When the marketing department successfully sells these goods, the revenue is recognized and so are the costs. We won't worry about the revenue side (for details, see Chapter 9), but let's assume that the costs of these sold items total $172,000. Thus, the entry is:

(8)	Cost of goods sold	$172,000	
	Finished goods		$172,000

The reader should understand that entries (5) and (6) occur throughout the year. In practice, entry (5) is recorded whenever the overhead items actually occur. Entry (6) for applied overhead is recorded when a job is completed (or when the fiscal period ends). If the actual overhead used in a job were known, the accountant would have no reason to estimate it.

In addition, the estimation process is never perfect, so actual overhead incurred will not equal applied overhead. In this example, the overhead incurred is $208,000 ($18,000 of indirect materials plus $110,000 of indirect labor plus $80,000 for other production resources). Applied overhead amounted to $200,000. Thus, the factory overhead account has a debit balance of $8,000. The last entry is to close it out by transferring this $8,000 to cost of goods sold.

(9)	Cost of goods sold	$8,000	
	Factory overhead		$8,000

Depreciation.   In Chapter 3 we explained that the journal entry for depreciation necessitates a debit to depreciation expense and a credit to accumulated depreciation. That statement is now updated for manufacturing concerns. When the depreciation relates to some asset used during the production process—for example, the factory building and the factory equipment—then the accountant observes that the depreciation is really part of the factory overhead. The depreciation represents the consumption of some plant or equipment, and it is neither direct materials nor direct labor, so by definition the depreciation is an element of factory overhead. Thus, the journal entry for depreciation of an asset used during production is:

Factory overhead	$XXX	
Accumulated depreciation		$XXX

Notice that the depreciation expense account no longer shows all of the depreciation of the firm. On the other hand, the indirect method of the cash flow statement must adjust for all of the depreciation of the entity. For a fuller explanation, see an intermediate accounting textbook.

Documents

The production cycle has three new documents: production orders, merchandise requisitions, and time tickets. Production control oversees the production process, and it determines which jobs to start and when they begin. Once they decide to commence a particular job, the department fills out a *production order*, a document issued by production control to begin some job. An example of a production order is given in Exhibit 11.9. The document shows the production order number and assigns the job a number as well. (If one production order always is associated with one job, then the production order number could be dropped.) The document minimally would show the date when production control initiates the job, the goods that will be produced, their product numbers, the quantities to produce, and the name of a manager who approves the decision to begin production.

The *materials requisition* is a document issued by production control that asks the warehouse to release certain raw materials to be used in a job. Exhibit 11.10 illustrates a materials requisition. It will indicate the job number and the requisition number. It also gives the date, description of the raw materials, inventory numbers, quantity desired, cost per unit, and total amount requisitioned. Finally, the document contains the signature of an approving supervisor.

Earlier we described the timecard, which is a document that shows when an employee has worked for the firm and how many hours he or she has worked. Its primary purpose is to determine how much to pay the employee. Time tickets are similar but have the purpose of helping to assign labor costs to particular jobs. So, the *time ticket* is a document in which workers indicate how many hours they worked on a specific job. Exhibit 11.11 displays a typical time ticket. It states the job number, time ticket number, employee's name, dates of the work, description of the work done, starting and ending times,

---

EXHIBIT 11.9

PRODUCTION ORDER

Date: _____   Production Order No. _____

Job No. _____

Goods to be produced	*Product No.*	*Quantity to produce*

Customer (if known): _____

_____

Approved by: _____

EXHIBIT *11.10*

MATERIALS REQUISITION

Job No. _____   Requisition No. _____

Date: _____

Description	Inventory No.	Quantity	Cost per Unit	Amount
			TOTAL	

Requested by: _____

number of hours worked, wage rate, and cost assigned to the job. A manager will sign off and thereby approve the time ticket.

Of course, the journal voucher will transcribe data from the various departments involved in production and send them to the general ledger department. The cost accounting department gathers and aggregates the data, and then sends the journal voucher to the general ledger department.

Summary

Although the accounting for production activities is more complicated than anything else we have tackled in this book, the AIS issues are not that difficult. We transfer raw materials from the warehouse, we work on them and transform them into finished goods, and then we hold them for sale. The control issues are obvious here and quite similar to those mentioned in the purchases cycle. Production also oversees labor expenditures and utilization of other resources, and these, too, must be controlled. The specific control objectives we leave as an exercise.

We also have a problem asking the reader to develop the production cycle flowchart. When you attempt the problem, keep in mind what is going on. Production control initiates the process, and there are only four documents to consider: production orders, materials requisitions, time tickets, and journal vouchers. (Although one could incorporate timecards, we leave them exclusively as belonging to the payroll cycle.) Consider who prepares the documents and who receives them.

EXHIBIT 11.11

TIME TICKET

Job No. _____   Time Ticket No. _____

Employee Name: _____
Dates of Work: _____
                    _____

Description of Work: _____
                    _____
                    _____

Date	Start time	End time	Hours worked	Wage rate	Cost
				TOTAL	

Approved by: _____

Once production is completed, the marketing department takes over as it attempts to sell the goods to customers. Actually, the customer might have initiated the transaction by sending a purchase order to the organization. In addition, the warehouse takes control of the finished goods until they are sold.

SIGHTS ALONG THE INTERNET

A few sites that cover software packages, especially with respect to payroll, are:

Accounting Web (click on "Human resources" and "Manufacturing & engineering")	www.accountingweb.co.uk/software
Accountants World (click on "Payroll" and "Finance")	www.accountantsworld.com
Electronic Accountant (click on "Fixed Assets" and "Payroll Software")	www.electronicaccountant.com

Go to the site and click the appropriate button to read about these software packages.

CHAPTER SUMMARY IN TERMS OF LEARNING OBJECTIVES

Define and Explain the Payroll Cycle. The payroll cycle is the accounting cycle dealing with the payment of wages and salaries to employees of the firm. Timekeeping tracks the hours worked by those paid by the hour. The payroll department uses these data to determine the amount of each employee's gross pay, it figures out the various deductions per employee, and then it computes each employee's net pay as the gross pay minus the deductions. The firm then pays the employees the net pay. The payroll cycle also calculates how much the employer must pay to others and then processes those payments.

Prepare Journal Entries in the Payroll Cycle and Use the Payroll Subsidiary Ledger. To set up a payroll fund, the firm debits payroll cash and credits cash. To recognize the labor expense, the company debits wages and salaries expense and credits employee federal income taxes payable, FICA (social security) taxes payable, and wages payable. When the payment is made, the accountant debits wages payable and credits payroll cash.

To recognize the additional expenses of the employer, debit payroll expenses and credit federal unemployment taxes payable and FICA taxes payable.

When the various payments to outsiders are made, the entity debits employee federal income taxes payable, FICA taxes payable, and federal unemployment taxes payable and credits cash.

A payroll subsidiary ledger has the employees as the subsidiary accounts. Fields within the records chronicle such data as the gross pay per period, the deductions per period, the year-to-date gross pay, and the year-to-date deductions.

Discuss the Payroll Cycle Flowchart. Timekeeping measures the hours worked by the employees. The payroll department prepares the payroll summary, sending one copy to accounts payable, and it posts the data to the payroll subsidiary ledger. The accounts payable department prepares the checks and payroll voucher. The unsigned checks go to cash disbursements for their approval and signature. Cash disbursements signs the checks and distributes them to the workers. It also writes a check for the total net pay and deposits this check into the payroll fund. The bank accepts this check and validates the deposit slip. The general ledger department updates the general ledger.

Describe the Facilities Cycle, Including the Facilities Subsidiary Ledger. The facilities cycle is the accounting cycle dealing with the acquisition and disposition of property, plant, and equipment. The function of this cycle is to make sure the firm has the needed long-term assets so it can conduct its business.

The facilities subsidiary ledger often is divided into a subsidiary ledger for property, plant, and equipment. The equipment subsidiary ledger has the pieces of equipment as its subsidiary accounts. Each piece of equipment is named, and its location is stated. Estimates of the asset's life and salvage value are noted. The date column shows the date of the transaction. The next three columns show what is in the asset's account, usually the original cost. The next three columns indicate the depreciation on the asset and its balance in accumulated depreciation. The book value is also computed.

Portray the Investments Cycle. The investments cycle is the accounting cycle dealing with buying the stock and bonds of other corporations. It attempts to make good investments that produce returns via dividends and interest and gains upon their sale.

Explain the Financing Cycle. The financing cycle is the accounting cycle dealing with obtaining money by borrowing funds or issuing stock. It attempts to obtain funds as cheaply as possible in the amount necessary for the firm to operate.

Perform Job-Order Costing, Including the Work-in-Process Subsidiary Ledger. Job-order costing attempts to measure the cost of each job carried out by the organization. When direct materials or direct labor are incurred, they are added to the job's work-in-process. The firm estimates the other resources incurred in the job by applying overhead, for example, by multiplying the number of direct labor hours by the overhead rate. Thus, each job displays its direct materials costs, its direct labor costs, and its factory overhead costs. When the job is completed, the costs are transferred out of work-in-process into finished goods. When the goods are sold, the costs are transferred out of finished goods and into cost of goods sold. At year-end the factory overhead account is closed out to cost of goods sold.

A work-in-process subsidiary ledger has jobs as the subsidiary accounts. Each job reveals its costs as categorized into direct materials, direct labor, and factory overhead.

Describe the Production Cycle Process. Production control issues a production order to start a particular job. It issues a materials requisition to the warehouse to obtain the materials used during the production process. Laborers fill out time tickets that show which jobs they worked on. Cost accounting processes these data and estimates the amount of factory overhead used and thereby obtains a cost for each job. Upon completion, the goods are sent to the warehouse.

GLOSSARY

Applied overhead—the assignment of factory overhead to a particular job.

Bond—a security in which the issuing corporation usually promises to pay interest periodically and, at the end of a certain time period, promises to pay the principal.

Capital asset proposal—a document that suggests the purchase of some property, plant, or equipment and has lines for appropriate managers or directors to approve the transaction.

Capital budgeting—the process of gathering data about possible capital projects and deciding which to undertake.

Cost accounting—that branch of the controller's department that determines the cost of products and services.

Coupon rate—the contractual interest rate on a bond, used to determine interest payments.

Direct labor—labor performed during the production process which can be traced to the products.

Direct materials—the raw materials that are used in the production of a product and become an integral part of the product.

Employee master file—a file that enumerates each employee of the firm and various details about each of them.

Enterprise resource planning (ERP)—software packages that integrate the various activities in the production process.

Face value of a bond—the principal amount of the bonds payable.

Facilities cycle—the accounting cycle dealing with the acquisition of property, plant, and equipment.

Factory overhead—resources employed in the production process except for direct materials and direct labor.

Factory overhead rate—the estimated factory overhead cost divided by the estimated number of direct labor hours.

Financing cycle—the accounting cycle dealing with obtaining money by borrowing funds or issuing stock.

Gross pay—the whole amount that the worker earns during some period of time.

Human resources department—the department of the firm that deals with such issues as hiring, retention, and firing of employees as well as training them and paying them wages and salaries and various benefits.

Indirect labor—labor during the production process that cannot be easily traced to the products.

Indirect materials—the raw materials that are used in production but are too small to keep track of.

Investments cycle—the accounting cycle dealing with buying stocks and bonds of other organizations.

Job—some work to be done or some specific task.

Job-order costing—an accounting method designed to measure the manufacturing cost of a job.

Limited liability—a feature of common and preferred stock that limits any losses to shareholders to the amount of their investments.

Materials requisition—a document issued by production control that asks the warehouse to release certain raw materials to be used in a job.

Net pay—the gross pay less the deductions paid by the employee during some period of time.

Payroll cycle—the accounting cycle dealing with the payment of wages and salaries to employees of the firm.

Payroll department—the department of a firm that processes the payment of wages and salaries to the employees.

Payroll fund—a special fund set up to make payments to employees for their net pay.

Payroll subsidiary ledger—a subsidiary ledger that provides details of the wages and salaries earned by each employee.

Payroll summary—a register (or special journal) that records the gross pay, deductions, and net pay to each employee.

Payroll voucher—a special type of journal voucher used to record wages and salaries.

Planning department—the department that oversees the planning process of the firm.

Production control—the department that manages the production process.

Production cycle—the accounting cycle dealing with the production of finished goods inventory.

Production department—a department that manufactures goods for the firm.

Production order—a document issued by production control to begin some job.

Timecard—a document that shows when an employee has worked for the firm.

Timekeeping—the group that keeps track of the time each hourly paid employee works.

Time ticket—a document in which workers indicate how many hours they worked on a job.

Title—a document that indicates ownership of the described property.

Zero-coupon bonds—bonds that have a zero-coupon rate of interest.

REVIEW QUESTIONS

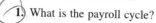

1. What is the payroll cycle?
2. What are the functions of the payroll cycle?
3. What business departments operate within the payroll cycle?
4. Describe the employee master file.
5. What deductions are taken out of the employee's paycheck?
6. How do employees pay their withholdings to the federal government?
7. What payroll fees do employers pay in addition to wages and salaries?
8. Describe the timecard, the payroll summary, and the payroll voucher.
9. Explain how a payroll subsidiary ledger works.
10. Briefly portray the payroll flowchart.
11. What is the facilities cycle and its functions?
12. Who makes the decisions in the facilities cycle? Who approves these decisions?
13. What is capital budgeting?
14. What documents exist in the facilities cycle?
15. Describe the equipment subsidiary ledger. What are the controlling accounts?
16. What is the investments cycle and its functions?

17. Who makes the decisions in the investments cycle? Who approves these decisions?

18. What is the financing cycle, and what is its function?

19. Who makes the decisions in the financing cycle? Who approves these decisions?

20. What is the production cycle?

21. What is ERP?

22. What are the functions of the production cycle?

23. What business departments are involved in the production cycle?

24. What are the basic steps in the production cycle?

25. Give an overview of job-order costing.

26. What items affect the work-in-process and the factory overhead accounts?

27. Why do accountants use the account payroll control? What kind of an account is it?

28. Explain why actual overhead is not put into job accounts. How do accountants handle this problem?

29. What happens at the end of the year when applied overhead does not equal actual overhead?

30. Where do the accounts payroll control and factory overhead appear on the financial statements?

31. What accounts have a portion of overhead in them?

32. Where does depreciation appear on the financial statements?

33. What documents exist in the production cycle?

DISCUSSION QUESTIONS

1. The word "register" often means the same thing as "special journal." The text mentions that the payroll summary is a register. In what ways does the payroll summary act like a special journal? In what ways is it different? What additional step must be added to make the payroll summary a special journal?

2. Let's reconsider how a payroll subsidiary ledger works. What are the records? What are the controlling accounts? How is the payroll subsidiary ledger organized differently from previous subsidiary ledgers that we have encountered? Why is it organized this way? How might we conceptualize the payroll subsidiary ledger to bring it into alignment with our normal interpretation of a subsidiary ledger?

3. (a) Managers often want to stay abreast of payroll expenditures. Design a management report that would assist managers in controlling payroll expenditures. What considerations help determine the information displayed on this report?

(b) Managers also like to keep on top of production costs. Design a management report that would assist managers in controlling production costs. What considerations help determine the information displayed on this report?

EXERCISES

1. Mindy Epstein, Inc. had the following payroll data for November:

Salaries and wages expense	$50,000	FICA taxes withheld	4,500
Federal income taxes withheld	12,000	Federal unemployment taxes	2,400

Present the journal entries to record the (a) salaries and wages expense, (b) payment of the payroll to the employees, (c) recognition of the employer's payroll taxes, and (d) payment of all liabilities related to the payroll.

2. Gannon Company reports the following balances in the following payroll-related accounts (prior to closing entries on December 31, 2003):

	January 1, 2003	*December 31, 2003*
Employee fed. inc. taxes payable	$7,000	$ 4,000
Fed. unemployment taxes payable	1,000	2,000
FICA taxes payable	9,000	8,000
Payroll expense		48,000
Salaries and wages expense		400,000
Wages payable	5,000	3,000

How much cash did Gannon Company pay during the year 2003 for payroll-related activities?

3. What are the control objectives for the payroll cycle?

4. Morley Jacobs and Company employs Ron Rufini (social security number 987-65-4321), who has worked the following hours during the week February 19–26:

Monday: 8–12 and 1–7   Thursday: 8–12 and 1–6
Tuesday: 8–12:30 and 1:30–5   Friday: 8–11:30 and 12:30–5.
Wednesday: 8–12 and 1–5

Design a timecard for Morley Jacobs and Company. Illustrate its usage with Ron Rufini's work week, and have Keith Brittain sign the card as the supervisor. Also show the calculation of the number of hours worked by Rufini.

5. The Jitterbug Mall has four employees. For the two-week period ended January 14, they worked the following hours:

Terry Blesh	SSN=111-11-1111	80 hours
Liz Pachecho	SSN=222-22-2222	100 hours
Sandy Simko	SSN=333-33-3333	90 hours
Stu Stringer	SSN=444-44-4444	85 hours

The Jitterbug Mall pays each employee $12 per hour up to 80 hours, and it pays time-and-a-half for each hour over 80 hours. Its fiscal year ends December 31. Assume that FICA taxes are 5% of wages and federal income taxes are 20% of wages. The employees are paid with checks beginning with number 11237.
   Prepare the payroll summary for The Jitterbug Mall.

6. Post the transactions in Exercise 5 to a payroll subsidiary ledger.

7. Prepare the journal voucher for the transactions in Exercise 5. The voucher is signed by Sami Son on January 14, and the voucher number is PR-12327.

8. What are the control objectives for the facilities cycle?

9. Aubrecht's Repair Shop has three automobiles tagged AUTO-1, AUTO-2, and AUTO-3. The first two both have a cost of $20,000, an estimated life of four years, and an estimated salvage value of $4,000. Aubrecht's acquired the first on January 1, 2002 and the second the following year. The third car costs $50,000, has a life of five years, and has a salvage value of $10,000. Aubrecht's purchased it on January 1, 2004. Aubrecht's applies the straight-line method to depreciate all long-term assets.
   Prepare the equipment subsidiary ledger for Aubrecht's Repair Shop.

10. Set up a record layout for the equipment master file. Use the data from the previous exercise to illustrate three records in the equipment master file. What is the key to this file?

11. (a) What are the control objectives of the investments cycle?
(b) What are the control objectives of the financing cycle?

12. On March 20 Craig Lee Fashions issues 1 million shares of common stock, par value of $1 per share, for $12 per share. On July 15 Craig Lee Fashions pays dividends of $0.50 per share. It does this again on September 15.
(a) Prepare the entries for Craig Lee Fashions.
(b) Aaron Carlson, Inc. buys 10,000 shares of Craig Lee Fashions on April 4. With respect to this investment, what entries does Aaron Carlson, Inc. make on its books for the year?
(c) Suppose Craig Lee Fashions had issued preferred stock instead of common stock on March 20. All other facts stay the same. What changes for Craig Lee Fashions? Aaron Carlson, Inc.?

13. John Fu, Ltd. issued 5,000 bonds at the face value of $1,000 each on January 2, 2003. The bonds carry a coupon rate of 8%, and the interest is paid each June 30 and December 31. The bonds have a life of five years.
(a) Prepare the year 2003 journal entries for John Fu, Ltd.
(b) Suppose Kitty Kites buys 100 of these bonds on January 2, 2003, and the firm still owns them at year-end. Prepare the journal entries for Kitty Kites for the year 2003.

14. What are the control objectives of the production cycle?

15. Steve Getto Leathers had the following materials issued during April:

Requisition No.	Raw Material No.	Job No.	Cost
9123	JK-107	105	$20,100
9124	QQ-055	106	3,200
9125	AM-982	107	9,800
9126	JK-102	108	12,000
9127	XY-669	indirect	4,500

Prepare the journal entry to record the issuance of these materials into the production process.

16. Time tickets for Steve Getto Leathers reveals the following labor employed during April:

Job No.	Cost
105	$10,000
106	1,900
107	2,700
108	6,000
indirect	43,900

Prepare the journal entry to record the production labor costs.

17. Steve Getto Leathers started business on April 1 of the current year. Use the data in Exercises 16 and 17, assume that no job is complete by the end of April, and ignore factory overhead. Draw T-accounts for the WIP-controlling account and each of the subsidiary accounts in the WIP subsidiary ledger. Post the journal entries recorded in the previous exercises to the general ledger and to the subsidiary ledger. Verify that the sum of the subsidiary accounts equals the balance in the controlling account.

18. The planning department of Chris Novak and Associates estimated for fiscal year 2004 that factory overhead costs would total $500,000 and that it would use 25,000 direct labor hours. The firm applies overhead to jobs on the basis of the number of direct labor hours. For the year, the production department worked 52,000 direct labor hours, and it actually encountered overhead costs of $505,000.

(a) What is the factory overhead rate?

(b) What is the journal entry for the applied overhead?

(c) What is the journal entry for the actual overhead?

(d) Is overhead overapplied or underapplied?

(e) Give the journal entry to eliminate the overhead account.

19. Job 982 has the following data in its account:

WIP-Job 982

Direct materials	$26,000
Direct labor	5,000

(a) Determine how much overhead should be charged to Job 982 if the factory overhead rate is $60 per direct labor hour and the job required 200 direct labor hours. Prepare the appropriate journal entry.

(b) Job 982 is finished. Prepare the journal entry at completion.

(c) Job 982 is sold for $52,000. Prepare the journal entries for this event.

20. Depreciation on the automobiles driven by the sales force comes to $25,000, and the depreciation on the factory building is $72,000. Make the journal entries for these two items. Where is the depreciation found on the financial statements?

21. On February 26, 2004 Sandy Simko, the production engineer at Applied Research, Inc., initiated production order number PROD-7116. This production order calls for the manufacture of 1,000 microcharms, product number MC-014, and 500 microcosms, product number MC-4U. The production manager Terry Blesh approved the production order. The microcharms will be manufactured with job number 5622, and the microcosms with job number 5623.

Required: Fill in the production order.

22. Pete Regel assigned Doug Tubbs, a production foreman at Applied Research, Inc., the responsibility to make 1,000 microcharms to fulfill part of production order number PRO-7116. The job is given the number 5622. His first decision is to request the following materials:

1,000 microchips (part no. AA-99) at $0.50 each

5,000 zappers (part no. ZP-50) at $0.10 each

250 do-dads (part no. DD-71) at $1 each

The materials requisition has the number RQ-5479 and is dated February 27, 2004.

Required: Fill in the materials requisition.

23. Charlene Dubois works for Applied Research, Inc. and earns $15 per hour. During the week March 1–5, 2004, she worked from 8 A.M. until 5 P.M., taking a lunch break each day from noon until 1 P.M. On March 1 and 2 and for half of March 3, Charlene worked on Job 5622, testing the parts and then assembling them together. (She worked on a different job the rest of Wednesday, March 3.) She records her work activities on time ticket number TT-6104, and it receives approval from Sherry Spurrier.

Required: Fill in the time ticket.

PROBLEMS

1. Draw an input-output model and an actors model of (a) the payroll cycle, (b) the facilities cycle (assume equipment), (c) the investments cycle, (d) the financing cycle, and (e) the production cycle.

2. (a) List all of the documents in the (i) payroll cycle, (ii) facilities cycle, (iii) investments cycle, (iv) financing cycle, and (v) production cycle. For each document, indicate who prepares it and who receives a copy.

(b) List all of the accounting journals and ledgers in the (i) payroll cycle, (ii) facilities cycle, (iii) investments cycle, (iv) financing cycle, and (v) production cycle. For each journal and ledger, state who has responsibility for it.

3. We can divide management assertions into five categories: existence or occurrence, completeness, valuation or allowance, rights and obligations, and presentation and disclosure. State management's assertions with respect to payroll expense, FICA taxes payable, payroll cash, equipment, investments, common stock, bonds payable, work-in-process inventory, and finished goods inventory.

4. Prepare a flowchart that covers the entity's determination of the payroll expenses and payment to the appropriate government agencies. To generalize the flowchart, have the payroll department prepare the appropriate government forms rather than specifying what forms to fill out. Assume that the payroll department does this on a quarterly basis. Let's also assume that there is no special journal for these transactions, so payroll prepares a journal voucher for them.

5. (a) How would the following errors likely be discovered?

(i) The payroll clerk credited John Smith with working 20 hours of overtime when it was John Smyth who did the overtime work.

(ii) FICA taxes have not been paid.

(iii) Richard Brown distributes the payroll checks to the employees. However, he keeps Richard Browne's check.

(b) How would the AIS prevent the following irregularities from occurring?

(i) Terminated employees remain on the payroll.

(ii) An employee falsifies how much he worked during some time period.

(iii) A payroll clerk writes a check to herself.

6. Klooster's Furniture creates custom-made furniture for hotels and motels. During the current year, Klooster's has the following transactions.

(a) It purchased on account $350,000 of raw materials.

(b) Production used $325,000 materials, consisting of $285,000 direct materials and $40,000 of indirect materials. (The rest of the materials is still in raw materials inventory.)

(c) It had factory payroll of $500,000. Of this amount, $45,000 was deducted for social security and $110,000 was deducted for federal income taxes. The payroll department prepares the entry.

(d) Payroll expenses amounted to $60,000, consisting of FICA taxes and federal unemployment taxes. All of this relates to factory payroll.

(e) Cost accounting determines that $400,000 of the factory payroll is direct labor, while the remaining $100,000 is indirect labor.

(f) Of the payroll expenses, cost accounting determines that 80% belongs to direct labor and 20% to indirect labor.

(g) Other factory overhead that was incurred amounts to $290,000.

(h) The firm applied factory overhead at the rate of $16 per direct labor hour. For the year, the firm utilized 25,000 direct labor hours.

(i) The cost of furniture completed during the year amounts to $1,200,000.

(j) The cost of goods sold during the fiscal year is $1,100,000.

(k) The general ledger department closed out the factory overhead account.

Required: Prepare the journal entries for these transactions.

7. David Jensen, Inc. has been building houses in the Park Forest (PF) and the College Heights (CH) divisions of Ponderosa. The company first signs a contract to build a customer a house, and then it begins construction. As a result, when the house is finished, it is transferred from work-in-process into cost of goods sold. Jensen employs a job-order cost system. The work-in-process subsidiary ledger contains the following entries. (The posting reference column is not shown.):

WORK-IN-PROCESS SUBSIDIARY LEDGER

Job PF-101

Year	Description	Debits	Credits	Balance
2004	Direct materials	81,000		81,000
2004	Direct labor	15,000		96,000
2004	Overhead	20,000		116,000
2005	Direct materials	42,000		158,000
2005	Direct labor	40,000		198,000
2005	Overhead	40,000		238,000
2005	Completed		238,000	0

Job PF-102

Year	Description	Debits	Credits	Balance
2005	Direct materials	85,000		85,000
2005	Direct labor	50,000		135,000
2005	Overhead	40,000		175,000
2005	Completed		175,000	0

Job PF-103

Year	Description	Debits	Credits	Balance
2005	Direct materials	65,000		65,000
2005	Direct labor	70,000		135,000
2005	Overhead	60,000		195,000
2005	Completed		195,000	0

Job PF-104

Year	Description	Debits	Credits	Balance
2005	Direct materials	50,000		50,000
2005	Direct labor	35,000		85,000
2005	Overhead	45,000		130,000

Job CH-101

Year	Description	Debits	Credits	Balance
2004	Direct materials	60,000		60,000
2004	Direct labor	25,000		85,000
2004	Overhead	15,000		100,000
2005	Direct materials	80,000		180,000
2005	Direct labor	55,000		235,000
2005	Overhead	65,000		300,000
2005	Completed		300,000	0

Job CH-102

Year	Description	Debits	Credits	Balance
2005	Direct materials	125,000		125,000
2005	Direct labor	100,000		225,000
2005	Overhead	85,000		310,000
2005	Completed		310,000	0

Job CH-103

Year	Description	Debits	Credits	Balance
2005	Direct materials	57,000		57,000
2005	Direct labor	40,000		97,000
2005	Overhead	37,000		134,000

Job CH-104

Year	Description	Debits	Credits	Balance
2005	Direct materials	50,000		50,000
2005	Direct labor	10,000		60,000
2005	Overhead	5,000		65,000

Required: From these data, answer the following questions:

(a) What is the beginning balance of work-in-process—control in 2005?

(b) What is the total of manufacturing costs during 2005?

(c) What is the cost of goods sold for 2005?

(d) What is the ending balance of work-in-process—control in 2005?

8. Sam Spurrier Manufacturing initiates the production process when production control issues a production order to the production departments. Production control also issues the materials requisition to inventory control, which fills the requisition by sending the raw materials to the appropriate production departments. Cost accounting receives a copy of the production order and opens a job account for the production order. It also receives a copy of the materials requisition and the time tickets. Cost accounting uses these data to post the costs to work-in-process. Assume that the time tickets contain the data about the number of direct labor hours, so that cost accounting can apply the factory overhead to the particular job.

When the job is finished, the production department turns the production order into a completed production order. It then sends this completed production order to inventory control, which updates the count of the finished goods. Inventory control then passes the completed production order to cost accounting. Cost accounting uses the data to transfer the costs from work-in-process to finished goods. Assume that inventory control has responsibility for raw materials subsidiary ledger, while cost accounting has responsibility for the work-in-process and finished goods subsidiary ledgers.

Prepare the production flowchart.

CHAPTER 12

RECOGNITION, MEASUREMENT, AND DISCLOSURE ISSUES

As we conclude our foray into the world of accounting systems and controls, we return to our original theme—financial accounting gains its significance in the world because it communicates information about some particular entity to investors and creditors and other interested parties. Because these users are outside the organization, they are not privy to the mass of data about the firm's activities, so they must rely on management's financial reports to them. Managers are also interested in these reports, even though they are aware of the company's activities, because managers are evaluated by the numbers in the financial statements. Their job security and salary raises and bonuses are based on how well they perform.

The major topics of this chapter are revenue recognition and measurement, especially the measurement of earnings, but also the measurement of assets and liabilities. Previously, we ignored the topic of measurement, even though it is of vital importance to financial reporting. For example, as we talked about purchasing and holding inventory in Chapter 10, the cost per unit was held constant. What happens when the cost per unit varies? In Chapter 11, we touched on bond investments and bond financing but always kept the price of the bond equal to the face amount of the bond. What happens when the price of the bond is not the same as its face amount? This chapter speaks to these questions.

Before addressing the measurement issue, the chapter begins with a review and an extension of the conceptual framework that was introduced in Chapter 1. This survey will help refresh the purpose of financial accounting, the qualitative characteristics of accounting information, and the elements of financial reports. We also introduce the recognition imperative and several measurement schemes. Then we describe revenue recognition. This topic has been briefly discussed before, for example in Chapter 9, but we formalize the discussion here. Afterward, the chapter moves to a more detailed discussion of measurement, focusing on the methods of historical cost, market value, and present value. We then briefly review the disclosure principle, an item of fundamental importance if the goals of accounting are to be reached. We conclude the chapter with some discussion about the auditing of recognition, measurement, and disclosure assertions by corporate managers.

After reading and studying this chapter, you should be able to:

- Discuss the conceptual framework, including the objectives, qualitative characteristics, elements of financial accounting, recognition imperative, and measurement attributes;
- State the conditions for revenue recognition;
- Compute income under the percentage of completion method, completed contract method, installment method, and cost recovery method;
- Describe the major measurement methods in accounting;
- Define historical cost accounting and use it for asset acquisition, depreciation, and disposal of a partial amount of some asset;

- Apply current market value accounting to inventories, trading securities, and available-for-sale securities;
- Compute present values of single sums and ordinary annuities;
- Apply present value accounting to bonds and leases;
- Define disclosure and explain its importance; and
- Discuss the auditing of management's assertions about revenue recognition, measurement, and disclosure.

THE CONCEPTUAL FRAMEWORK: A REPRISE AND AN EXTENSION

As explained in Chapter 1, the Financial Accounting Standards Board created a conceptual framework of accounting and reporting. Presently, it consists of seven documents, termed Statements of Financial Accounting Concepts (SFAC), and they encompass the objectives of financial accounting, the qualitative characteristics of information, the elements of financial accounting, and recognition and measurement, including usage of present values. The FASB addressed the concerns of both nonbusiness organizations (e.g., state and local governments) and business enterprises; we'll restrict the interchange to business enterprises.

The conceptual framework is sketched in Exhibit 12.1. This synopsis lists the major objectives, qualitative characteristics, elements of financial statements, recognition imperative, and measurement attributes contained in these documents. (The elements in the cash flow statement actually come from the Statement on Financial Accounting Standards No. 95.) There is no attempt to summarize all the major details in the conceptual framework; more particulars may be found in Intermediate Accounting textbooks.

Objectives

The conceptual framework begins with the objectives of financial reporting. The primary objective of financial accounting is to furnish investors and creditors with information to assist them in making rational decisions. Generally, in this context the focus is on investment decisions, such as buying or selling or holding securities like bonds, preferred stock, and common stock. Although there may be some strategic issues at hand, the FASB concentrates on the financial aspects of the investment activity. In their collective eyes, they see investors and creditors concerned about the cash flows they will receive in the future. More specifically, they are concerned about the amount of cash they will collect, the timing of these cash flows, and the risks or uncertainty they face. This observation implies that the investors and creditors need information to assist them in estimating the amounts, timing, and uncertainty of these cash flows. Traditionally, this has been accomplished by periodically releasing a balance sheet, an income statement, a statement of changes in stockholders' equity, and, more recently, a cash flow statement.

Qualitative Characteristics

The next aspect of the conceptual framework addresses the information itself and its qualitative characteristics. Although the FASB portrays several attributes, it primarily promotes relevance and reliability. Recall that relevance refers to the information's pertinence to a particular decision that needs to be made and that reliability refers to the property that the

EXHIBIT *12.1*

A SKETCH OF THE CONCEPTUAL FRAMEWORK

Panel A: Objectives (SFAC No. 1)

1. Financial reporting should provide information to help investors and creditors. This information should:

   a. Help them make rational decisions.

   b. Help them assess the amounts, timing, and uncertainty of prospective cash receipts from their investments.

2. Financial reporting helps investors and creditors by providing information about the entity's assets and claims to those assets by creditors (i.e., liabilities) and investors (i.e., stockholders' equity).

Panel B: Qualitative characteristics (SFAC No. 2)

1. Relevance—the property that the information is pertinent to a particular decision.

   a. Predictive value

   b. Feedback value

   c. Timeliness

2. Reliability—the property that the information represents what it is supposed to represent and that it is free from bias and measurement error.

   a. Representational faithfulness

   b. Neutrality

   c. Verifiability

Panel C: Elements of financial statements (SFAC No. 3 and 6 and SFAS No. 95)

1. Balance sheet

   a. Asset—a resource owned or controlled by the firm that probably has future economic value.

   b. Liability—an obligation of the firm that can be discharged by disbursing assets, providing services in the future, or creating new obligations.

   c. Stockholders' equity—the residual interest that stockholders have in the assets of the corporation.

2. Income statement

   a. Revenue—an inflow of assets (or outflow of liabilities) that arises because the firm sells a product or provides a service.

   b. Gain—an inflow of assets (or outflow of liabilities) that arises from some peripheral activity of the business.

   c. Expense—an outflow of assets (or inflow of liabilities) that arises from acquiring or manufacturing goods, providing services, or some other activity that is part of the major activities of the business.

   d. Loss—an outflow of assets (or inflow of liabilities) that arises from some peripheral activity of the business.

   e. Net income—revenues and gains minus expenses and losses.

3. Statement of changes in stockholders' equity

   a. Distributions to owners—decreases in stockholders' equity that result from transferring net assets or providing services to owners.

   b. Investments by owners—increases in stockholders' equity that result from an owner's transferring net assets or providing services to the business.

4. Cash flow statement

   a. Cash flow from financing activities—cash flows from transactions and events pertaining to borrowing money and to common and preferred stock.

   b. Cash flow from investing activities—cash flows from transactions and events pertaining to the making of loans and to the long-term assets of the firm.

   c. Cash flow from operating activities—cash flows from transactions and events other than financing and investing activities.

Panel D: Recognition and measurement (SFAC No. 5)

1. Recognize an element if:

   a. It meets the definition of the element.

   b. It can be measured reliably.

   c. Information about the element is relevant.

   d. Information about the element is reliable.

2. Measurement methods

   a. Historical cost

   b. Replacement cost

   c. Current market value

   d. Net realizable value

   e. Present value of future cash flows (also the subject of SFAC No. 7) information represents what it is supposed to represent and that it is free from bias and measurement error.

To give flesh to the concept of relevance, the FASB claims that three aspects of relevance are predictive value, feedback value, and timeliness. If information helps investors and creditors predict some important event, then it has predictive value and is relevant to them. If they predict something, investors and creditors can determine how well they predicted the activity. They can then use this analysis to help them better predict things next time. If information helps investors and creditors confirm or correct earlier predictions, then it has feedback value and is relevant to them. Finally, information can be relevant only if it reaches the user prior to the time when a decision is made. In this case, the information is timely and it is relevant to the investors and creditors.

The FASB also states that there are three aspects of reliability: representational faithfulness, neutrality, and verifiability. If information accurately records some underlying phenomenon, then it is representationally faithful and so is reliable. If the information does not bias the behavior of the investors and creditors, then it is neutral and so it is reliable. If different measurers can gauge the event or transaction and obtain the same value, then the information is verifiable and so is reliable.

Elements of Financial Statements

The four financial statements are the balance sheet, income statement, statement of changes in stockholders' equity, and cash flow statement. Their components are referred to as the elements of financial accounting.

The balance sheet states that assets equal liabilities plus stockholders' equity. Assets are resources owned or controlled by the firm that probably have future economic value. Liabilities are obligations of the firm that can be discharged by disbursing assets, providing services in the future, or creating new obligations. Stockholders' equity is the residual interest that stockholders have in the assets of the corporation.

The income statement computes net income as revenues plus gains minus expenses and losses. A revenue is an inflow of assets (or outflow of liabilities) that arises because the firm sells a product or provides a service. A gain is an inflow of assets (or outflow of liabilities) that arises from some peripheral activity of the business. An expense is an outflow of assets (or inflow of liabilities) that arises from acquiring or manufacturing goods, providing services, or some other activity that is part of the major activities of the business. A loss is an outflow of assets (or inflow of liabilities) that arises from some peripheral activity of the business.

The statement of changes in stockholders' equity indicates that ending stockholders' equity equals the beginning stockholders' equity plus net income plus any additional investments by owners minus distributions to owners. Investments by owners are increases in stockholders' equity that result from an owner's transferring net assets or providing services to the business. Distributions to owners are decreases in stockholders' equity that result from transferring net assets or providing services to owners; in a corporation, distributions to owners are called dividends.

The cash flow statement displays the change in cash during a period of time as equal to the cash flows from operating activities plus the cash flows from financing activities plus the cash flows from investing activities. Financing activities refer to those transactions and events pertaining to borrowing money and to common and preferred stock. Investing activities refer to those transactions and events pertaining to the making of loans and to the long-term assets of the firm. Operating activities refer to those transactions and events pertaining to the profit-making activities of the firm, that is, the delivery of goods and services to the customers. Pragmatically, operating activities encompass anything that is not a financing or an investing activity.

Recognition and Measurement

The recognition imperative is easy. The FASB claims that an entity should recognize an element in the financial statements whenever it meets the definition of the element, when it can be measured reliably, and when the information about the element is relevant and reliable. In practice, however, there are a number of gray areas. We will consider some of these difficulties in the next major section of the text on revenue recognition.

Measurement involves the assignment of a number to some attribute. Of course, we would like to assign meaningful numbers to the accounting elements! According to the FASB, there are five possible measurement bases for assets: historical cost, replacement cost, current market value, net realizable value, and present value. (Although we focus on assets, some simple adjustments can be made to the definitions so that we can discuss the measurement of liabilities.)

Measurement issues have been among the most contentious areas of accounting policy making. Some accountants have proposed historical cost accounting for everything, whereas others have advocated either replacement cost accounting or current market value accounting. More advanced books discuss these issues in details. In addition, the measurements can be adjusted for the effects of inflation, a method termed constant dollar accounting. Constant dollar accounting was a required disclosure several years ago when the United States faced relatively high inflation rates. With today's low inflation rates, the FASB has dropped the requirements. (Details about constant dollar accounting are beyond the scope of this book.)

Today, rather than utilizing only one measurement method, assets and liabilities are measured under several schemes. Each of the five measurement methods listed above is used in practice. We define the methods here and briefly indicate where they are employed. Later in the measurement section of the chapter, we provide greater explanation.

Historical cost is the amount of cash (or its equivalent) paid to obtain the asset. This original cost may be amended later for depreciation, depletion, or amortization. Property, plant, and equipment are typically measured at their historical cost.

Replacement cost is the amount of cash (or its equivalent) needed to replace the asset with an equivalent asset today. Replacement cost is sometimes called current entry value, for it is the current price to buy or produce something. Sometimes, when the lower-of-cost-or-market rule is applied, inventories are measured at their replacement cost. The lower-of-cost-or-market rule is described later in the chapter.

Current market value, sometimes termed current exit value, is the amount of cash (or its equivalent) needed to sell the asset. Investments accounted for as trading securities and available-for-sale securities are measured at current market value.

Net realizable value is the current market value less any direct costs to bring about the sale of the item. As with replacement cost, sometimes inventory is measured at net realizable value when the lower-of-cost-or-market rule is employed.

Present value is the value today of some stream of cash flows. In other words, it is the amount of cash today that is equivalent to a series of future cash flows, adjusted for the timing and uncertainty of the cash flows. How to make these adjustments is discussed later in this chapter. Long-term receivables and most long-term liabilities should be measured at their present value. SFAC No. 7 tells us that present values are not prized intrinsically but as approximations for current market values when it is difficult to obtain current market values.

Summary

We have briefly described the fundamental points of financial accounting and given a sketch of it in Exhibit 12.1. See Chapter 1 for more details about the objectives of financial accounting and the qualitative characteristics of accounting information. See Chapter 2 for more details about the balance sheet, income statement, and statement of changes in stockholders' equity. Similarly, see Chapter 5 for more information about the elements of the cash flow statement. Revenue recognition is discussed further in the next part of this chapter. The section after that expands the dialogue on measurement in accounting.

REVENUE RECOGNITION

One of the more problematic areas in practice, as seen in the number of lawsuits and SEC proceedings, is that of revenue recognition. Too frequently, managers want to recognize revenue and thus income before the proper time. As with fine wine, managers and their accountants should let their "wine" age fully so that they can savor the taste and avoid any bitter aftertaste.

The Recognition Imperative

Basically, three conditions surround the question of when revenue ought to be recognized. A business enterprise may recognize revenue when:

1. The amount and timing of the revenues are reasonably determinable.
2. The earnings process is complete or nearly complete.
3. There are no major uncertainties about the collection of cash.

The first condition basically says that the firm must have a reasonable idea of how to measure the revenue. If there are significant contingencies still awaiting resolution, then the firm should not recognize the revenue. If, for example, a franchiser gets a percentage of a franchisee's sales, the franchiser should wait to find out what the franchisee's revenue is instead of guessing the amount.

The second provision keeps the definition of revenue in mind and insists that the company do something to justify the revenue. Merely signing a contract or making a deal with a customer is insufficient. The business enterprise must provide goods or services to the customer before booking the revenue. This condition also implies that, if the customer might cancel the deal, then the firm must wait until the period of the cancellation right expires before recognizing the revenue. If the firm has significant experiences with customer returns, at year-end it must estimate the amount of sales returns and allowances and reduce that amount from sales.

One practical consideration for determining whether the revenue has been earned is to ask who has the risks and rewards of ownership of the product. As long as the corporation maintains these risks and rewards, it has the property rights to the inventory and should not recognize any revenue. The firm can recognize the revenue when it transfers the risks and rewards of product ownership to the customer.

The third requirement suggests that the revenue not be recognized if cash collection problems might exist. This proviso also considers the definition, for a revenue has an inflow of net assets as a result of providing a good or a service. If that net asset is a receivable but the customer might not pay off its debt, it is unclear whether or not there is actually an inflow of net assets.

Some Methods of Revenue Recognition

As a result of these considerations, accountants have come up with several alternative methods of revenue recognition: the percentage of completion method, the completed contract method, the installment method, and the cost recovery method. The time line in Exhibit 12.2 will help to clarify the differences. As a template, we can think of the sales process as producing goods (if a manufacturer), holding the goods for sale (inventory), selling the goods on credit, and collecting the cash from the customer. The question is when, along this time line, the company can book revenues. Throughout this text we have assumed that revenue is to be recognized when the sale is made, as evidenced by a purchase order from the customer. Other possibilities exist, and we consider them next.

Sometimes, the entity obtains a contract to build a large item, such as a bridge or a jumbo jet. With a definite contract in hand, these corporations might recognize revenue as they produce the bridge or jumbo jet. The *percentage of completion method* is a revenue recognition method that recognizes a fraction of the income equal to the amount of work done in proportion to the total work to be done. The amount of work that has been completed relative to the total amount can be measured either by engineering estimates or by accounting estimates of the project's costs.

On the other hand, some firms take a more conservative approach and wait until the production process is concluded before recognizing the revenue. This method is termed the completed contract method. The *completed contract method* is a revenue recognition method that recognizes no income until the project is finished.

Accountants developed the next two approaches to handle concerns about the collection of cash from customers. The *installment method* is a revenue recognition method that recognizes a fraction of the total gross profit equal to the amount of cash received from the customer in proportion to the total cash to be received. Each cash receipt allows partial recognition of the total revenues and total expenses. The *cost recovery method* is a revenue recognition method that recognizes no income until the cash flows from the customer recoup all of the project costs. Early cash flows merely recover the expenses. After all expenses are recovered, then any additional cash collections go into earnings.

Exhibit 12.3 illustrates these new procedures. Assume that Sally Smithfield, Inc. signs a contract in 2002 with a customer to build a ship for $400 million. The project manager anticipates total costs for the project will amount to $240 million, so the gross profit equals $160 million. The timing of the cost incurrences is (in millions): $90, $120, and $30 in 2002–2004, respectively. The cash flows occur (again in millions): $50, $100,

---

EXHIBIT 12.2

TIME LINE FOR REVENUE RECOGNITION

		Awaiting cash collection
Production	Awaiting sales	
|------------------|	|------------------|	|------------|
Production begins	Production ends	Sale (transfer to customer)	Cash collection

	Percentage of completion	Completed contract	Installment; Cost recovery

EXHIBIT *12.3*

REVENUE RECOGNITION EXAMPLE

Sally Smithfield, Inc. constructs ships. In 2002 the company contracts with a customer to build a particular ship at a contract price of $400 million. Sally Smithfield, Inc. expects that the project will cost $240 million and that it will be completed in 2004. The costs and cash flows are as follows (in millions):

	Costs	*Cash Flows*
2002	$ 90	$ 50
2003	120	100
2004	30	150
2005	0	100

Required: Compute the income for each year if Sally Smithfield accounts for the contract with (a) percentage of completion, (b) completed contract, (c) installment method, and (d) cost recovery method.

Answer:

	Percentage of Completion	*Completed Contract*	*Installment Method*	*Cost Recovery Method*
2002	$150 − 90 = $60	$ 0 − 0 = $ 0	$ 50 − 30 = $20	$ 50 − 50 = $ 0
2003	$200 − 120 = $80	$ 0 − 0 = $ 0	$100 − 60 = $40	$100 − 100 = $ 0
2004	$ 50 − 30 = $20	$400 − 240 = $160	$150 − 90 = $60	$150 − 90 = $ 60
2005	$ 0 − 0 = $ 0	$ 0 − 0 = $ 0	$100 − 60 = $40	$100 − 0 = $100

$150, and $50 during 2002–2005, respectively. With these data, let's determine the revenue, expense, and gross profit earned under the percentage completion, completed contract, installment, and cost recovery methods.

Let's begin with the percentage of completion method. In 2002, utilizing the cost numbers as signals of how much work has been accomplished, 37.5% ($90 / $240) of the project is completed. We do similar calculations in the rest of the years, dividing the costs incurred by the total estimated costs. In 2003, it is 50% ($120 / $240), and in 2004, it is 12.5% ($30 / $240).

Next, take these percentages and multiply them by the contract price ($400) to obtain the revenue for that year. During the first year it is $150 (37.5% of $400), during the second $200 (50% of $400), and during the third $50 (12.5% of $400).

To get the gross profit from the project, simply subtract the costs, which are given, from the revenues just calculated. Thus, in 2002, the gross profit is $60 ($150 − $90). Similarly, in 2003 the gross profit is $80, and in 2004 it is $20.

Notice that there is no revenue or expense in 2005, even though some of the cash flows occur in 2005. That is because the percentage of completion method recognizes these elements during the period in which the work occurs and does not even consider the timing of the cash flows. This, of course, is consistent with accrual accounting.

The second method that Exhibit 12.3 illustrates is the completed contract method. This method is simple, for it recognizes all $400 million revenue and all $240 million expense in 2004, the year in which the project is finished. (By implication, the project is finished in 2004 since the last dollar spent on the project occurred in 2004.) In all other years, the revenue, expense, and gross profit are zero.

The installment method is the third technique shown in Exhibit 12.3. The first thing to do when applying this method is to calculate the gross profit rate on the project. In this example, the gross profit is 40% (($400 − $240) / $400).

The accountant uses this gross profit rate to compute the amount of gross profit to recognize on the project in any year. Simply multiply the gross profit rate by the amount of cash received during the year. In 2002 the gross profit is $20 (40% of $50); in 2003 it is $40 (40% of $100); in 2004 it is $60 (40% of $150); and in 2005 it is $40 (40% of $100).

The revenue is made equal to the cash inflow. Then the bookkeeper backs out the expense as the revenue minus the gross profit. Thus, in 2002 the expense is $30 ($50 − $20). Alternatively, we could take one minus the gross profit rate—60% in this case— and multiply the cash inflow by this percentage. We again obtain $30 (60% of $50) as the expense. In like manner, we compute the expenses for all of the years, as shown in Exhibit 12.3.

The fourth method, the cost recovery method, is an ultraconservative method employed only in extreme circumstances, such as when the customer has entered into bankruptcy. All of the early cash flows recoup the costs of the project. During these periods, the revenues equal the expenses which in turn equal the cash flows. In 2002 revenues and expenses are $50, and in 2003 they are both $100.

This process continues until all of the costs are recovered. In this example, the full recovery takes place during 2004. Once they are recovered, all cash flows go into revenues and there are no more expenses to book. Thus, in 2004, $90 more of expenses are recognized but no more. This is because all $240 of costs have been recovered at that point. All $150 of cash flows belong to revenues. Thus, in 2004, revenue is $150, expense is $90, and the gross profit is $60.

In 2005, revenue is $100, the amount of the cash flow. The expense is zero, for no more costs need recognition. This leaves the gross profit as $100.

The main thing to remember about revenue recognition is that all three conditions (the amount and timing of the revenues are reasonably determinable; the earnings process is complete or nearly complete; and there are no major uncertainties about the collection of cash) must be met. The four new methods discussed in this section merely meet particular issues that have come up in practice. The percentage of completion and the completed contract approach address concerns about what to do with long-term contracts. Both the installment method and the cost recovery method attempt to deal with problems of any major uncertainties surrounding whether the customer is going to pay.

The astute reader will notice that the assumptions made by management in our examples were always correct. If the actual numbers differ from the estimations, then the accountant uses a more complicated process in the percentage of completion method and in the gross profit method. These complexities are left for other courses.

MEASUREMENT ISSUES

As mentioned earlier, the FASB in SFAC No. 5 stated that five measurement bases are used in practice today: historical cost, replacement cost, current market value, net realizable value, and present value.

Historical Cost

The historical cost method values the asset at the amount of cash (or its equivalent) paid to obtain it. This historical or original cost includes the costs of everything necessary to obtain the asset and make it useful. If you pay a sales tax when you purchase something, include the sales tax as part of the asset. If you buy securities and pay a brokerage fee, include it as part of the cost of the securities. If you purchase a building, include the various closing costs and legal fees as the historical cost of the building.

Historical Cost at Acquisition. Generally, at the date of acquisition, historical cost starts at the market value of the asset plus the additional charges necessary to obtain the asset and put it in a useful state. After the date of acquisition, historical cost typically does not match the market value.

Historical Cost Depreciation. Often, the accountant depreciates (or depletes or amortizes) assets with a determinable finite life, including buildings, equipment, and prepaid items. The straight-line method computes depreciation as cost minus salvage value, all divided by the life, which is usually measured in time. Of course, the salvage value with such things as prepaid insurance is zero. There are other methods of depreciation, but the straight-line is the most used method in practice.

Bonds not issued at their face amount provide a new example. As discussed later in the chapter, this situation arises when the coupon rate differs from the market interest rate. Upon issuance of the bonds, if the cash proceeds are greater than the face amount, the difference is called the premium on bonds payable. This premium is amortized over the life of the bond, and the offsetting entry goes to bond interest expense. If the cash proceeds are less than the face amount, the difference is a discount on bonds payable. It, too, would be amortized over the life of the bond. Amortization of a bond premium reduces the bond interest expense, whereas amortization of a discount increases the bond interest expense.

Exhibit 12.4 gives an illustration of this amortization. Panel A shows a firm that issues a bond with a $4,000 premium (a credit account; on the balance sheet it would be added to bonds payable). The premium is amortized over the remaining life of four years, so that amounts to $1,000 per year. By itself, the journal entry is a debit to the premium account and a credit to interest expense. The rationale for reducing interest expense is that the company borrowed $104,000 but only has to pay back cash interest plus the face amount $100,000.

Panel B of Exhibit 12.4 handles a discount example. Accounting for bond investments that are held to maturity are mirror images of these examples, though in practice the premium or discount is often combined with the investments account.

Partial Disposal. If an asset measured at historical cost is sold in its entirety, then the accounting records the assets received at their historical cost, removes the carrying value of the disposed asset (including accumulated depreciation, if any), and recognizes a gain or loss for the difference. A problem arises if a partial amount is disposed and if the original amounts have different costs. The problem arises because of the uncertainty of which cost to remove from the books.

Specific identification is possible. If there are several items of one type of asset and one is sold, and if the accountant can specify which one it is and therefore knows its specific cost, then the accountant has no problem in determining the cost of the disposed asset. But suppose that specific identification either is not possible or is prohibitively expensive to implement. What then?

The most important example of this issue involves inventory. The solution typically requires some assumption about the flow of inventory in the company. The first-in, first-out (FIFO) method assumes that the beginning inventory and early purchases are the first

EXHIBIT 12.4

BONDS WITH STRAIGHT-LINE AMORTIZATION

Panel A: Bond premium example

Ian MacDonald and Company issues bonds on January 1, 2002. The bonds have a face amount of $100,000, and they are issued for $104,000. Maturing on December 31, 2005, the bonds pay interest once per year on December 31 and have a coupon rate of 10%.

Required: Prepare a bond amortization table if Ian MacDonald and Company amortizes the bond discount with the straight-line method. Then give the journal entries for the transactions.

Answer:

Date	Payment	Interest	Principal Reduction	Principal (EOY)
01-01-2002				104,000
12-31-2002	10,000	9,000	1,000	103,000
12-31-2003	10,000	9,000	1,000	102,000
12-31-2004	10,000	9,000	1,000	101,000
12-31-2005	10,000	9,000	1,000	100,000
12-31-2005	100,000	0	0	0

January 1, 2002:

Cash	$104,000	
Bonds payable		$100,000
Premium on bonds payable		$ 4,000

December 31, 2002–2005:

Premium on bonds payable	$ 1,000	
Bond interest expense	$ 9,000	
Cash		$ 10,000

December 31, 2005

Bonds payable	$100,000	
Cash		$100,000

(continued)

that get sold. As the name indicates, you assume that the item sold was the earliest one into the system. The last-in, first-out (LIFO) method makes the opposite assumption. The items that are sold are the last ones into the system. The earliest items stay in inventory. Though counterintuitive, this method is popular for tax purposes because it generally gives the biggest tax deductions. A third method, called the weighted average method, computes a weighted average per unit as the cost of goods available for sale divided by the number of units available for sale. You then multiply this average by the number of units in ending inventory or the number of units sold to obtain the cost of ending inventory or the cost of goods sold.

Exhibit 12.5 presents an example. Jeannette Mittra, Inc. has 100 units of beginning inventory and has three purchases during the year, each of 100 units. Of these 400 units

EXHIBIT *12.4*

BONDS WITH STRAIGHT-LINE AMORTIZATION (continued)

Panel B: Bond discount example

Ian MacDonald and Company issues bonds on January 1, 2002. The bonds have a face amount of $100,000, and they are issued for $92,000. Maturing on December 31, 2005, the bonds pay interest once per year on December 31 and have a coupon rate of 10%.

Required: Prepare a bond amortization table if Ian MacDonald and Company amortizes the bond premium with the straight-line method. Then give the journal entries for the transactions.

Answer:

Date	Payment	Interest	Principal Reduction	Principal (EOY)
01-01-2002				92,000
12-31-2002	10,000	12,000	(2,000)	94,000
12-31-2003	10,000	12,000	(2,000)	96,000
12-31-2004	10,000	12,000	(2,000)	98,000
12-31-2005	10,000	12,000	(2,000)	100,000
12-31-2005	100,000	0	0	0

January 1, 2002:

Cash	$ 92,000	
Discount on bonds payable	$ 8,000	
Bonds payable		$100,000

December 31, 2002-2005:

Bond interest expense	$ 12,000	
Discount on bonds payable		$ 2,000
Cash		$ 10,000

December 31, 2005

Bonds payable	$100,000	
Cash		$100,000

available for sale, 250 are sold and the remaining 150 units belong to ending inventory. The question is how to cost the units in ending inventory and the units sold.

FIFO assumes that the 150 units in ending inventory consist of 50 units from the next-to-last purchase and all of the 100 units in the last purchase. The other units are those that are sold. LIFO presumes that the 150 units in ending inventory contain the 100 units in beginning inventory plus 50 units from the first lot purchased. The other units make up those that are sold. Weighted average works out to an average of $2.50 (COGAS of $1,000/number of units available for sale, 400). This method then multiplies the average cost per unit $2.50 by 150, the number of units in ending inventory, and by 250, the number of units sold, to arrive at the answers.

EXHIBIT 12.5

INVENTORY MEASUREMENT METHODS

Jeannette Mittra, Inc. has 100 units in beginning inventory at $1 each. Jeannette Mittra, Inc. purchases inventory during the year as follows:

March 1	100 units at $2 each
September 1	100 units at $3 each
December 1	100 units at $4 each

The ending inventory consists of 150 units.

Required: Compute the cost of the ending inventory and the cost of goods sold under FIFO, LIFO, and weighted average.

Answer:

Note that cost of goods available for sale is 100 * $1 + 100 * $2 + 100 * $3 + 100 * $4 = $1,000. Also note that the number of units sold is 400 units available less 150 units in ending inventory for 250 units.

FIFO

Ending inventory is 50 * $3 + 100 * $4 = $550.

Cost of goods sold is 100 * $1 + 100 * $2 + 50 * $3 = $450.

Alternatively, COGS is $1,000 − $550 = $450.

LIFO

Ending inventory is 100 * $1 + 50 * $2 = $200.

Cost of goods sold is 50 *$2 + 100 * $3 + 100 * $4 = $800.

Alternatively, COGS is $1,000 − $200 = $800.

Weighted average

Weighted average per unit is COGAS / units available for sale = $1,000 / 400 = $2.50.

Ending inventory is 150 * $2.50 = $375.

Cost of goods sold is 250 * $2.50 = $625.

Alternatively, COGS is $1,000 − $375 = $625.

Market Value Method

Replacement cost, net realizable value, and current market value are three variants of using market values to measure the accounting object, whether assets, liabilities, or earnings. Inventories, measured under lower of cost or market, make use of replacement cost and net realizable value. Investments that are accounted for as trading securities or as available-for-sale securities employ current market values.

Replacement Cost and Net Realizable Value. Frequently, accountants assign inventories a value by applying the lower-of-cost-or-market rule. This rule gets complicated because the market value, initially set as the replacement cost, must abide within certain limits. The upper limit, also known as the ceiling, equals the net realizable value; the lower limit, sometimes called the floor, is the net realizable value less a normal profit margin. In other words, if the replacement cost is greater than the net realizable value, "market" becomes the net realizable value. If the replacement cost is lower than the net realizable value less a normal profit margin, then "market" is set equal to net realizable value less a normal profit margin. Otherwise, "market" stays at replacement cost. Once the bookkeeper determines the proper number for market, he or she then compares the cost with market and assigns the lower value to inventory.

Displayed in Exhibit 12.6 is an exercise that demonstrates this application. Six independent cases are given. Notice that in each case, the accountant first establishes the market number. After this, you compare cost to market and choose the lower number.

Securities. Trading securities and available-for-sale securities are valued at current market values. For example, assume that Snow Shoe, Inc. has acquired 100 shares of Python Company's stock at $45 per share. Let's assume these shares are trading securities. At year-end the shares have a value of $60 per share. Next year the shares are sold for $67 per share.

The original journal entry recognizes the acquisition cost of the securities:

| Trading securities | $4,500 | |
| Cash | | $4,500 |

At year-end, the adjusting entry updates the value of the investments:

| Trading securities | $1,500 | |
| Unrealized gain on investments | | $1,500 |

You should notice that trading securities obtains a new value, $6,000, which is 100 shares at $60 per share. The last entry becomes:

Cash	$6,700	
Trading securities		$6,000
Gain on sale of investments		$ 700

The net effect is to place $1,500 of the profit into the first year's income statement and $700 profit in the second year's.

Available-for-sale securities also records the investments at their current market value on the balance sheet but defers recognition of the profit until the period in which they are sold. Consider the previous example, but assume that the investments are available-for-sale securities. Both methods place the investments on the balance sheet at $6,000 at the

EXHIBIT 12.6

AN EXAMPLE OF THE LOWER-OF-COST-OR-MARKET RULE

Case	Cost	*NRV Less Normal Profit Margin*	*Replacement Cost*	*Net Realizable Value*	*"Market"*	*Lower of Cost or Market*
1	10	9	11	14	11	10
2	10	8	9	12	9	9
3	10	8	13	12	12	10
4	10	6	12	9	9	9
5	10	11	9	14	11	10
6	10	8	7	11	8	8

end of the first year. Unlike trading securities, the available-for-sale method recognizes no income during the first year and $2,200 during the second year, when they are sold. Notice that both methods measure the same amount of profit over the life of the investment but recognize them differently in the different years.

The journal entries for the available-for-sale securities are a bit more complicated, and we leave them for more advanced accounting courses.

Present Value

The last valuation technique relies on the notion of present value, which takes dollars from different time periods and discounts their value for the implied interest. After briefly discussing how to compute present value, we turn our attention to bonds and leases and apply the present value method to these topics.

Computing Present Value. If you were offered $100,000 today or $1 million in five years, which would you take? How would you compare the two cash streams, given the difference when you would receive them? The answer relies on the *time value of money*, which implies that a dollar received today is more valuable than a dollar received in the future. This truth can be seen by recognizing that the dollar received today can be placed in a bank account and earn interest.

Suppose that you have $100 today. If this amount is put into the bank at an interest rate of 9%, then one year later you will have earned interest of $9. One determines this amount by using the simple interest formula $I = PRT$ where P = principal, R = interest rate, and T = time. In this case, $I = 100 * 0.09 * 1 = \$9$. Add the interest to the amount put in originally and there is $100 + $9 or $109. This amount is referred to as the *future value* because it tells how much the original can grow when left intact.

In the second year, the principal becomes $109 instead of the original $100. (As the principal changes and one calculates the interest on this adjusted principal, this technique is called compound interest.) The reader can verify that the interest during this second year is $9.81, so the ending amount in the bank account is $118.81 ($109 + $9.81).

You can continue the process. The interest in each year is 9% of the beginning-of-the-year balance. The ending balance is obtained by multiplying the beginning balance by $(1 + .09)$. Another way of looking at this process is to notice that the balance at the end of n years is the original $100 multiplied by $(1 + 0.09)$ n times, which equals $100 * (1.09)^n$. In general, the future value of $X in n periods at an interest rate of r is: $X (1 + r)^n$.

Present value is the opposite situation, for it gives the value today of some set of cash flows. For example, we might want to purchase some item that costs $10,000 in two years and desire to know how much we have to stash away in the bank today to buy it. If the interest rate is 8%, the present value of $10,000 in one year is $10,000 / (1 + 0.08) or $9,259.26. Then, we can find the present of $9,259.26, again at 8%, as $9,259.26 / (1 + 0.08), which equals $8,573.39. Thus, one has to save $8,573.39 and let it sit in the bank account for two years at 8% to have $10,000 in two years.

To find the present value of $10,000 n years from now at 8%, just divide by $(1 + 0.08)$ n times. More generally, the present value of $X in n periods at an interest rate of r is $X / (1 + r)^n$. You could use your calculator to compute such values, but tables are also available, such as the one shown in Exhibit 12.7. The table calculates the term $[1 / (1 + r)^n]$. Just look up the row that contains the number of periods n and then find the column for a specific interest rate r. The intersection of the row and the column has the value for the term $[1 / (1 + r)^n]$. To find the present value, you simply multiply the cash flow X by the interest factor given in the table (Exhibit 12.7). In the example above, with two

EXHIBIT 12.7

PRESENT VALUE OF $1

Periods	0.50%	1%	2%	3%	4%	5%	6%	8%	10%	12%	15%	20%
1	0.99502	0.99010	0.98039	0.97087	0.96154	0.95238	0.94340	0.92593	0.90909	0.89286	0.86957	0.83333
2	0.99007	0.98030	0.96117	0.94260	0.92456	0.90703	0.89000	0.85734	0.82645	0.79719	0.75614	0.69444
3	0.98515	0.97059	0.94232	0.91514	0.88900	0.86384	0.83962	0.79383	0.75131	0.71178	0.65752	0.57870
4	0.98025	0.96098	0.92385	0.88849	0.85480	0.82270	0.79209	0.73503	0.68301	0.63552	0.57175	0.48225
5	0.97537	0.95147	0.90573	0.86261	0.82193	0.78353	0.74726	0.68058	0.62092	0.56743	0.49718	0.40188
6	0.97052	0.94205	0.88797	0.83748	0.79031	0.74622	0.70496	0.63017	0.56447	0.50663	0.43233	0.33490
7	0.96569	0.93272	0.87056	0.81309	0.75992	0.71068	0.66506	0.58349	0.51316	0.45235	0.37594	0.27908
8	0.96089	0.92348	0.85349	0.78941	0.73069	0.67684	0.62741	0.54027	0.46651	0.40388	0.32690	0.23257
9	0.95610	0.91434	0.83676	0.76642	0.70259	0.64461	0.59190	0.50025	0.42410	0.36061	0.28426	0.19381
10	0.95135	0.90529	0.82035	0.74409	0.67556	0.61391	0.55839	0.46319	0.38554	0.32197	0.24718	0.16151
11	0.94661	0.89632	0.80426	0.72242	0.64958	0.58468	0.52679	0.42888	0.35049	0.28748	0.21494	0.13459
12	0.94191	0.88745	0.78849	0.70138	0.62460	0.55684	0.49697	0.39711	0.31863	0.25668	0.18691	0.11216
13	0.93722	0.87866	0.77303	0.68095	0.60057	0.53032	0.46884	0.36770	0.28966	0.22917	0.16253	0.09346
14	0.93256	0.86996	0.75788	0.66112	0.57748	0.50507	0.44230	0.34046	0.26333	0.20462	0.14133	0.07789
15	0.92792	0.86135	0.74301	0.64186	0.55526	0.48102	0.41727	0.31524	0.23939	0.18270	0.12289	0.06491
16	0.92330	0.85282	0.72845	0.62317	0.53391	0.45811	0.39365	0.29189	0.21763	0.16312	0.10686	0.05409
17	0.91871	0.84438	0.71416	0.60502	0.51337	0.43630	0.37136	0.27027	0.19784	0.14564	0.09293	0.04507
18	0.91414	0.83602	0.70016	0.58739	0.49363	0.41552	0.35034	0.25025	0.17986	0.13004	0.08081	0.03756
19	0.90959	0.82774	0.68643	0.57029	0.47464	0.39573	0.33051	0.23171	0.16351	0.11611	0.07027	0.03130
20	0.90506	0.81954	0.67297	0.55368	0.45639	0.37689	0.31180	0.21455	0.14864	0.10367	0.06110	0.02608
21	0.90056	0.81143	0.65978	0.53755	0.43883	0.35894	0.29416	0.19866	0.13513	0.09256	0.05313	0.02174
22	0.89608	0.80340	0.64684	0.52189	0.42196	0.34185	0.27751	0.18394	0.12285	0.08264	0.04620	0.01811
23	0.89162	0.79544	0.63416	0.50669	0.40573	0.32557	0.26180	0.17032	0.11168	0.07379	0.04017	0.01509
24	0.88719	0.78757	0.62172	0.49193	0.39012	0.31007	0.24698	0.15770	0.10153	0.06588	0.03493	0.01258
25	0.88277	0.77977	0.60953	0.47761	0.37512	0.29530	0.23300	0.14602	0.09230	0.05882	0.03038	0.01048
26	0.87838	0.77205	0.59758	0.46369	0.36069	0.28124	0.21981	0.13520	0.08391	0.05252	0.02642	0.00874
27	0.87401	0.76440	0.58586	0.45019	0.34682	0.26785	0.20737	0.12519	0.07628	0.04689	0.02297	0.00728
28	0.86966	0.75684	0.57437	0.43708	0.33348	0.25509	0.19563	0.11591	0.06934	0.04187	0.01997	0.00607
29	0.86533	0.74934	0.56311	0.42435	0.32065	0.24295	0.18456	0.10733	0.06304	0.03738	0.01737	0.00506
30	0.86103	0.74192	0.55207	0.41199	0.30832	0.23138	0.17411	0.09938	0.05731	0.03338	0.01510	0.00421

periods and 8% interest, you find out that the interest factor is 0.85734. Multiply this by $10,000 and you obtain the present value of $8,573.40, correct within one penny. (Tables are also available for future value computations, but since we concentrate on the present value concept, we do not show them in this text.)

If there are several different cash flows, then take the present value of each cash flow and add up the present values. This process always works, but it can be simplified in certain cases. One special stream of cash flows, termed an *annuity*, has several cash flows in equal amounts and occurs at equal intervals. For example, a mortgage might require payment of $800 each month for 360 months. An *ordinary annuity* is an annuity in which the cash flows occur at the end of the period. A mortgage typifies an ordinary annuity. An *annuity due* is an annuity in which the cash flows occur at the beginning of the period. Leases usually require the first payment up front, so they exemplify an annuity due.

Exhibit 12.8 gives a table with the interest factors for the present value of an ordinary annuity. As with a single cash flow, you would look for the number in the intersection of the column that gives the interest rate and the row that indicates the number of cash flows that occur. For example, if a customer pays you $10,000 each year for six years at 12% interest, what is the value of the receivable? Look up the interest factor for an ordinary annuity in Exhibit 12.8. With six cash flows and an interest rate of 12%, the interest factor is 4.11141. The present value is $10,000 * 4.1141 or $41,114.

One more wrinkle needs discussion before we look at a couple of applications. The interest rate and the number of periods or cash flows must be measured in the same time units. The above examples are all in yearly terms, but they could be measured in months or half-years or some other time unit, as long as both the interest rate and the number of periods or cash flows are compatible. Conventionally, interest rates are stated in annual amounts unless otherwise stated. If the time period is different, then one must adjust the rate.

For example, if a customer pays $500 each month for one year at an interest rate of 12%, what is the present value of the receivable? Since the payments are made monthly, the interest rate must be converted from an annual to a monthly basis by dividing by 12. Thus, we find a monthly interest rate of 1% in this exercise. Look up the appropriate interest factor in Exhibit 12.8 for 12 months at 1% and you get 11.25508. The present value, therefore, is 500 * 11.25508 = $5,627.54.

Bonds. The last chapter discussed bonds, but in all cases the face amount equals the price of the bonds, and thus there is no premium or discount on the bonds. Earlier in the chapter we introduced premiums and discounts but did not discuss why they arise. Not only do we now address this issue, but also we tackle the issue of bond pricing and how to construct a bond amortization table.

In theory, the price of the bonds equals the present value of the future cash flows. Unlike most situations, the cash flows are known (unless there is a default) because the cash flows are contractually stated. Specifically, the bond issuer promises to make two types of cash flows—the cash interest that in practice is usually paid every six months and a repayment of the face amount at maturity.

Exhibit 12.9 provides several possibilities for examination. Assume that the face amount of the bonds is $100,000, the coupon rate of interest is 10%, payments are made every six months, and the bonds mature in three years. The cash interest or coupon payments are determined with the simple interest formula: $I = PRT = 100,000 * 0.10 * \frac{1}{2} = $5,000.

We will consider three cases, beginning with the situation in which the discount or market rate of interest equals the coupon rate. As an aside, there is no rule requiring firms to issue bonds at the market rate of interest; thus, they can choose any coupon rate they

EXHIBIT 12.8

PRESENT VALUE OF AN ANNUITY

Periods	0.50%	1%	2%	3%	4%	5%	6%	8%	10%	12%	15%	20%
1	0.99502	0.99010	0.98039	0.97087	0.96154	0.95238	0.94340	0.92593	0.90909	0.89286	0.86957	0.83333
2	1.98510	1.97040	1.94156	1.91347	1.88609	1.85941	1.83339	1.78326	1.73554	1.69005	1.62571	1.52778
3	2.97025	2.94099	2.88388	2.82861	2.77509	2.72325	2.67301	2.57710	2.48685	2.40183	2.28323	2.10648
4	3.95050	3.90197	3.80773	3.71710	3.62990	3.54595	3.46511	3.31213	3.16987	3.03735	2.85498	2.58873
5	4.92587	4.85343	4.71346	4.57971	4.45182	4.32948	4.21236	3.99271	3.79079	3.60478	3.35216	2.99061
6	5.89638	5.79548	5.60143	5.41719	5.24214	5.07569	4.91732	4.62288	4.35526	4.11141	3.78448	3.32551
7	6.86207	6.72819	6.47199	6.23028	6.00205	5.78637	5.58238	5.20637	4.86842	4.56376	4.16042	3.60459
8	7.82296	7.65168	7.32548	7.01969	6.73274	6.46321	6.20979	5.74664	5.33493	4.96764	4.48732	3.83716
9	8.77906	8.56602	8.16224	7.78611	7.43533	7.10782	6.80169	6.24689	5.75902	5.32825	4.77158	4.03097
10	9.73041	9.47130	8.98259	8.53020	8.11090	7.72173	7.36009	6.71008	6.14457	5.65022	5.01877	4.19247
11	10.67703	10.36763	9.78685	9.25262	8.76048	8.30641	7.88687	7.13896	6.49506	5.93770	5.23371	4.32706
12	11.61893	11.25508	10.57534	9.95400	9.38507	8.86325	8.38384	7.53608	6.81369	6.19437	5.42062	4.43922
13	12.55615	12.13374	11.34837	10.63496	9.98565	9.39357	8.85268	7.90378	7.10336	6.42355	5.58315	4.53268
14	13.48871	13.00370	12.10625	11.29607	10.56312	9.89864	9.29498	8.24424	7.36669	6.62817	5.72448	4.61057
15	14.41662	13.86505	12.84926	11.93794	11.11839	10.37966	9.71225	8.55948	7.60608	6.81086	5.84737	4.67547
16	15.33993	14.71787	13.57771	12.56110	11.65230	10.83777	10.10590	8.85137	7.82371	6.97399	5.95423	4.72956
17	16.25863	15.56225	14.29187	13.16612	12.16567	11.27407	10.47726	9.12164	8.02155	7.11963	6.04716	4.77463
18	17.17277	16.39827	14.99203	13.75351	12.65930	11.68959	10.82760	9.37189	8.20141	7.24967	6.12797	4.81219
19	18.08236	17.22601	15.67846	14.32380	13.13394	12.08532	11.15812	9.60360	8.36492	7.36578	6.19823	4.84350
20	18.98742	18.04555	16.35143	14.87747	13.59033	12.46221	11.46992	9.81815	8.51356	7.46944	6.25933	4.86958
21	19.88798	18.85698	17.01121	15.41502	14.02916	12.82115	11.76408	10.01680	8.64869	7.56200	6.31246	4.89132
22	20.78406	19.66038	17.65805	15.93692	14.45112	13.16300	12.04158	10.20074	8.77154	7.64465	6.35866	4.90943
23	21.67568	20.45582	18.29220	16.44361	14.85684	13.48857	12.30338	10.37106	8.88322	7.71843	6.39884	4.92453
24	22.56287	21.24339	18.91393	16.93554	15.24696	13.79864	12.55036	10.52876	8.98474	7.78432	6.43377	4.93710
25	23.44564	22.02316	19.52346	17.41315	15.62208	14.09394	12.78336	10.67478	9.07704	7.84314	6.46415	4.94759
26	24.32402	22.79520	20.12104	17.87684	15.98277	14.37519	13.00317	10.80998	9.16095	7.89566	6.49056	4.95632
27	25.19803	23.55961	20.70690	18.32703	16.32959	14.64303	13.21053	10.93516	9.23722	7.94255	6.51353	4.96360
28	26.06769	24.31644	21.28127	18.76411	16.66306	14.89813	13.40616	11.05108	9.30657	7.98442	6.53351	4.96967
29	26.93302	25.06579	21.84438	19.18845	16.98371	15.14107	13.59072	11.15841	9.36961	8.02181	6.55088	4.97472
30	27.79405	25.80771	22.39646	19.60044	17.29203	15.37245	13.76483	11.25778	9.42691	8.05518	6.56598	4.97894

EXHIBIT *12.9*

BOND AMORTIZATION TABLES

Face amount = $100,000. Coupon rate of interest = 10%. Payments each six months for 3 years. Thus, the coupon payments are $100,000 * 10% * $\frac{1}{2}$ = $5,000.

Panel A: Coupon rate equals the discount rate

Payment Number	Principal (beginning of period)	Cash Payment	Bond Interest Expense	Reduction of Principal	Principal (end of period)
1	100,000	5,000	5,000	0	100,000
2	100,000	5,000	5,000	0	100,000
3	100,000	5,000	5,000	0	100,000
4	100,000	5,000	5,000	0	100,000
5	100,000	5,000	5,000	0	100,000
6	100,000	5,000	5,000	0	100,000
6	100,000	100,000	0	100,000	0

Panel B: Coupon rate is less than the discount rate (12%)

Payment Number	Principal (beginning of period)	Cash Payment	Bond Interest Expense	Reduction of Principal	Principal (end of period)
1	95,083	5,000	5,705	(705)	95,788
2	95,788	5,000	5,747	(747)	96,535
3	96,535	5,000	5,792	(792)	97,327
4	97,327	5,000	5,840	(840)	98,167
5	98,166	5,000	5,890	(890)	99,057
6	99,056	5,000	5,943	(943)	100,000
6	100,000	100,000	0	100,000	0

Panel C: Coupon rate exceeds the discount rate (8%)

Payment Number	Principal (beginning of period)	Cash Payment	Bond Interest Expense	Reduction of Principal	Principal (end of period)
1	105,242	5,000	4,210	790	104,452
2	104,452	5,000	4,178	822	103,630
3	103,630	5,000	4,145	855	102,775
4	102,775	5,000	4,111	889	101,886
5	101,886	5,000	4,075	925	100,961
6	100,961	5,000	4,039	961	100,000
6	100,000	100,000	0	100,000	0

want, sometimes even choosing to pay no interest. Bonds that pay no coupon interest are called zero-coupon bonds. Often corporations try to estimate the market rate, but there could be changes in the market rate of interest after the firm chooses an interest rate and has a printer type out the bond certificates.

In the first case the discount rate is 10%, the same as the coupon rate, and the price is $100,000. The present value of the cash interest payments, which form an ordinary annuity, comes to 5,000 * 5.07569 = $25,378. The 5.07569 is the interest factor found in Exhibit 12.8 for six periods and an interest rate of 5%. The present value of the payment of $100,000 equals 100,000 * 0.74622 = $74,622. The price of the bonds is $25,378 plus $74,622 or $100,000. When the coupon rate equals the discount rate, the bonds will always sell at their face amount, and there is no premium or discount.

Panel A of Exhibit 12.9 gives the bond amortization table for this example. A bond amortization table shows the balance in the bonds account, the cash paid, the bond interest expense, and the amount of reduction in the debt. The table shows these things for each payment made. Note that the last payment consists of both the interest and the principal, a fact that is emphasized by placing this last payment in two rows. The next-to-last row gives the data for the coupon payment; the last row gives the data for repayment of the face amount.

Panel B takes up the second case in which the coupon rate is less than the discount rate. Let's assume that the discount or market rate of interest is 12%. The price of the bonds is equal to $95,083 (the reader should verify this number). Indeed, whenever the coupon rate is lower than the discount rate, the bonds will sell below their face amount and give rise to what is called a discount on bonds payable.

(When determining the price of a bond or constructing a bond amortization table, we do not round when performing the calculations but will round the answers to the nearest dollars. If you are more than (say) $10 off, you have made a mistake.)

The beginning principal starts with the price when issued; thereafter, it is equal to the ending principal from the previous period. The cash payment is the $5,000 coupon payments plus, at the end, the payment of the face amount. The bond interest expense is found by multiplying the beginning principal by the discount rate and the time period (6/12 months). In the first case, it is $95,083 * 12% * $\frac{1}{2}$ = $5,705. Notice that the calculation of the coupon payment depends on the coupon rate of interest, whereas the determination of the bond interest expense is a function of the discount rate.

The cash payment in every case (except at the end) is less than the bond interest expense. When this occurs, the accountant adds the unpaid portion to the old principal. For the first period, note that this amounts to $705, shown in the table as a reduction of $(705). We actually add $705 to the old principal of $95,083 to obtain the new principal of $95,788. This latter number becomes the beginning principal for the second period. The process continues until maturity. Immediately after the last interest payment has been made, the principal becomes $100,000, the face amount of the bonds. Then this amount is paid off and everybody is happy.

Once we add the $705 to the old principal at the end of the first six months, again notice that the new principal becomes $95,788. This implies that, at this time, the discount on the bonds payable equals $100,000 − $95,788 = $4,212. As the discount goes from the original $4,917 to $4,212, we say that the discount is amortized $705. This process continues until the discount achieves a zero balance. Unlike the earlier example under historical cost depreciation, this method does not have an equal amount amortized in each period. This method, termed the interest rate method, is considered superior because it uses the market rate of interest on the date the bonds were issued.

Panel C covers the case when the coupon rate is greater than the discount rate. Let's assume the latter is only 8%. You can ascertain that the price of the bonds is $105,242. In fact, when the coupon rate is greater than the discount rate, the price of the bonds will exceed the face amount of the bonds. In this case, the bonds are said to sell at a premium.

The amortization table works in a manner similar to panel B, except that the bond interest expense is less than the cash payment. In this case, the additional cash paid reduces the principal amount that is owed. This, of course, reduces the principal, and eventually it is reduced to $100,000, the face amount. The interest rate method of amortizing the premium on bonds payable works similarly to the amortization of a bond discount. At maturity, the premium on the bonds payable becomes zero.

The reader is encouraged to verify each number in Exhibit 12.9 for all three cases. The journal entries are left as a problem.

Leases. A lease is an arrangement by which the lessor allows the lessee to borrow or use something the lessor owns in exchange for something from the lessee, usually cash. Students who rent apartments frequently must sign a lease agreement that will give them use of the apartment in exchange for monthly cash payments to the landlord.

If a lease is merely a rental, then the accounting proceeds in a simple fashion. The lessee records a rental expense, and the lessor records rental income and continues to depreciate the asset. Sometimes, however, the lease acts more as a financing device by which the lessee purchases the item. In this case, the accounting gets a bit more complicated by requiring the parties to treat it as a capital lease. The lessee records the leased asset at its present value and over time depreciates it. The lessee also discloses the interest expense embedded in the lease over time. The lessor, on the other hand, records a sale and recognizes a gain or loss on the sale. In addition, the lessor records the interest revenue over the life of the lease. Interestingly, even if the lessor has legal title to the resource, the lessor does not depreciate the asset any more.

Several criteria decide whether one should treat the lease as an operating or a capital lease. We leave these criteria and other items to later courses. Here we concentrate on finding the present value of the lease and filling out a lease amortization table.

Exhibit 12.10 provides an example. The lessee acquires usage of some item by agreeing to pay six annual payments of $60,000, always at the beginning of the year. If the interest rate is 8%, the present value of the lease is $60,000 (the present value of the first payment) plus 60,000 * 3.99271 (the present value of the remaining five payments, which constitute an ordinary annuity); the total present value is $239,563.

Exhibit 12.10 also contains the lease amortization table. In spirit it is very much like the bond amortization tables, though it is set up slightly differently to accommodate the fact that the cash flows occur at the beginning of the years. The column titled "Be-

EXHIBIT **12.10**

LEASE AMORTIZATION TABLE

The lessee agrees to make six annual payments at an annual interest rate of 8%. Each payment equals $60,000 and takes place at the beginning of the year. The present value of the lease is $299,563.

Payment Number	Cash Payment	Beginning Lease Obligation (after payment)	Interest Expense	Ending Lease Obligation
1	60,000	239,563	19,165	258,728
2	60,000	198,728	15,898	214,626
3	60,000	154,626	12,370	166,996
4	60,000	106,996	8,560	115,556
5	60,000	55,556	4,444	60,000
6	60,000	0	0	0

ginning Lease Obligation" is the amount immediately after the cash payment is made. Initially, it is the present value of the lease minus the first payment. Thereafter, it is the ending lease obligation from the previous period minus the cash payment. Interest accrues on the lease after the cash payment until the next one is made. Thus, the interest equals the beginning-of-the-period lease obligation times the interest rate times the amount of time. During the first year the interest is $239,563 * 8\% * 1 = $19,165. The ending lease obligation equals the beginning balance plus the interest accrued during the period. This process continues until the last payment is made, when the balance becomes zero.

Journal entries for a lease are left as a problem for the reader.

Summary

According to the FASB, five measurement bases are employed in practice today: historical cost, replacement cost, current market value, net realizable value, and present value. Historical cost is applied in most situations, which is why the accounting system is called historical cost accounting. Accountants apply replacement cost and net realizable value only as modifiers of inventory valuation, though net realizable value is also used when the organization is going out of business. Firms utilize the current market value in circumstances that have active markets such as stocks and bonds. The present value method is applied when cash flows are contractually set, as with most liabilities.

DISCLOSURE

Financial accounting provides information to the users of the financial report, primarily investors and creditors, to help them make rational investment decisions. In this manner, managers communicate the financial results about the corporation and fulfill their obligations to their users if they provide all relevant financial information. As defined in Chapter 1, this ethical principle is called the disclosure principle.

We can group disclosures into four categories: transaction-based disclosures, disclosures about accounting methods, disclosures about other important events or conditions, and disclosures of management's analysis of the financial reports. Accountants must assure that corporate managers make each type of disclosure.

Disclosures about transactions encompass the determination, measurement, and communication of the financial effects of the firm's transactions. Transaction-based disclosures follow naturally by recording accurately and completely the financial effects in the ledgers and journals of the corporation and later summarizing these effects in the financial statements themselves. These disclosures have been a major focus of this book. Footnotes to the financial statements provide additional details and clarifications about these transactions and their financial effects.

Disclosures about accounting methods concern those areas in which the firm has various alternatives from which to choose. For example, the company can value its inventory by FIFO, LIFO, or weighted average. It can choose whichever method it wants, but the firm has an obligation to tell outsiders which method it selects. This type of disclosure is so important that one accounting regulation requires a full discussion of the accounting methods either as a prelude to the footnotes or as the first footnote to the financial statements.

Besides transactions, other important events or conditions might occur that have, or may have, significant effects on the corporation. Examples include the possibility of declaring bankruptcy, major customers who are in financial trouble, a discovery or an invention with significant economic potential, major declines in value of certain assets, expropriations of assets, and lawsuits. Managers need to state these events or conditions and discuss the possible ramifications.

Finally, managers know a lot more about the organization than is revealed in the financial reports. With their greater understanding, managers should discuss the results depicted in the financial statements and place them in context. They should also disclose the future prospects of the company.

By providing all these disclosures, the managers can adequately communicate with investors and creditors about the firm.

AUDITING MANAGEMENT'S ASSERTIONS

We conclude this textbook with a reminder and an admonition that managers have self-interests that can run counter to the economic interests of investors and creditors. External auditing and internal auditing play major roles in verifying the disclosures by managers. After all, the four types of disclosures just portrayed are worthwhile and meaningful only when investors and creditors can trust management's assertions.

Throughout this text we have emphasized that the bookkeeping aspects of transactions involve assertions about those transactions. Managers make assertions about existence or occurrence, completeness, valuation or allowance, rights and obligations, and presentation and disclosure. In the accounting cycle chapters, we described these assertions and the control objectives for verifying these assertions. In the present chapter, we explained some revenue recognition methods, the major measurement methods, and, briefly, some disclosure issues. External and internal auditors must also study managers' assertions with respect to these items. We leave the details to later accounting and auditing courses, but the reader should recognize that evidence must exist to support these assertions. More importantly, an internal control system must operate in such a way that it gives credence to management's statements.

SIGHTS ALONG THE INTERNET

To learn more about finance, take a look at:

Association for Investment Management and Research	www.aimr.com
Ohio State Virtual Finance Library	www.cob.ohio-state.edu/dept/fin/overview.htm

Recall the firms listed in Chapters 2 and 5: Apple Computer (AAPL), Banc One Corporation (ONE), Chevron Corporation (CHV), GATX Corporation (GMT), General Motors (GM), J. C. Penney Company (JCP), Mellon Bank (MEL), Tribune Company (TRB), and Wendy's International (WEN). Go to the following site:

Investor Relations Information Network	www.irin.com/index.html

Click on "On-line annual reports and shareholder info." You can find stock quotes, news, shareholder information, and annual reports for these business enterprises. For some of them, you will also find links to SEC documents.

Let's take another look at the SEC's site.

Securities and Exchange Commission	www.sec.gov

There is a lot of data on firms that have not complied with SEC regulations. Go to the site and click on "Enforcement Division." Examine the administrative proceedings, litigation releases, and Internet enforcement program. What do you learn?

Finally, managers are often accused of managing earnings. See a summary of a book on this subject at:

Studies in the Development of Accounting Thought	www.corpcom.org/dot/index.htm

See also *The Earnings Management Literature* by Dale Buckmaster.

CHAPTER SUMMARY IN TERMS OF LEARNING OBJECTIVES

Discuss the Conceptual Framework, Including the Objectives, Qualitative Characteristics, Elements of Financial Accounting, Recognition Imperative, and Measurement Attributes. The objective of financial accounting is to help investors make rational investment decisions as they assess the amounts, timing, and uncertainty of their cash flows. Accountants accomplish this objective by issuing financial statements. The chief qualitative characteristics of information that accountants are concerned with are relevance—having pertinence to a particular decision—and reliability—representing what it is supposed to represent and being free from bias and measurement error. The elements of financial statements are assets, liabilities, stockholders' equity, revenues, gains, expenses, losses, distributions to owners, investments by owners, and cash flows from financing, investing, and operating activities. The recognition imperative states that one ought to recognize an element when it meets the definition of the element, it can be measured reliably, and the information is relevant and reliable. Five measurement attributes are historical cost, replacement cost, current market value, net realizable value, and present value.

State the Conditions for Revenue Recognition. A business enterprise may recognize revenue when: (1) the amount and timing of the revenues are reasonably determinable; (2) the earnings process is complete or nearly complete; and (3) there are no major uncertainties about the collection of cash.

Compute Income Under the Percentage of Completion Method, Completed Contract Method, Installment Method, and Cost Recovery Method. The percentage of completion method is a revenue recognition method that recognizes a fraction of the income equal to the amount of work done in proportion to the total work to be done. The amount of work that has been completed relative to the total amount can be measured either by engineering estimates or by accounting estimates of the project's costs. The completed contract method is a revenue recognition method that recognizes no income until the project is finished.

The other two approaches handle concerns about the collection of cash from customers. The installment method is a revenue recognition method that recognizes a fraction of the total gross profit equal to the amount of cash received from the customer in proportion to the total cash to be received. The cost recovery method is a revenue recognition method that recognizes no income until the cash flows from the customer recoup all costs of the project.

Describe the Major Measurement Methods in Accounting. The five measurement methods found in accounting practice are historical cost, replacement cost, current market value, net realizable value, and present value. Historical cost is the amount of cash (or its equivalent) paid to obtain the asset. This original cost may be amended later for depreciation, depletion, or amortization. Replacement cost is the amount of cash (or its equivalent) needed to replace the asset with an equivalent asset today. Current market value is the amount of cash (or its equivalent) needed to sell the asset. Net realizable value is the current market value less any direct costs to bring about the sale of the item. Present value is the value today of some stream of cash flows. In other words, it is the amount of cash today that is equivalent to a series of future cash flows, adjusted for the timing and uncertainty of the cash flows.

Define Historical Cost Accounting and Use It for Asset Acquisition, Depreciation, and Disposal of a Partial Amount of Some Asset. At the date of acquisition, historical cost starts at the market value of the asset plus the additional charges necessary to obtain the asset and put it in a useful state. After acquisition, the accountant depreciates assets with a determinable finite life. The straight-line method computes depreciation as cost minus salvage value, all divided by the life, which is usually measured in time. If an asset measured at historical cost is partially sold, if the parts have different costs, and if specific identification cannot be used, then a flow assumption must be invoked. The first-in, first-out (FIFO) method assumes that the early items are sold and the later items are still part of the asset. The last-in, first-out (LIFO) method assumes that the early items are still part of the asset while the later items are sold. The weighted average method assumes that a bundle of early and late items is sold and a bundle of each is unsold.

Apply Current Market Value Accounting to Inventories, Trading Securities, and Available-for-Sale Securities. When inventory is measured with the lower-of-cost-or-market rule, market is replacement cost. Market cannot exceed the ceiling, the net realizable value. In addition, market should not be smaller than the floor, the net realizable value less a normal profit margin. The appropriate market number is compared with the inventory cost to assess which is lower.

Trading securities and available-for-sale securities are reported on the balance sheet at their current market value. Increases in the market values of the trading securities are reported as gains in the income statement, but similar increases for available-for-sale securities are not.

Compute Present Values of Single Sums and Ordinary Annuities. To find the present value of $X, a single sum, look up in a table for the present value of $1 the row that contains the number of periods n and the column for a specific interest rate r. The intersection of the row and column gives the present value factor. Multiply this factor by the cash flow to get its present value.

An annuity is a set of cash flows, equal in amount and occurring at equal intervals, and an ordinary annuity has the cash flows occur at the end of the period. To find the present value of such an ordinary annuity, look up in a table for the present value of an annuity the row that contains the number of periods (which is also the number of cash flows) n and the column for a specific interest rate r. The intersection of the row and column gives the present value factor. Multiply this factor by the amount of one cash flow to get its present value.

Apply Present Value Accounting to Bonds and Leases. The price of
bonds equals the present value of the future cash flows discounted at the market rate of
interest. This price is the total of the present value of the coupon interest payments, discounted at the market rate, plus the present value of the face amount, also discounted at
the market rate. A bond amortization table shows the balance in the bonds account, the
cash paid, the bond interest expense, and the amount of reduction in the debt as each payment is made. The beginning principal starts with the price when issued; thereafter, it is
equal to the ending principal from the previous period. The cash payment equals the face
amount times the coupon rate times the time between coupon payments. The bond interest expense is found by multiplying the beginning principal by the discount rate and the
time period. The amount of principal reduction equals the cash payment minus the bond
interest expense. The ending principal equals the beginning principal minus the amount
of principal reduction.

A lease is an arrangement by which the lessor allows the lessee to borrow or use
something the lessor owns in exchange for something from the lessee, usually cash. The
present value of the lease is the present value of whatever cash flows are contracted, discounted at an appropriate interest rate. It is possible to construct a lease amortization table.
The column titled "Beginning Lease Obligation" is the amount immediately after the cash
payment is made. Initially, it is the present value of the lease minus the first payment.
Thereafter, it is the ending lease obligation from the previous period minus the cash payment. The interest equals the beginning-of-the-period lease obligation times the interest
rate times the amount of time. The ending lease obligation equals the beginning balance
plus the interest accrued during the period. This process continues until the last payment
is made, when the balance becomes zero.

Define Disclosure and Explain Its Importance. Disclosure is the communication of important pieces of information to investors and creditors. Disclosures about
transactions encompass the determination, measurement, and communication of the financial effects of the firm's transactions. Disclosures about accounting methods concern
those areas in which the firm has various alternatives to choose from. It can choose
whichever method it wants, but the firm has an obligation to tell the outsiders which
method it finally selects. Other important events or conditions might occur that have, or
potentially may have, significant effects on the corporation. Managers need to state these
events or conditions and discuss the possible ramifications. Managers should also discuss
the results depicted in the financial statements and place them in context.

***Discuss the Auditing of Management's Assertions About Revenue
Recognition, Measurement, and Disclosure.*** Managers make assertions
about existence or occurrence, completeness, valuation or allowance, rights and obligations,
and presentation and disclosure. Besides transactional data, managers also make assertions
about revenue recognition, measurement methods, and disclosure. External and internal auditors must evaluate and verify the managers' assertions with respect to these items.

GLOSSARY

Annuity—a set of cash flows, equal in amount and occurring at equal intervals.

Annuity due—an annuity in which the cash flows occur at the beginning of the period.

Completed contract method—a revenue recognition method that recognizes no income until the project is finished.

Cost recovery method—a revenue recognition method that recognizes no income until the cash flows from the customer recoup all costs of the project.

Current market value—the amount of cash (or its equivalent) to sell the asset.

Future value—the value at a future time of some stream of cash flows.

Historical cost—the amount of cash (or its equivalent) paid to obtain the asset.

Installment method—a revenue recognition method that recognizes a fraction of the total gross profit equal to the amount of cash received from the customer in proportion to the total cash to be received.

Measurement—the assignment of a number to some attribute.

Net realizable value—the current market value less any direct costs to bring about the sale of the item.

Ordinary annuity—an annuity in which the cash flows occur at the end of the period.

Percentage of completion method—a revenue recognition method that recognizes a fraction of the income equal to the amount of work done in proportion to the total work to be done.

Present value—the value today of some stream of cash flows.

Replacement cost—the amount of cash (or its equivalent) to replace the asset with an equivalent asset today.

Time value of money—the principle that a dollar received today is more valuable than a dollar received in the future.

REVIEW QUESTIONS

1. What is the conceptual framework of accounting?

2. What are the objectives of financial reporting?

3. Name and define the two most important qualitative characteristics of information.

4. Sketch the elements of the balance sheet, income statement, statement of changes in stockholders' equity, and cash flow statement.

5. When should an accountant recognize an element of the financial statements?

6. What is meant by the term "measurement"?

7. Name and define the five measurement bases for assets.

8. What are the three criteria for deciding when to recognize revenue?

9. Generally, revenue is recognized at the time of sale. What conditions give rise to considering other points in time for recognizing revenue?

10. Explain the percentage of completion method.

11. When does the completed contract method recognize revenue?

12. What is the installment method, and how does it work?

13. When is revenue recognized under the cost recovery method?

14. What does historical cost mean at and after acquisition of the asset?

15. Explain why accountants invoke cost flow assumptions.

16. Distinguish between FIFO and LIFO.

17. How does the average cost method assign cost to inventory and to cost of goods sold?

18. Explain step by step the lower-of-cost-or-market rule for inventory valuation.

19. How is the accounting for trading securities and available-for-sale securities alike? How do they differ?

20. What is meant by the time value of money?

21. Distinguish between future value and present value.

22. Suppose that you want to find the present value of $X at an interest rate of r over n periods. Explain how you can apply the table in Exhibit 12.7 to compute the number.

23. What is an annuity? What is the difference between an ordinary annuity and an annuity due?

24. Suppose that you need to find the present value of an ordinary annuity that has periodic cash flows of $X at an interest rate of r over n periods. Explain how you can apply the table in Exhibit 12.8 to compute the number.

25. If you need to find the present value of an annuity due that has periodic cash flows of $X at an interest rate of r over n periods, how can you use the table in Exhibit 12.8 to compute the number?

26. Under what condition will a premium on bonds payable exist? a discount?

27. How is a bond amortization table constructed?

28. Sometimes a lease is considered a capital lease. Describe the lease amortization table in this case.

29. What are the four types of disclosures that managers make?

30. Do managers assert anything when they disclose something other than a transaction?

DISCUSSION QUESTIONS

1. Some accountants have advocated the use of current market values for the measurement of all assets and liabilities. What are the advantages and disadvantages of such a policy?

2. Sometimes students complain that the completed contract method is deficient because it shows no revenues and expenses in some years. They forget that real-life firms usually have multiple projects ongoing at any point in time. Consider: Manikowski Inc. signs a contract in 2001 for $390 million that will require three years to complete, ending in 2003. The project incurs $100 million during each year of construction. Manikowski signs another contract in 2002 for $390 million, and it, too, incurs $100 million during each year of construction and takes three years to complete. In fact, Manikowski signs such a contract each year for eight years in total.

Required: Compare the income statements of Manikowski Inc. of 2005–2008 under (a) the percentage of completion method and (b) the completed contract method.

3. Previous discussion of the sales journal, purchases journal, and inventory subsidiary ledger assumed no changes in prices. Now that we allow prices to vary, the accountant must employ some cost flow assumption. If the firm uses (a) FIFO or (b) the weighted average method, what changes must be made to the sales journal, purchases journal, and inventory subsidiary ledger? (You may ignore LIFO. In the real world, firms that use LIFO actually keep the books on a FIFO basis and, at year-end, apply a sophisticated technique called dollar-value LIFO. The journals and ledgers nonetheless follow a FIFO assumption.)

4. The text says that, to find the present value of an annuity due for n periods, you should consider two sets of cash flows: the very first one and all the rest. The first one occurs today, so it is already in present value terms. The remaining cash flows comprise an ordinary annuity for $n - 1$ periods. The present value of the annuity due is the sum of these two present values. If X is the periodic cash flow and if Y is the interest factor found in the present-value-of-an-(ordinary)-annuity table, then the present value of an annuity due is:

$$X * 1 + X * Y = X (1 + Y)$$

In other words, you could create a table for the annuity due. The numbers would equal one plus the factor found in the table for present value of an ordinary annuity for one period less. *Required:* Use these facts to create a table for an annuity due. Consider interest rates 2%, 3%, 4%, and 5% and for periods from 1 to 5.

5. Concerns over the Y2K bug—the problem of what would happen to computers and to computer chips that represented years with only the last two digits—led the SEC in the late 1990s to require corporations to disclose what they were doing to mitigate the Y2K bug. Why did the SEC do this? Would these statements be useful disclosures to investors and creditors? Could their assertions be audited?

EXERCISES

1. Boalsburg Construction Company signs a contract to build a bridge for $90 million. The project is expected to take two years and cost $60 million. Specifically, Boalsburg Construction Company incurs costs of $20 million in 2003 and $40 million in 2004. It receives $45 million in 2003 and another $45 million in 2004.

Required: Compute the income for 2003 and 2004 if Boalsburg Construction Company uses (a) percentage of completion, (b) completed contract, (c) installment method, and (d) cost recovery method.

2. Smithfield Inc. signs a construction contract for a price of $360 million in 2001. It expects that the project will cost $240 million and that it will be completed in 2003. The costs and cash flows are as follows (in millions):

	Costs	Cash flows
2001	$ 30	$ 60
2002	150	120
2003	60	180

Required: Compute the income for 2001–2003 if Smithfield Inc. uses (a) percentage of completion, (b) completed contract, (c) installment method, and (d) cost recovery method.

3. The Bradford Company bought a parcel of land for $1,200,000. The firm paid its lawyer $15,000 to arrange the deal, write the contract, and represent the firm in the transaction. Bradford Company paid $250,000 cash and borrowed the rest in the form of a mortgage. It had to pay the bank closing costs of $5,000 and to pay transfer taxes of $2,000. What is the cost of the land? What is the journal entry for this transaction?

4. The Lovin' Fork and Knife buys a widget for $1,000 cash on January 1, 2002. It sells the widget on December 31, 2005 for $100. Calculate the depreciation per year (using the straight-line method), the gain or loss on the sale, and the earnings impact over the entire period in which The Lovin' Fork and Knife owned the widget under each of the following conditions:

(a) life = 4 years; salvage value = $0 (c) life = 10 years; salvage value = $0
(b) life = 4 years; salvage value = $200 (d) life = 10 years; salvage value = $100

What can you conclude? (You can try any life and any salvage value. If you know other depreciation techniques, you can also try any depreciation method.)

5. Franklin Inc. applies the periodic method to its inventory. On January 1 the beginning inventory consists of 120 units at $1 each. During the year Franklin Inc. acquires inventory in four lots:

March 1	200 units @ $2 each
May 30	300 units @ $3 each
September 4	250 units @ $4 each
October 8	130 units @ $5 each

The number of units in inventory at December 31 is 150 units.
Required: Determine the cost of goods sold if Franklin Inc. uses (a) FIFO, (b) LIFO, or (c) weighted average.

6. Using the figures in the previous exercise, prepare the journal entries if Franklin Inc. uses (a) FIFO, (b) LIFO, or (c) weighted average.

7. Emerald Inc. uses the lower-of-cost-or-market method of measuring its inventory. With the following data, compute the inventory value.

Product	Cost	Replacement Cost	Net Realizable Value	Profit Margin
A	$100	$ 90	$ 95	$8
B	100	90	97	5
C	100	90	85	6
D	100	101	105	7
E	100	102	95	6
F	100	110	115	4
G	100	110	105	6
H	100	110	98	6

8. In 2001 Schwartz Consulting acquires 10,000 shares in Williams International for $43 per share. Schwartz Consulting holds on to these 10,000 shares until 2004 when all of them are sold for $64 per share. Shares in Williams International have year-end values of $39 in 2001, $48 in 2002, and $55 in 2003.

(a) Assume that Schwartz Consulting considers these shares trading securities. What is shown in the assets' section of the balance sheet and on the income statement in each year 2001–2004?

(b) Assume that Schwartz Consulting considers these shares available-for-sale securities. What is shown in the assets' section of the balance sheet and on the income statement in each year 2001–2004?

(c) In what way do these two methods differ in terms of the earnings shown across all of the years that the firm owns the shares?

9. Joe and Kelli will receive $10,000 from a fund paying 6%. What is the fund worth today if they will get the cash in:

(a) three years; **(b)** four years; **(c)** five years; and **(d)** ten years?

10. Janet and Doug want to save $30,000 for new furniture, which they plan to buy in three years. How much must they invest today if the bank is paying:

(a) 3%; **(b)** 5%; **(c)** 8%; and **(d)** 12%?

11. Adam and Emily want to save $25,000 for a new car. Desiring to purchase the car in one year, how much must they put into the savings account today if the 12% interest rate is compounded:

(a) annually; **(b)** semiannually; **(c)** quarterly; and **(d)** monthly?

12. Kathleen and John will receive $5,000 each year from a fund paying 10%. What is the present value of these cash flows if they will receive them for:

(a) 5 years; **(b)** 10 years; **(c)** 15 years; and **(d)** 20 years?

13. Brian and Vallerie obtained a loan and are repaying it at $2,000 per year for five years. How much did they borrow if the interest rate is:

(a) 3%; **(b)** 6%; **(c)** 8%; and **(d)** 12% set?

14. Bob and Pat obtained a loan and are repaying $1,200 per year for two years, though the cash flow may be divided up into several payments. The interest rate is 12%. How much did they borrow if the interest rate is compounded and payments are made:

(a) annually; **(b)** semiannually; **(c)** quarterly; and **(d)** monthly?

15. Lloyd and Lou buy a $50,000 car. Although there is no down payment, the loan required monthly payments for two years. How much is the monthly payment if the monthly interest rate is (a) 1% or (b) 2%?

16. James Corporation issues bonds with a face amount of $100,000 and a coupon rate of 8%. Payments are required every six months and the bonds mature in three years. The market rate of interest at the date of issuance is 6%.

(a) What is the price of James's bonds?

(b) Prepare a bond amortization table in which the premium or discount is amortized with the interest rate method.

17. James Corporation issues bonds with a face amount of $100,000 and a coupon rate of 8%. Payments are required every six months and the bonds mature in three years. The market rate of interest at the date of issuance is 12%.

(a) What is the price of James' bonds?

(b) Prepare a bond amortization table in which the premium or discount is amortized with the interest rate method.

18. van der Wink Inc. leases an automobile for five years from Golan Inc. The lease agreement calls for van der Wink to make five annual payments of $15,000, each payment at the beginning of the year. The interest rate implicit in the lease is 12%.

(a) What is the present value of the lease?

(b) Prepare a lease amortization table for this particular lease.

19. Classify the following 10 items into one of the following disclosure categories: (a) transaction-based disclosures; (b) disclosures about accounting methods; (c) disclosures about other events or conditions; and (d) management's analysis of the financial reports. The items are:

    (1) Sales are $50 million.

    (2) Firms filing with the SEC are expected to include a section entitled management's discussion and analysis (MDA).

(3) LIFO is used to value inventory.
(4) Mortgage liability amounts to $5 million.
(5) The firm is facing a variety of lawsuits.
(6) The company indicates the possible effects from Y2K.
(7) The firm tells how it accounts for barter transactions.
(8) The company is negotiating the purchase of another firm.
(9) The firm indicates the likely impact of interest rate changes.
(10) The corporation says what it is doing about environmental cleanup.

PROBLEMS

1. Consider each of the following independent situations concerning revenue recognition.

Case 1. McLeod Company has products available to ship to customers prior to the end of its current fiscal year. Lewis, Ltd. places an order for the products, and McLeod Company delivers them prior to the end of the fiscal year. McLeod's customary business practice is to enter into a written sales order that requires the signatures of the authorized representatives of McLeod and the customer. McLeod prepares the sales order, but Lewis, Ltd. does not sign the agreement because Lewis, Ltd. is waiting for approval by its legal department. Lewis's purchasing department has orally agreed to the sale and thinks the contract will be approved during the first week of McLeod's next fiscal year. Can McLeod recognize the revenue in the current fiscal year?

Case 2. D'souza Inc. enters into an arrangement with Jensen Hardware to deliver D'souza's products to Jensen Hardware on a consignment basis. This means that title to the products does not pass from D'souza to Jensen until Jensen either consumes the products in its operations or sells them to a third party. D'souza Inc. delivers products to Jensen Hardware on December 31 under the terms of the arrangement. Can D'souza recognize revenue upon delivery of its product to Jensen Hardware?

Case 3. Rice & Sons receives purchase orders for products it manufactures. At the end of its fiscal year, customers may not yet be ready to take delivery of the products for various reasons such as insufficient space or delays in customers' production schedules. May Rice & Sons recognize revenue for the sale of its products once it has completed manufacturing if it segregates the inventory of the products in its own warehouse from its own products?

Case 4. Fried Corporation is a retailer that offers "layaway" sales to its customers. Fried retains the merchandise, sets it aside in its inventory, and collects a cash deposit from the customer. Although Fried may set a time period within which the customer must finalize the purchase, Fried does not require the customer to enter into an installment note or other fixed payment commitment when the initial deposit is received. The merchandise generally is not released to the customer until the customer pays the full purchase price. In the event that the customer fails to pay the remaining purchase price, the customer forfeits its cash deposit. In the event the merchandise is lost or damaged, Fried either must refund the cash deposit to the customer or provide replacement merchandise. When may Fried Corporation recognize revenue for merchandise sold under its layaway program?

2. On December 14, 2003 Michael Dupuis, CEO of Craters Inc., pored over the preliminary income statement with his CFO Billy Shoemaker. He read (numbers in millions of dollars):

	2002	2003
Revenues		
Construction projects	$200	$200
Services	60	60
	$260	$260
Expenses		
Costs of projects	$100	$100
Other operating exp.	70	80
Income taxes (40%)	36	32
	$206	$212
Net Income	$ 54	$ 48

"This is a bunch of b.s.!" exclaimed the CEO. "We can't show these numbers to our stock-holders. Are you out of your mind?"

The CFO stood there fidgeting. "But those are the preliminary results, sir."

The CEO said, "We need more income. The shareholders want some growth and you've given them a decline. That's disgraceful." He thought for a few more seconds and got an idea. "Billy, don't we account for the project revenues with the percentage-of-completion method?"

"Yes, Mike."

"Would you happen to have those numbers?"

"Yes, I do. Here they are." Then he produced the following table:

	2002	2003	2004
Revenues	$100	$200	$200
Expenses	50	100	100
Gross income	$ 50	$100	$100

The CFO explained, "In 2002 we had two projects, but we finished one last year. During this year we have had only one construction project, the one these numbers are for. According to our engineers, we did 40% of the work on that project this year, so we can recognize $200 of revenue and $100 of gross income."

Dupuis examined the table quickly and smiled. "Yes, we can improve the income state-ment." He handed the documents back to Shoemaker and said, "Find an engineer who will es-timate that we did 50% of the work and then redo the numbers. That should give us the growth in earnings we need to report."

Billy walked out of the room, went to his office, and prepared the second version of the preliminary in-come statement. He knew that he really didn't need to talk with an engineer at this time. He could always do that later if it became necessary.

Required:

(a) Prepare the new preliminary income statement for 2003. (Keep in mind that you also have to change the income taxes.)

(b) What is the chief weakness of the percentage of completion method?

(c) What is the consequence of a change in estimate from 40% to 50% in 2003 for the 2004 income statement?

(d) How can external auditors catch this ruse?

3. On March 9, 2004 the Lemont Suiteheart purchases a parcel of land for $4 million and pays legal fees of $200,000 for this transaction. On August 8 the corporation also acquires a second parcel of land for $3 mil-lion, which also includes an old building, and it removes the old building at a cost of $300,000. Legal fees for this transaction amount to $200,000. On December 30, 2004, Lemont Suiteheart sells the second parcel of land for $5 million.

(a) What is the historical cost of the two parcels of land?

(b) What is the cost of the land sold under FIFO? LIFO? weighted average?

(c) Do accountants normally make a cost flow assumption when they account for parcels of land? Why or why not?

4. Anne Beatty, Inc. has 100 units in beginning inventory at $1 each in 2002. The firm purchases inventory during 2002 as follows:

March 1	100 units at $2 each
September 1	100 units at $3 each
December 1	100 units at $4 each

The ending inventory consists of 150 units. In 2003 Anne Beatty, Inc. purchases inventory as follows:

February 2	100 units at $5 each
June 5	100 units at $6 each
August 25	100 units at $7 each
October 1	150 units at $8 each

At the end of 2003 the company has 200 units in ending inventory.

Required: Compute the cost of ending inventory and cost of goods sold in 2003 under the (a) FIFO, (b) LIFO, and (c) weighted average methods.

5. Sometimes investments are not measured at their current value but at cost. A typical reason for this change occurs when the stock is privately, not publicly, traded. Consider the following case.

Eagle Grip buys 10,000 shares of Gelcrap common stock on January 22, 2003 for $39 per share. On March 30, 2003 Eagle Grip buys another 10,000 shares of Gelcrap for $47 per share. Then on October 29, 2003 it buys yet another 10,000 shares of Gelcrap, this time for $64 per share. On December 30, Eagle Grip sells 5,000 shares of Gelcrap for $57 per share.

Required:

(a) What is the gain or loss on the sale of these shares if Eagle Grip applies FIFO to these investments? if it utilizes LIFO? if it uses the weighted average method? (Actually, firms are not allowed to use LIFO to account for investments. Ignore this detail in solving the problem.)

(b) Instead of employing either FIFO or weighted average, managers prefer to apply the specific identification method. Why?

(c) When companies sell securities during the last week or so of a fiscal year, it is called "window dressing." Given your answer to (b), why is this practice referred to as "window dressing"?

6. The chapter describes the basics of the lower-of-cost-or-market method for valuing inventories. We applied this rule on an item-by-item basis in the text of the chapter, but the rule can be implemented either (a) item by item, (b) by groups of items (e.g., departments), or (c) the total inventory. Which implementation scheme produces the lowest and which the highest inventory valuation? Why?

As a help to answering the question, consider the following example. Disc Company has five inventory items with the following costs and market values. (Market has already been adjusted for the upper and lower limits.)

Product Number	Department	Cost	Market
001	Hardware	$2,000	$2,100
002	Hardware	1,400	1,450
003	Hardware	3,900	3,300
004	Software	2,500	2,450
005	Software	3,100	3,200

Compute the inventory amount to display on the balance sheet under the lower-of-cost-or-market rule, implementing it under each of the three ways.

7. On July 1 Chaser, Inc. acquired 100 shares of Gardner Company's common stock at $52 per share and classified them as trading securities. At year-end the shares have a value of $50 per share. Next year Chaser sells the shares at $59 per share. Prepare the journal entries for Chaser, Inc.

If the shares had been classified as available-for-sale, how much would be recognized as income in the first year and how much in the second year?

8. Prepare the journal entries for all transactions related to the bonds payable examples in panels B and C in Exhibit 12.8. Amortize the premium or discount under the interest rate method instead of the straight-line method. Assume that the bonds are issued on January 1, 2001, that the coupon payments are each made on June 30 and December 31, and that the bonds mature on December 31, 2003. *Hint:* Use the template in Exhibit 12.4 but the numbers from Exhibit 12.9.

9. Consider the lease example in Exhibit 12.10. Assume that the cash payments occur on January 1 of each year from 2001 to 2006. The original cost to the lessor is $250,000, and the asset has an accumulated depreciation of $70,000 with a remaining life of six years.

(a) Prepare all the journal entries for the lessee if it is considered a rental.

(b) Prepare all journal entries for the lessor if it is considered a rental. (Include depreciation, assuming a remaining life of 10 years and no salvage value.)

(c) Prepare all journal entries for the lessee if it is considered a capital lease.

(d) Prepare all journal entries for the lessor if it is considered a capital lease. At the end of the lease, the asset reverts back to the lessor, and the asset has a market value of $20,000.

INDEX

Q

Qualitative characteristics of information, 3–4, 359–361
Quality of earnings, 136–137
Quality, product, 294
Query, 180, 187–188

R

Raw materials inventory, 25, 33–34, 339–340, 342, 344
Realization principle, 71
Receiving department, 257, 270, 294, 311
Receiving report, 270, 307, 311
Recognition, 362–366
Reconciliation, 206, 209–211
Record, 184
Record layout, 184–185
Records symbol, 235–236
Reference column. *See* folio column.
Reference file, 186–187
Relevance, 4, 359–361
Reliability, 4, 359–361
Remittance advice, 180–181, 272–273
Replacement cost, 362, 370–371
Report file, 186
Responsibility, 203–204
Retained earnings, 6, 28, 37–38, 141
Revenue, 5, 29, 58, 143–145, 360–361, 363–364
Revenue cycle, 177, 255–280
Revenue recognition, 363
Reversing entry, 97, 118–119
Rights and obligations, assertions about, 198–199. *See also* Manager assertions.
Risk assessment, 200–201

S

Safeguarding, 202–203
Sales, 31, 79, 104–107, 265–269

Sales analysis report, 182
Sales cycle, 177, 202, 255–272
Sales discounts, 31, 108
Sales invoice file, 269
Sales journal, 104–106, 266
Sales order, 261–262, 265
Sales order department, 256–257, 265
Sales order file, 269
Sales returns and allowances, 31, 269–272
Sales returns and allowances file, 271
Sales returns and allowances report, 182–183
Sales returns memos, 269–270
Salvage value, 73
Securities and Exchange Commission (SEC), 2, 14
Segregation of duties, 207
Selling expense, 32
Service company, 22, 29–30, 110–114
Shipping department, 257, 265–266, 294
Social security taxes. *See* FICA taxes.
Sole proprietorship, 5, 22, 37
Solvency, 136
Sorting a file, 187
Source document, 179–182. *See also* Input document and Output document.
Special journal, 56, 98, 104–109
Specific identification, 367
Standard accounting entries, 229–230
Statement of changes in stockholders equity, 3, 36–39, 97
Statement of retained earnings, 38
Stockholders equity, 5, 23, 27–28, 58, 360–361
Subsidiary account, 99, 298

Subsidiary ledger, 64, 98, 99–104, 298
Subsidiary schedule, 99, 298, 301
Subsystem, 173
System, 173–176

T

T-account, 57, 65
T-account method
   Direct method, 154–157
   Indirect method, 147–153
Taxes payable, 26
Temporary account, 58
Time card, 181, 330
Time ticket, 346, 348
Time value of money, 372
Timekeeping, 328, 333
Title, 336
Transaction, 1, 7, 53–54, 179
Transaction cycle, 176–178
Transaction file, 185–186
Transactions processing, 1, 7–8, 54–55, 97, 178–184
Transactions processing system (TPS), 178–184
Transformation. *See* Process.
Treasurer, 239
Treasury department, 239–240, 256, 338
Treasury stock, 28, 38
Trial balance, 55, 70. *See also* Adjusted trial balance; Post-closing trial balance; and Unadjusted trial balance.

U

Unadjusted trial balance, 70, 97
Unearned revenue, 26, 72
Unemployment taxes, 330
Unqualified audit opinion, 12–13
Updating a file, 187

V

Valuation adjustment, 73–74
Valuation, assertions about, 197–198. *See also* Manager assertions.